CONTESTED COMMUNITIES
SMALL, MINORITY AND MINOR LITERATURES IN EUROPE

LEGENDA

LEGENDA is the Modern Humanities Research Association's book imprint for new research in the Humanities. Founded in 1995 by Malcolm Bowie and others within the University of Oxford, Legenda has always been a collaborative publishing enterprise, directly governed by scholars. The Modern Humanities Research Association (MHRA) joined this collaboration in 1998, became half-owner in 2004, in partnership with Maney Publishing and then Routledge, and has since 2016 been sole owner. Titles range from medieval texts to contemporary cinema and form a widely comparative view of the modern humanities, including works on Arabic, Catalan, English, French, German, Greek, Italian, Portuguese, Russian, Spanish, and Yiddish literature. Editorial boards and committees of more than 60 leading academic specialists work in collaboration with bodies such as the Society for French Studies, the British Comparative Literature Association and the Association of Hispanists of Great Britain & Ireland.

The MHRA encourages and promotes advanced study and research in the field of the modern humanities, especially modern European languages and literature, including English, and also cinema. It aims to break down the barriers between scholars working in different disciplines and to maintain the unity of humanistic scholarship. The Association fulfils this purpose through the publication of journals, bibliographies, monographs, critical editions, and the MHRA Style Guide, and by making grants in support of research. Membership is open to all who work in the Humanities, whether independent or in a University post, and the participation of younger colleagues entering the field is especially welcomed.

ALSO PUBLISHED BY THE ASSOCIATION

Critical Texts
Tudor and Stuart Translations • New Translations • European Translations
MHRA Library of Medieval Welsh Literature

MHRA Bibliographies
Publications of the Modern Humanities Research Association

The Annual Bibliography of English Language & Literature
Austrian Studies
Modern Language Review
Portuguese Studies
The Slavonic and East European Review
Working Papers in the Humanities
The Yearbook of English Studies

www.mhra.org.uk
www.legendabooks.com

STUDIES IN COMPARATIVE LITERATURE

Editorial Committee
Chair: Professor Wen-chin Ouyang (SOAS, London)
Dr Ross Forman (University of Warwick)
Professor Angus Nicholls (Queen Mary, University of London)
Dr Henriette Partzsch (University of Glasgow)
Dr Ranka Primorac (University of Southampton)

Studies in Comparative Literature are produced in close collaboration with the British Comparative Literature Association, and range widely across comparative and theoretical topics in literary and translation studies, accommodating research at the interface between different artistic media and between the humanities and the sciences.

ALSO PUBLISHED IN THIS SERIES

20. *Aestheticism and the Philosophy of Death: Walter Pater and Post-Hegelianism*, by Giles Whiteley
21. *Blake, Lavater and Physiognomy*, by Sibylle Erle
22. *Rethinking the Concept of the Grotesque: Crashaw, Baudelaire, Magritte*, by Shun-Liang Chao
23. *The Art of Comparison: How Novels and Critics Compare*, by Catherine Brown
24. *Borges and Joyce: An Infinite Conversation*, by Patricia Novillo-Corvalán
25. *Prometheus in the Nineteenth Century: From Myth to Symbol*, by Caroline Corbeau-Parsons
26. *Architecture, Travellers and Writers: Constructing Histories of Perception*, by Anne Hultzsch
27. *Comparative Literature in Britain: National Identities, Transnational Dynamics 1800-2000*, by Joep Leerssen
28. *The Realist Author and Sympathetic Imagination*, by Sotirios Paraschas
29. *Iris Murdoch and Elias Canetti: Intellectual Allies*, by Elaine Morley
30. *Likenesses: Translation, Illustration, Interpretation*, by Matthew Reynolds
31. *Exile and Nomadism in French and Hispanic Women's Writing*, by Kate Averis
32. *Samuel Butler against the Professionals: Rethinking Lamarckism 1860–1900*, by David Gillott
33. *Byron, Shelley, and Goethe's Faust: An Epic Connection*, by Ben Hewitt
34. *Leopardi and Shelley: Discovery, Translation and Reception*, by Daniela Cerimonia
35. *Oscar Wilde and the Simulacrum: The Truth of Masks*, by Giles Whiteley
36. *The Modern Culture of Reginald Farrer: Landscape, Literature and Buddhism*, by Michael Charlesworth
37. *Translating Myth*, edited by Ben Pestell, Pietra Palazzolo and Leon Burnett
38. *Encounters with Albion: Britain and the British in Texts by Jewish Refugees from Nazism*, by Anthony Grenville
39. *The Rhetoric of Exile: Duress and the Imagining of Force*, by Vladimir Zorić
40. *From Puppet to Cyborg: Pinocchio's Posthuman Journey*, by Georgia Panteli
41. *Utopian Identities: A Cognitive Approach to Literary Competitions*, by Clementina Osti
43. *Sublime Conclusions: Last Man Narratives from Apocalypse to Death of God*, by Robert K. Weninger
44. *Arthur Symons: Poet, Critic, Vagabond*, edited by Elisa Bizzotto and Stefano Evangelista
45. *Scenographies of Perception: Sensuousness in Hegel, Novalis, Rilke, and Proust*, by Christian Jany
46. *Reflections in the Library: Selected Literary Essays 1926–1944*, by Antal Szerb
47. *Depicting the Divine: Mikhail Bulgakov and Thomas Mann*, by Olga G. Voronina
48. *Samuel Butler and the Science of the Mind: Evolution, Heredity and Unconscious Memory*, by Cristiano Turbil
49. *Death Sentences: Literature and State Killing*, edited by Birte Christ and Ève Morisi
50. *Words Like Fire: Prophecy and Apocalypse in Apollinaire, Marinetti and Pound*, by James P. Leveque

Contested Communities

Small, Minority and Minor Literatures in Europe

Edited by Kate Averis, Margaret Littler,
and Godela Weiss-Sussex

Studies in Comparative Literature 57
Modern Humanities Research Association
2023

Published by Legenda
an imprint of the Modern Humanities Research Association
Salisbury House, Station Road, Cambridge CB1 2LA

ISBN 978-1-83954-223-7 (HB)
ISBN 978-1-83954-224-4 (PB)

First published 2023

All rights reserved. No part of this publication may be reproduced or disseminated or transmitted in any form or by any means, electronic, mechanical, photocopying, recording or otherwise, or stored in any retrieval system, or otherwise used in any manner whatsoever without written permission of the copyright owner, except in accordance with the provisions of the Copyright, Designs and Patents Act 1988, or under the terms of a licence permitting restricted copying issued in the UK by the Copyright Licensing Agency Ltd, Saffron House, 6–10 Kirby Street, London EC1N 8TS, England, or in the USA by the Copyright Clearance Center, 222 Rosewood Drive, Danvers MA 01923. Application for the written permission of the copyright owner to reproduce any part of this publication must be made by email to legenda@mhra.org.uk.

Disclaimer: Statements of fact and opinion contained in this book are those of the author and not of the editors or the Modern Humanities Research Association. The publisher makes no representation, express or implied, in respect of the accuracy of the material in this book and cannot accept any legal responsibility or liability for any errors or omissions that may be made.

Trademark notice: Product or corporate names may be trademarks or registered trademarks, and are used only for identification and explanation without intent to infringe.

© Modern Humanities Research Association 2023

Copy-Editor: Richard Correll

CONTENTS

	Acknowledgements	ix
	Notes on the Contributors	x
	Introduction MARGARET LITTLER	1

PART I: RE-MAPPING EUROPE

1. Francophone Latin American Writing: Between Two Major Traditions   13
   KATE AVERIS

2. German-Jewish Women's Writing in Early Twentieth-Century Berlin: Claiming Space for a (Multiple) Minority   25
   GODELA WEISS-SUSSEX

3. Land, Art and Activism in Galician Writing by Women: Teresa Moure's *A intervención* (2010)   39
   CATHERINE BARBOUR

4. Peripheries of the Revolution and Geographies of Exclusion in Djaimilia Pereira de Almeida's *Luanda, Lisboa, Paraíso* (2018)   51
   MARGARIDA RENDEIRO

5. Representations of Greenland: Danish and Greenlandic Literary Perspectives   65
   CHRISTINNA HAZZARD

PART II: CIRCULATION AND READERSHIP

6. A Move Towards the Mainstream? New Perspectives on the Public Reading of Minority Writing in the UK   85
   BRIONY BIRDI

7. Small Literature, Big Ambition: Basque Literature of the Present   97
   MARI JOSE OLAZIREGI

8. *Land un Lü*: Low German Diversities   109
   STEFAN WILLER

9. *Lontano da Mogadiscio* and *Nuvole sull'equatore*: Belonging, Language and the Market   121
   SIMONE BRIONI AND SHIRIN RAMZANALI FAZEL

PART III: EMERGENT COMMUNITIES

10 Translating the Dead Other? The Politics of Minority Writing, Non-Identity and the Inoperative in Terézia Mora's *Das Ungeheuer* 139
    TERESA LUDDEN

11 Futurity and the People to Come: *futuristen-epilog — poeme* by Berkan Karpat and Zafer Şenocak 157
    MARGARET LITTLER

12 Minor Literature, Minor Discourse and the Representation of Eastern Europeans Working in Britain: Monica Ali's *In the Kitchen* and Marina Lewycka's *Two Caravans* 173
    PAMELA MCCALLUM

13 Reinventing Europe from the Margins: Theatre on the Periphery 187
    MADELENA GONZALEZ

14 Of Boiled Eggs and Rocket Science: Sharon Dodua Otoo's *Herr Gröttrup setzt sich hin* 203
    ÁINE MCMURTRY

Bibliography 217

Index 235

ACKNOWLEDGEMENTS

We acknowledge the generous support of the AHRC's Open World Research Initiative (OWRI) programme, which enabled the exchange of scholarship and expertise beyond the boundaries of linguistic fields by sponsoring a series of conferences that led to this publication: Interpreting Communities (October 2015, ILCS); Minor, Minority and Small Literatures in European Fields (April 2016, King's College, Cambridge); Unsettling Communities (February 2017, ILCS). These events were part of the 'Cross-Language Dynamics: Reshaping Community' project led by the Universities of Manchester and Durham and the School of Advanced Study, University of London. We want to express our gratitude to Cathy Collins, Jane Lewin and Jenny Stubbs, whose administrative and organizational support in setting up the conferences at the ILCS was invaluable, as well as to King's College, Cambridge for their generous support of the event that took place there.

Finally, our warmest thanks go to Dr Malachi McIntosh, who was one of the initiators of this joint project and whose input in developing and steering it has been crucial for its success.

NOTES ON THE CONTRIBUTORS

Kate Averis teaches European literatures at the Universidad de Antioquia (Colombia). Her research lies in the field of contemporary literatures in French and Spanish and, in particular, women's writing of transnational mobility, female ageing, and the intersections between them. She is the author of *Exile and Nomadism in French and Hispanic Women's Writing* (Legenda, 2014) and has edited several collections on contemporary women's writing, including: *Exiles, Travellers and Vagabonds: Rethinking Mobility in Francophone Women's Writing*, with Isabel Hollis-Touré (2016); *Women's Ageing in Contemporary Women's Writing*, with Maria-José Blanco (special issue of *Journal of Romance Studies*, 2017); *Nancy Huston* (special issue of *Nottingham French Studies*, 2018); and *Trangression(s) in Twenty-First-Century Women's Writing in French*, with Eglė Kačkutė and Catherine Mao (2021).

Catherine Barbour is Assistant Professor in Hispanic Studies at Trinity College Dublin. She specializes in contemporary Iberian literary and cultural studies, with particular interests in Galician Studies, multilingual literature, gender and migration studies. Her work has been published in the *Bulletin of Spanish Studies*, *English in Education*, *International Journal of Iberian Studies*, *Journal of Romance Studies* and *Parallax* and she is author of the monograph *Contemporary Galician Women Writers*, published by Legenda in 2020. With Danny Barreto (Colgate University), she recently guest edited a special issue of the *International Journal of Iberian Studies* entitled '(Re)Producing Galician Femininities: Women's Creative Praxis in 21st-Century Galicia' (2022). Catherine is an elected member of the Modern Language Association Galician Forum executive committee (2020–24).

Briony Birdi is a Professor in Library and Information Science at the Information School, University of Sheffield. Her research and teaching explore the social, political and educational roles of public and youth libraries, with a particular emphasis on social justice and diversity, and the engagement of all age groups with literature and reading. Since 1999 she has been involved in a wide range of research projects, funded by organizations including the AHRC, the Arts Councils of England and Wales, the British Council, the Museums, Libraries and Archives Council and local authorities (individual and consortia). She is also regularly consulted on public library policy and practice, reading and diversity for regional, national and international academic and professional organizations.

Simone Brioni is an Associate Professor in the Department of English at Stony Brook University and affiliated faculty in the Department of Africana Studies and the Department of Women's, Gender and Sexuality Studies. His research focuses on the literary and cinematographic representation and self-representation of migrants. His publications include the monographs *The Somali Within: Language, Race and Belonging in 'Minor' Italian Literature* (2015) and *L'Italia, l'altrove: luoghi, spazi e attraversamenti nel cinema e nella letteratura sulla migrazione* (2022). He has also edited Geneviève Makaping's *Reversing the Gaze: What If the Other Were You?* (2023) and Shirin Ramzanali Fazel's *Islam and Me: Narrating a Diaspora* (forthcoming 2023).

Madelena Gonzalez studied at the universities of Birmingham, Aix-en-Provence and Vienna before settling in France. She is currently Professor of Anglophone Literature at the University of Avignon and head of the multidisciplinary research group Cultural Identity, Texts and Theatricality (ICTT). She is also in charge of the Masters programme in English Studies. She has published widely on contemporary Anglophone literature, theatre and culture, including several volumes on minority theatre. Her most recent publication, *Le Théâtre à l'ère du numérique: convergences et paradoxes* (2022), deals with theatre in the digital age.

Christinna Hazzard is a Lecturer in International Relations and Politics at Liverpool John Moores University. Her research is interdisciplinary and comparative, exploring the postcolonial politics and literature of the Nordic region, literary representations of national movements, and the relationship between capitalism and culture in world literature. She has published a book chapter on the postcolonial politics of 'Nordic Noir' crime dramas and is working on a monograph about the literary significance of the semi-periphery in world literature. She is also part of a joint project researching the impact of Arts and Humanities Foundation years on diversity and social justice in Higher Education.

Margaret Littler is Professor Emerita of Contemporary German Culture at the University of Manchester. Her research interests include gender studies, minority culture in German and the new materialist philosophy of Gilles Deleuze. She is a long-standing editor of the journal *German Life and Letters*. She is editor of *Gendering German Studies* (1997) and co-author (with Brigid Haines) of *Contemporary Women's Writing in German: Changing the Subject* (2004). Her more recent publications on the authors Zafer Şenocak, Emine Sevgi Özdamar and Feridun Zaimoglu are part of a project informed by Deleuze and Guattari's formulation of minor literature, viewing these writers' work as a transformative force in contemporary German literature.

Teresa Ludden is Senior Lecturer in German Studies at the University of Newcastle upon Tyne. She is a philosopher of literature, especially interested in phenomenology and aesthetics, gender theory, feminist philosophies, deconstruction, and twentieth- and twenty-first-century German-language literature and poetry. Recent publications have been on Decoloniality and the Austrian writer Anna Kim, Pluralization and Difference and the Austrian philosopher Isolde Charim, Vegetal Ontology and the poet Oswald Egger, Relational Ontologies and texts by Verena Stefan.

Pamela McCallum is Professor Emerita at the Department of English, University of Calgary. She is the author of *Cultural Memories and Imagined Futures: The Art of Jane Ash Poitras* (2011) and co-editor (with Wendy Faith) of *Linked Histories: Postcolonial Studies in a Globalized World* (2005). She has recently published articles on 'Art and Artists in Claire Messud's *The Woman Upstairs*' (2022); '1968 and Nationalism' in *Cultural Critique* (2019); on Marina Lewycka in *Negative Cosmopolitanism* (2017); on Chris Abani in *Mosaic* (2015); on Biyi Bandele in *Ethnic Literatures and Transnationalism* (2015); and on Nancy Huston in *Trans/Acting Culture, Writing, and Memory* (2013). Her research interests are in cultural memory, the representation of globalization, and literary theory. From 2001–11, she was editor of the journal *ARIEL: A Review in International English Literature*.

Áine McMurtry is Senior Lecturer in German at King's College London. Her research field is modern literature with specialization in twentieth- and twenty-first-century experimental writing. Her first book, *Crisis and Form in the Later Writing of Ingeborg Bachmann*, appeared in the MHRA's Bithell Series in 2012; it draws on extensive archival work to cast new light on one of the most important German-language writers of the post-1945 period. Her current work employs materialist and decolonial perspectives to explore contemporary multilingual writings; she publishes on such authors as Herta Müller, Emine Sevgi Özdamar, Kathrin Röggla, Tawada Yōko, José F. A. Oliver and Uljana Wolf. In 2018, she was awarded the essay prize of the Critical Theory journal *Paragraph* for an article on the cross-disciplinary artist Caroline Bergvall.

Mari Jose Olaziregi is Professor of Basque literature at the University of the Basque Country (Spain). She holds a PhD in Basque literature (University of the Basque Country) and an MA in Studies in Fiction (University of East Anglia). She has lectured at various universities, among them the University of Nevada-Reno, the University of Konstanz, the Bordeaux Montaigne University, the University of Chicago and the CUNY Graduate Center. She is a specialist in contemporary Basque and Iberian literatures, gender studies, and the politics of memory. She is the author of 11 books on Basque literature, 92 book chapters, 18 edited books, and 81 articles in indexed journals. Since 2013, she has coordinated the *Historical Memory in Iberian Literatures Consolidated Research Group*, MHLI, at the University of the Basque Country <www.mhli.net>.

Shirin Ramzanali Fazel is an Italian writer of Somali and Pakistani origins. Her first novel, *Lontano da Mogadiscio* (1994), which is considered a milestone in Italian postcolonial literature, describes her experience of migration to Italy and the effects of Italian colonialism in her native Somalia. Shirin's second novel, *Nuvole sull'equatore* (2010), fleshes out the issue of *meticciato* and race discrimination, a crude legacy of the Italian colonial government. *Lontano da Mogadiscio / Far from Mogadishu*, an extended and bilingual version of the 1994 edition, was published in 2013 as an ebook. Her publications also include the collection of poems *Wings* (2017) and *I Suckled Sweetness* (2020).

Margarida Rendeiro is a Researcher at the Centre for the Humanities (CHAM), FCSH-NOVA Lisbon and an Assistant Professor at Lusíada University of Lisbon.

She gained a PhD in Portuguese Studies from King's College London (2008). Her research broaches questions related to contemporary cultural and literary studies in Portuguese-speaking countries, women's and Black studies. She has co-edited *Challenging Memories and Rebuilding Identities* (2019) and authored *The Literary Institution in Portugal: An Analysis under Special Consideration of the Publishing Market* (2010). She is the Principal Researcher of the project Women's Literature: Memories, Peripheries and Resistance in the Luso-Afro-Brazilian Atlantic (PTDC/LLT-LES/0858/2021), funded by the Foundation for Science and Technology (FCT) in Portugal.

Godela Weiss-Sussex is Professor of Modern German Literature at the Institute of Languages, Cultures and Societies (ILCS), University of London. She is also a Fellow of King's College, Cambridge. Her main research interests lie in the culture and literature of the twentieth and twenty-first centuries in the following areas: women's writing, German-Jewish cultural production, multi- and translingualism, concepts of *Heimat* and belonging, and minor and minority literatures. Recent publications include *Barbara Honigmann*, co-edited with Robert Gillett (2023), *Rethinking Minor Literatures: Contemporary Jewish Women's Writing in Germany and Austria* (special issue of *Modern Languages Open*, co-edited with Maria Roca Lizarazu, 2020) and *Women Writing Heimat in Imperial and Weimar Germany* (special issue of *German Life and Letters*, co-edited with Caroline Bland and Catherine Smale, 2019).

Stefan Willer has been Professor of Modern German Literature at the Humboldt-Universität, Berlin since 2018. From 2010 to 2018 he was Associate Director of the Centre for Literary and Cultural Research (ZfL) in Berlin and held a professorship in Cultural Research at the Humboldt-Universität from 2014 to 2018. His research interests include theories of inheritance, genealogy, and cultural transfer across generations. Recent book publications are: *Das Konzept der Generation* (2008); *Erbfälle* (2014), *Futurologien* (2016), on the history of future knowledge and fiction; *Zukunftssicherung* (2019); and *Selbstübersetzung als Wissenstransfer* (2020), on theories of language and translation.

INTRODUCTION

Margaret Littler

This volume is conceived as a contribution to the current shift towards expansion and diversification of the disciplinary field of Modern Languages. In the first two decades of the twenty-first century scholarship in the discipline has decisively moved beyond the limitations of single-language, nation-bound enquiry and expanded its remit instead into a transnational exploration of literary, cultural and social phenomena.[1] The understanding of the national as multilingual, intersectional and dynamic in an increasingly globalized world underlies our stance — and while recognizing cultural and socio-political specificity, the contributors to this volume build their work on an inclusive and comparative perspective and methodology. The notion of community itself is not taken for granted, but is itself a contested term, one that is subject to resistance, redefinition and experimentation in myriad new forms.

By focusing on small, minority and minor literatures in Europe from the early twentieth century to today, we turn, in this collection, to those authors and communities that have existed on the fringes of Europe's conception of itself, despite being long present within its borders and spheres of activity. Positioning migration as central rather than marginal to society,[2] we investigate diversity both between and within European nations, exploring the productive porosity of cultural and linguistic boundaries, and the transnational potential inherent in all supposedly homogeneous national communities. Our focus on peripheral literature is thus a continuation of the transnational reconception of cultures by means of a challenge to the boundaries of the European literary canon.[3]

We seek to add nuance to the perception of minority and peripheralized writing to better understand the interaction between 'central' and 'marginal' as a charged field of cultural production. To this end, we explore the strategies that literary authors use to express the relationship between their texts and their position in the world. We also explore the institutional and material contexts in which their texts are produced and that both enable and constrain their access to a public sphere, and the range of reading strategies adopted aims to illuminate the variety of interventions enacted by the works discussed.

One way of viewing this book is that it is concerned with three spheres of inquiry that are reflected in the volume's three sections: 'the world in the text' ('Re-Mapping Europe'), 'the text in the world' ('Circulation and Readership') and 'beyond the text/world distinction' ('Emergent Communities'). Sections I and II adopt a more representational approach to literature and its embeddedness in cultural and institutional settings, while section III departs from representational approaches and experiments with new materialist thinking, both about language and about the relationship between text and world. However this characterization of each section is too crude, obscuring the overlaps and continuities between them, just as it suggests a far too absolute distinction between 'text' and 'world', representation and non-representation, even between 'small', 'minority' and 'minor', which emerge more as points on a continuum than as discrete categories. Each of the three sections also adopts a distinctive perspective, moving from the topographical concept of re-mapping through the socio-political framing of multilingualism, reading and circulation to the temporal anticipation of future worlds. Yet from these different perspectives commonalities can be seen, in terms of the dynamism and innovation emerging from them all.

This Introduction attempts to chart some of the overlaps, divergences, and tensions between the concepts and approaches deployed in the chapters of the book. On one level almost all of the contributors to the volume are concerned with the conditions of emergence of 'small' literatures in an increasingly globalized Europe. This is a Europe characterized both by the homogenizing force of transnational commerce and global capital flows, and by what Stuart Hall has called 'the subaltern proliferation of difference' in which 'vernacular modernities' assert themselves in the midst of neoliberal hegemony.[4] It is a Europe in which the drive towards ever greater integration coincides with the anxious reassertion of national boundaries in the face of mass migrations, renewed imperialist claims and global pandemics.

It is a very different Europe from that of the Prague-German writer Franz Kafka, who posed a similar question about the emergence of 'small' literatures in his famous diary entry of 25 December 1911.[5] As a German-speaking Jewish writer in the Austro-Hungarian Empire, cut off from a national German speech community, witnessing the emergence of Czech nationalism, and encountering Yiddish theatre in Prague, Kafka pondered the value of literary culture for small nations or peoples, perhaps conjuring an ideal literary community for himself. Such 'small literatures' had a peculiar vitality that could provide an integrative, unifying consciousness for a people as yet unformed, and they possessed an immediacy that was directly political, rather than existing in a rarefied literary sphere detached from politics. They were sustained by a dynamic ecology of publishing, magazines and conflict, rather than consensus and canon-building.

This enigmatic diary entry on 'small literatures' has been interpreted in vastly differing ways, from Pascale Casanova's view that in Kafka's Prague 'a nascent literature existed only through its claim to national identity',[6] to Gilles Deleuze and Félix Guattari's formulation of minor literature as linguistic activism taking flight from all such identity politics. Indeed Deleuze and Guattari's *Kafka: Toward a Minor Literature*, inspired by Kafka's musings on 'small literatures', has exerted an enormous influence on scholars of minority and minoritized literatures, including several contributors to this volume.[7] As Scott Spector points out in his magisterial *Prague Territories*, their formulation of minor literature offers an analysis of the political effects of literature beyond author intention or the representation of ethnic difference, which is as liable to appropriation as it is likely to liberate: 'Minor literature is precisely not a multicultural absorption of marginality into a cultural canon, but instead posits an indigestible particle into the core of territorialized language, the concord of artist, work and setting'.[8] The representation of ethnic and linguistic difference can of course seem fundamental to the emergence and even survival of small literatures, but arguably does little to alter their minoritized status in relation to a majoritarian norm. For Deleuze and Guattari it was Kafka's appropriation of a major language to make it resonate with new intensity and wrest from it new meanings that constituted its 'minor' force. For them, minor literature is not a representation of minority subjects, but a liberation of language from its anchorage in an existing subjectivity, national or otherwise, so that it paves the way for a new people to be formed. Minority is used here mainly to refer to communities defined in relation to a majoritarian norm, whereas minor is used here in the sense inaugurated by Deleuze and Guattari to refer to all that disrupts such normative notions of identity, community and codified meaning.[9] It designates as much a non-representational approach to reading as a classification of literature itself.

There are those who mistrust the philosophers of difference such as Derrida and Deleuze who resist its grounding in community or subjectivity. Françoise Lionnet and Shuh-mei Shih criticize poststructuralist thinking for seeking to contain marginality, even as it privileges it, and for ultimately denying a reality to the other: 'The marginal or the other remains a philosophical concept and futuristic promise: the other never "arrives", he or she is always "a venir"'.[10] The consistent conflation of minor and minority in their study of 'minor transnationalism' shows a commitment to representational thinking that conceives of the minor only in terms of existing minoritized identities.[11] Their debt to Deleuze and Guattari is actually more visible in their view of the rhizomatic connections between minority communities, as a more productive alternative to the verticality of margins and centre. This perspective on lateral connections is shared by contributors to the 2019 volume *Translating the Literatures of Small European Nations*, which adopts Mette Hjort's definition of 'small' as more than a quantitative designation when applied to cultural production: '*Small* points at least as much to the dynamics of recognition, indifference, and participation, nationally and transnationally, as it does to various forms of *mathesis* or quantification'.[12] Thus it matters whether we persist in viewing small literary cultures always in relation to a centre–periphery model, or whether we consider also their rhizomatic relations to other marginalized literatures, with which they may share strategies in the struggle for transnational recognition (see Olaziregi, Gonzalez and Barbour in this volume).

Our topic encompasses both 'small' literatures, which issue from linguistic communities that are based in countries where their ancestral language and regional cultures are rendered peripheral (Cornish, Breton, Basque, Galician, Low German or 'Plattdeutsch'), and 'minority' communities of migrants and their descendants whose cultural allegiances and practices are continuously considered through the lens of difference. These include historic diasporas (German Jewish writing), histories of actual colonization (Italian-Somalian, Black and Asian British), including those that self-identify as 'benevolent colonialism' (Portuguese Africa, Danish Greenland), and yet others that have their roots in labour migration (Eastern Europeans in UK, Turks in Germany) or globalization more generally (Eastern Europeans in the post-Cold War West, Latin Americans in Europe).

While these different histories of minority are distinct, their shared peripheralized status offers grounds for comparison, and their literary strategies may overlap as much as they diverge. In our interest in minority literatures, we are attentive to the specificity of minority identities and their mutations across time and space/place, to their assertion of (more or less strategic) minority identities, or their resistance to any identity defined by a majoritarian norm. We also consider how they may summon similar reactions within the fields of literary production, circulation and reception.

Inevitably the diverse cultural contexts addressed in this volume call for a plurality of conceptual approaches, which might be best viewed on a continuum ranging from the assertion and definition of minority identities at one end to the questioning of all concepts of identity at the other. Thus the visibility and promotion of minority literatures in public lending libraries depends on their classification as such by librarians who also make judgements on the identities of potential readers (see Birdi in this volume). Online publishing platforms and reading potentially liberate minority and multilingual writing from the constraints of the conventional publishing and circulation of texts that target a specifically defined readership, while also distributing meaning-giving agency across multiple sites (see Brioni and Shirin).[13] The cultural politics of protecting regional and minority languages may also appear to depend on the identification of fixed language communities, though several contributors to the volume discuss strategies that counteract the potential provincialism thus promoted, be they an emphasis on plurilingualism and ethnic diversity (Willer), engagement with global themes (Barbour), or an insistence on rhizomatic relations across minority literatures rather than a hierarchy of centre and periphery (Gonzalez, Olaziregi).

The performative rewriting of diasporic, ancestral and postcolonial narratives concerns several contributions to the volume, which explore the creative potential of disrupting existing categories of identity. The rootedness of the traditional model of diaspora is unsettled by nomadic subjectivity (Weiss-Sussex); shared Celtic mythologies straddling multiple regions and languages are brought to new and unpredictable life in experimental live performance (Gonzalez); polyphonic collective memory is invoked to unsettle dominant narratives of decolonization (Rendeiro) and persisting colonial clichés betray the enduring hierarchies structuring postcolonial literatures (Hazzard). While the impulse of some of the chapters could be said to be decolonial in their exposure of enduring Eurocentric hierarchies of power, others are more aligned with the postcolonial critique of representation, both in its aesthetic and ethical senses. Arguably this too is a binary opposition that is ripe for deconstruction, rather than an absolute categorical divide.[14]

Building on mobile and hybridized models of identity, some contributions to the volume work with non-foundational philosophies that break with autonomous notions of identity altogether. Drawing on philosophers such as Gilles Deleuze, Félix Guattari and Jean-Luc Nancy, they explore how ideas of inoperative community and minor literature help to conceive of a radical openness and incompletion of being, or of dynamic becoming rather than an existing state of the world. Rather than seeking a representation of existing minority subjects in literature they seek out experimental writing which resists reduction to a single set of cultural coordinates or a singular interpretation (Littler, Ludden); the supposed link between language and identity is disrupted by minor discourse and multilingualism (McCallum, Littler); rhizomatic bonds are formed across national and linguistic boundaries through the intensity of live performance (Gonzalez); and even the anthropocentrism of representational narrative is challenged by a science-fictional egg-narrator, whose status of sheer intensive potential points to a state of the world to come (McMurtry). Encompassing the entirety of this spectrum of approaches our volume proposes that each has its validity in the project of reconceiving European cultures in a globalized world.

Discussions of small, minority and minor literatures encompass multiple attitudes to space and place, from the celebration of space as relational and dynamic,[15] to place-making that stakes a claim to a territorial home,[16] or indeed the move from extensive notions of space that can be 'inhabited' to the intensive states of becoming associated with deterritorialization.[17] As already noted, for those existing on the periphery, hierarchical relations with a cultural and political centre can be less important than lateral connections with other marginal and minoritized nodes in a transnationally networked world. Time is also conceptualized in radically different ways by peoples for whom the absence of a national literary history renders cultural memory all the more significant for both its formative and its normative force: it can produce a sense of community and testify to traumatic pasts.[18] As Michael Rothberg has shown, cultural memory can take on transcultural significance when thought beyond conventional identity politics.[19] Such an understanding of multidirectional memory informs Rendeiro's essay on Black Portuguese writing in this volume. But equally significant is the challenge of these literatures to chrononormative time, and their projection of the conditions for future communities not yet actualized but no less real. Deleuze's characterization of political cinema is predicated on the absence of the people whom it might represent: 'The moment the master, or the colonizer, proclaims "There have never been people here", the missing people are a becoming'.[20]

Small, minority and minor literatures proliferate linguistic strategies, from the fight for visibility of small, even only recently codified language cultures,[21] to the drive for translation as a route into world literatures.[22] A text in a major language may be hybridized with heteroglossia, as a challenge to the monolingual norm,[23] or it can tap into the foreignness of the major language itself, destabilizing and deforming the dominant power structures inherent in major language use. This is what Deleuze and Guattari call an 'asignifying *intensive utilization* of language', that unmoors meaning from existing stratified social norms.[24] At its limits minor language becomes untranslatable, more akin to a cry than to syntax when it pushes language beyond representation (see Ludden in this volume).²⁵ Minority literatures can willingly adopt the burden of representation of marginalized communities, or they can resist such representational status by experimenting with language, adopting an apersonal perspective, and implicating the reader in the unfolding of an unpredictable world.²⁶ This question of representation is fraught with tensions that resonate throughout this book, perhaps most strongly where minoritized perspectives coincide with histories of racist colonialism. Here the tension between claims to ethnic and geo-political specificity and the need to unite under agreed (and contested) banners of solidarity has gained renewed urgency since the international Black Lives Matter movement of 2020.

All of these issues resonate in the essays collected here, ranging from the struggle for visibility of small language cultures, to their claims to world literature status via translation, to the hybridization of major European language cultures by the mass migrations of the neoliberal, postcolonial world. Yet in setting out the distinct strategies above, our discussion risks becoming polarized and static, as most of the works of literature under discussion here participate in many of them simultaneously. Serious claims for political representation may find expression in narrative realism, poetry, humour, multilingualism and science-fictional worlds. Such claims may be promoted by public libraries, by online publication platforms, by translation, or by language preservation policies. The contributors to this volume adopt a range of methodologies, from literary criticism to sociological analysis, and from dialogic exchange between author and scholar to original composition, in order to gain a greater understanding of the complexity of contemporary Europe from the perspective of its small, minority and minor literatures.

Re-Mapping Europe

In this first section of the book, Europe is viewed obliquely from the literary imagination of the peripheries, from which a number of recurring themes emerge: firstly, the dangers of provincialism arising from assumptions about the links between language, territory and identity versus the assertion of multilingual, rhizomatic and diverse communities; and secondly, the persistence of colonial hierarchies in supposedly postcolonial Europe. In this section's opening chapter, Francophone Latin American literature is shown to exist at the intersection of two major literatures, its writers unusual among their Latin American peers for adopting the French language, whether as a liberation from monolingual minority community identity, as identification with adopted French culture, or as indicative of the linguistic and cultural hybridity of Latin American as well as of European communities. The writers discussed by Kate Averis in this chapter display an ambiguous distance from singular identity, expressed in liminal imagery and third-person narrative voice. In the following chapter, Jewishness is shown to be both an oppressive community of origin (diaspora) and an intellectual resource, even impetus, for nomadic subjectivity in early twentieth-century German women's writing, where Godela Weiss-Sussex reveals how a dialectic between relational space and territorial place plays out. In this way, her chapter demonstrates how the experience of marginalization offers a fertile ground for the reconceptualization of space, community and belonging. Ecofeminism in Galician women's writing is then read as a challenge to both provincialism and patriarchy in Catherine Barbour's chapter, which analyses writing that advocates a more progressive, inclusive and intersectional brand of regional autonomy. Through recourse to elements of magic realism and the theme of organic growth, such writing is also shown to pose a challenge to both realist representation and to the dominance of the digital in a globalized world, and posits the power of female-authored texts of small literatures that push back against both linguistic and gender biases. Margarida Rendeiro's chapter concerns the rewriting of the European city from its excluded postcolonial peripheries. In her analysis, Black Portuguese writing about Lisbon invokes polyphonic collective memory as a corrective to the predominantly white narrative of Portuguese democracy. A similar corrective to postcolonial cliché is proposed in recent Greenlandic literature, in contrast to more mainstream Danish literature about Greenland, in the final chapter of this section by Christinna Hazzard.

Circulation and Readership

This, the second section of the volume, explores the material conditions of writing, distribution and readership of minority literatures, reflecting centrally on the question of language choice and translation, as well as institutional frameworks such as language preservation policies that promote minority languages, and lending libraries and publishing houses that act as gateways to readership. Briony Birdi adopts a sociological approach in her chapter that discusses public libraries as spaces in which Black and Asian British writing is accessed, as investigated by surveys of readers (adopting reader response theory) and librarians (applying personal construct theory) to determine the expectations shaping both the promotion and reception of this writing. In the subsequent chapter, Mari Jose Olaziregi views Basque-language literature in Spanish translation in the context of multilingual and plurinational Iberian literatures, where translation is deemed essential to a place in world literature. Here, promotion of translation across regional languages is advocated in order to break the centre–periphery hierarchy with Spanish, a focus on lateral relations that echoes that already seen in the dynamics and stakes of Galician translation discussed in Barbour's chapter and foreshadows the multilingual productions of Welsh, Cornish and Breton theatre in Gonzalez's chapter (Section III). The danger of provincialism in language preservation is subsequently explored in the Low German 'Plattdeutsch' revival, characterized by multilingualism and a diversification of regional language communities that unsettle the bonds linking language, people and territory. Stefan Willer's chapter thus confronts provincialism in ways that echo similar challenges made in Catherine Barbour's chapter on Galician ecofeminism. In the closing chapter of this section, plurilingual Somali-Italian writer Shirin Ramzanali Fazel reflects on the relationship between author, critic and publisher in a dialogue with Simone Brioni, where they also discuss the new opportunities offered by small and online publishing platforms for marginalized writers.

Emergent Communities

The third and final section of the volume brings together essays that adopt a non-representational approach to literature as imaginative and linguistic experimentation, not representations of existing communities but explorations of emergent properties of language as well as life. Most work with the Deleuzo-Guattarian concept of minor literature as linguistic disruption, political immediacy and anticipation of an as yet absent collective. In Teresa Ludden's opening chapter, minor literature and Jean-Luc Nancy's inoperative community are introduced as frameworks to give voice to the silenced other in a German Hungarian writer's work, which also resists the commodification of ethnicity as 'enrichment' of major culture. In the following chapter Margaret Littler explores futurity not as a temporal dimension but as an opening to the Deleuzean virtual in experimental poetry by two Turkish German artists whose work resists a representational aesthetic in favour of the asignifying and translingual force of poetic language. Their poetry also harnesses the dynamism of earlier futurisms to envisage the conditions of emergence of a people. In the chapter by Pamela McCallum, linguistic disruption and political immediacy are explored in English novels about Eastern European migrants, where vernacular language (easily reterritorialized on recognizable identities) contrasts with minor discourse in which language is detached from identitarian rootedness. The lateral, rhizomatic dynamics of Welsh, Cornish and Breton theatre form the focus of the chapter by Madelena Gonzalez, in an analysis that demonstrates multilingual theatre's challenge to both national language cultures and the ready consumption of the digital age. The privileging of regional over national alliances, cross-cultural collaboration, multilingual production and live performance are explored here as powerful instances of linguistic action and minor style. In Áine McMurty's chapter, German Afrofuturism is viewed from a posthuman perspective that challenges the epistemological privilege of white male German subjectivity. A short story in which one narrative voice is that of a disruptive egg de-centres the human and even the stability of organic wholeness, in the sense of Deleuze and Guattari's Body without Organs, opening up a space for silenced and unnoticed difference to emerge.

★ ★ ★ ★ ★

As a whole this volume presents multiple and interlocking perspectives on the literary landscape of Europe, not as a solid set of hierarchically organized, discrete language cultures but as an entity more readily conceived in terms of a mechanics of fluids, or the turbulence of a weather map, so fluid and mobile are its constituent parts. It requires a model of viscosity rather than solidity, as the basis of understanding the world, similar to the Lucretian model proposed by Michel Serres:

> A viscosity takes over. It comprehends. It creates comprehension. It teaches. But one must concede that everything is not solid and fixed and that the hardest

solids are only fluids that are slightly more viscous than others. And that edges and boundaries are fluctuating. Fluctuating fluid. [...] Yes, it is an advancement in the very notion of comprehension. Relations spawn objects, beings and acts, not vice versa.[27]

Instead of discrete identities seeking expression in literary form, therefore, we conceive of a dynamic relationality giving rise to Europe's literary life. *Contested Communities* charts the resistance to, the circulation amongst and the emergent properties of communities that are less stable, more mutable entities than generally assumed. From the representational identitarian claims of small and minority literatures to the post-representational, even posthuman resistance to identity politics, the affirmation of difference is central to our vision of a liveable European future. In place of the top-down mapping of political jurisdictions, these literary interventions form new lines of affiliation from which emergent communities may arise.

Notes to the Introduction

1. See Paul Jay, *Global Matters: The Transnational Turn in Literary Studies* (Ithaca, NY: Cornell University Press, 2010).
2. Erol Yildiz and Marc Hill, 'Einleitung', in *Nach der Migration: Postmigrantische Perspektiven jenseits der Parallelgesellschaft*, ed. by Yildiz and Hill (Bielefeld: Transcript Verlag, 2015), pp. 9–16 (p. 11).
3. This approach is exemplified in book series such as Transnational Modern Languages published by Liverpool University Press; see <https://www.liverpooluniversitypress.co.uk/series/series-13275/> [accessed 15 September 2022].
4. Stuart Hall, 'Conclusion: The Multicultural Question', in *Un/Settled Multiculturalisms: Diasporas, Entanglements, 'Transruptions'*, ed. by Barnor Hesse (London: Zed Books, 2000), pp. 209–41 (p. 215).
5. Franz Kafka, *Diaries, 1910–1923*, ed. by Max Brod, trans. by Joseph Kresh, Martin Greenberg and Hannah Arendt (New York: Schocken Books, 1976), pp. 148–53.
6. Pascale Casanova, *The World Republic of Letters*, trans. by M. B. DeBevoise (Cambridge, MA: Harvard University Press, 2004), p. 202.
7. Gilles Deleuze and Félix Guattari, *Kafka: Toward a Minor Literature*, trans. by Dana Polan, (Minneapolis: University of Minnesota Press, 1986) (French 1975).
8. Scott Spector, *Prague Territories: National Conflict and Cultural Innovation in Franz Kafka's fin de siècle* (Berkeley: University of California Press, 2000), p. 28. Spector also finds that Deleuze and Guattari's analysis of the interplay of literature and political context is just as relevant in post-Cold War Europe, with its 'violent return of repressed ethnoterritorial visions' as it was to *fin-de-siècle* Prague (p. 30). Lene Rock also draws interesting parallels between the cultures of early twentieth-century and early twenty-first-century Europe in *As German as Kafka* (Leuven: Leuven University Press, 2019).
9. The distinction is less rigorously upheld by some authors in the volume.
10. Françoise Lionnet and Shu-mei Shih, 'Introduction: Thinking through the Minor, Transnationally', in *Minor Transnationalism*, ed. by Lionnet and Shih (Durham, NC: Duke University Press, 2005), pp. 1–23 (p. 3).
11. Lionnet and Shih define minor literature in terms of the themes of exile, mobility, displacement, idealization of homelessness, and free-floating subjectivity rooted only in language (Lionnet and Shih, 'Introduction', p. 18).
12. Mette Hjort, cited in Rajendra Chitnis and Jakob Stougaard-Nielsen, 'Introduction', in *Translating the Literatures of Small European Nations*, ed. by Rajendra Chitnis, Jakob Stougaard-Nielsen, Rhian Atkin and Zoran Milutinuvic (Liverpool: Liverpool University Press, 2019), pp. 1–8 (p. 3).

13. As the authors point out in their chapter in this volume, Somali proper names are referred by using the first name, a convention also adopted here to refer to the Italian-Somali author, Shirin Ramzanali Fazel.
14. On the overlaps between decolonial and postcolonial knowledge see K. Asher and P. Ramamurthy, 'Rethinking Decolonial and Postcolonial Knowledges beyond Regions to Imagine Transnational Solidarity', *Hypatia*, 35 (2020), 542–47.
15. Henri Lefebvre, *The Production of Space*, trans. by Donald Nicholson Smith (Oxford: Blackwell, 1991); Doreen Massey, *For Space* (London: Sage, 2005).
16. Barbara E. Mann, *Space and Place in Jewish Studies* (New Brunswick, NJ: Rutgers University Press, 2012).
17. Deleuze and Guattari, *Kafka*, p. 22.
18. Jan Assman, 'Collective Memory and Cultural Identity', trans. by John Czaplicka, *New German Critique*, 65 (1995), 125–33.
19. Michael Rothberg, *Multidirectional Memory: Remembering the Holocaust in the Age of Decolonisation* (Stanford, CA: Stanford University Press, 2009).
20. Gilles Deleuze, *Cinema 2: The Time Image*, trans. by Hugh Tomlinson and Robert Galeta (London: Continuum, 2005), p. 209.
21. Gayatri Chakravorty Spivak, *An Aesthetic Education in the Era of Globalization* (Cambridge, MA: Harvard University Press, 2012). Spivak sees language learning as an ethical as well as a political imperative, due to the link between first-language learning and the establishment of an ethical awareness: 'You enrich your ability to become ethically active [...] through the exercise of language learning', 'Occupy Education: An Interview with Gayatri Chakravorty Spivak', 8 January 2012, <https://politicsandculture.org/2012/09/25/occupy-education-an-interview-with-gayatri-chakravorty-spivak/> [accessed 12 October 2021].
22. David Damrosch, *What Is World Literature?* (Princeton, NJ: Princeton University Press, 2003).
23. Yasemin Yildiz, *Beyond the Mother Tongue: The Postmonolingual Condition* (New York: Fordham University Press, 2012).
24. Deleuze and Guattari, *Kafka*, p. 22.
25. Deleuze and Guattari, *Kafka*, p. 23.
26. Pamela McCallum notes the intensity of an apersonal perspective in her discussion of Monica Ali's novel *In the Kitchen* in this volume.
27. Michel Serres and Bruno Latour, *Conversations on Science, Culture, and Time*, trans. by Roxanne Lapidus (Ann Arbor: University of Michigan Press, 2011), p. 107.

PART I

Re-Mapping Europe

CHAPTER 1

Francophone Latin American Writing: Between Two Major Traditions

Kate Averis

Latin American literature has long-standing, historical ties with the French literary tradition, ties anchored in the prestige accorded to France as a cradle of the arts, letters and sciences since the founding of the Latin American republics in the early nineteenth century. Paris's global appeal as the nineteenth century's capital of culture[1] extended to Latin American creole populations, whose ruling classes sought cultural and social education in the city, contributing to the 'myth of Paris' in the Latin American cultural imaginary.[2] Such was its pull that by the end of the nineteenth century it had become the essential site of pilgrimage for Latin America's political, social and cultural elite, and the 'Grand Tour' became an obligatory rite of passage 'para el criollo que como un adolescente primitivo se prepara para poder entrar a la edad adulta de hombre hecho y derecho, con cultura europea, y más concretamente, francesa' [for the creole [the locally born descendant of European colonizers in Latin America] who, as a primitive adolescent, prepares to enter adulthood as a fully formed man, replete with European, and more precisely, French culture].[3]

As well as a site of pilgrimage to which the ruling classes have historically turned for the cultural and social education of their younger (and principally male) members, Paris has also represented a significant literary hub as a site of production, reception and circulation of Latin American literature. In addition to playing a key role in maintaining Latin American literature's historical and sustained ties with French literature, Paris has also been instrumental in the consecration of Latin American authors and literary works: as a site of reception, translation, and circulation of their works.[4] Throughout the nineteenth and twentieth centuries Latin American authors in Paris were able to reach wider publics beyond their respective local audiences, coming into contact and exchange with authors from other countries in their home continent, a contact formerly hampered by the reliance on bilateral publishing and distribution channels between Latin America and the former colonial centre, Spain.[5]

Since the emergence of the foundational texts of Latin American literature in the nineteenth century that looked towards France as a model of civilization,[6] many of its most celebrated works have been written in France (and frequently in Paris), although relatively few of them in French. The highly influential modernist poet and renowned Francophile Rubén Darío wrote many of his poems and chronicles during his residency in the French capital at the onset of the twentieth century (1900–1915), yet going only so far as to 'think in French while writing in Spanish'.[7] Throughout the remainder of the twentieth century many of the poets and novelists who would have the greatest impact on contemporary Latin American literature — amongst them Miguel Ángel Asturias, Alejo Carpentier, Julio Cortázar, Gabriel García Márquez, Octavio Paz, Juan José Saer and Mario Vargas Llosa — wrote some of their best-known works in France, yet not in French. In spite of the important role that Franco-American exchanges have played in the Latin American literary tradition, and the significant Latin American presence in France since the nineteenth and throughout the twentieth century,[8] only very few writers from Latin America have adopted French as a language of literary expression, a trend that can still be observed in an ongoing albeit diminishing practice of contact with Paris and France for Latin American writers.[9]

This chapter takes as its starting point the question posed and left unanswered by Ursula Mathis-Moser and Birgit Mertz-Baumgartner in the introduction to their annotated dictionary of migrant writers in France from 1981 to 2011: 'Why do Latin American migrant authors continue, for the most part, to write in Spanish, barely seeking to enter the field of French literature?'[10] The following analysis approaches this question from its obverse by examining two authors who constitute exceptions to this trend: the anomalous cases of Silvia Baron Supervielle (1934–) and Héctor Bianciotti (1930–2012). By examining two of the very few writers from Latin America to have taken up residence in France and to have published some or all of their works in French, it proposes to examine the quantitatively reduced but stylistically rich field of Francophone Latin American writing that has emerged in the interstices of the two major traditions of French and Latin American literatures.[11] Focusing on writers who have published some or all of their works in France and in French in the late twentieth and early twenty-first century, this chapter traces the historical, cultural and linguistic encounters that have led to the development of a reduced but ongoing tradition of Francophone Latin American writing, thus adopting the methodology proposed by Pascale Casanova in *The World Republic of Letters* to propose an interpretation that is both literary and historical. By exploring the historical conditions under which their texts are produced, as well as paying close attention to their internal, aesthetic qualities, the analysis examines the highly variant routes that led Baron Supervielle and Bianciotti to write in French and their divergent contributions to shaping France's literary landscape.

Echoing Mathis-Moser and Mertz-Baumgartner, Sara Kippur observes that writers from Latin America are underrepresented amongst the translingual writers from around the world who have contributed to the great range and richness of the canon of French literature, which has a long tradition of accommodating writers from a wide range of cultural and linguistic traditions. Kippur notes that of the forty-four writers who co-signed the 2007 manifesto, 'Pour une "littérature-monde" en français', published in the French newspaper *Le Monde* and which calls for a '"World Literature" in French', 'not a single signatory was Latin American'.[12] By contrast with many other writers who made their way to France and French from such varied global locations as Ireland, Spain, Romania, China, Russia and North America,[13] as well as multilingual writers from the formerly colonized nations of France's colonial empire in North and Sub-Saharan Africa, the Caribbean, the Middle East and South-East Asia who have more postcolonial reasons for writing in the French language,[14] Latin American writers have demonstrated a reluctance to adopt French as their language of literary expression. Baron Supervielle and Bianciotti are thus set apart from both their Latin American peers, as Francophone authors, as well as being in a minority amongst their translingual, transnational peers in the French literary space, in which Latin Americans are underrepresented.

It is no coincidence that the two Francophone Latin American writers examined here both hail from Argentina, given the pivotal role of European immigration in the Southern Cone. Nor is it incidental that their unconventional literary choices depart from a Latin American literary and critical tradition steeped in gendered and sexual orthodoxy, where even today some literary and critical works still fail to recognize the phallocentric and heteronormative bias of Latin American literary culture. A further aim of the current chapter, then, is to expand the understanding of the important role that writing in French and in France has played for these Southern Cone writers in enabling the expression of gendered and sexual identities that were repressed or even punished in the place of origin. As such, it builds on efforts, like that of Milagros Palma, to counter the historical invisibility of Latin American women in canonical literary history that has largely focused on its male authors, and like those of Robert Richmond Ellis, to focus on literary acts of resistance to the literal and social policing of non-normative sexualities in Latin America.[15]

The following section turns to the role that a family history of migration and personal experience of translingual culture played in these authors' presence in the field of Francophone Latin American writing. The analysis then focuses on the transnational, translingual manoeuvres in Baron Supervielle's *La Ligne et l'ombre* [The Line and the Shadow] (1999) and Bianciotti's *Ce que la nuit raconte au jour* [What the Night Tells the Day] (1992), two texts that are particularly revealing of the ways in which these authors handle their mixed cultural and linguistic inheritance.[16]

Southern Cone *Francophonies*

Key to becoming a practitioner of Francophone literary writing is the context of cultural and literary exchanges between France and Latin America that form the backdrop to Baron Supervielle's upbringing in the Southern Cone nations of Argentina and Uruguay. While Paris, as the nineteenth-century global capital of culture, attracted the privileged classes of Latin America, Argentina and Uruguay concurrently received an influx of predominantly Italian, Spanish, and French immigration, facilitated through state policies that offered passage, work, and often land in the development of the newly founded republics. The rate of European immigration to the Southern Cone during the course of the nineteenth century was such that the overseas-born population outnumbered the locally born population by the 1890s.

It was during this period that Baron Supervielle's paternal French and maternal Spanish ancestors arrived in Uruguay, triggering what Baron Supervielle would later refer to in *La Ligne et l'ombre* as a hereditary desire for departure passed on from generation to generation that would lead to an inevitable, deferred 'return' to the ancestors' homeland:

> L'émigrant ne vient jamais à bout de son voyage. Il n'a pas la capacité de s'enraciner à nouveau. Fonderait-il une famille dans la terre qui l'accueille, un jour, si ce n'est lui un de ses enfants ou petits-enfants ou arrière-petits-enfants, éprouvera encore une fois le désir de se mettre en marche: de génération en génération, le goût du départ perdure dans le sang des siens. (*La Ligne et l'ombre*, p. 210)

> [The emigrant never reaches the end of their journey. They are not capable of setting down new roots. If they raise a family in the land that welcomes them, one day, they or one of their children or grandchildren or great-grandchildren will feel the desire to set off again: from generation to generation, the desire for departure remains in the blood of their descendants.][17]

Baron Supervielle's linguistic and cultural proximity to France, then, can be traced to her paternal great-grandfather, who arrived in Uruguay before her parents eventually settled in Buenos Aires where Baron Supervielle was born in 1934. Upon the death of her Uruguayan mother in childbirth, the infant was largely raised by her paternal grandmother, who was herself educated in Paris and had an extensive library of works by French authors. Raising the future author in the French cultural tradition, her grandmother passed on not only the French language and culture she had acquired from her own father and education, but also a certain nostalgia for the France she had experienced in her youth. Not solely the result of family inheritance, Baron Supervielle's linguistic and cultural heritage can also be attributed to her membership of a River Plate cultural elite in Montevideo and Buenos Aires that prized the French language and cultural tradition, and in which they educated their children. Her mother's family, born in Montevideo and of Spanish Basque origin, was equally fluent in French and familiar with French culture as her paternal family, thus indicating that the particular appeal of France for the Argentine elite also extended to the wider River Plate region.

By contrast with Baron Supervielle's urban, cosmopolitan background, Bianciotti's parents and grandparents, from the agricultural Piedmont region of northwestern Italy, settled in rural Argentina near Córdoba where they discouraged their children from learning their Piedmontese dialect, motivated by a well-intentioned insistence on their children's assimilation into the newly adopted national language and culture. Bianciotti thus learnt neither the Piedmontese dialect nor the Italian language of his family heritage and, as he recounts in *Ce que la nuit raconte au jour*, reading in the family home was restricted to Sundays and rainy days. It was only upon discovering the poetry of Paul Valéry in a newspaper supplement issued on the occasion of the poet's death that the adolescent Bianciotti was inspired to teach himself French out of a desire to read Valéry's poetry in the original, thus illustrating Baron Supervielle's somewhat withering claim that, in Argentina:

> la langue française, aimée de tous, n'éta[i]t pas seulement réservée à une élite: des personnes simples, de peu de moyens, l'apprenaient avec ferveur, comme si elle avait le pouvoir de leur offrir une existence plus digne.[18]
>
> [the French language, loved by all, was not solely the preserve of an elite: humble people, of few resources, learned it eagerly, as though it had the power to offer them a more dignified existence.]

While Baron Supervielle's eventual departure for Paris at the age of twenty-seven followed a well-trodden path for the young men and to a lesser extent, women, of her background, Bianciotti's trajectory from rural Argentina to Paris, via Córdoba, Buenos Aires, Rome and Madrid, arriving in Paris at thirty-one, is a highly atypical one. In *La Ligne et l'ombre* and *Ce que la nuit raconte au jour*, Baron Supervielle and Bianciotti respectively evoke their positioning within these broad historical and cultural trends. Each describes their upbringing in a multilingual household in which the languages of their ancestors were present to differing degrees: French in Baron Supervielle's case cohabiting with — and Italian and Piedmontese in Bianciotti's case superseded by — the local Argentine Spanish, itself marked by the European languages, and particularly Italian, that disembarked along with their speakers in the Southern Cone. For Baron Supervielle, then, the use of French was consistent with her family background and social milieu in which multilingualism (and particularly knowledge of French) was a valued cultural trait, while for Bianciotti it represented a radical departure from the environment in which he was raised, where multilingualism (and, in particular, use of the regional Italian dialect) was perceived as a hindrance to assimilation for new migrants and their offspring.

By the time Baron Supervielle and Bianciotti departed from Argentina and arrived in Paris, both in 1961, the Latin American presence in Paris was undergoing a rapid transformation.[19] The quest for 'civilization' and 'edification' that in the nineteenth century had driven Latin America's political and cultural elite to France, and in particular to Paris, was giving way to rapidly evolving patterns of mobility that reflected twentieth-century political and economic developments in Latin America, notably, the 1959 Cuban revolution, the Southern Cone military dictatorships in the 1970s and '80s, and conflict and economic decline in the Andean region towards the end of the century. These two writers, then, are situated on the cusp of a long period of cultural and social contact with France that was initially restricted to a Latin American elite but was now opening towards more widespread modes of mobility and exchange between Latin America and Europe. Their highly divergent strategies of telling stories of intercultural belonging are revealing of these wider changes.

The Francophone, Autobiographical Return

Baron Supervielle's *La Ligne et l'ombre*, a lyrical reflection on memory, writing and her own geographic and linguistic crossings, penned at sixty-five years of age, escapes easy classification. Its lyrical style echoes the fluid motion of the River Seine that flows past her writing desk, both of which are repeatedly evoked in this non-fictional, autobiographical text. The first in a series of four reflective autobiographical texts, it forms part of a prodigious corpus that includes over fifty works of poetry, prose and translation, almost all published in French over five decades.[20] From Baron Supervielle's first publication, a collection of poetry entitled *Les Fenêtres* [*The Windows*] (1977), to her most recent (at the time of writing), a novel entitled *Le Regard inconnu* [*The Unfamiliar Gaze*] (2020), her works have persistently traced the contours of a writerly life spent between nations, languages and cultures.[21] Having composed poetry in Spanish while living in Buenos Aires, it was not until she settled in Paris that she published her first collection, this time written in French. Baron Supervielle describes her switch to writing in French as being for practical reasons, in order to share her poetry with friends in Paris unfamiliar with Spanish, such that the origins of her translingual writing project is less a gesture of Francophile reverence than a pragmatic deployment of the linguistic tools available to her. She recounts this linguistic shift with considerable detachment:

> Je me remis à écrire, les mots ne pouvant pas me voir. Ils appartenaient à la langue française, mais ils auraient pu appartenir à une langue différente, me serais-je retrouvée dans un autre pays. (*La Ligne et l'ombre*, p. 53)
>
> [I began writing again, the words being unable to see me. They belonged to the French language, but they might have belonged to another language, had I found myself in another country.]

Her apparently dispassionate switch from Spanish to French might be more precisely characterized, then, as a detachment from particular languages, and a move towards a space between languages, which for her comes to represent the necessary condition for writing, as she rather haughtily declares:

> celui qui n'éprouve pas le besoin de sortir de sa langue, en utilisant celle-ci ou une autre, pour en inventer une nouvelle qui ne réponde qu'à son étrange monde, n'est que l'imitation d'un écrivain. (*La Ligne et l'ombre*, p. 75)
>
> [he who does not feel the need to step outside his language, using this one or another, to invent a new one that responds only to his strange world, is but the imitation of a writer.]

For Baron Supervielle, a writer must detach him- or herself from an unreflective use of the language(s) available to them in order to create their own language, to express their own being, a sentiment also expressed by Mohamed Kacimi, an author born in Algeria who lives in Paris and writes in French, when he says: 'Je n'écris pas en français. J'écris en "moi-même"' [I don't write in French. I write in 'myself'].[22]

The Argentine writer Jorge Luis Borges — with whom Baron Supervielle was acquainted and a number of whose works she translated from Spanish into French

— is cited in *La Ligne et l'ombre* as being emblematic of the polyglot who writes beyond any particular language to create his own. She cites by way of example his tendency to:

> place[r] les adjectifs avant les noms comme il est d'usage en anglais, de sorte que sa langue en vient ni de l'Espagne, ni de l'Argentine ou d'un autre pays d'Amérique du Sud, mais uniquement de lui (*La Ligne et l'ombre*, p. 81)

> [place adjectives before nouns as is customary in English, so that his language comes neither from Spain nor from Argentina, nor any other country in South America, but only from him.]

Baron Supervielle can be said to create her own literary language through the crafting of an interstitial style that dwells on the in-between spaces and elements that unite 'here' and 'there', as is strikingly illustrated by a selection of her publication titles over the last five decades: the aforementioned *Les Fenêtres* [*The Windows*] (1977), *Espace de la mer* [*The Space of the Sea*] (1981), *La Frontière* [*The Frontier*] (1995), *Autour du vide* [*Around the Void*] (2008), and *Sur le fleuve* [*On the River*] (2013). In *La Ligne et l'ombre*, Baron Supervielle employs a number of her favoured motifs of simultaneous separation and approximation — the window, the river, the sea — to trace a return, via the waters that flow between them, from her adopted city to those of her childhood, adopting a syntax that mimics the lapping of water:

> ...Et la fenêtre près de la Seine, dont les eaux se jettent dans l'Atlantique et dans un autre fleuve, le Río de la Plata, au bord duquel je suis née. Sur l'une de ses rives, Buenos Aires, ma ville, sur l'autre, Montevideo, la ville de ma mère [...]. (*La Ligne et l'ombre*, p. 7).

> [...And the window by the Seine, whose waters flow into the Atlantic and into another river, the River Plate, alongside which I was born. On one of its banks, Buenos Aires, my city, on the other, Montevideo, my mother's city [...].]

If the writing desk features as a figurative point of anchorage in the 'here' and 'now', it is also the material site of production of Baron Supervielle's interstitial, lyrical prose and also of her many translations from Spanish into French of the works of predominantly Argentine writers. In her capacity as both writer and translator she acts as a vector of transcultural exchange, drawing the expression of Southern Cone experience and identity — both her own and others' — into the French literary space. In this sense, she might be compared to the singular Argentine literary figure, Victoria Ocampo, arguably better known as a highly influential editor, publisher and literary patron in mid-twentieth-century Buenos Aires than for her own considerable body of writing. For both Baron Supervielle and Ocampo, translation and literary mediation form a significant part of their respective writing projects alongside their own writing, and both act as transnational literary agents in fomenting channels of literary contact and exchange between Argentina and France, albeit in opposite directions across the Atlantic, as observed by Axel Gasquet:

> Victoria Ocampo cherche à amener le monde en Argentine, en donnant à sa maison d'édition *Sur*, une envergure cosmopolite; Baron Supervielle veut rapprocher l'Argentine de la France à travers ses traductions.[23]

> [Victoria Ocampo seeks to bring the world to Argentina, by giving her publishing house *Sur* a cosmopolitan scope; Baron Supervielle wants to draw Argentina and France closer together through her translations.]

This role is of course available to Baron Supervielle only through her privileged, life-long access to both the French and Spanish languages, her inheritance of the literary traditions expressed in these languages, and her contact with Parisian critics, publishers and other writers. It is perhaps also her privileged access and mobility which relegates her corpus to a particular, and somewhat restricted, receptive framework in a contemporary critical environment that (rightly) has been keen to make up for the historical neglect of overlooked and underrepresented minority voices, as indicated by the very limited critical attention her work has received. As mentioned above, Baron Supervielle's arrival in Paris came at the end of a long period of contact with France that was largely restricted to Latin America's economically and socially privileged classes and preceded the arrival of political exiles expelled by the military dictatorships of the 1970s and '80s and other mobile subjects displaced by conflict and economic decline who would provide literary history with a rich vein of innovative and influential works. Baron Supervielle's publications might equally be considered to have landed at a critical turning point when they began appearing in the 1970s, corresponding neither to local, French expectations of the 'exiled Argentine writer', nor to the tastes of readers 'at home', many of whom rejected the class structures that led Baron Supervielle to Paris in the first place. Her works have more recently garnered recognition through prestigious awards in France — the *Prix de littérature francophone Jean Arp* (2012), the *Prix spécial Roger Caillois* (2013), and the *Prix du rayonnement de la langue et de la littérature françaises* (2019) of the *Academie française*. These, as well as the 2013 publication of her collected poetry in Argentina — in the bilingual *Al margen/En marge: poesía reunida/poésie réunie* [*On the Margin: Collected Poetry*][24] — testify to her institutional recognition as a prominent figure in a francophone literary space that spans both French and Latin American literatures and who, as a solitary female migrant, disrupted gender and class expectations to attain such prominence.

If Baron Supervielle's 'choice' to publish her first collection of poetry in French in 1977 was primarily an editorial and practical decision, Bianciotti's adoption and use of French indicates a more deferential, even reverential approach to the language that he began to study on his own as a boy in rural Argentina. Bianciotti began writing in French only after publishing four novels, one collection of short stories and one play that were written in Spanish but published first in their French translation; the remainder of his corpus, comprising six novels, one collection of essays and one of letters, were written directly in French. This linguistic shift was accompanied by a generic shift towards the autobiographical, and *Ce que la nuit raconte au jour* is the first volume of an autobiographical trilogy published between 1992 and 1999.[25] Its opening line bears witness to a pressing need to turn to life-writing while also self-consciously drawing attention to the first-person writing project: 'Aujourd'hui, c'est ma vie qui me cherche' [Today, my life has come looking for me] (*Ce que la nuit raconte au jour*, p. 7). Bianciotti's striking use of a split narrating subject notably shifts the agency away from the present narrating self to a past life ('ma vie') that begs to be told ('qui me cherche'), a subjective compartmentalization shared by Baron Supervielle in *La Ligne et l'ombre* where the narrator refers throughout to 'celle qui écrit' [she who writes], implying the great distance traversed by both authors from the past to the present self. Indeed, Ellis describes *Ce que la nuit raconte au jour* as 'an extended metaphor of escape',[26] insofar as it recounts a gradual journey away from what Bianciotti's narrator describes as a restrictive physical landscape — despite its limitless confines — on the Argentine plains of his childhood, experienced by the young boy as a culturally barren environment:

> Dans ces matinées de l'enfance, au galop du Colorado, je vis devant moi la terre en allée et le ciel reculer sans cesse et, prenant conscience de ma captivité, je sentis s'accroître jusqu'à l'insoutenable, la requête d'une limite, d'une frontière, voire d'un obstacle. (*Ce que la nuit raconte au jour*, p. 76)

> [Galloping on Colorado in these mornings of my childhood, I saw the earth stretching away and the sky incessantly receding before me, and becoming aware of my captivity, I felt within me the growing and unbearable need for a boundary, a frontier, an obstacle even.]

Ce que la nuit raconte au jour describes Bianciotti's rural childhood in the Argentina *pampa* as the son of Italian immigrant parents, his awakening homosexuality, his departure from the family home to study at a seminary where he experiences his first sexual encounters, and his years as a young gay man in a politically and socially repressive Buenos Aires during the Peronist era, before closing with his departure for Europe in 1955. While this autobiographical text describes the subject's gradual movement away from Latin America and towards Europe, the adoption of French conversely brings the author back to his Argentine life for the first time in his writing, while also reversing the historical channels of cultural influence between France and Latin America as he, like Baron Supervielle, transposes Argentine experience into the francophone literary text.

Bianciotti's description of an austere and culturally impoverished childhood in rural Argentina — what he describes as 'ce monde à la fois si vaste et si étroit' [this world at once so vast and so narrow] (*Ce que la nuit raconte au jour*, p. 110) on the plains of his childhood — only more forcefully highlights his symbolic as well as physical flight from the cultural and literary margins through the excessively lyrical, grammatically sophisticated, and highly literary style that he adopts in its narration:

> Il s'en fallait de quinze ans que Perón ne prît le pouvoir, quand je suis né au mois de mars, dans cette plaine argentine que j'ai essayé de décrire, ou d'exorciser tant de fois. (*Ce que la nuit raconte au jour*, p. 14)

> [Fifteen years would pass before Peron came to power when I was born, in the month of March, on this Argentine plain that I have tried to describe, or to exorcise, so many times.]

Such an overt demonstration of mastery of French — in the lengthy syntactical constructions, the ternary rhythms, and the use of the historical past and the negative subjunctive in the above two extracts — also emulates the epitome of a certain style of highly literary French prose. Critics such as Ellis and Gasquet have drawn comparisons between Bianciotti's memory-driven prose and that of Proust in *À la recherche du temps perdu* (1913–27). Such canonical echoes alongside textual references in *Ce que la nuit raconte au jour* to popular works by Max du Veuzit and Delly, which constitute some of the narrator's earliest readings in French, provide an indication of his autonomous and varied immersion in French literature and culture that, as mentioned, included the poetry of Paul Valéry and which provided the future author with some relief from the cultural claustrophobia and homophobia experienced in Argentina.

Bianciotti's emulative, deferential style largely failed to connect with a wide readership in France and he similarly remained practically unknown in Argentina,[27] the resistant identity and sexual politics of his autobiographical writing perhaps overshadowed by his reverence towards the canonical forms to which he showed himself indebted. He nevertheless garnered consecration and accolades from France's most prestigious literary institutions: upon arrival in Paris he almost immediately entered cultural and literary circles, taken on as a reader at Gallimard from 1962 and subsequently as a literary critic at *La Quinzaine littéraire*, *Nouvel observateur* and *Le Monde*; he reaped major literary awards in France, including the *Prix Femina*, the *Prix Médicis étranger* and the *Prix du meilleur livre étranger*; and he eventually attained membership, in 1996, of the ultimate bastion of French literary culture, the *Académie française*. Recognition of Bianciotti's adoption of the French language and contribution to French literature by this notorious institution not only gives a sense of his engagement with French literary culture but also signals a stark contrast with what he experienced as his expulsion from 1940s and '50s Argentina and a lack of recognition in Argentina as a critically acclaimed writer and Franco-American transcultural agent from the 1960s until his death in 2012.

The institutional recognition that both Bianciotti and Baron Supervielle enjoyed in France, paired with their relative lack of widespread academic and public attention both in France and Argentina, is suggestive of a national literary culture in France that is flattered by and keen to reward the adoption of French and a concurrent difficulty to accommodate Francophone Latin American writing within existing national, linguistic or literary categories, in both France and Argentina. While exceptional, Baron Supervielle and Bianciotti's status as Francophone Latin American writers is not unique, given the field's history which dates back to the nineteenth century, as shown, and the ongoing, twenty-first-century practice of writers who provide more recent iterations of the field, one notable example being Laura Alcoba's developing corpus of work. Of note is Alcoba's transposition into the French literary text of the child's experience of the military dictatorship in Argentina and exile to France in the 1970s, and the young adolescent's subsequent account of learning French and adapting to life in a Parisian housing estate, testifying to the evolution of the field in light of the material, historical circumstances that led to its production, as have also seen to be instrumental in the francophone works of Baron Supervielle and Bianciotti.[28]

Compelling readers to review any existing assumptions that they might hold concerning the 'choice' of adopting the position of linguistic and 'literary interloper',[29] and rendering impossible the adoption of linguistically or regionally defined reading frameworks, Francophone Latin American writing raises important questions about the linguistic and literary hierarchies that govern literary consecration and the variable climates in which literary texts are read and circulate. Concurrently 'Latin American', 'French' and 'Francophone', while also exceeding or failing to fully inhabit any of these qualifiers, Latin American authors who write in French express the play of cultural and linguistic legacies and hierarchies that inform the production, circulation and reception of a contemporary tradition of Francophone Latin American writing that is produced in the interstitial spaces between France and Latin America and that illustrates the dynamism and hybridity of European literary space.

Notes to Chapter 1

1. Walter Benjamin, 'Paris, Capital of the Nineteenth Century' (1939), in *The Arcades Project*, trans. by Howard Eiland and Kevin McLaughlin (Cambridge, MA: Harvard University Press, 1999), pp. 14–26.
2. As sustained by Patrice Higonnet, *Paris: Capital of the World*, trans. by Arthur Goldhammer (Cambridge, MA: Harvard University Press, 2002); Jason Weiss, *The Lights of Home: A Century of Latin American Writers in Paris* (New York: Routledge, 2003); and Milagros Palma, *El mito de París: entrevistas con escritores latinoamericanos en París* (Paris: Indigo and Côté-femmes, 2004).
3. Palma, *El mito de París*, p. 9.
4. Jean-Claude Villegas, *Paris: capitale littéraire de l'Amérique latine* (Dijon: Éditions universitaires de Dijon, 2007).
5. Pascale Casanova, *The World Republic of Letters*, trans. by M. B. DeBevoise (Cambridge, MA: Harvard University Press, 2007), pp. 126–63.
6. See Domingo F. Sarmiento's *Facundo: civilización y barbarie* (1845) for a canonical example of this.
7. Mariano Siskind, *Cosmopolitan Desires: Global Modernity and World Literature in Latin America* (Evanston, IL: Northwestern University Press, 2014), p. 214.
8. Milagros Palma's anthology, *Le Paris latino-américain: anthologie des écrivains latino-américains à Paris* (Paris: Indigo and Côté-femmes, 2006) includes over one hundred Latin American writers in Paris up until the end of the twentieth century.
9. In recent decades, the Colombian writers Juan Gabriel Vásquez, Pablo Montoya and Héctor Abad Faciolince report having spent formative periods in Paris while the Argentine writers Elsa Osorio and Laura Alcoba, and the Cuban writer Zoé Valdés, have settled and established literary careers there. Of these writers, only Laura Alcoba has published works in French.
10. Ursula Mathis-Moser and Birgit Mertz-Baumgartner, *Passages et ancrages: dictionnaire des 'écrivains migrants' en France depuis 1981* (Paris: Champion, 2011), p. 115.
11. From the nineteenth century to the present, the most frequently cited authors of the reduced field of Francophone Latin American literature include Enrique Gómez Carrillo, Jules Supervielle, Vicente Huidobro, César Moro, Alfredo Gangotena and Copi (Raúl Damonte), and to a lesser extent, Julio Quiñones, Ramón Fernández, Gloria Alcorta, Eduardo Manet, Alicia Dujovne Ortiz, Santiago Amigorena and Laura Alcoba.
12. Sara Kippur, 'Pour ou contre une littérature-monde? Héctor Bianciotti, Silvia Baron Supervielle, and the Case of Argentina', *Contemporary French and Francophone Studies*, 13.2 (2009), 211–22 (p. 211).
13. Such as James Joyce, Samuel Beckett, Jorge Semprun, Eugène Ionesco, Emil Cioran, Dai Sijie, François Cheng, Andreï Makine, Nancy Huston and Jonathan Littell.
14. Such as Assia Djebar, Hélène Cixous, Tierno Monénembo, Alain Mabanckou, Patrick Chamoiseau, Maryse Condé, Amin Maalouf, Vénus Khoury-Ghata and Anna Moï.

15. Robert Richmond Ellis, 'Homoeroticism and the Ever-Recurring Illusion of Selfhood: The Argentine "Life" of Hector Bianciotti', *Revista Canadiense de Estudios Hispánicos*, 22.3 (1998), 431–46.
16. Silvia Baron Supervielle, *La Ligne et l'ombre* (Paris: Seuil, 1999); Héctor Bianciotti, *Ce que la nuit raconte au jour* (Paris: Grasset, 1992) [*What the Night Tells the Day*, trans. by Linda Coverdale (New York: New Press, 1995)].
17. All translations throughout are my own.
18. Silvia Baron Supervielle, *L'Alphabet du feu: petites études sur la langue* (Paris: Gallimard, 2007), p. 43.
19. Olga González, 'La Présence latino-américaine en France', in *Migrations latino-américaines*, special issue of *Hommes et migrations*, ed. by Olga González, 1270 (2007), 8–18.
20. The other three works being *Le Pays de l'écriture* (Paris: Seuil, 2002); *L'Alphabet du feu* (2007); *Journal d'une saison sans mémoire* (Paris: Gallimard, 2009).
21. Silvia Baron Supervielle, *Les Fenêtres* (Paris: Hors commerce, 1977); *Le Regard inconnu* (Paris: Gallimard, 2020).
22. Mohamed Kacimi, cited in Martine Paulin, 'Langue maternelle et langue d'écriture', in *Langues et migrations*, ed. by Claire Extramania, special issue of *Hommes et migrations*, 1288 (2010), 118–28 (p. 120).
23. Axel Gasquet, *L'Intelligentsia du bout du monde* (Paris: Kimé, 2002), p. 291.
24. Silvia Baron Supervielle, *Al margen/en marge: poesía reunida/poésie réunie* (Buenos Aires: Adriana Hidalgo, 2013).
25. The two subsequent volumes of the autobiographical trilogy being *Le Pas si lent de l'amour* (Paris: Grasset, 1995) and *Comme la trace de l'oiseau dans l'air* (Paris: Grasset, 1999).
26. Ellis, 'Homoeroticism and the Ever-Recurring Illusion of Selfhood: The Argentine "Life" of Hector Bianciotti', p. 433.
27. Alberto Giordano, 'Situación de Héctor Bianciotti: el escritor argentino y la tradición francesa', *Hispamérica*, 28.84 (1999), 3–12 (p. 3).
28. See, in particular, her autobiographical trilogy: *Manèges: petite histoire argentine* (Paris: Gallimard, 2007); *Le Bleu des abeilles* (Paris: Gallimard, 2013); and *La Danse de l'araignée* (Paris: Gallimard, 2017).
29. Steven G. Kellman, *The Translingual Imagination* (Lincoln: University of Nebraska Press, 2000), p. 8.

CHAPTER 2

German-Jewish Women's Writing in Early Twentieth-Century Berlin: Claiming Space for a (Multiple) Minority

Godela Weiss-Sussex

By the early twentieth century, German Jews had long held a markedly fraught minoritized position within German society. Centuries of progressive legal emancipation had not changed this, and neither had the huge contribution German Jews had made to German cultural production. During the first two decades of the 1900s, a time of accelerated social and cultural change, the project of assimilation was, by and large, continued: most German Jews, especially from the highly educated middle classes, regarded themselves as Germans first and foremost; though, as anti-Semitic discourses gathered momentum too, movements of dissimilation, primarily in the form of Zionism, gained ground as well. Literary and autobiographical texts by male authors of the time exploring their place in society have achieved some prominence — Kafka, Schnitzler, Wassermann and Freud are cases in point — but German-Jewish women writers have received far less attention.[1]

This chapter will consider three novels by female authors of great energy and intellectual acuity, who used their writing to actively participate in important societal discourses of their time; they are Auguste Hauschner's two Lowositz novels (*Die Familie Lowositz* [*The Lowositz Family*], 1908, and *Rudolf und Camilla* [*Rudolf and Camilla*], 1910), Grete Meisel-Hess's *Die Intellektuellen* [*The Intellectuals*] (1911), and Elisabeth Landau's *Der Holzweg* [*The Dead End*] (1918). All three texts are firmly rooted in their authors' autobiographical experience and may be read as reactions to their precarious social position, as they were marginalized as Jews and as women. Auguste Hauschner, indeed, speaks of the 'doppelte[] Martyrium des Weibseins und des Judentums' [twofold martyrdom of being a woman and being a Jew].[2] Concentrating on authors who wrote in and about Berlin, Germany's first metropolis and a hub of German-Jewish intellectual and artistic activity, and focusing on a decade of rapid change in the position of German Jewry in Germany, allows us to identify strategies and crystallize differences in literary responses to clearly defined socio-cultural circumstances.

Specifically, this chapter will show the novels' varied approaches to asserting claims for liberation from minoritarian marginalization and to positively articulating a space for German-Jewish women on the cultural map of Europe. A central question to be raised in this context is to what extent these authors conceive of space not simply as static but as 'the product of interrelations', 'always under construction',[3] and therefore intrinsically connected with time and with an assumption of openness to transition, change and futurity. This understanding, put forward by Doreen Massey, among others, resonates with the well-established concept of Jewish non-territoriality. However, Barbara E. Mann, following Daniel and Jonathan Boyarin, makes the case for a re-evaluation of the importance of making a home and investing space with a sense of belonging, i.e. of 'place-making', in geographer Yi-Fu Tuan's terms:[4] 'Jews are always a "displaced" people', Mann argues, 'and therefore conscious of the need to turn space into place'.[5] We shall therefore think of space in relational as well as territorial terms in order to do justice to the texts under discussion.[6]

Literature is at the heart of the symbolic act of 'claiming space' because, as Massey explains, both the political act of claiming space and the concept of place 'depend[] crucially on the notion of articulation'.[7] German women's literary writing of the early twentieth century, in particular, is a fertile field for new, and often utopian, conceptualizations of space and place, as a number of authors at the time were questioning the static concepts of home and belonging encapsulated in the traditional spatially-bound concept of 'Heimat'.[8]

Focusing on German-Jewish women's writing here, the following questions will thus be at the centre of this chapter's enquiry: To what extent do these authors critique or even reject their allocated position in geographical and social terms? What strategies do they develop of claiming space? What spaces are claimed? What alternative concepts of belonging are developed, what communities aligned with or posited? And to what extent do the novels presented here use concepts of territorial fixity and/or make a case for conceiving of a space of belonging inscribed with mobility and change?

The first texts considered here, Auguste Hauschner's *Die Familie Lowositz* (1908) and *Rudolf und Camilla* (1910), tell the story of a German-Jewish pair of siblings growing up in Prague and moving to Berlin as young adults. Of particular importance here is the narrative strand concerned with Camilla Lowositz, and her experience of a loveless childhood and an arranged marriage. Hauschner explicitly addresses her female protagonist's position as member of a triple minority — a German speaker in Prague, a Jew and a woman — but focuses *not* on her marginalization as a speaker of German or a Jew (these aspects, which refer to cross-community social interactions, are reserved for the narrative strand dedicated to her brother's life), but on her situation as a young woman in a Jewish minority community holding on to traditionally prescribed gender roles and practices.

Camilla's life is marked by neglect and restriction. Hauschner presents a harsh indictment of the social sphere of middle-class German Jews in Prague, a community in which girls grow up in a highly restricted social radius, with no support for their intellectual growth and with no prospect of a fulfilling future apart from marriage, seen as their life's goal.

Through the sensitive and psychologically sophisticated portrayal of her young protagonist, Hauschner elicits the reader's empathy with her situation as one of spatial, social and intellectual restriction and of subjugation by the rules of a patriarchal community. Focusing on the practice of the arranged marriage, still then a custom of the traditional German-Jewish minority culture this novel reflects, Hauschner critiques a *status quo* that denies her protagonist any agency. Indeed, she highlights how the psychological pressure wrought on the young woman has hardened into a deep-seated character trait: a sense of 'Gebundenheit' [bondage] that stands in the way of any liberating emotion or action.[9] She makes sure to extend her narrative beyond that of an individual concern and to claim a representative character for her text: positing a general Jewish tendency to melancholic yearning, she explains it, *not* as caused by the experience of oppression or persecution endured by generations of Jews — a trope that might be expected here[10] — but, in a highly unusual turn, by the Jewish practice of the arranged marriage. 'Wer weiß', Camilla's brother Rudolf muses, 'ob er seinen sehnsüchtigen Sinn nicht irgend einer Frau verdankte, deren Sehnsucht, an einen ungeliebten Mann verhandelt, hatte ungestillt verbrennen müssen' [Who knows whether he might not have inherited his yearning mind from a woman whose longing had burnt out unfulfilled, as she was sold to an unloved husband] (*RuC*, 316). Camilla's story of oppression takes on significance as communal enunciation, first, in relation to German-Jewish women, but secondly also as cause for a general 'Jewish' consciousness or characteristic shared by both genders.

Hauschner's protagonist does not have the strength to resist the arranged marriage; she cannot voice her desire to break out from the constraints of the traditional German-Jewish customs and the state of boundedness that her community imposes on her. Over the course of the novel, however, the author describes a trajectory from suffering and oppression in a destructive, restrictive environment, via a number of failed attempts at liberation, towards the protagonist's dawning consciousness of the possibility of a different future, a 'natural' new beginning, culminating in an attempt to claim — even if the act is unrealistic and utopian — a place of freely chosen belonging.

When, following the birth of her daughter, Camilla suffers a nervous breakdown — in the wake of Sigmund Freud's and Josef Breuer's *Studien über Hysterie* ([*Studies on Hysteria*], 1895) a well-used trope in contemporary women's literature for feminine resistance[11] — and is sent to stay with a cousin in Berlin to recover, the reader is led to expect that the big city with its loosened ties of family and community and its promises of intellectual and cultural activity might provide the liberation the protagonist longs for.

In the novel's narrative arc, however, the city of Berlin stands for a blind alley in the search for a positive cultural space to be claimed: Hauschner paints a picture of a place in which immorality, duplicity and morphine abuse are rife. We can see the influence here of contemporary psychiatrist Richard von Krafft-Ebing, who, in his treatise *Psychopathia Sexualis* of 1886, had condemned the world's metropoles as breeding grounds of the unnatural and the degenerate: 'Dass die Großstädte Brutstätten der Nervosität und entarteten Sinnlichkeit sind, ergibt sich aus der

Geschichte von Babylon, Ninive, Rom, gleichwie aus den Mysterien des modernen großstädtischen Lebens' [Large Cities are hotbeds in which neuroses and low morality are bred, *vide* the history of Babylon, Nineveh, Rome and the mysteries of modern metropolitan life].[12]

Krafft-Ebing also provides the template for Camilla's eventual vision of a better future, as he sets the ideal of motherhood up as counterpoint to and remedy for the evils of modern civilization and, specifically, as the cure for nervous diseases such as hysteria; following Darwin, he describes 'Mutterliebe' [motherly love] as the natural instinct that will preserve the species.[13] Echoing his thinking, Hauschner conceives of her protagonist's redemption in a state of freedom beyond the confines of any particular society: by acknowledging her 'unermeßlich reiche[]' [immeasurably rich] (*RuC*, 372–73) love for her child, Camilla embraces the biological commonality of motherhood, while at the same time rejecting the social obligations of family and community life that patriarchal society places on mothers: she resolves to accept her motherhood but to separate from her husband.

The commitment to motherhood thus provides the impetus to rejecting notions of home that entail not only restriction but also objectification and the denial of voice. This may seem surprising, as the emphasis on gendered responsibility that informs the idea of motherhood is rooted in the conservative thinking of Krafft-Ebing. However, referring to the feminist politics of Luce Irigaray, Rosi Braidotti explains this two-faced character of the idea: 'in more recent feminist readings [...] [m]otherhood is seen as both one of the pillars of patriarchal domination of women and one of the strongholds of female identity'.[14] As Irigaray, who thus reclaims motherhood and sexual difference as a resource for women, contends, motherhood allows the positive conceptualization of sexual difference in a future-oriented context grounded in a sense of female humanity.[15]

It is this commonality of female humanity that is claimed here as a new space of belonging lying outside the constraints of the patriarchal community, into which Camilla and her fellow members of the multiple minority of German-Jewish women were born. The claim is based in a shared sense of identity and it is supported and given substance through the biological argument of a 'natural' way of life but, beyond a very vague evocation of an idyllic rural location far from the corruptions of civilization, it is not connected with a territorially — or indeed, socially — defined space.

Hauschner seems well-aware of the unrealistic, utopian dimension to her protagonist's decision; the act of claiming a space does not (yet) seem possible for her. It remains unclear where this idyllic, rural space, free of all restrictions, might be found and how the unworldly Camilla could possibly provide for herself and her daughter. Even more importantly, the reader is left asking how likely it is for Camilla to shed the character trait of 'Gebundenheit' that has defined her for so long. Even if a new claim for belonging can be made, what chance is there to escape from the self? The author herself clearly wrestled with this question, as we can see from a review of Arthur Schnitzler's novel *Der Weg ins Freie* [*The Road to the Open*], which she published in 1909, while working on *Rudolf und Camilla*, and which she ended with the question: 'Gibt es einen Weg zur Selbstbefreiung? Und ist nicht das die Frage, die der Dichter stellen wollte?' [Is there a road to self-liberation? And is this not the question the author wanted to ask?].[16]

Only three years later, a very different voice was to be heard: Grete Meisel-Hess's novel *Die Intellektuellen* (1911) traces the emotional and intellectual journey to maturity of her *alter ego*, Olga, in a novel that brims over with self-confidence and optimism. Meisel-Hess claims a space for the German-Jewish community at the heart of the German nation, and she does so on two levels: firstly, by emphasizing her protagonist's at-homeness in the political and cultural centre, Berlin, and secondly by asserting a crucial role for German Jews in national and international endeavours to improve no less than the future of humanity.

Olga's story is the narrative of her migration from a petit-bourgeois Jewish community in an (unnamed) small town in Silesia, via Vienna, to Berlin. It is conceived as a trajectory of liberation and, rather than expanding on the boundedness and oppression of the home environment, as Hauschner does, Meisel-Hess's positive and optimistic narrative focuses on the place of arrival, the congenial space for the strident, self-confident protagonist. Olga's arrival in Berlin, the description of which fills ten pages, is developed in a downright explosive way, as the release of a life-long accumulation of frustration: entering Berlin on the train, Olga immediately feels 'freer'; she looks forward to being able to work 'freely' and unrestrained, to let her will 'roam free' — and even the fields she sees on her way into the city are described as 'free'.[17]

The sense of liberation is mainly conceived in contrast to the petit-bourgeois norms and expectations linked to class and gender that Olga experienced in Silesia and in Vienna, but it is also related to the protagonist's Jewishness. Olga's new home city — or at least the milieu of intellectuals in which the novel's characters move — is curiously free of anti-Semitism. We may criticize this as an act of wilful blindness on the part of the author or a lack of sensitivity to social reality, but Meisel-Hess was not alone in this perception.[18] Georg Hermann, for instance, a German-Jewish author whose knowledge and understanding of Berlin was second to none, described Berlin as a congenial home for 'wurzellose intellektuelle Großstadtjuden' [rootless intellectual metropolitan Jews] in the years before the First World War.[19]

Hermann's is only one in the chorus of voices asserting this affinity between metropolis and intellectual Jew, but he is more acute than most when it comes to explaining the reason: it is the opportunity the metropolis provides to its inhabitants 'sich nicht an den seienden Dingen begnügen zu lassen [*sic*], sondern über die seienden Dinge hinaus zu-schaffende-Möglichkeiten zu sehen' [to not simply be contented with things as they are but to see possibilities to be explored beyond the current state of affairs] that he highlights as particularly resonant with the German-Jewish mindset.[20] Jewishness is here firmly linked with intellectual and/or creative energy and a future-oriented will to promote reform; and Berlin, the ever-changing place of encounters, the place without tradition — a trope that has a history reaching back far before cultural historian Karl Scheffler made it commonplace in his 1910 volume *Berlin, ein Stadtschicksal*[21] — is thus posited as the German Jews' obviously congenial home.

Indeed, it is precisely this sense of openness and contingency that makes Olga experience Berlin as 'Zuhause' (*I*, 510), a place to be at home in. The choice of vocabulary is significant here: she avoids the loaded term 'Heimat' and thus defines her home not in reference to an idealized construct of origin and familial togetherness,[22] but to the freely chosen and actively constituted relationship with 'Menschen, die nach ähnlichen Zielen ringen' [people who are striving for similar goals] (*I*, 44). Race and geographical origin play no role in this community so determinedly oriented towards the future — and neither does gender. There is no need, in Meisel-Hess's positive world view, to claim a particular space for women; Olga's integration as an equal in the reformist circles in which she moves and her success as a journalist and inspirational public speaker are never in question.

In fact, in contrast to Hauschner, Meisel-Hess shows us the German-Jewish woman as an individual with agency rather than a victim of social conditions and forces; her Olga actively constructs place in the sense of Doreen Massey's definition — as a significant space 'formed out of social interrelations'.[23] Olga's claim of belonging in Berlin is touchingly supported by a little poem, in which she professes her understanding of and affinity with the city and which ends with the words 'ich glaube ich verstehe dich, — Berlin' [I believe I understand you, — Berlin] (*I*, 241–42). By thus adding a second authorial voice, that of her protagonist, to her own, Meisel-Hess effectively adds another layer here to the literary articulation of claiming space.

Meisel-Hess not only stresses her protagonist's at-homeness in Germany's intellectual and political centre, though; she also accords her a prominent role in an avant-garde movement that combines the promotion of reforms in reproductive ethics with post-racial and post-national thinking.[24] She thus places Olga firmly at the centre of early twentieth-century post-Darwinist debates around supporting human evolution,[25] not just nationally but internationally: her place of work, the 'Zentralstelle zur Durchforschung der Probleme der Entwickelung [sic]' [central research institute for problems of development] (*I*, 409) operates in a 'globische' [global] (*I*, 409) framework, with the goal to provide 'eine verbindende Brücke über die[...] verschiedenen Völker' [a bridge joining different peoples] (*I*, 475).

The 'Zentralstelle' promotes a concept of assimilation that conceives of different cultures and ethnicities as complementary aspects contributing to the further development of humanity through — and only through — their combination. In this optimistic social model, a cultural symbiosis of equals is proposed as the instigator of 'ein allgemeines Europäertum, oder besser gesagt, Weltbürgertum' [a community of Europeans or, indeed, a community of world citizens].[26]

Jewishness, which Meisel-Hess defines in purely cultural and intellectual terms while sharply rejecting the concept of race,[27] is, in this view, a fully integrated, indeed necessary, element in the broad stream of 'kosmopolitische[] Kultur' [cosmopolitan culture].[28] Deploying a contemporary trope that had established the intelligence and intellectuality of the Jews as a common cultural assumption,[29]

Meisel-Hess describes her German-Jewish protagonists as the embodiment of 'voraussetzungslose Intellektualität' [pure intellectuality] (*I*, 52). She adds her own interpretation to this trope, however, by explaining it as a successful amalgamation of Jewish-oriental (emotional) and western (rational-oriented) culture in the ideal type of the assimilated Jew: 'Sein Herz birgt noch die alte Inbrunst vom Sinai — aber seine Vernunft klettert kühn auf die Gipfel westlicher Kultur, bis zu Darwin, Nietzsche und Kant' [His heart still harbours the old fire from the Sinai — but his mind boldly climbs the summits of western culture, up to Darwin, Nietzsche and Kant] (*I*, 501). Conceived in this way as a model of successful cultural hybridization, the German-Jewish intellectual has indeed earned his — or her — place at the heart of the nation.

In *Die Intellektuellen*, the self-confident claim of space goes a long way beyond the vague utopia that was sketched, somewhat hesitantly, in Hauschner's Lowositz novels. Grounding her political vision in concrete socio-cultural context, Meisel-Hess presents a case of positive, diasporic placemaking as posited in the Boyarin brothers' 'admittedly idealized' concept of diaspora as '[...] those situations in Jewish history when Jews were both relatively free from persecution and yet constituted by strong identity — those situations, moreover, within which Promethean Jewish creativity was not antithetical, indeed was synergistic with a general cultural activity'.[30]

Meisel-Hess's German Jews are integrated into German society and culture; they are not subsumed under it but maintain difference and claim leadership. Her novel is a reminder of the relative cosmopolitan openness of pre-First World War Berlin. While anti-Semitic prejudice was certainly part of everyday life — historian Shulamit Volkov speaks of a 'cultural code' of anti-Semitism at the time, a phenomenon that was no longer 'mit echtem Haß gepredigt' [preached with real hatred] but had become '[ein] Bestandteil einer ganzen Kultur' [an integral part of an entire culture][31] — it could be downplayed, and largely ignored in intellectual circles.

A few years later, at the end of the First World War, the climate for German Jews had changed drastically, as Elisabeth Landau's novel *Der Holzweg* shows. *Der Holzweg* was written in the final months of the war, as the author grappled with the wave of anti-Semitism that German Jews were facing, because military defeat was looming and a scapegoat needed to be found. What Landau's female protagonist shares with those of Hauschner and Meisel-Hess, is the urgent recognition of the need to break free and claim a space outside the place of origin that is — or has become — a place of marginalization; now, however, it is (again) Berlin that must be left behind.

Der Holzweg is a sweeping, panoramic, social novel, but one of its main concerns is the discussion of the relationship between German Jews and their home country, the German nation. Through her two main protagonists, Karl Hinrichsen and Elise Frank, Landau explores the options of either staying on and, in solidarity with fellow Jews, opposing the anti-Semitic aggression and exclusion with heightened energy — or leaving Germany and starting a new life elsewhere.

The novel is built on a dialectical engagement with the Heimat concept. The male protagonist, Hinrichsen, embraces the conventional Heimat ideology, a fundamental constituent of hegemonic German ideas of nation and identity, grounded in a specific geographic attachment, a sense of regional and national rootedness. He experiences the fact that Germany has turned against him in an anti-Semitic surge ('daß meine Heimat also handelt'; [that my homeland would act in this way])[32] as humiliation and as an incomprehensible act, especially in view of his deep emotional attachment to what he sees as his home nation.

In line with Freudian thinking on the Heimat concept, Landau represents his attachment to Germany as an affect and, decidedly critically, as a somewhat regressive need. In this, she reflects contemporary critical views on the subject, such as that voiced by the geographer and free-thinker Paul Krische, who, in the same year as the novel's publication, described the attachment to Heimat as 'einen stark instinktmäßigen Drang, den wir [...] Trieb nennen' [a strongly instinctual compulsion, which we call drive]. 'Die Erfüllung eines solchen Triebes', he continues, 'erfolgt ohne Besinnen und Nachdenken, [...] lediglich, um ein Bedürfnis des rein Persönlichen, des Triebmenschen zu befriedigen' [The satisfaction of such a drive occurs without thought or reflection, simply to assuage a need of purely personal nature, of a person controlled by their drives].[33]

Landau links Hinrichsen's Heimat attachment with an active, altruistic and courageous struggle for the acceptance of his fellow Jewish Germans as members of the 'Volksgemeinschaft', but she makes clear how flimsy the base of his stance and how inappropriate his judgement of the position of the Jews in Germany is, in her view, by criticizing his activism as 'Kampf mit Windmühlen' [a battle with windmills] (H, 106).

Elise, in contrast, the main female protagonist and Hinrichsen's counterpart, bases her approach to her German homeland on a rational, critical evaluation of the current situation. She has cut her emotional ties to Germany and is preparing the physical step of emigrating to Britain with her young son Konrad. 'Sie glauben dem deutschen Judenleid Abhilfe schaffen zu können', she points out to Hinrichsen, 'ich gebe diese Sache verloren [...] — das Elend setzt seinen unseligen Kreislauf fort, hält nur ein, wenn der letzte Jude der Verfolgung zum Opfer fällt [...]' [You believe that you can end the suffering of the German Jews, I am resigned to having lost this battle, [...] this misery continues its vicious circle, it will only stop when the last Jew falls victim to the persecution [...]] (H, 105). Elise's pessimism may have sounded like defeatism to contemporary readers, but from our perspective today, her understanding of the situation, which is also that of the author, is remarkably clear-sighted.

For Elise, the notion of belonging is not a static, but a dynamic and geographically transposable concept, and one that is rooted not in reference to a given community, but in the subjectivity of the individual, the possibility of innumerable new acts of self-positioning and, crucially, a set of cultural values that are not determined by the place of her birth: namely her religion and her claim to the right 'frei und gleichberechtigt unter den anderen zu stehen' [to be free and equal among all others] (*H*, 106). The understanding of religion as the basis of belonging is reminiscent of Heinrich Heine's reference to the Torah as his 'portatives Vaterland' [portable fatherland].[34] The ideas of tolerance and equality, on the other hand, are values of the Enlightenment, and specifically also of the German Enlightenment of Kant, Lessing and Goethe. But Elise recognizes that the Germany she lives in is no longer 'das Deutschland Goethes' [the Germany of Goethe] (*H*, 272), and consequently her bond with the German nation is revocable. Because she embraces a freedom and an agency that Hinrichsen cannot grasp and because her rational and value-oriented thinking allows the idea of a new beginning in another community built on Enlightenment principles and western European culture, Elise can choose a third option beside those of 'being German' and being 'heimatlos' [without homeland]: the option of being a European.[35]

Elise's and Konrad's emigration is of course a reaction to the social exclusion they experience as German Jews — but Elise also actively and positively initiates her departure and understands it (at least in part) as an opportunity for a re-orientation in the world: '[...] in jenem berüchtigten Nomadentum der Kinder Israels', she explains, 'liegt der Segen ihres Fluches, ein großer Schwung geht durch den Wanderer, der ihm Sinn und Augen öffnet [...]' [in the infamous nomadism of the children of Israel lies the blessing of their curse, a great momentum fills the wanderer, opening his mind and eyes] (*H*, 106). Landau's naming of her main female protagonist may be no coincidence then. After all, in the foundation myth of the city of Carthage, 'Elissa' (not Dido) is the name of the Phoenician, i.e. Semitic, princess, who, having fled violence and persecution in her homeland, builds a new and better world on foreign shores.[36] Landau's choice of name, whether conscious or not, thus supports the power of Elise's story as a narrative of female vision, migration, leadership and new beginnings.[37]

It is no coincidence, either, that Landau's dialectical discussion is allocated to a male and a female interlocutor. Landau, like Braidotti and Irigaray, posits a feminist consciousness that builds on an understanding of female difference, in which motherhood plays an important role — as specifically female form of experience and perspective, but also as a concept with strategic and political potential. Elise's way of thinking about belonging is specifically coded as female: motherliness is Elise's defining character trait, it is motherliness that marks her position as superior (repeatedly, she addresses Hinrichsen as 'mein armer Junge' [my poor boy]) and motherly love that provides her main reason for emigrating, as she is seeking to secure a future for her son. Maternal responsibility is, in Landau's eyes, of greater import than the more abstract solidarity with the group of the German Jews as a whole as a persecuted people, which (at least partly) motivates Hinrichsen's actions. 'Ihre Sorge gilt der Gegenwart', Elise points out to Hinrichsen, 'die meine der Zukunft' [Your concern is with the present, mine is with the future] (*H*, 104); again, as in Hauschner's Lowositz novels, motherhood and futurity are firmly linked.

From our vantage point today, and in the light of philosophical and political theory of the late twentieth century, we can read Landau's Elise as the embodiment of a 'nomadic subject' in Rosi Braidotti's sense of the word: an identitarian model into which mobility, the liberation from restrictive norms, and the openness to an unlimited number of re-constitutions of belonging are inscribed. Braidotti highlights two aspects that are of central importance to the 'nomadic subject' — and which are also key to Landau's Elise: first, the aspect of resistance against restrictively binary ways of thinking, against any claims of power and oppression, against the pressure to conform to hegemonic perspectives of world and self and, crucially, against exclusion of any kind: '[t]he critical intellectual camping at the city gates is not seeking readmission', Braidotti writes, 'but rather taking a rest before crossing the next stretch of desert'.[38]

The second aspect she emphasizes is that of responsible, independent agency and the creative development of alternative models of a future life. Nomadism as a political stance is conceived as the possibility of transporting and thus saving ideas that are under threat from oppression or exclusion — as a political project that is fed by narratives of hope and change. Concurringly, Elise denies contemporary German culture its Enlightenment credentials and claims a space for the Jewish people outside Germany: in a Europe constituted by the values of religious tolerance, equality and personal dignity.

In the two sequels to *Der Holzweg*, the novels *Ahasver* (1920) and *Die Brandfackel* [*The Incendiary Torch*] (1929), Landau fleshes out the idea of a post-national European identity in some detail and goes on to develop a visionary, utopian concept of a 'Vereinigte Staaten Europas' [United States of Europe][39] that culminates in a somewhat messianic pledge:

> So eng verwurzelt sind die [europäischen] Kulturen, daß sie sich wiederum vereinen müssen, denn unser Erdteil wird und kann noch nicht untergehen. [...] Ich halte es für meine Pflicht, jenem Gesundungswillen zu leben.[40]
>
> [[European] cultures are so closely intertwined that they will by necessity unite again, for our continent will and cannot yet founder. [...] I see it as my duty to devote my life to this will to recovery].

The unification of cultures and peoples should be carried and led by Jewish thinkers in Landau's vision because, she argues, they have learnt to think in supra-national, internationalist ways as a result of anti-Semitic persecution, and are thus, as a consequence of their experience, 'Friedensbringer in jedem Kulturvolk' [bringers of peace in every culture].[41] Like Meisel-Hess, then, she evokes Jewish leadership in an international context, though the cultural and historical background from which this claim arises is very different. Where Meisel-Hess, stridently promoting the recognition of the Jewish contribution to the German nation, argued for a leading role for Jewish intellectualism in a symbiosis of cultures and ethnicities, Landau reclaims agency after the hardships of persecution and projects a new realm of belonging in which the experience of marginalization is a qualification for leadership.

As I have shown, the novels considered in this chapter present three markedly different narrative strategies. They reflect very specific cultural and historical contexts; indeed, it is possible to read them as expressions of three consecutive stages of claiming space for German-Jewish women in the years before and after the First World War. While for Hauschner's protagonist, rooted in the bounded German-Jewish minority in Prague, an articulation of positive space-claiming is not yet possible, Meisel-Hess, writing from the vantage point of the Berlin intellectual avant-garde, projects the self-confidence of a cosmopolitan German citizen claiming their place at the heart of the nation. Landau, finally, writing in response to the final war years' wave of anti-Semitic exclusion and violence, has presciently given up hope for a space to be claimed for the German-Jewish minority in Germany and can but turn the bitter recognition of the need to emigrate into a claim for a space outside her home nation.

All three authors, however, forcefully emphasize the need to break away from oppressive communities of origin that threaten their individual development, dignity and freedom. They turn the tables, then, on the traditional association of the feminine with a static, bounded 'Heimat' and articulate and claim a space allowing them the agency to play a leading role in shaping the future and new concepts of community.

The spaces they claim through their writing are defined by values and ideas, and by opportunities for change. While remaining vague in territorial terms (except in Meisel-Hess's affiliation of her heroine with Berlin), all three authors stress the idea of openness and transcendence of boundaries and posit new configurations of community based on post-racial, post-national and post-patriarchal social visions. Interrelationality, rather than boundedness, is the guiding concept of space we encounter in these novels; and it is presented in two exemplary modes here: firstly, that of motherhood — with Hauschner emphasizing the mother–child bond as the route to a 'natural' life, whereas Landau focuses on the mother's responsibility and clear-sighted rationality — and secondly, that of supra- or post-national unity — in the form of a cultural symbiosis (Meisel-Hess) or a vision of a 'United States of Europe' (Landau). These documents of minoritarian writing can thus be read as early enunciations of feminist thinking as developed by Massey, Braidotti and others — and as powerful reminder that the experience of marginalization is a fertile ground for the reconceptualization of space, community and belonging.

Notes to Chapter 2

1. For an overview, see Andreas Kilcher, *Metzler Lexikon der deutsch-jüdischen Literatur* (Stuttgart: J. B. Metzler, 2012).
2. Auguste Hauschner, 'Rahel Levins Sendung', *Das literarische Echo*, 17 (1914/15), cols 267–70 (col. 268).
3. Doreen Massey, *For Space* (London: Sage, 2005), p. 9.
4. See Yi-Fu Tuan, *Space and Place: The Perspective of Experience* (Minneapolis: University of Minnesota Press, 2001), p. 6.
5. Barbara E. Mann, *Space and Place in Jewish Studies* (New Brunswick, NJ: Rutgers University Press, 2012), p. 110. See also Daniel Boyarin and Jonathan Boyarin, 'Diaspora: Generation and the Ground of Jewish Identity', *Critical Inquiry*, 19.4 (1993), 714–23.
6. In this, we follow Massey, who consistently maintained that the 'binary opposition between territorial and relational approaches cannot be sustained'; Richard Meegan, 'Doreen Massey (1944–2016): A Geographer Who Really Mattered', *Regional Studies*, 51.9 (2017), 1285–96 (p. 1290).

7. Doreen Massey, *Space, Place and Gender* (Cambridge: Polity, 1994), p. 8.
8. See Caroline Bland, Catherine Smale and Godela Weiss-Sussex (eds), *Women Writing Heimat in Imperial and Weimar Germany*, special issue of *German Life and Letters* (72.1, January 2019).
9. Auguste Hauschner, *Rudolf und Camilla* (Berlin: Egon Fleischel & Co, 1910), p. 245. From here on, this text will be referenced with the abbreviation *RuC*. All translations in this chapter are my own, unless otherwise indicated.
10. In a well-established German-Jewish discursive tradition of the nineteenth and early twentieth centuries, negative modes of behaviour that are stereotypically associated with 'Jewishness' are explained as resulting from the history of persecution of the Jewish community. Ostentation, for instance, is explained by the long periods of want and destitution the Jewish people had to suffer, loud and compulsive speaking by long periods of enforced silence. See, for instance, Nahida Ruth Lazarus, *Das jüdische Weib* (Berlin: Siegfried Cronbach, 1896) or Else Croner, *Die moderne Jüdin* (Berlin: Axel Juncker, 1913).
11. See, for example, Elaine Showalter, 'Hysteria, Feminism, and Gender', in *Hysteria Beyond Freud*, ed. by Sander Gilman et al. (Berkeley: University of California Press, 1993), pp. 286–344.
12. Richard von Krafft-Ebing, *Psychopathia Sexualis: Mit besonderer Berücksichtigung der conträren Sexualempfindung. Eine klinisch-forensische Studie* [1886] (Stuttgart: Ferdinand Enke, 1894), p. 7. Translation: Richard von Krafft-Ebing, *Psychopathia Sexualis*, trans. by F. J. Rebman (Chicago, IL: Keener, 1901), p. 7.
13. See Krafft-Ebing, *Psychopathia Sexualis*, p. 1.
14. Rosi Braidotti, *Nomadic Subjects: Embodiment and Sexual Difference in Contemporary Feminist Theory* (New York: Columbia University Press, 1994), p. 129.
15. Braidotti, *Nomadic Subjects*, pp. 99–100. The reference is to Luce Irigaray's *Ce sexe qui n'en est pas un* (1977) and *Ethique de la différence sexuelle* (1984).
16. Auguste Hauschner, '[review of] *Der Weg ins Freie*', *Die Hilfe*, 15 (1909), 39–40 (p. 40).
17. 'freier zumute', 'frei den Dingen zuzuwenden', 'Willensgeister [...] sich freier tummeln', 'frei' (Grete Meisel-Hess, *Die Intellektuellen* (Berlin: Oesterheld & Co. 1911), p. 132. Henceforth referred to as *I*.
18. For further exploration of this, see Emily D. Bilski (ed.), *Berlin Metropolis: Jews and the New Culture, 1890–1918* (Berkeley: University of California Press, 1999).
19. Georg Hermann, 'Der deutsche Jude und das Großstadtproblem', undated typescript, Georg Hermann Collection, Leo Baeck Institute New York, section V, 9 pages, here p. 4. See also Hermann's novel *Die Nacht des Doktor Herzfeld* (1912), in G. Hermann, *Doktor Herzfeld: Die Nacht / Schnee* (Berlin: Das Neue Berlin, 1997), pp. 7–265, in which he discusses at length the affinity between the Jewish intellectual and the city of Berlin.
20. Hermann, 'Der deutsche Jude', p. 9.
21. Karl Scheffler, *Berlin: Ein Stadtschicksal* [1910] (Berlin: Fannei und Walz, 1989). See his definition of Berlin as 'dazu verdammt: immerfort zu werden und niemals zu sein' [condemned for ever to become, but never to be] (p. 219).
22. See Peter Blickle, *Heimat: A Critical Theory of the German Homeland* (Rochester, NY: Camden House, 2002), particularly pp. 3–6.
23. Massey, *Space, Place and Gender*, p. 5.
24. The policies of this movement reflect those of the Bund für Mutterschutz [League for the Protection of Mothers], of which Meisel-Hess was an active member.
25. See Malcolm Humble, 'Monism and Literature in the Later Years of the *Kaiserreich*', in *Science, Technology and the German Cultural Imagination*, ed. by Christian Emden and David Midgley (Oxford: Peter Lang, 2005, pp. 57–79.
26. Grete Meisel-Hess, *Die sexuelle Krise: Eine sozialpsychologische Untersuchung* (Jena: Eugen Diederichs, 1909), p. 372.
27. See Grete Meisel-Hess, 'Die Judenfrage in romantischer Behandlung', *Der Weg*, 3 (1911), cols 801–05 (col. 802).
28. Meisel-Hess, 'Die Judenfrage', col. 805.
29. See Sander Gilman, *The Smart Jew: The Construction of Jewish Superior Intelligence* (Lincoln: University of Nebraska Press, 1996).

30. Boyarin and Boyarin, 'Diaspora', p. 711.
31. Shulamit Volkov, 'Antisemitismus als kultureller Code' [1978], in S. Volkov, *Antisemitismus als kultureller Code: Zehn Essays* (Munich: C. H. Beck, 2000), pp. 13–36 (pp. 23 and 33).
32. L. Audnal (pseudonym for Elisabeth Landau), *Der Holzweg* (Berlin: Erich Reiss, 1918), p. 102. From here on referenced as *H*.
33. Paul Krische, *Heimat! Grundsätzliches zur Gemeinschaft von Scholle und Mensch* (Berlin: Paetel, 1918), p. 50.
34. For further discussion of this concept, see Anat Feinberg, 'Abiding in a Haunted Land: The Issue of Heimat in Contemporary German-Jewish Writing', *New German Critique*, 70 (1997), 161–81.
35. Gabriel Rießer, a prominent nineteenth-century advocate for Jewish emancipation, described the position of assimilated German Jews in these terms: 'wenn [...] der Deutsche uns Deutsche fremd nennen dürfte, so wären wir ohne Heimat und Vaterland' [If the Germans were allowed to call us Germans 'foreigners', we would be without homeland and fatherland]. Gabriel Rießer, *Gesammelte Schriften*, 4 vols, 1867–68, vol. IV, p. 303, cited in Hans G. Adler, *Die Juden in Deutschland: Von der Aufklärung bis zum Nationalsozialismus* (Munich: Kösel, 1961), p. 71.
36. For the foundation myth of Carthage, see Werner Huß, *Geschichte der Karthager* (Munich: C. H. Beck, 1985), pp. 41–42.
37. Carol Gilligan offers a similar re-writing of the myth in her novel *Kyra* (2008), in which the protagonist, a female American architect, founds a city on an island off the shores of Massachusetts in order to build a new society based on communal living and the renunciation of violence.
38. Braidotti, *Nomadic Subjects*, p. 56.
39. L. Audnal (pseudonym for Elisabeth Landau), *Die Brandfackel* (Dresden: Piersons, 1929), p. 361.
40. Audnal, *Die Brandfackel*, p. 361.
41. Audnal, *Die Brandfackel*, p. 173.

CHAPTER 3

Land, Art and Activism in Galician Writing by Women: Teresa Moure's *A intervención* (2010)

Catherine Barbour

If small literatures have been consistently overlooked, their women's voices have been doubly silenced. Narrative by women writing in the language of Galician from the non-state Atlantic nation of Galicia, north-western Spain, represents a case in point, demonstrating the persistent and multifaceted tensions between language, nation, gender and genre.[1] In this chapter, through analysis of the 2010 novel *A intervención* [*The Operation*] by influential writer Teresa Moure (born Monforte de Lemos, 1969), I examine how creativity is presented as a form of resistance to the heteropatriarchal neoliberal order of the nation state, demonstrating how women in minoritized linguistic and cultural contexts write against the hegemonic social, political and economic discourses that have endeavoured to stifle them. Navigating the binds relating to their linguistic, cultural and literary heritage, as well as their gender, many contemporary women writers of fiction in Galician have set out to defy state hegemony and reclaim space in the historically patriarchal Galician literary sphere, renegotiating and redefining discourses of Galician culture more generally.

The Unsteady Trajectory of the Galician Novel by Women

In Galicia's linguistically diglossic society, the autochthonous Romance language of Galician, which is closely related to Portuguese, has been under threat from the imperialist imposition of Spanish since the Early Modern period, culminating in the repression of Galician language, culture and identity during the Franco dictatorship of 1939–1975. The political and cultural spheres tend to be more mutually dependent in non-state nations where access to institutional support is precarious, and literature written in Galician has been fundamental to asserting Galician national consciousness. As a result of centuries of Spanish centralization, literature written in the language 'enfronta un contexto diglósico, está fortemente ligada a unha ideoloxía concreta, e convive con eivas na institucionalización política que a realidade galega aínda conserva' [faces a situation of diglossia, is strongly linked to a concrete ideology, and maintains an unsteady coexistence in the political institutionalization that continues to define the Galician reality].² It was during the rise of the nation state and national identities in the nineteenth century that Galicia's distinct sense of self came into being; a shift which, critically, was driven forward by a Romantic woman poet and novelist. In 1863, Rosalía de Castro published the first literary work in the Galician language, a collection of poems entitled *Cantares Gallegos* [*Galician Songs*]. Her bold decision to defy centuries of linguistic and cultural repression by writing in Galician triggered the *Rexurdimento* [Renaissance], the cultural revival of Galician-language literature and a pivotal moment in Galicia's self-discovery that was especially revolutionary given her gender. De Castro's pioneering poetry vindicated the Galician landscape, culture and psyche, challenging the subjugation of her people by the Spanish nation state, highlighting widespread impoverishment and the plight of emigrants, and, crucially, drawing attention to the oppression of women. Along with the work of other *Rexurdimento* writers such as Eduardo Pondal and Manuel Curros Enríquez, De Castro's focus on Galician cultural specificity, penned in the Galician language, worked in tandem with the political discourse on Galician regional identity being circulated by intellectuals such as her husband, Manuel Murguía, and Alfredo Brañas. This would ensure a flurry of literary and cultural activity written in a language hitherto consigned to the medium of orality, and set the foundation stones for early Galician nationalism, which gained ground in the early twentieth century.

The Galician literary canon was developed during this period by mostly male intellectuals who were challenging linguistic, political and cultural oppression whilst adhering to the acutely conservative and patriarchal norms of the time. The ensuing masculinist perception of novels authored by men as instrumental to nation-building has had lasting ramifications for women writing narrative fiction in Galician, with their contributions often dismissed or overlooked. In spite of the evidence that women have been writing narrative in the language since Rosalía de Castro paved the way in the nineteenth century, it has only been since the turn of the new millennium that women's contributions to the genre can be said to have achieved visibility, recognition and commercial success. Narrative by women writers has been consistently ignored by Galician cultural institutions, as has been well documented in feminist scholarship in Galician Studies.³ Moreover, appropriation of De Castro's legacy has meant that the poetic genre continues to be perceived as quintessential to Galician identity (even though she was also a prolific writer of prose), and women writers especially have been expected to uphold the Rosalían tradition by writing poetry. Francisca Herrera published the novel *Néveda: Historia dunha dobre seducción* [Néveda: Story of a Double Seduction] in 1920, whilst many Galician women succeeded in publishing narrative in Spanish during the intense linguistic imperialism of the dictatorship, yet most women writers who achieved success publishing in the Galician language in the twentieth century did so through poetry.⁴ Women writers also maintained a presence in Galician-language children's literature, a phenomenon again reinforced by patriarchal associations between women and this particular genre. At the height of the dictatorship in the 1960s,

María Xosé Queizán and Xohana Torres were an exception to the rule, as they managed to publish feminist adult novels which contributed to the male-dominated mid-twentieth-century wave of radical, experimental novels labelled *Nova Narrativa Galega* [New Galician Narrative]. However, their efforts had been censored by the Francoist establishment on the one hand and derided or ignored by conservative (male) Galician nationalist critics on the other, as seen for example in the scathing reviews that targeted the provocative, anachronistic themes of Queizán's path-breaking radical feminist novel *A orella no buraco* [The Ear on the Hole] (1965) which underwent Falangist censorship.[5]

The apparent androcentrism of Galician-language narrative has nonetheless been derailed in the new millennium, as a proliferation of novels by women writers has encroached on the Galician literary market with much success, so that nowadays 'falar numa narrativa de autoria femenina no contexto galego não significa necesariamente falar de literatura nas margens' [speaking of women-authored narrative in the Galician context doesn't necessarily mean speaking of literature at the margins].[6] The dissemination of women-authored work defies not only the systematic repression of the Galician language and women's voices that characterized the Franco dictatorship, but also the patriarchal tenets of Galician nationalism and Galician literature. A new generation of women writers has consolidated women's perspectives in Galician-language narrative throughout the past two decades to much critical acclaim, though this has been contingent on intersections such as race, class, sexuality and disability.[7] Galician literature continues to face the at times insurmountable political and commercial challenges that threaten small literatures, namely the cultural and linguistic hegemony of established national literatures and the highly competitive, globalized neoliberal market. Yet minoritized groups working within this context, whether they be women, LGBTQ+, racialized or immigrant writers, are continually managing to forge new paths, to varying degrees of success, prominence and longevity.

New Directions: Teresa Moure

I turn now to consideration of the ways in which the novel *A intervención* by Teresa Moure contests capitalist, state-sanctioned oppression through its focus on an ecofeminist act of civil disobedience, shedding light on the role of creativity as resistance in Galician-language narrative by women. Moure, who stands as arguably one of the best-known contemporary Galician writers in Spain, has been a driving force in establishing a foothold for women writing novels in Galician. She stands as a key spokesperson of Galician nationalism, which has historically relied on cultural intervention due to political subjugation, and is a staunch supporter of Galician independence, gender and LGBTQ+ equality and eco-activism. Moure has published novels, journalistic and academic essays, children's stories, poetry and two plays and is an Associate Professor in Linguistics at the University of Santiago de Compostela. In 2005, her novel *Herba moura* [*Black Nightshade*], published in self-translation to Spanish as *Hierba mora*, made a splash in the Galician literary scene with an unprecedented level of critical and commercial success, leading to translations into Catalan, English, French, Italian, Dutch, Portuguese and Serbian — a rare phenomenon for Galician-language writers, especially women. It won the prestigious Xerais prize for Galician fiction and was also the first book by a woman to win the Galician-language category of Spain's national literary prize, the Premio de la Crítica Española. Though the novel was lauded in the local press as a triumph for Galician feminism and Galician women writers, Helena Miguélez-Carballeira has influentially argued that its supposed innovation had been exemplified decades before by writers such as Queizán and Torres, who dared to pen radical feminist discourse in Galician during Francoism.[8] It is indeed crucial to note that any furore surrounding female-authored works can obscure the engrained gender imbalance that continues to plague certain facets of the Galician literary market.

Moure herself is an avid social justice activist, in favour of an ecofeminist Galician nationalism that resists conservative, heteropatriarchal place-based politics. Her third novel, *A intervención*, was the last she would publish in 'standard Galician'. In 2013, she penned a well-publicized manifesto for the Galician nationalist newspaper *Praza Pública* announcing her decision to revert to the use of Galician-Portuguese, a minority, lesser-used variant of written Galician that is also known as *galego internacional* [international Galician].[9] She signalled her support for the ideological movement of *reintegrationismo* [reintegrationism], which calls for the reassertion of Galicia's linguistic, social, political and economic links to Lusophone cultures as a means to resist oppression by the Spanish state. Moure's subscription to this marginal movement within the broader minority context of Galician nationalism represents an ideological stand against not only the state-imposed infiltration of Spanish, but also the more institutionalized, conservative factions of Galician nationalism that are represented by standardized Galician and mainstream publishing. There is undeniably a tangible contradiction in Moure's insistence on contesting Spanish sovereignty and rejecting standardized Galician to write in a marginal language variety yet simultaneously self-translating her novels to the hegemonic language of Spanish. Indeed, the writer herself admits that publishing her work in standard Spanish has considerably broadened her readership, given that her work is known throughout Spain and further afield as a result of her self-translations, collaboration with mainstream publishing houses, successful application for Spanish-language prizes, and interviews given in Spanish about her work.[10] The process of self-translation from Galician to Spanish allows for exportation of the minority culture into the dominant one, and can serve to contest hegemonic discourses, given that 'self-translators' double affiliation in multilingual contexts places them in a privileged position to problematize power and to negotiate identities', as Olga Castro, Sergi Mainer and Svetlana Page assert.[11] However, the process can be equally problematic for the minoritized language and culture, seen for example in the failure to clarify in the foreign language translations of Moure's texts that the originals were written in Galician, in addition to the omission of certain markers of cultural specificity in her self-translations, such the reduction in references to local place names, which assumes that the non-Galician reader will not be familiar or wish to be made familiar with aspects of Galician cultural specificity.[12] The Spanish translation of the title of *A intervención*, *Artes subversivas para cultivar jardines* [Subversive Arts for Growing Gardens], arguably dilutes its political potential, possibly due to editorial pressures. This linguistic and cultural modification undermines not only the author's dissident publishing strategy of writing in Galician-Portuguese, but also her broader commitment to promoting Galician cultural distinctiveness and contesting state hegemony that drives the plot of *A intervención*.

A intervención: Galician Ecological Artivism

Tension between political interests and commercial pressures notwithstanding, Moure asserts the radical ideological positioning first put forward in her provocative ecocritical essay *O natural é político* [*The Natural is Political*] (2008) in *A intervención*. This is a semi-utopian tale of environmental artivism — 'artivism' being the conscious intermingling of art and political activism that stems from the work of Chicanx artists in Chiapas, Mexico and Los Angeles, USA, in the 1990s.[13] The novel was published in Galician in 2010, with the author's self-translation into Spanish, *Artes subversivas para cultivar jardines*, released in 2014, and an English-language translation by Philip Krummrich, *The Operation*, published in 2021. Themes such as collective memory, ecoactivism and artistic practice merge in a plot that centres on an unconventional group of individuals who collaborate to protest at the destruction of the environment due to mining. When university student Leandro Balseiro is looking for a creative outlet for his political activism, his mother Clara suggests devising a piece of land art that mimics her late father Leandro Senior's extravagant garden by planting flowers over an abandoned quarry, this illegal reclaiming of commodified land being the artistic and political 'intervention' referred to in the title of the novel. They enlist the help of Candela, with whom Leandro is romantically involved, and Sampaio, an Austrian pianist who is suffering from acute amnesia. Sampaio's long-lost daughter Ingrid, a psychiatrist, unexpectedly arrives in Galicia looking for her father, and encourages the group to document the experience. The textual metanarrative is composed of the five protagonists' diary entries leading up to the intervention.

Since Galician society has historically been largely agrarian, the rural sphere continues to be idealized as a significant and indeed stereotypical marker of its distinct collective identity. *A intervención* diverges from traditional bucolic narratives, serving as 'a further example of how the rural landscape has been suffused with more complex social and political dynamics' through attempts to reclaim the Galician attachment to the land as a site of artistic, ecofeminist revolution.[14] Conceived of by Françoise d'Eaubonne in 1974, ecofeminism can be understood as feminist environmental consciousness which denounces the patriarchal commodification of women and the natural world, reclaiming the essentialist conflation of the land, the nation and the female body.[15] Clara suggests staging the intervention in an abandoned quarry in the remote mountainous area of O Courel on Galicia's eastern border with Castile as it is a symbolic representation of the natural environment being threatened by global capitalism:

> non moi lonxe, a pouco máis de douscentos quilómetros, unha comarca enteira estaba a ser borrada do mapa. Transmitiunos coa voz quebrada que se trataba dun lugar dunha beleza emocionante, con fragas centenarias e ríos abrollando entre montañas magníficas e bravas[16]
>
> [not very far away, little more than two hundred kilometres away, an entire region was about to be wiped off the map. She told us in a broken voice that it was a place of incredible beauty, with centuries-old ravines and rivers running between wild, breathtaking mountains]

There have been numerous examples of environmental destruction provoked by capitalist exploitation in Galicia in recent years, with examples including mass industry, deforestation, wildfires, mining and marine pollution that have been met with widespread protests in Galician society. The textual focus on an intervention in an abandoned quarry in O Courel, an area negatively impacted by extractive industries, is therefore especially resonant.

Moure insists on the need to protect Galicia's natural environment through a magical realist exposé of its effects on generations of Clara's family, the Balseiros, whose attachment to the land perpetuates a typical Galician cliché: 'os galegos, por moito que teñamos as casas a medio derrubar, chantamos á porta fermosísimas plantas nun xesto de tenrura fóra do razoábel' [Even though we have houses that are half falling down, we Galicians grow really beautiful plants with care that goes far beyond what is usual] (*AI*, 283). When in his youth Clara's late father Leandro Senior had lost his job, his mother had encouraged him to take up gardening because of the healing power of nature, evoking the ecofeminist conflation of femininity, maternity and the earth. This environmental potential is thrown into contrast with the weakness of humanity, which depends on nature for survival, 'as flores dispuxeron o goberno de todas as cousas' [the flowers arranged the governing of all things] (*AI*, 22), whilst the sheer force of nature in Leandro Senior's garden is rumoured to have brought about climate change. Even as a talented gardener Leandro Senior was not always able to fulfil the needs of his supernatural garden: 'as flores, todas as súas flores benqueridas, estaban dando gritos desesperados que el non podía ouvir polas limitacións inherentes aos sentidos da súa especie' [the flowers, all his darling flowers, were giving out desperate cries that he couldn't hear due to the limitations of the senses inherent to his species] (*AI*, 124). Both large- and small-scale acts of resistance challenge state oppression and the commodification of the land, often with elements of the fantastic genre:

> As violetas pechábanse de golpe cando facía rolda a parella da garda civil e as dúas flores sempre contrapostas do hippeastrum retorcíanse nunha viraxe imposíbel até se miraren con tal de sinalar o paso do cura don Simón, que disque coqueteara coa Falanxe (*AI*, 22)
>
> [the violets closed suddenly when a couple of civil guard officers were doing their rounds and two always opposing flowers of the hippeastrum twisted in an impossible contortion until they could signal that the priest Don Simón, who it was said was in league with the Falange, was passing by]

When Clara's mother abandoned the family (this plot point contrasting with the feminist emphasis on the adult Clara's maternal instinct), her father set the house on fire in a fit of rage and left the child to fend for herself, with the garden serving for her as a source of sustenance, protection and emotional solace, vindicating the intrinsic relationship of the Galician community, and women, to the earth. She shelters in a bed of hydrangeas and feeds herself by sucking petals, in an ecofeminist image of Mother Earth: 'as flores facían oficio de nai e decidían con plena xustiza o goberno de todas as cousas' [the flowers did the job of a mother and decided with complete justice the governing of everything] (*AI*, 127). Her deep-seated attachment to the environment as an adult stems from this early dependence on it in the face of parental rejection and imminent danger: 'foi difícil de explicar no hospital, mais para curaren a nena tiñan que deixar entrar canda ela á árbore á que se abrazaba' [it was difficult to explain in the hospital, but to cure the child they had to bring in the tree that she was hugging] (*AI*, 129). These enmeshed themes of community, maternity and ecology highlight Moure's concern for the protection of Galicia's natural spaces.

The place-based activism in the novel is implicitly linked to global social movements, evoking political dialogue. Arif Dirlik has emphasized the role of social movements in redefining static conceptions of place, suggesting that they

> offer a means to linking places in larger wholes that are important not only for overcoming the parochialism that is the predicament of place-based politics but also to answer to the demands of sustenance within political economic spaces that of necessity transcend places.[17]

By instigating political activism in a space that has been commodified, the characters in Moure's novel and the text itself adhere to Michael Keith and Steve Pile's call for 'a commitment to the continual questioning of location, movement and direction — to challenging hegemonic constructions of place, of politics and of identity'.[18] Their activism captures the spirit of the global 'Extinction Rebellion' environmental movement (2018–) and avant-garde performance movements such as 'Reclaim the Streets', a series of unauthorized counter-culture street parties which began in London in 1995 and spread throughout the world. Evoking Moure's implicit criticism of the conservatism of Galician institutions, Candela and Leandro break into the University of Santiago de Compostela, cover the carpet in soil and write in Galician 'a terra tamén é arte' [the land is also art] (*AI*, 131), harking back to the environmental creations of artist couple Cristo and Jeanne-Claude.[19] Even so, Candela insists on her autonomy as a woman activist, reflecting Moure's feminist activism: '[Candela] detestaría que a presentase así, como alguén secundario, alguén que incita outro á acción mentres se mantén nas marxes' [Candela hated being introduced like that, as someone secondary, someone who incites someone else into action while remaining on the margins] (*AI*, 47). Moure herself rebelled against the subjugation of Galician culture by carrying out small-scale artivism. In 2009, when the conservative former Galician Minister for Culture Roberto Varela made the inflammatory comment, 'a cultura galega limita' [Galician culture is limiting], the writer and some friends painted his words on windmills, seeking to challenge stereotypes of Galician insularity.[20] A group of Galician writers signed a petition demanding the politician's resignation for committing 'unha descualificación da nosa mesma identidade' [a denouncement of our very identity].[21]

Moure has commented that the characters' cathartic process of introspection which is provoked by their activism can be considered a metaphorical revision of the history of Galicia, a key means of contesting centuries of Spain's annihilation of otherness.[22] As Neil Anderson argues, 'through the processes of creative forgetting, family re-membering, and artistic maternity, Clara performs a political intervention by inventing a home that is less hierarchical, less rigid in its roles, and more conducive to happiness than the lost "paradise" of her infancy'.[23] As a woman leading the project outside institutional culture, Clara also reaffirms Galician women's creativity beyond the patriarchal confines of institutions, exposing how, as Linda Nochlin has famously claimed, 'art is not a free, autonomous activity of a super-endowed individual, "influenced" by previous artists, and, more vaguely and superficially, by "social forces", but rather, that the total situation of art making, both in terms of the development of the art maker and in the nature and quality of the work of art itself, occur in a social situation, are integral elements of this social structure, and are mediated and determined by specific and definable social institutions'.[24] Planning the intervention becomes a means for her to come to terms with her turbulent past, emphasizing the potential of an ecofeminist political activism for working through the collective trauma relating to Galicia's subjugation and 'poñer orde na memoria colectiva' [putting collective memory in order] (*AI*, 21). The intervention is rooted in the customs and traditions of the local community, in defiance of the influence of globalization. The instigators ridicule Candela's husband's insistence that the project should receive institutional recognition, '*Merchandising*. Podedes vender de todo' [Merchandising. You can sell everything] (*AI*, 254), for he is perpetuating the very capitalist values they seek to overhaul, and indeed Candela's affair with Leandro undermines the heteropatriarchal values he represents. By adopting the method of laying floral carpets that is typical of the religious celebration of Corpus Christi in many Galician towns, the activists entrench their activism in the local area, as Leandro insists that 'non fomos quen de rachar coas nosas ataduras' (*AI*, 80) [we haven't broken our ties]. He mounts Celtic sculptures of torc, a totem of a wolf's head and a yew tree which harks back to the purity of Galicia's disputed Celtic past, the pre-industrial period when culture was intrinsically linked to nature: 'esas formas conéctannos co pasado remoto e coas culturas que algún día habitaron este territorio antes de o colonizaren os romanos e de nos converteren en parte do occidente industrial' [these shapes connect us with the remote past and with the cultures which once inhabited this land before it was colonized by the Romans and they converted us into part of the industrial West] (*AI*, 247). They carry out the intervention between the summer solstice and the Galician festival of San Xoán, in keeping with local Celtic and Catholic traditions.

One of the participants is the Austrian pianist, Daniel Sampaio, who is suffering from acute amnesia having been knocked down whilst walking the iconic Camiño de Santiago [Way of St James] pilgrimage. Through collaborating to recover the

Galician landscape, Sampaio regains his lost memories of a childhood spent in Galicia during the Civil War when his family were forced to flee to Austria. His flashbacks to the lavish cultural scene he has left behind in Vienna, representative of capitalist spoils, are merged with the old town of Santiago de Compostela and its university history department, the Ortigueira, Moeche and Pardiñas folk festivals, the night of San Xoán and, most significantly, the rural setting of O Courel. The project, rooted in the earth and defined by a greater purpose, is portrayed as more 'authentic' and less superficial than the milieu of the European high arts. In an allusion to Moure's reintegrationist ideology and an early indication of his suspected Galician ancestry, Sampaio's surname is Portuguese, a combination of São and Paulo [Saint Paul] — the Apostle who converted to Christianity. Sampaio, once known for his extravagant capitalist excesses in Viennese high society, has undergone a symbolic conversion, becoming enlightened by eco-activism in rural Galicia. The organic means of carrying out the intervention stands as a rejection of the negative influence of globalization and digital technology:

> Quizais este obxectivo non sería de todo estraño en Berlín ou en Nova York mais, fóra das grandes urbes e dos seus circuítos bohemios, era case impensábel que ninguén cambiase a súa vida auténtica para consagrarse a un proxecto delirante, e moito menos que pretendesen facelo sen un patrocinador ou unhas canales de comunicación axeitadas e, por riba, na clandestinidade (*AI*, 204–05)
>
> [perhaps this objective wouldn't be altogether out of place in Berlin or in New York, but outside the big cities and their bohemian scenes, it was almost unthinkable for someone to transform their authentic life to throw themselves into a crazy project, and much less to try to do it without an investor or some appropriate communication channels and above all, in secret]

Clara and Candela bond over their desire to ingest compost, with the symbolic consumption of organic matter, in an ecofeminist act that renders them quite literally at one with the earth, but conversely reinforces patriarchal, colonial stereotypes associating woman, and Galicians, with nature. The group are helped by a young man called Tomé, who unlike so many of Galicia's rural youth has not moved away to find employment opportunities, and retains the traditional attachment to the land that is integral to Moure's vision for Galicia: 'tan apegado á terra coma nós' [as tied to the land as us] (*AI*, 178). This grass-roots approach to inciting the local community into action corresponds to Moure's insistence on locally driven resistance: 'Agora estaban rexenerando e remodelando artisticamente o terreo: a súa terra recuperaba esa estima colectiva' [now they were regenerating and artisitically remodelling the terrain: their land was recuperating that collective esteem] (*AI*, 245). Their aim to produce radical art embedded in the local community is envisaged as provocative resistance to the establishment: 'debía denunciar a inepcia dos gobernantes, enraizarse no país, tirar do que é do seu, debía conmover as conscencias durmidas e dispoñelas á actuación, ademais de alertalas sobre os problemas reais do tempo que nos tocou vivir' [it had to denounce the ineptitude of governments, be rooted in the nation, take back what belongs to it, it had to mobilize sleeping consciences and prepare them for action, as well as alert them to the real problems of our times] (*AI*, 66). When, towards the end of the novel, Sampaio passes away, his ashes are scattered over the quarry garden, marking the climax of the text, as he is bound to both the artistic movement and the Galician land from which he came. The Balseiro line of horticultural artists will be continued, ensuring that the struggle to preserve Galicia's natural spaces and contest state capitalist exploitation continues, as the last line of the text reveals that Candela is pregnant with Leandro's child, conceived during the intervention.

Yet although the participants in the intervention break the law, setting out to challenge the environmental negligence of the Spanish state, their artistic social disturbance ultimately fails. Succumbing to a fate that might recall Clara's father's garden project, they gain recognition for their cause, but ultimately don't succeed in what they set out to achieve. The project's outcome arguably destabilizes its utopian mission and diminishes its ideological resonance, though it can also be read in terms of Jack Halberstam's theorization of failure as a 'queer art' — itself a mode of resistance as it 'allows us to escape the punishing norms that discipline behavior and manage human development'.[25] In an implicit allusion to the Spanish trope of Quixotic madness, the group escapes prosecution due to a plea of insanity proven by their diary entries, thereby destabilizing the strong arm of authority.

Whilst it is cause for celebration that Moure's fictional account of environmental artivism is circulating in translation beyond Galicia's borders, the limits of the translation and marketing processes with regard to the sensitive exportation of the minority culture should not be overlooked. The tensions surrounding creative resistance in this novel by one of Galicia's most well-known women writers reflect the complex standpoint of Galician-language writers, and indeed women writers, in the negotiation of their contested history and identity. Though *A intervención* admittedly falls into certain traps of cultural essentialism, reinforcing the age-old associations between Galicia, woman and nature, Moure proactively draws on and engages with global feminist, environmental, political and aesthetic movements through a textual focus on community-based ecofeminist artivism in rural Galicia. This novel serves as just one example to demonstrate the essential role of Galician women cultural producers in resisting heteropatriarchal global and state capitalism to assert a collective identity that is decolonial and feminist as well as environmentally conscious. For even if they must negotiate market pressures and write against the confines of linguistic and gender bias, women writing in Galician in the twenty-first century continue to prove that they are a force to be reckoned with, like many others before them.

Notes to Chapter 3

1. This chapter draws on material in my monograph *Contemporary Galician Women Writers* (Cambridge: Legenda, 2020). Reproduced here with generous permission of the publisher.
2. Mario Regueira, 'Editorial', *Galicia 21*, Issue J (2020), 3–6 (p. 3).
3. For further reading on the perceived lack of narrative written by women in Galician, see Catherine Barbour, *Contemporary Galician Women Writers* (Cambridge: Legenda, 2020), Helena González Fernández, *Elas e o paraugas totalizador: escritoras, xénero e nación* (Vigo: Xerais, 2005); Kirsty Hooper, 'Girl, Interrupted: The Distinctive History of Galician Women's Narrative',

Romance Studies, 21.2 (2003), 101–14; María Liñeira, 'Literary Citizenship and the Politics of Language: The Galician Literary Field between 1939 and 1965' (unpublished doctoral thesis, University of Oxford, 2015); María Xesús Nogueira, Laura Lojo and Manuela Palacios (eds), *Creation, Publishing and Criticism: The Advance of Women's Writing* (New York: Peter Lang, 2010).
4. See Liñeira.
5. Dolores Vilavedra, *A narrativa galega na fin de século* (Vigo: Galaxia, 2010), p. 312.
6. Lorena López López, *Ainda invisíveis? Narradoras e margens na literatura galega contemporânea* (Santiago de Compostela: Através Editora, 2022), p. 18.
7. Eva Moreda Rodríguez, 'Addressing Gender Gaps in Contemporary Galician-Language Fiction: The Cases of Úrsula Heinze, Silvia Bardelás and Beatriz Dacosta', in *Women's Lived Experiences of the Gender Gap*, ed. by Angela Fitzgerald (Singapore: Springer, 2021), pp. 59–71 (p. 60).
8. Helena Miguélez-Carballeira, 'Inauguar, reanudar, renovar: a escrita de Teresa Moure no contexto da narrativa feminista contemporánea', *Anuario de estudos galegos* (2006), 72–87.
9. Teresa Moure, 'Sobre encrucilhadas, normas ortográficas e independência', *Praza Pública*, 27 March 2013 <http://praza.com/opinion/981/sobre-encrucilhadas-normas-ortograficas-e-independencia/> [accessed 20 March 2022].
10. Moure's self-translations include *Hierba mora* (Barcelona: Lumen, 2006); *La jornada de las mujeres-árbol* (Barcelona: Ronsel, 2006), *La palabra de las hijas de Eva* (Barcelona: Lumen, 2007) and *Artes subversivas para cultivar jardines* (Gijón: Hoja de Lata, 2014). Teresa Moure cit. in Montse Dopico, 'O amor de mãe tópico tem uma leitura antipolítica', *Praza Pública*, 13 October 2014 <http://praza.gal/cultura/7994/lo-amor-de-mae-topico-tem-uma-leitura-antipoliticar/> [accessed 10 March 2022].
11. Olga Castro, Sergi Mainer and Svetlana Page, 'Introduction: Self-Translating, from Minorisation to Empowerment', in *Self Translation and Power: Negotiating Identities in European Multilingual Contexts*, ed. by Olga Castro, Sergi Mainer and Svetlana Page (New York: Palgrave Macmillan, 2017), pp. 1–22 (p. 11).
12. See Olga Castro, 'Apropriación cultural en las traducciones de una obra (autotraducida): la proyección exterior de Herba Moura, de Teresa Moure', in *Aproximaciones a la autotraducción*, ed. by Xosé Manuel Dasliva and Helena Tanqueiro (Vigo: Editorial Academia del Hispanismo, 2011), pp. 23–44.
13. See, for example, Arcadi Poch and Daniela Poch, *Artivism* (London: Carpet Bombing Culture, 2018).
14. Maria Reimóndez, 'The Rural, Urban and Global Spaces of Galician Culture', in *A Companion to Galician Culture*, ed. by Helena Miguélez-Carballeira (Woodbridge, Suffolk: Tamesis, 2014), pp. 157–74 (p. 162).
15. See Françoise d'Eaubonne, *Le Féminisme ou la mort* (Paris: Pierre Horay, 1974).
16. Teresa Moure, *A intervención* (Vigo: Xerais, 2010), p. 143. Further references to this edition are given in the text, marked *AI*. Translations into English are my own unless otherwise indicated.
17. Arif Dirlik, 'Globalization, Indigenism, Social Movements, and the Politics of Place', *Localities*, 1 (2011), 47–90 (p. 51).
18. Michael Keith and Steve Pile, *Place and the Politics of Identity* (London: Routledge, 2004), p. 217.
19. See Burt Chernow, *Cristo and Jeanne-Claude: A Biography* (New York: St Martin's Press, 2002).
20. Roberto Varela cit. in Isabel Bugallal, 'La cultura gallega está bien pero limita, prefiero la cultura hecha en Galicia', *Faro de Vigo*, 23 April 2009 <http://www.farodevigo.es/galicia/2009/04/23/cultura-gallega-limita-prefiero-cultura-17946155.html> [accessed 26 March 2023].
21. 'Once autores rexeitan a "análise negativa da cultura galega" de Varela', *La Voz de Galicia*, 25 January 2010 <http://www.lavozdegalicia.es/ocioycultura/2010/01/26/0003_8252185.htm> [accessed 10 March 2022].
22. Teresa Moure cit. in 'Teresa Moure "Os prexuízos contra o galego aumentan por mor da inepcia dos gobernantes"', *La Opinion Coruña*, 23 May 2010 <http://www.laopinioncoruna.es/cultura/2010/05/23/teresa-moure-prexuizos-o-galego-aumentan-mor-da-inepcia-gobernantes/387141.html> [accessed 10 March 2022].
23. Neil D. Anderson, 'A Critical Geography of Home: Teresa Moure's *A intervención*', *Modern Languages Open* (2016), DOI: <http://doi.org/10.3828/mlo.v0i0.111>.

24. Linda Nochlin, 'Why Have There Been No Great Women Artists?' in *The Feminism and Visual Culture Reader*, ed. by Amelia Jones (London: Routledge, 2003), pp. 229–33 (p. 232).
25. Jack Halberstam, *The Queer Art of Failure* (Durham, NC: Duke University Press, 2011), p. 3.

CHAPTER 4

Peripheries of the Revolution and Geographies of Exclusion in Djaimilia Pereira de Almeida's *Luanda, Lisboa, Paraíso* (2018)

Margarida Rendeiro

> This is the trauma of the Black subject; it lies in this state of absolute Otherness in relation to the *white* subject.
> — GRADA KILOMBA, *Plantation Memories*, p. 20

Imagining the future possibilities of Portugal in present-day postcolonial Europe cannot be a successful enterprise without acknowledging and discussing its colonial and imperial past.[1] Only then can a truly inclusive future be reconfigured. Albeit this argument concerns the history of the country, this is mainly an argument about the more fluid concept of cultural memory. Remembrance of a collective is polyphonic, closely linked to the nature of experience of the individuals that form that collective and, as Michael Rothberg argues, 'remembrance is freed from the (never actually) homogeneous space-time of the nation state'.[2] In this chapter, I argue that Djaimilia Pereira de Almeida's prizewinning *Luanda, Lisboa, Paraíso*, a novel set among the Angolan diaspora community in Lisbon, charts the emergence of a Black Portuguese literature, rooted not in the former colonies but in Portugal itself. This is a necessary step towards the Portuguese recognition of a Portuguese-language postcolonial literature because remembering in the postcolonial nation is always rooted in a polyphonic experience.

Postcolonial Portuguese Geographies of Exclusion

In Portugal, remembrance of the colonial past has encountered systematic resistance to its polyphonic possibilities. An example of this concerns the public policies of memory associated with the 25 April 1974 revolution that overthrew the four-decade-long dictatorial and nationalist Estado Novo, the last guardian of the Portuguese colonial empire, and also put an end to a colonial war that had lasted over a decade. This revolution would not have happened without the national liberation movements in the former Portuguese African colonies. However, as historian Manuel Loff contends, the 1974 revolution has been remembered as a Portuguese event that happened in Portugal with causes and effects that concerned only the nation state.[3] There is no memorial to the victims of Portuguese colonialism in Lisbon yet and much less in the rest of the country, whilst there is a war memorial in Lisbon to the soldiers of the Portuguese army who died in the Colonial War.[4] Not surprisingly, it is located in Belém, very near the Tower of Belém, and within a walking distance to the Jerónimos Monastery, the Imperial Square and the Monument to the Discoveries; the latter two are remnant sites of the Exhibition of the Portuguese World, set up in 1940 by the regime led by Salazar to celebrate eight centuries of Independence of Portugal and three centuries of Restoration (of Independence), and whose imperial memories of the grandeur of Portugal have not yet been challenged by the public policies of memory in Portuguese democracy. The war memorial is part of an array of ancient and modern buildings that celebrate the memory of the heyday and the fading of Portugal's imperial past. It is true that the Colonial War killed thousands of conscripted Portuguese soldiers, but also undeniable is the profound impact of decolonization in 1975, which caused massive flows of immigration of thousands of Portuguese former settlers (also known as 'retornados' [returnees]) and colonized Africans, and the flows of immigration from the newly independent African countries, fleeing civil war and economic hardship during the late 1970s; these facts alone altered the present-day ethnic composition of the Portuguese, particularly the composition of those living in the Lisbon area.

The postcolonial nation has had little to offer to African minorities, in that nothing includes them in the public policies of memory of the imperial and colonial past; in other words, public remembrance of this past has not been polyphonic, notwithstanding the ethnic diversity of its population and the variable exposure of younger and older generations of African minority communities to the experience of the Portuguese colonial past. To put it simply, multiculturalism has essentially been a word used in Portuguese history textbooks to characterize the consequences of Portuguese maritime and imperial expansion in the fifteenth and sixteenth centuries and in travel brochures to highlight Lisbon's promotion as a cosmopolitan city to tourists. African minorities almost never hold publicly prominent positions in Portugal, such as presenters on the mainstream television channels, occupying company management-level positions or political posts, and they can hardly relate their own ethnic ancestry and history to expressions such as 'cultural encounters' between Portuguese seafarers and African natives to describe colonial violence and the transatlantic slave trade, or representations of African communities as examples of primitive culture that have pervaded history textbooks to date.[5]

In fact, in the 1990s Portuguese memory culture evolved in line with national memory projects in other western European countries, such as France, Spain or the Netherlands, as their integration into the European Union sparked nationalist reactions and interest in national history, and culture was put on the research agenda.⁶ This shows the extent to which Pierre Nora's seminal project on French *lieux de mémoire* (1989) could be exported and used in other countries for comparable projects, often boosted by nostalgia.⁷ As far as the history of Portugal is concerned, after having been used during the last decades of the nineteenth century to enhance the image of an imperial and strong nation state following the British Ultimatum in 1890, it was again used during the Estado Novo, as a key part of its national project to instil nationwide pride. The history and growth of the nation state was celebrated and glorified with the reconstruction of monuments, such as Saint George's Castle in Lisbon during the 1930s, with the organization of the Exhibition of the Portuguese World mentioned above, and the construction of the miniature park *Portugal dos Pequenitos* [Portugal for the Little Ones] in Coimbra, also inaugurated in 1940, with diminutive versions of Portuguese houses and monuments, and pavilions dedicated to the former Portuguese African colonies. Nowadays, this park still remains open to the public, practically unchanged.

The implementation of democracy in 1974 did not constitute a disruption to the long-standing effects of a four-decade long project founded on nationalist pride and in the narrative of a not so violent colonialism, known as Lusotropicalism.⁸ The decision to join what is now the European Union, in a process that formally started in 1977 and was concluded in 1985, also generated nationalist reactions, particularly led by political parties that did not agree with the integration into the so-called European Economic Community (EEC); however, and apart from these reactions, the integration into the EEC was concluded by the right-wing government, headed by Prime Minister Aníbal Cavaco Silva, whose policies were also grounded in a national identity project that was not radically different from that of the Estado Novo, and whose sites of memory also stemmed from the official narrative of Portuguese uniqueness and historical contribution to the world. Several historical urban centres were refurbished across the country and the glorification of the Portuguese Discoveries continued to constitute the core of that official narrative, as shown in the commemorative regatta in 1988 to celebrate the 500th anniversary of explorer Bartolomeu Dias's achievement of sailing around the southernmost tip of Africa, and the recreation at Expo92 in Seville of King Manuel I's Embassy to the Vatican. The construction of the Belém Cultural Centre offers an insight into the way the reinforcement of the sites of memory intermingled with the affirmation of Portugal's integration into the European Union. It is a complex of venues aligned with the Jerónimos Monastery and near the Monument to the Discoveries, built to accommodate the administration of Portugal's Presidency of the European Council in 1992 but with the long-term purpose of providing permanent venues for conferences, exhibitions and performance arts. At the time, the public tender process conveyed the government's determination to establish a link between the future cultural centre and the Imperial Square and, at the same time, serve as a facility that would encourage tourists to stay longer in that historical area.

The end of the twentieth century marks the beginning of the contestation of the sites of memory projects across Europe. Pim de Boer contends that the rise of postcolonial studies encouraged various kinds of present tensions to infuse interpretations of the past so that 'from the postcolonial perspective the memory boom is memory-war'.⁹ In Portugal, a noteworthy case is the recent controversy over the statue of Father António Vieira unveiled in Lisbon city centre in 2017. This monument was the result of a protocol between Lisbon City Council and the Lisbon *Santa Casa da Misericórida* and was the subject of an organized protest by anti-racist advocacy group Descolonizando [Decolonizing], who claimed that the statue was offensive in its representation of infantilized indigenous peoples of the Americas. The patriarchal representation of Vieira as the guardian of Amerindian children ignores the fact that the Catholic Church — and the Jesuits in particular — were complicit in the Atlantic slave trade to Brazil, whilst the description of this statue identifies Vieira as an advocate of human rights, an anachronism because the concept of human rights was non-existent in the seventeenth century. This statue shows the extent to which the politics of memory of the colonial and imperial past remains essentially Lusotropicalist in Portugal in the twenty-first century, regardless of the fact that historical research has already shown the complex relations between the Catholic Church and slave trade in the past. The Lusotropicalist approach has had implications for a persistent widespread denial that racism is a structural problem in Portuguese society. In her Portuguese edition of *Plantation Memories*, Portuguese artist Grada Kilomba argues that postcolonial Portugal is still in denial, preventing new configurations of power that would enable marginalized subjects (and identities) from reconfiguring the collective knowledge of the colonial past.¹⁰

However, African minorities have lately been challenging their invisibility and silencing, reclaiming their right to participate in the wider discussion about the Portuguese colonial past and advocating a decolonial approach to the collective memory. In the recent past, several street demonstrations decrying discriminatory police violence have taken hundreds of Afrodescendant Portuguese to Lisbon's city centre; on 6 June 2020, more than six thousand protested against racism on the streets of Lisbon, Porto and Coimbra, in what was considered the most significant demonstration organized by anti-racist organizations in Portugal. Although demonstrators expressed solidarity with North American cases of police violence, such as the one that victimized George Floyd, protesters wielded posters with the names of Portuguese black victims of police violence. At the end of July 2020, hundreds went back to the streets after Bruno Candé, a Portuguese actor of Guinean descent, was shot dead in broad daylight in a central avenue in Moscavide, on the eastern periphery of Lisbon, by a veteran of Portugal's colonial war, in a case that was described as a 'racial hate crime'. The court was told that, before he shot Candé, the accused shouted that the actor should go back to the *sanzala*.¹¹ These words illustrate the scope of Kilomba's words when she states: 'within racism, black bodies are constructed as inappropriate bodies, as bodies that are out of place'.¹²

Lisbon is yet to have its first memorial to slavery, though there are plans to locate one at Campo das Cebolas, in downtown Lisbon, the site of a slave market in the sixteenth and seventeenth centuries. The sculptural installation entitled *Plantation: Prosperity and Nightmare* by Angolan artist Kiluanji Kia Henda was selected for the construction of this memorial to enslaved people and it recreates a plantation of

540 three-metre-high sugar canes built in black-lacquered aluminium flanked by circular concrete benches, where visitors will be able to sit, contemplate and reflect upon the Portuguese colonial past. The creation of this memorial was proposed to the Participatory Budget of Lisbon in 2017 by Djass, the Portuguese association of Afrodescendants, and was announced as one of the winning projects of that Lisbon City Council initiative which included it in its budget. Participatory budgeting was adopted by Lisbon City Council in 2008 and was designed to encourage people to engage — face-to-face and through an online platform — in public decision-making. Following the announcement of this memorial as one of the winning projects, Henda's design received the most votes tallied over six public sessions that also showed the blueprints by four other African and Afro-descendant artists from Portuguese-speaking countries. Djass organized these sessions across several locations around Lisbon where there is a strong presence of African and Afrodescendant communities. This is the first time Lisbon will have a memorial that tells part of the history that has been made invisible in the public space.

As regards Nora's *lieux de mémoire* project, despite being hailed as a scholarly achievement, critics have also expressed reservations; one particularly relevant to this chapter is the fact that this has fundamentally led to Eurocentric memory projects, making the imperial and colonial history part of the *non-lieux de mémoire*. Despite Nora's avowed interest in a polyphonic approach to memory, his collection puts forward a Gallocentric conception of a nation purged of its imperial past.[13] Aligned with this strand of criticism, and in view of the limits of Nora's *Les Lieux de mémoire*, Rothberg suggests a new model of remembrance, calling this new approach knots of memory or *noeuds de mémoire*.[14] This model conveys the foremost characteristic of collective memory: its multidirectional dynamics. This is also implied in Portuguese sociologist Sheila Khan's *Portugal a lápis de cor*. In her monograph, Khan points out the gap between the daily experience of the communities of African descent in Portugal and Portuguese academic and literary circles. Portuguese literature published after 1974 does discuss the social and political implications of postcolonial Portuguese cultural identity; various scholarly contributions by authors such as Ellen Sapega ('No Longer Alone and Proud', 1997), Ana Paula Ferreira ('Lusotropicalist Entanglements', 2014) and Patrícia Martinho Ferreira (*Órfãos do Império*, 2021) show the extent to which a discussion about the revolution and decolonization and the image of Portugal as the colonizer has been accomplished by Portuguese literary authors and, as Ferreira contends, is making up for the lack of a wider political discussion in Portugal about these issues.[15] Nevertheless, the life experiences of the African minorities have rarely been addressed and the few cases have always been fictionalized by Portuguese white writers. Khan draws the reader's attention to those invisible minorities who, despite living side by side with the Portuguese population — and we have to read this as the Portuguese white population — are not heard, as if they were not part of the same society. She insists it is high time that the voices of these minorities were heeded: 'Hoje, mais do que nunca, pensar a pós-colonialidade como uma postura, uma opção moral, tem de inevitavelmente assumir-se como um compromisso com a História desta nação [...]. Os narradores desta História terão de ser também os Outros, aqueles ainda remetidos ao esquecimento e à invisibilidade sociais [Today, more than ever, thinking postcoloniality as a stance, a moral choice, must inevitably be associated with the history of this nation [...]. The narrators of this history also have to be the *Others*, those already consigned to social oblivion and invisibility].[16] Portuguese postcolonial research has counted on the participation of a new generation of researchers of African descent who contribute to a gradual decolonization of the academic debate.[17]

Hence, when the juries of the Inês de Castro Foundation Literary Prize (2018), the Eça de Queirós Foundation Literary Prize (2019) and the Oceanos Prize (2019) justified their awards for Djaimilia Pereira de Almeida's *Luanda, Lisboa, Paraíso* on the grounds that this novel conveyed both the profound loneliness and the illusions and disillusionment of postcolonial Portugal (Notícias de Coimbra, DGLAB and Oceanos), they actually failed to mention what makes this novel stand out in post-1974 prizewinning Portuguese literature: this is a novel by an Afro-Portuguese author, about an ethnic community within Portugal whose voices have until now been unheard in Portuguese literature; these awards represent the recognition of a Black Portuguese literature. Despite being the first Afro-Portuguese author with an award-winning novel after 1974, Djaimilia Pereira de Almeida is not alone in the Portuguese literary scene that has also seen the recent publication of fiction exposing the experience of Otherness in postcolonial Portugal by other authors of African descent, such as Kalaf Epalanga, Telma Tvon, Yara Monteiro and Luísa Semedo.[18] Their writing focuses less on Portuguese decolonization and various African independences than on daily experience as part of the Afro-Portuguese communities; it is the experience of racism, but it is also the experience of building their cultural identity as a mingling of the Africanness of their ancestry and their daily experience as citizens in postcolonial Portugal. After all, as Almeida concluded in an interview following the publication of *Esse Cabelo*, her debut novel in 2015, published in Eric M. B. Becker's translation as *That Hair* by Tin House in 2020: 'a girl like me will always be an African girl in Lisbon'.[19] This is part of a process of self-affirmation that entails 'the understanding and the study of one's own marginality' to create 'the possibility of emerging as a new subject'.[20] Renegotiating postcolonial cultural memory has to be founded upon a compromise of various social and cultural identities, ways of thinking and diversity in knowledge.[21]

A Postcolonial Memory in *Luanda, Lisboa, Paraíso*

The topic explored in *Luanda, Lisboa, Paraíso* develops themes from *Esse Cabelo* (2015), which is a hybrid novel between an essay and autobiographical fiction.[22] There, Almeida developed a number of visual and narrative tropes, some of which are expanded in her subsequent novels. For example, the unpacked suitcases kept in Mila's bedroom and the fact that her Angolan grandfather travelled to Lisbon so that one of his sons could receive medical treatment are further explored in *Luanda, Lisboa, Paraíso* (2018); and the long intercontinental phone calls between

Mila and her mother in Luanda and her sporadic holidays in that city become a central topic in *As telefones* [*The Telephones*] (2020). In her later novels, these topics are explored in the third person: as their Afro-Portuguese author argues, her story is very similar to that of many Africans who came to Portugal and telling stories like this in the third person enables her to explore them as stories about the African communities and identities, living on the peripheries of metropolitan Lisbon, as a central topic in Portuguese literature.[23] In fact, *Esse Cabelo* is the beginning of a trajectory of self-consciousness explored in consonance with the theory and praxis of the *wake work*.[24] Mila's personal experience of having her hair done and being confronted with her African ancestry also becomes a way of assuming a process of identity reconstruction and memory recovery as an African girl living in Lisbon.[25] In *Luanda, Lisboa, Paraíso*, this process is shown as a story of exclusion; not only socially speaking, but also because it concerns the public policies of memory in post-1974 Portugal. This novel exposes the need to challenge the exclusionary and univocal cultural memory of the end of Portuguese colonialism. This end has been a predominantly heroic white narrative, obscuring the trauma of the colonized.

This novel tells the story of Cartola de Sousa, an Angolan male midwife who in 1984 leaves Luanda with his 14-year-old son, Aquiles, to have the latter's congenital ankle disorder treated in Lisbon. His wife, Glória, who is bed-ridden and partially paralysed, stays in Luanda with the rest of the family. Cartola and Aquiles believe they will be welcomed as ordinary Portuguese citizens. However, with little money to support themselves, and unable to return to Luanda, they endure the hardships of undocumented African immigrants. They end up working in construction sites and living in Paraíso, a slum on the outskirts of Lisbon. This story epitomizes real stories of undocumented African immigrants in Lisbon, and many who travel to the Portuguese capital every year to receive medical treatment. Cooperation agreements signed between Portugal and the former African colonies in 1975 established a fixed number of African patients per year who can be treated in Portuguese hospitals, but research has shown that most of these patients and their families are destitute, their condition aggravated by lack of support from their local embassies, and by the fact that many are not fluent in Portuguese. They eventually have to accept precarious jobs to eke out a living.[26]

The story of Cartola and Aquiles conveys the extent to which the discourse about racial integration, part of the Portuguese colonial propaganda, was a delusion. Cartola is an *assimilado*, the son of a shepherd from M'Banza, Congo, and educated in a Portuguese mission.[27] He is the male midwife who assists the white Portuguese doctor, Dr Barbosa da Cunha, at the Moçâmedes local hospital during the last years of Portuguese colonialism. Angolan independence coincides with the birth of his son Aquiles. Cartola and Aquiles belong to two different periods in the history of Angola; while Cartola is a black man of colonial Portugal, Aquiles is a son of the Angolan diaspora in Portugal.

In colonial Angola, Cartola emulates the habits and tastes of Dr Barbosa da Cunha, including his clothes, food tastes and way of speaking. The memories of the relationship between the two men and their families convey the fading of an era that offered an apparently established order and the illusion that an *assimilado* could secure his social status in colonial Portugal:

> Através das cortinas de linho de duas janelas altas, as sombras dos quatro adultos eram as de quatro defuntos a dançarem numa moldura, numa casa a óleo, fora do tempo, para lá do lugar onde uma excepção pode salvar o que não tem de pedir desculpa por ser doce.[28]
>
> [Through the linen curtains of two high windows, the shadows of the four adults were those of four corpses dancing inside a framed oil painting of a house, out of time, far from the place where the exception can save what one does not have to apologize for because it is sweet.]

Cartola is a proud Portuguese speaker, a 'gentle' man who can recite Camões's epic poem, the *Lusíadas*. He is moved when he hears the Portuguese national anthem, and continues to feel this way after decolonization (p. 89). However, these things that gave him the illusion of being an ordinary Portuguese, make him a ghostly presence in postcolonial Lisbon, a 'portuguesão dispensado do império' [true Portuguese repudiated by the empire] (p. 42) and 'um homem que ninguém conheceu nem ninguém viu, que não foi mas poderia ter sido' [a man nobody knew, nobody saw, who was nobody but could have been somebody] (p. 70).

In *Luanda, Lisboa, Paraíso*, the narrator describes the African minority community as being very close to social outcasts, vulnerable and easily manipulated by those who are socially integrated. African immigrants roam around Lisbon and are pushed to the periphery of the city, where they can barely live with dignity; multigenerational families of African ethnic minorities have worked on construction sites that have modernized a city whose benefits they cannot enjoy. They save money to call their families in Africa from the central telephone station and get glimpses of family life back home (p. 62). The marginalization experienced by this minority is of a deeper dimension because its scope is beyond social segregation; this minority is fluent in Portuguese but there is apparently nothing in postcolonial Lisbon that relates their existence to the history of the nation and of this city; it is as if 'estão desligados de uma história [...] não sabem dizer quem são' [they are disconnected from history [...] unable to say who they are] (p. 130).

Cartola eventually becomes another of the undocumented African immigrants in Lisbon with little or no prospects, always expecting 'serem enganados e atraiçoados' [to be fooled or betrayed] (p. 73). The disconnectedness between African minorities and the postcolonial city is conveyed in the way the protagonist feels himself among Lisboners. In the eyes of Cartola, the Portuguese mainstream population is also an indifferent mass: apart from Dr Barbosa da Cunha, pinpointing any Lisboner is pinpointing 'alguém' [someone], 'um estranho' [a stranger], or 'outra' [another] (p. 68); people Cartola is literally unable to reach out to. Black minorities and the mainstream population cannot find a way to see each other's face and recognize each other. This is especially illustrated when the Barbosa da Cunha couple come across Aquiles in the street and mistake him for a street beggar. Only in the Prazeres cemetery in Lisbon does Cartola experience moments of delusionary equality while strolling among the tombs of Portuguese people (pp. 87, 96).

The narrative symbolically shows that Lisbon progressively rejects Cartola and Aquiles and they are pushed away to the periphery. The boarding house near the hospital where they are first accommodated is partly destroyed by a fire, killing an African mother and her child who are living in a similarly destitute situation, and the only place they can afford to live in is in Paraíso. Postcolonial Lisbon emerges as a totally different city from the one they had imagined back in Luanda; after the first moments of their arrival, when 'o quotidiano ainda não subtraíra a fantasia' [daily life had not taken away the fantasy] (p. 34), the Portuguese capital gradually evolves into a city that is 'perigosa' [dangerous] and 'incognita' [unfamiliar] (p. 39); its widely acclaimed light 'não iluminou' [did not illuminate them] (p. 78); it is a city that is at first 'silenciosa' [silent], then 'barulhenta' [noisy]: an inscrutable city they cannot integrate into (p. 67). The only place Cartola frequents regularly is the Rossio in downtown Lisbon, where he has a *"ginginha"* (bitter cherry liqueur), chats occasionally with other African immigrants, and looks in the shop windows (pp. 63, 97). The narrative reproduces the opacity that covers the historical memory of African minorities' presence in Lisbon.[29] Although there is no official reference to the presence of African communities in the Rossio, such as a city plaque, the silenced memory of the African presence in this part of the city is nevertheless preserved by a continuum of African communities who also sell their goods there. *Luanda, Lisboa, Paraíso* does not provide an explanation for the presence of Cartola and of the other African immigrants in the Rossio, so their presence there remains unaccounted for and, thus, unintegrated. The postcolonial capital emerges as a city haunted by imperial memory. When Justina, Aquiles's eldest sister, visits them in the early 1990s, she finds all the statues, fountains and pavements 'gastos, velhos, sem interesse, sujos' [old, worn out, uninteresting and dirty] (p. 125). The empire does not exist anymore, but Lisbon remains its ghostly capital. The full recognition of this anachronism is conveyed at the end of the narrative, when Cartola throws his newly purchased top hat into the river Tagus and walks away. He looks the river in the face but it is 'como se o rio não supportasse olhá-lo a direito' [as if the river could not to bear to look back at him] (p. 229).

In an impasse between his memories as the son of an African shepherd in M'Banza, Congo, and those of his adult life in Moçâmedes, Cartola is a man who 'perdera poder sobre o seu passado' [had lost power over his past] (p. 88). From a proud user of the Portuguese language, Cartola evolves into a character whose communication skills regress to the level of that of a child, while at the same time he feels unable 'vomitar Luanda' [to vomit Luanda] (p. 52). Throughout the narrative, indications of his articulate speech and fine manners, signs of an inculcated "civilization", are gradually replaced by various references to his state of decline that include choking as he speaks, having lost his manners, and eventually showing signs of dementia (p. 153). Alcohol and shame of what he has become diminish him to the point where the roles of father and son are reversed, and Aquiles is obliged to take care of his own father. This transformation is intensified by the deterioration of his physical appearance throughout the narrative. After he starts working as a bricklayer, his torso becomes muscled, his impeccable midwife's hands become hardened and calloused, his feet become swollen, his spine curves, and his clothing is always worn out and untidy (p. 69).

Interviewed by Portuguese historians Miguel Bandeira Jerónimo and José Pedro Monteiro, Elizabeth Buettner argues that in Europe postcolonial ethnic minorities have largely been treated as second-class citizens, second-generation immigrants, or as foreigners with a passport.[30] In Portugal, the concept of naturalization differs from its usage in other EU countries and it does not apply to the attribution of Portuguese nationality to a child because their parent has acquired Portuguese nationality nor to people who acquire Portuguese nationality by marriage or adoption. Nationality by naturalization in the Portuguese legislative context refers to foreign citizens who acquire Portuguese nationality by residing in the country legally for six years, by completing the first four years of schooling, by being born in the country and residing there for ten years, or by having a parent who has resided legally in the country for five years prior to the application. Moreover, the amendments to the Portuguese nationality law in 1975 and in 1981 left Africans who had come to Portugal after the independence of the former colonies in a precarious situation.[31] In Almeida's novel this is shown when Cartola's chances of obtaining his citizenship grow dimmer when Dr Barbosa da Cunha, to whom he had given his own and his son's documents, simply disappears and Cartola cannot get through to him. Aquiles and Cartola are literary representations of the plight of those who struggle to obtain Portuguese citizenship. Aquiles, in particular, grows from adolescence to adulthood as an invisible citizen. Eventually, the lack of prospects as a result of his undocumented immigrant status lead him to work with Cartola in construction sites in Lisbon's metropolitan area.

Aquiles conveys the extent to which the false consensus of the policies of memory grounded upon a univocal approach leads to an identity in suspension. Metaphorically, this idea is conveyed by the suitcases kept in Cartola's and Aquiles's bedrooms which have never been unpacked. They bring them when they move to Lisbon and later to Paraíso, but they are not unpacked and are eventually destroyed by a fire that destroys their slum house. Aquiles is involved between his Angolan ancestry and his growth into adulthood in Lisbon. As an *assimilado*, Cartola decides to not pass on to Aquiles his memories of M'Banza in Congo, or teach him Kikongo, his mother tongue: 'Tinha condenado o filho a não ter história por medo que ele não se conseguisse erguer se a conhecesse' [He had condemned his son to having no history, fearing that he could not succeed if he learned it] (p. 152). After leaving Luanda, Aquiles has little contact with the family he has left behind, as they can only afford a monthly call to his mother Glória. His African memories are basically what he remembers from his mother's expressions and manners (p. 56): 'Luanda tornara-se para ele uma miragem e Lisboa era uma cidade sem árvores' [For him, Luanda had become a mirage and Lisbon was a city without trees] (p. 78). While in the hospital where he is being treated when they first arrive in Lisbon, already Aquiles 'tenha deixado de se sentir angolano' [had stopped feeling himself Angolan], and seven years later he does not identify with his immigrant status, a status he associates with his father (pp. 57, 153). Aquiles's identity is a complex cultural construct that entails resistance and negotiation in postcolonial times:

> Perto dos dezoito anos, era um mensageiro entre dois mundos. Aos novos trazia o segredo dos velhos, que lhe vinha de uma vida inteira com um pai desajustado ao presente. Aos velhos, os seus modos acriançados e uma vergonha silenciosa lembravam a magia da meninice quando já a tinham esquecido. (p. 76)
>
> [On the verge of celebrating his eighteenth birthday he was a messenger between two worlds. To the youngsters he brought the secret of the old people that had come to him from a lifetime with a father ill-adapted to the present. For the elder, Aquiles's childish manners and silent shame were reminders of the magic of childhood when they had already forgotten about it.]

This character is built upon the idea of long-standing endurance to the violence of racism that depicts Black people as dangerous. Aquiles's introverted personality impedes him, in his daily life, from establishing friendships with street youngsters. He is afraid of taking the wrong steps and getting into trouble, and is ashamed of his outward signs of poverty (p. 77); he is seen as 'o nativo' [the native] but he is not regarded as an African man by his own family (p. 169): when Justina visits them, she is startled by Aquiles's manners: 'Não, Papá tem razão, não é anemia, Papá, *esse miúdo é que virou mesmo um branco* [No, Daddy is right, it's not anaemia, Daddy, *it's the child himself that's turned into a white man*] (p. 132, my italics).

Aquiles is a son of the Angolan diaspora that postcolonial Lisbon does not acknowledge as an integral part of its population. This character is gradually built up on the idea of orphanhood: his mother is physically absent, and his father is increasingly alienated. Orphanhood is a trope that has recurrently been used in Portuguese literature in the last few decades to refer to the broken relation between Portugal and the former African colonies. Patrícia Martinho Ferreira shows the extent to which the orphan figure has been used in Portuguese fiction to challenge the imperial propaganda of the Estado Novo and as a metaphor for the end of the colonial empire. Furthermore, the orphan is a dystopic figure that conveys the not yet sufficiently discussed complex postcolonial heritage and multiculturality.[32] It is implicitly used to describe Mila's identity conflicts in *Esse Cabelo*, and in *Luanda, Lisboa, Paraíso*, Aquiles is the Afro-Portuguese young man for whom, the narrator writes: 'Não há pressa nem de ter casa nem de ter pai nem de ter mãe [There is no hurry to have a house, or to have a father, or to have a mother] (p. 170); in other words, he is a young man with his life in suspension. The use of this same trope used in the Portuguese literature published after 1974 to convey the idea of loss comparable to that experienced by Portuguese returnees and soldiers is indicative of the need to expand the debate on the complex heritage of the memory of colonialism to other voices and, thus, decolonize the idea of loss.[33]

Paulo de Medeiros contends that although *Luanda, Lisboa, Paraíso* fits into the Portuguese literary tradition, it also inherits the legacy of Portuguese Angolan José Luandino Vieira's *Luuanda*, because both works deal with issues that concern the ending of Portuguese colonialism and its persistent effects in the postcolonial nation.[34] In this novel, the imperial and colonial memory that links Portugal and Angola is a spectre that still haunts the postcolonial nation and is responsible for the emergence of what Inocência Mata identifies as 'an identity in exile', an expression this scholar draws from Julie Lussier.³⁵ The relations that can be established with these literary traditions and works show that discussing memory of the colonial and imperial past affects the way the heirs of Portuguese colonialism see themselves as citizens of the postcolonial history and that there is a duty of reparation that implies making postcolonial memory a polyphonic discussion. The fact that *Luanda, Lisboa, Paraíso* and Djaimilia Pereira de Almeida have received literary recognition shows the extent to which literature plays an important role in this discussion.

Notes to Chapter 4

1. This chapter was written for the Project *Women's Literature: Memories, Peripheries and Resistance in the Luso-African-Brazilian Atlantic* (PTDC/LLT-LES/0858/2021), funded by the Foundation for Science and Technology (FCT) in Portugal.
2. Michael Rothberg, 'Between Memory and Memory: From Lieux de mémoire to Noeuds de mémoire', in *Noeuds de mémoire: Multidirectional Memory in Postwar French and Francophone Culture*, special issue of *Yale French Studies*, 118/19 (2010), 3–12 (p. 12).
3. Manuel Loff, 'Estado, democracia e memória: políticas públicas e batalhas pela memória da ditadura portuguesa (1974–2014)', in *Ditaduras e Revolução: democracia e políticas de memória*, ed. by Manuel Loff, Filipe Piedade and Luciana Castro Soutelo (Coimbra: Almedina, 2015), pp. 23–143 (p. 31).
4. The name of this memorial is Monumento aos Combatentes do Ultramar [Monument to the Fighters in the Overseas Territories]. It was inaugurated in 1994 by the former Minister for Overseas Territories during the Estado Novo, Adriano Moreira, and explicitly avoids reference to the phrase 'colonial war'. 'Overseas' was the term used by the Estado Novo propaganda to refer to the Portuguese colonial empire comprising a territory 'from the Minho to Timor'.
5. Worthy of mention is the work on this topic published by Marta Araújo, researcher of the Centre for Social Studies at the University of Coimbra, as part of a joint project with the Faculty of Education of the Minas Gerais Federal University (UFMG) that analysed Eurocentric representations of race and Africa in Portuguese history textbooks.
6. Pim den Boer, 'Lieux de mémoire in a Comparative Perspective', in *The Theoretical Foundations of Hungarian 'lieux de mémoire' Studies/Theoretische Grundlagen der Erforschung ungarischer Erinnerungsorte*, ed. by Pál S. Varga et al. (Debrecen: Debrecen University Press, 2013), p. 45.
7. Den Boer, 'Lieux de mémoire in a Comparative Perspective', p. 47.
8. The idea of a not so violent colonialism, also known as Lusotropicalism, was a theory created by Brazilian anthropologist Gilberto Freyre during the 1930s. According to this theory, the Portuguese had been more successful colonizers than their European counterparts because they naturally accepted miscegenation with colonized women; the reason for this acceptance, he claimed, was the fact that Portugal had been occupied by the Moors and the biological temperament of the Portuguese grew more suitable for the tropics than that of any other white Europeans. Freyre created this theory to account for what he believed was the successful blending of races in Brazilian society. This theory was later adopted by Salazar's Estado Novo to maintain colonial power in Africa as international pressure against the Portuguese colonial empire grew in the 1950s and 1960s. Lusotropicalism has eventually dominated the Portuguese cultural mindset in relation to race and colonization to date.
9. Den Boer, 'Lieux de mémoire in a Comparative Perspective', p. 46.
10. Grada Kilomba, *Plantation Memories: Episodes of Everyday Racism* (Münster: Unrast Verlag, 2010), pp. 5–6.
11. Borrowed from Kimbundo, the term 'sanzala' refers to an African slave camp in Colonial Brazil. It is also worth mentioning the recent episode involving Joacine Katar Moreira, a Portuguese MP of Guinean descent, elected on an anti-racist and feminist platform, and one of the three Black MPs of African descent elected in the last legislative elections. During parliamentary

discussions in January 2020 about colonial reparations, a debate that has hardly begun in Portugal, the far-right MP André Ventura suggested that Moreira should be sent back to Guinea-Bissau. The political parties with parliamentary seats decided not to condemn Ventura officially, so that his words would not be 'echoed'.
12. Kilomba, *Plantation Memories*, p. 30.
13. Perry Anderson, *The New Old World* (London: Verso, 2009), p. 161.
14. Rothberg, 'Between Memory and Memory', p. 7.
15. Patrícia Martinho Ferreira, *Órfãos do Império: heranças coloniais na literatura portuguesa contemporânea* (Lisbon: ICS, 2021), p. 213.
16. Sheila Khan, *Portugal a lápis de cor: a sul de uma pós-colonialidade* (Coimbra: Almedina, 2015), p. 91 (original emphasis). Translations are mine unless otherwise mentioned.
17. Three relevant research projects are *Memoirs: Filhos de Império e Pós-Memórias Europeias/Children of Empires and European Postmemories* (2015–21), coordinated by Margarida Calafate Ribeiro, based in the CES (Centre for Social Studies), Coimbra University, and financed by the European Research Council; *Afro-Port: African Descent in Portugal: Sociabilities, Representations and Sociopolitical and Cultural Dynamics. A Study in the Lisbon Metropolitan Area* (2018–21), coordinated by Iolanda Évora, based in the CSG [Centre for Research in Social Sciences & Management] at ISEG [Lisbon School of Economics & Management] and financed by the FCT (Foundation for Science and Technology); and *Amílcar Cabral, from Political History to the Politics of Memory* (2016–19), coordinated by Rui Lopes, based in the Institute of Contemporary History at FCSH-NOVA Lisbon and, also, financed by the FCT.
18. In 1965, José Luandino Vieira's *Luuanda* received the Society of Portuguese Authors' Literary Prize. At the time, and because Angola was part of the Portuguese empire, Angolan citizenship was non-existent, but Luandino Vieira later maintained dual citizenship. Recent works by Afro-Portuguese authors include Kalaf Epalanga's *Também os brancos sabem dançar (Um romance musical)* (Caminho, 2017), *Angolano que comprou Lisboa (por metade do preço)* (Caminho, 2014), and *Estórias de amor para meninos de cor* (Caminho, 2011); Telma Tvon's *Um preto muito português* (Chiado Editora, 2018); Yara Monteiro's *Essa dama bate bué!* (Guerra e Paz, 2018), and Luísa Semedo's *O Canto da Moreia* (coolbooks, 2019).
19. Isabel Lucas, '"Uma rapariga africana em Lisboa": interview with Djaimilia Pereira de Almeida', *Público*, 2 October 2015, <http:www.publico.pt/2015/10/02/culturaipsilon/entrevista/uma-rapariga-africana-em-lisboa-1709352>.
20. Kilomba, *Plantation Memories*, p. 38.
21. Inocência Mata, 'Estranhos em permanência: a negociação da identidade portuguesa na pós-colonialidade', in *Portugal não é um país pequeno: contar o 'império' na pós-colonialidade*, ed. by Manuela Ribeiro Sanches (Lisbon: Cotovia, 2006), pp. 285–315 (p. 288).
22. *Esse Cabelo* received the 2016 New Talents Prize, sponsored by the Gulbenkian Foundation, under the category of 'Literature'.
23. Isabel Lucas, '"Djaimilia Pereira de Almeida: não é só raça nem género, é querer participar na grande conversa da literatura": interview with Djaimilia Pereira de Almeida', *Público*, 20 December 2018, <https://www.publico.pt/2018/12/20/culturaipsilon/noticia/djaimilia-1854988>.
24. Patrícia Martinho Ferreira, *Órfãos do Império*, p. 234. In her book *In the Wake: On Blackness and Being* (Durham, NC: Duke University Press, 2016), Christina Sharpe explains the concept of 'wake work' to contend the imperative of a new consciousness that rethinks the past because the political, racial and cultural exclusion experienced by Black people perpetuates slavery's violence, with repercussions such as police violence against Black communities and social and economic inequality that affects primarily these communities.
25. Ferreira, *Órfãos do Império*, p. 235.
26. See Maria Adelina Henriques, 'A emigração PALOP em Portugal: o caso dos doentes evacuados', *Sociológico*, 22 (2012), 53–62 <http://doi.org/10.4000/sociologico.573>.
27. The Colonial Statute of 1954 determined that in order to be considered for *assimilado* status, African subjects should have a Catholic education, obtain a civil marriage licence, secure a Portuguese sponsor, be an employee in any business accepted by the Portuguese colonizer, and live like a Portuguese. History shows that very few actually gained this status and those who did

never had the same rights and civil status as white Portuguese citizens. See Maria da Conceição Neto, 'A República no seu estado colonial: combater a escravatura, estabelecer o "indigenato"', *Ler História*, 59 (2010), 205–25.
28. Djaimilia Pereira de Almeida, *Luanda, Lisboa, Paraíso* (São Paulo: Companhia das Letras, 2018), p. 44. Further page references to *Luanda, Lisboa, Paraíso* are given in the text. All translations are mine unless otherwise mentioned.
29. In the sixteenth century, the first Black brotherhood (of slaves and manumitted slaves), initially a branch of the *Confraria do Rosário* before becoming an autonomous brotherhood, was established in the Church of S. Domingos in Rossio. Moreover, in the seventeenth century, African women sold corn, rice and vegetables at the steps of Rossio hospital (which no longer exists).
30. Miguel Bandeira Jerónimo and José Pedro Monteiro, *História(s) do presente: os mundos que o passado nos deixou* (Lisbon: Tinta-da-china, 2020), pp. 42–43.
31. The Law of Nationality approved in 1975, based on the principle of *jus soli* [birthright citizenship], removed Portuguese nationality from those born in the African ex-colonies who did not have Portuguese (or Goan) ancestry. In 1981, changes introduced into this law were oriented by the principle of *jus sanguinis* [depending on parents' nationality]. This was an opportunity to give Portuguese nationality to Portuguese emigrants born abroad. Although this new law combined the principle of *jus domicile*, thus giving Portuguese citizenship to foreign residents in the country, it privileged Portuguese ancestry.
32. Ferreira, *Órfãos do Império*, p. 43.
33. Ferreira, *Órfãos do Império*, p. 230.
34. Paulo de Medeiros, 'Memórias Pós-Imperiais: *Luuanda*, de José Luandino Vieira, e *Luanda, Lisboa, Paraíso*, de Djaimilia Pereira de Almeida', *Língua-Lugar: Literatura, História, Estudos Culturais*, 1 (2020), 136–49, <http://doi.org/10.34913/journals/lingua-lugar.2020e211>.
35. Inocência Mata, 'Uma implosiva geografia exílica', *Público*, 14 December 2018, <https://www.publico.pt/2018/12/14/culturaipsilon/critica/implosiva-geografia-exilica-1854334>.

CHAPTER 5

Representations of Greenland: Danish and Greenlandic Literary Perspectives

Christinna Hazzard

Introduction

Located within the Arctic Circle, Greenland may not be part of the continental European landmass, but through its political history as a Danish colony and its status as one of the Overseas Countries and Territories (OCT) of the European Union (EU), it forms the northernmost border of geo-political Europe. This chapter will consider how Greenland's position on the periphery of Europe, as well as its history as a colony and autonomous region of the Kingdom of Denmark, continue to have an impact on its literature, causing it to be viewed as a minority literature in relation to both Nordic and European writing more broadly. Contextualizing the analysis provided in this chapter, this short introduction will situate contemporary Greenlandic writing within the history of Danish colonialism and imperialism in Greenland and illustrate the lasting impact of Danish colonial rule on the culture, language, and politics of Greenland.

The minority status of Greenlandic literature needs to be considered in relation both to the history of colonialism and to ongoing imperialism in the Arctic region. The colonial history of Greenland can be traced back to 1262, when Norse Viking settlers who had populated southern parts of the island since the tenth century, living separately from the Inuit population in the north, accepted the rule of the Norwegian King.[1] Although the Norse settlements in Greenland were wiped out by the sixteenth century, the territory remained part of the Kingdom of Norway and it was not until 1721, when Hans Egede (1686–1758) led a mission to Greenland in an attempt to re-establish contact with the lost Norse settlements, that interest in recolonizing the island was renewed. Once they realized the Norse population no longer existed, Egede's mission, 'partly financed by colonial trade, quickly changed its focus to the conversion of the Greenlanders', and by 1780 the Royal Greenlandic Trading Department was established to administer the colony's trade.[2] Greenland remained part of the Danish-Norwegian realm until the Treaty of Kiel in 1814, when Norway was ceded to Sweden and the Norwegian overseas possessions were transferred to Denmark.

In 1953 the Danish *Grundlov* (constitution) was updated and Greenland's official status as a colony ended. The remaining Danish possessions in the North Atlantic — Greenland and the Faroe Islands — were integrated into the Kingdom of Denmark, reclassified as autonomous Danish provinces, and given representation in *Folketinget* (the Danish Parliament).[3] This was partly in response to international pressure to decolonize; however, it did little to satisfy the national independence movements that had been growing in both the Faroe Islands and Greenland throughout the twentieth century. In a referendum in 1979 Greenlanders voted in favour of independence and the Greenlandic government was established. The Greenland Home Rule Act handed over responsibility for the day-to-day governing of Greenland to the Greenlanders, while foreign affairs, the legal system and defence remained overseen by the Danish government. Due to continued pressure for autonomy another referendum was held in 2008 and Greenlanders once again voted in favour of independence, which resulted in the 2009 Act on Greenland Self-Government. The act extended the powers of the Greenlandic home rule government, including control of the legal system, but kept responsibility for foreign policy and security under the Danish government. The relationship between Denmark and Greenland continues to raise debate in Greenland but independence remains 'the ultimate political goal for the Greenlandic nation'.[4] The current debates about independence tend to focus on the issue of the Greenlandic national economy, which is still subsidized by the Danish state, and is framed by the issue of funding economic growth and national independence via the extraction of natural resources at a time when the effects of climate change are undeniable.[5] Thus, the Greenlandic context troubles any straightforward notion of decolonization leading to sovereignty, but instead offers a valuable opportunity to consider how new forms of political and cultural domination continue to shape Greenland's postcolonial condition after colonialism is supposed to have officially ended.[6]

Danish political and cultural imperialism in Greenland has also had a profound effect on the Greenlandic language and its cultural production, and the close ties between Denmark and Greenland continue to shape the way Greenlandic literature is written, read, and circulated. The Greenlandic language consists of four main dialects, with Kalaallisut, the West-Greenlandic dialect, as the official language since 2009. However, for much of the twentieth century Danish was the primary language of public life, culture, and learning, and it continues to be spoken widely in Greenland today. This was due in part to the changes in the *Grundlov* in 1953, when the Danish *grønlandspolitik* (Greenlandic policy) moved to a policy of 'Danification' and Danish was made the official language of Greenland. However, it was also the early colonial administration that was initially responsible for making Greenlandic a written language, with the Danish Mission and other Christian groups producing hymn books in Greenlandic and teaching the Greenlanders to read and write in both Danish and Greenlandic.[7] It was not until the start of the twentieth century that the first Greenlandic novels were written, a moment that coincided with increased influence from the outside world and rapid social change in Greenland, including improvements in education leading to an increase in literacy and the creation of local and regional councils that enabled Greenlanders to participate in the political and cultural life of their country.[8] Prior to this, Greenland had an oral literary culture, which was made up of stories, songs, poetry, spells and fables that were shared by Inuit people across the arctic region.[9] The process of Danification was met with protest, expressed in political songs and poetry as well as in the Greenlandic newspapers. A project of cultural and linguistic revival accompanied the country's increased political autonomy in the late 1970s and '80s, which led to an increasing number of literary works being published in Greenlandic.[10]

Today Greenlandic authors continue to write and publish in both Danish and Greenlandic, but the literary output remains small and international circulation tends to be restricted to Denmark and the Nordic region. Furthermore, until 2021, when Niviaq Korneliussen was awarded the prize for her second novel *Naasuliardarpi* [*Flower Valley*], in the fifty-year history of the prestigious Nordic Council's Literature Prize no Greenlandic writer had ever won, despite regular nominations. However, Greenland has been an important subject in Danish literature, including in the internationally bestselling novel by Peter Høeg, *Frøken Smillas Fornemmelse for Sne* [*Miss Smilla's Feeling for Snow*] (1992), and in the recent works of Danish-Norwegian author Kim Leine, whose historical novel set in Greenland, *Profeterne i Evighedsfjorden* [*The Prophets of Eternal Fjord*] (2012) was awarded the Nordic Council's Literature Prize in 2013. Indeed, the Danish literary tradition of writing novels about Greenland stretches back to the nineteenth century, and includes works such as Bernhard Ingemann's *Kunuk og Naja* [*Kunuk and Naja*] (1842), and Nobel Prize-winning author Henrik Pontoppidan's *Isbjørnen- et Portræt* [*The Polar Bear- a Portrait*] (1887). Cultural historian Kirsten Thisted calls this body of literature 'den danske grønlandslitteratur' [Danish Greenland literature], and the fact that it is more widely read, translated and circulated than Greenlandic literature points to a lasting imbalance of power between the two countries.[11]

Drawing on this distinction between Greenlandic literature and Danish literature, this chapter will compare the representation of Greenland and Greenlanders in recent Greenlandic and Danish Greenland literature and question what is gained and lost in the majority representation of the Greenlandic minority. I shall first consider some of the reasons for the lack of critical engagement with Danish colonialism. Secondly, I will explore Peter Høeg's *Frøken Smillas Fornemmlse for Sne* and Kim Leine's *Kalak* (2007) and show that even though both authors are critical of Danish colonialism, they nonetheless default to negative stereotypes of Greenlanders and Greenland that reflect attitudes still prevalent in Danish society. The final section will focus on two recent novels by Greenlandic authors, Niviaq Korneliussen's *HOMO Sapienne* (2014) and Juaaka Lyberth's *Godt i Vej* [*Well on Our Way*] (2014),[12] in order to consider the different ways they represent Greenland and engage with the history and legacies of Danish colonial rule.

Nordic Colonialism

Despite centuries of colonial rule in the North Atlantic, as well as in the Caribbean, Africa, and India, Denmark is still rarely thought of as a colonial power and is usually excluded from discussions about the European imperial project. This is also largely the case within Denmark, where the image of a 'democratic and peace-loving country is a central part of the Danish national narrative'.[13] Furthermore, the idea that Danish colonialism was somehow more benign than that of other European empires has tended to characterize the discussion of Danish involvement in Greenland, focusing on the subsidies paid by the Danish government to Greenland and the modernization programs introduced in the 1950s and '60s, as opposed to the violence (in its many forms) entailed in colonial domination.[14] Although Greenlanders have repeatedly protested against Danish colonial rule and voted in their majority for independence in several referenda, this attitude remains firmly in place in most parts of Danish society. This is illustrated, as Thisted has recently argued, in the lack of public debate in Denmark over the 2009 Act on Greenland Self-Government:

> [...] at the time when the act was formulated, most Danes — including most Danish politicians — thought it completely unrealistic that Greenland would ever want full independence. The power relationship between Denmark and Greenland has been so unequal, and from a Danish point of view, Greenland has been so underdeveloped and completely dependent on Danish assistance, that such a solution has seemed barely conceivable.[15]

Indeed, Lars Jensen has suggested that the character of postcolonial Denmark can be defined precisely by this 'lack of attention [...] towards the colonies and the idea of Denmark as part of an overseas imperial enterprise', an oversight that is 'matched by an equally underrated significance granted to the remnants of the Danish empire, Greenland and the Faroe Islands, as a formative influence on contemporary Danish history'.[16] Jensen also draws attention to the negative attitude of many Danes towards the people of the Faroe Islands and Greenland, who are seen as 'ungrateful and somehow lacking citizen[s] (and therefore never quite ready for autonomy)'.[17] This idea is repeated through 'education, media representation and the Danish political establishment', alongside negative stereotypes that portray Greenlanders as benefit scroungers, alcoholics, and drug addicts without due consideration of the profound and violent disruption caused by colonialism to traditional ways of life.[18]

It is noteworthy, therefore, that Greenland remains a topic of interest for Danish writers, and it is contradictory, as Thisted has highlighted, that while much of Danish society has avoided participating in the reconciliation process recently set in motion by the Greenlanders to recover and work through the colonial past, the reading public have flocked around authors such as Kim Leine, whose novels deal directly with the colonial past. Leine follows in the footsteps of Peter Høeg, who in 1992 brought the issue of Nordic colonialism to public attention, both in Denmark and internationally, with his postcolonial crime thriller *Frøken Smillas Fornemmelse for Sne*. It is this disconnect between the popularity of Greenland as a trope in Danish literature versus the 'cultural amnesia' of Danish colonialism in Danish society that is the focus of this chapter.[19] In order to understand this situation further, the following section will consider the representation of Greenland and Greenlanders in Høeg's and Leine's novels and show that despite being critical of Danish colonialism both authors continue to rely on negative stereotypes of Greenlanders.

Danish Greenland Literature: Peter Høeg's *Frøken Smillas Fornemmelse for Sne* and Kim Leine's *Kalak*

Published in Danish in 1992, Peter Høeg's critically acclaimed novel *Frøken Smillas Fornemmelse for Sne* (*Smilla*), was translated into English in 1993, made into a feature-length film in 1997, and has since become a key text in the Nordic noir literary canon. The novel deals with the mysterious death of a young Greenlandic boy called Esajas, who the police believe has fallen from the roof of his apartment block in Copenhagen whilst playing. On analysing the footprints left in the snow, the protagonist, Smilla, a neighbour and friend, believes Esajas may have been running away from someone. With the help of Peter, a mechanic living in her apartment block, Smilla starts an investigation of her own, which leads her all over Copenhagen and eventually back to Greenland where she was raised. Through her investigations, Smilla reveals a violent history related to a series of Danish scientific expeditions to Gela Alta, an island off the coast of Greenland, where a valuable meteorite has been found. She discovers that Esajas's father, a diver on a previous expedition, died of a parasite he contracted from the waters surrounding the meteorite, and that Esajas, having accompanied his father to Gela Alta, has been murdered because of his possible knowledge of the meteorite's location. Drawing on the narrative conventions of noir, Høeg presents a nuanced critique of Danish colonialism in the novel, illustrating both the violence of the past and new manifestations of colonial exploitation and oppression.

The protagonist, Smilla, is central to the novel's postcolonial critique. Smilla's mother was a Greenlandic Inuit hunter who had died when she was a young child, and her father is a middle-class Danish doctor from Copenhagen. The novel is permeated with both joyful memories of her childhood in Greenland and the trauma of her relocation and institutionalization in Denmark after the death of her mother, an experience that echoes a well-known social experiment in the 1950s, when twenty-two Greenlandic children from disadvantaged families were removed from their families and relocated for re-education in Denmark.[20] Smilla is represented as highly intelligent but prone to bouts of depression, a loner, estranged emotionally from her father, but dependent on his money, with a failed career that does not live up to her intellectual potential. In their essay on Høeg's novel, Prem Poddar and Cheralyn Mealor describe Smilla as 'a hybrid', and suggests that her hybridity manifests itself in several ways, including 'in her passion for ice which is fuelled by a combination of her instinctive (Eskimo) "feeling for snow" and expert (Western) knowledge in glacial morphology'.[21] They argue that through the character of Smilla Høeg presents an essentialist perspective on identity as 'closed, secured within its boundaries and only [...] fractured or repressed by the various forms of subjugation which [...] are exercised by the colonial regime', and that '[i]ndigenous resistance' therefore takes 'the form of an attempt to regain or rediscover the authentic pre-colonial identity'.[22] Smilla's dislocated sense of self, they argue, is rooted in her 'frustrations as a hybrid', and her inability to recover this 'true identity'.[23] This argument underestimates the complexity of postcolonial identity formation, which is not a matter of return to some originary pre-colonial state. It also significantly undervalues Smilla's determination to find out the truth about Esajas, and her willingness to put herself at risk by joining the return expedition to Gela Alta under the guise of a ship's stewardess in order to confront those involved. Poddar and Mealor are also dismissive of Høeg's emphasis on colonialism as part of capitalist imperialism, suggesting (in a later version of the essay) that while Høeg is critical of Danish colonialism, it is 'presented essentially as one of capitalism's evils'.[24] I argue that one of the strengths of Høeg's postcolonial critique in the novel is precisely that it reveals capitalism, globalization and colonialism to be intimately connected by showing that exploitation and oppression of the Greenlandic population continues through institutions such as the Cryolite Corporation, the company behind the scientific expeditions to Gela Alta and the death of Esajas and his father.

Indeed, this is captured in an illuminating description towards the end of the novel of Sonne, a Danish sailor onboard the *Kronos* who takes it upon himself to protect Smilla from the other crewmen. After mocking him affectionately for being typically Danish, Smilla describes his reactions:

> Han rødmer. Han vil gerne protester. Gerne tages højtideligt. Gerne hævde sin autoritet. Som Danmark. Med blå øjne, røde kinder, og reelle hensigter. Men uden om ham er der store kræfter, pengene, udviklingen, misbruget, killisionen mellem den nye of den gamle verden. Han har ikke forstået hvad der foregår. At han kun bliver tålt så længe han følger med.[25]
>
> [He blushes. He wants to protest. Wants to be taken seriously. Wants to raise his authority. The same way as Denmark does. With blue eyes, pink cheeks, and honourable intentions. But all around him are powerful forces, money, development, abuse, the clash between the new and the old world. He doesn't understand what is happening. That he will only be tolerated as long as he keeps in line.]

By suggesting that it is the 'powerful forces' of capitalism that keep Smilla and Sonne, a 'pæn ung Dansker' [nice young Dane], locked in the same uneven relations of power as during colonial rule, Høeg shows that the violence and oppression of colonialism continue, despite its official end in 1953.[26] Furthermore, through the Gela Alta plot, Høeg makes it clear that the pursuit and domination of knowledge and resources at the heart of the colonial project are still present and active through the 'new imperialism' of late capitalism.[27]

However, despite Høeg's nuanced representation of capitalist imperialism, he nonetheless defers to stereotypes about Greenlanders that are common in Danish society, particularly the widespread idea that Greenlanders have alcohol and social problems and, as suggested by Jensen, are 'somehow lacking citizen[s]'. Juliane, Esajas's mother for instance, is represented as a dysfunctional alcoholic who is unable to care for Esajas properly and vulnerable both to the bureaucracy of the Danish welfare state and the cronies of the Cryolite Corporation. Although alcohol abuse is seen as the biggest public health concern in Greenland and the root cause of other social problems such as violence, sexual assaults, and suicides, alcohol consumption has decreased steadily in Greenland since the 1980s, a trend that is very similar in Denmark, where alcohol has also been the primary health and social concern since the mid-twentieth century.[28] However, despite this, the idea that all Greenlanders are problem-drinkers is still widespread in Danish society, and although Høeg represents both Smilla and Juliane sympathetically, and wields a clear critique of Danish colonialism, he nonetheless fails to leave these damaging stereotypes behind.

Like Høeg, the Danish-Norwegian author Kim Leine relies on similarly problematic representations of Greenlanders in his recent novels. Leine has become an important voice in Denmark about issues relating to Greenland and both his debut novel *Kalak* and his highly acclaimed historical novel *Profeterne I Evighedsfjorden* (2012) deal with the history and legacies of colonial rule.[29] Leine describes *Kalak* as an *Erindringsroman* [autobiographical novel] — a novel based on his experience of working as a nurse in Greenland for fifteen years. The novel deals closely with the social problems in both Danish and Greenlandic society, including alcoholism, suicide, and sexual abuse. The protagonist, Kim, is born in Norway in a community of Jehovah's Witnesses. At the age of seventeen he runs away to live with his sexually abusive father who has moved away to Copenhagen earlier in the novel. Kim decides to study nursing so he can escape Copenhagen and fulfil his dream of working in Africa. During his studies Kim meets Lærke, they marry and have two children together. Once qualified, Kim is offered work in Nuuk, Greenland's capital, an opportunity that offers him an 'arktisk version af den gamle drøm om Afrika og bushen' [arctic version of the old dream of Africa and the bush].[30] Despite warnings about 'danskerhadet, volden, drikkeriet, fjendtligheden' [hatred of the Danes, the violence, the drinking, the hostility], Kim feels at home in Nuuk, learning the language quickly, and entering into numerous affairs with co-workers and neighbours.[31] Halfway through the novel Lærke and Kim divorce, she returns to Denmark with the children and, in what is almost a mirror image of Høeg's Smilla, Kim is left trapped between the two countries.

The Greenland of *Kalak* is urban, nocturnal, with dingy nightclubs and women who are all too willing to have sex with Kim. When he first moves to Nuuk, Kim describes it as a place that it takes a while to fall in love with, with its 'lange rækker af betonblokke, våde, ramponerende og affaldsstinkende, og det hvileløst skiftende vejr' [long rows of cement blocks, wet and smelling of rubbish, and the restless, ever-changing weather].[32] This representation of Greenland is in stark contrast with that of *Smilla*, where Greenland is visualized through Smilla's memories of a traditional nomadic life with her mother. Unlike Leine's descriptions of the socially deprived capital, Nuuk, Smilla's memories focus on traditional ways of life in the artic landscape creating a romanticized image of Greenland untouched by the modern world. Before arriving in Nuuk, Kim is also warned not to go out alone at night, because a Dane was recently attacked and beaten badly, with no other reason than '[d]e hader os' [they hate us], another very different image to that of the Greenlanders of Høeg's novel who are almost universally victims of violence.[33] However, despite the warnings, when Kim arrives in Greenland he is welcomed with a 'brysk og næsten familiær elskværdighed' [a brusque and almost familiar kindness].[34]

An important aspect of *Kalak* is Leine's description of the Greenlandic language, which Kim learns, one word at a time, and eventually masters. He suggests that '[a]t tale grønlandsk er at ændre sin måde at tænke på, ændre sit billed af verden' [to speak Greenlandic involves changing the way you think, the way you understand the world around you], and he finds the complexities of tone and grammar both intriguing and challenging:

> Hvis jeg havde forstillet mig at grønlandsk var en slags natursprog, så bliver jeg skuffet. Jeg forsøger at regne ud hvor mange bøjningsformer et udsagnsord har og når til 600. [...] En sætning med kryds, bolle og firkant består tit kun af et enkelt ord, der til gengæld er sat sammen af kæder på fem til ti stavelser, noget der gør det næsten umuligt at læse en tækst.[35]

> [If I had imagined that Greenlandic would be a kind of natural language, I was sorely mistaken. I try to calculate the inflections of a verb and reach nearly 600. [...] A sentence describing a cross, circle and square consists of just a single word, which in turn is made up of five to ten different spellings, making it almost impossible to read a text.]

Such descriptions not only emphasize the complexity of the Greenlandic language but contribute to the sense of Kim's foreignness in Nuuk at the start of the novel. However, he works hard to integrate and his attempts to communicate in Greenlandic with patients and colleagues in the hospital offer one of the few sympathetic representations of him.

He soon finds, however, that being a foreigner in Greenland in fact gives him a kind of power, as his female co-workers are almost universally attracted to him and he realizes that he only needs to 'række handed frem og sige ordene' [reach out and say the words] to get what he wants from them.[36] He initially tries to remain faithful to Lærke, wanting to avoid the stereotype he himself describes as 'hvid man på besøg i tidligere koloni' [white man visiting a former colony], but despite this he becomes involved in a number of sexual relationships with Greenlandic women.[37] Leine is thus clearly aware of and uncomfortable with the position of power that Kim, as a Dane, holds in the Greenlandic community, but he does little to challenge this, showing only how he takes advantage of it to steal painkillers from the hospital without suspicion, and how it gives him access to as many women as he likes. Greenland is thus represented as a place for hedonistic and self-destructive behaviours, where the uneven power dynamics at the heart of the colonial encounter between Greenlanders and Danes remains cemented in place.

Where in Høeg's *Smilla* Greenland is represented as an arctic colonial frontier and the indigenous people as nomadic hunters, in Kim Leine's *Kalak* Greenland is a place that the rapid postcolonial modernization has left crumbling in its wake, full of concrete buildings and rife with alcoholism and drug abuse. Although both these works undoubtedly take a critical stance towards Danish colonialism and the continued imbalance of power between the two countries, they ultimately reproduce stereotypes about Greenland and Greenlanders, without adequately considering these in relation to the disruption to the traditional way of life caused by colonialism in the first place. Having discussed the ways in which Danish authors engage with the history and legacies of Danish colonialism in their representations of Greenland and Greenlanders, the final section of this chapter will move on to consider the key themes and formal features of two recent Greenlandic novels, Juaaka Lyberth's *Godt i Vej* (2014) and Niviaq Korneliussen's *HOMO Sapienne* (2014), to show the very different ways they represent Greenland and the experience and legacies of Danish colonial rule.

Greenlandic Literature: Juaaka Lyberth's *Godt i Vej* and Niviaq Korneliussen's *HOMO Sapienne*

Juaaka Lyberth's coming-of-age novel *Godt i Vej* explores the changes to Greenlandic society and culture in the early 1970s and was nominated for the Nordic Prize for Literature in 2014. The novel follows the life of Paul Erik, nicknamed Pauli, a teenager from Uummannaq in Northern Greenland, who, like other academically promising youths from around the country, attends high school in Nuuk at the College of Education, the centre of the Greenlandic education system.[38] The story takes place in the years before home rule and registers the stirring rebellion against Danish authorities that eventually led to the vote for greater independence in 1979. The novel also depicts the development of a Greenlandic youth culture, shaped by international influences, including bands such as the Rolling Stones and the Beatles.[39] It opens with Pauli's journey from his village Uummannaq to the college in Nuuk onboard the coastal ship *Disko*. The school is run entirely by Danish teachers, who assert their authority at every opportunity, making sure the students stick to the strict rules governing college life, including the most important rules of all: no drinking and no mixing between the girls' and boys' dormitories. The students are also kept separate from the rest of the population of Nuuk, meaning they rarely interact with anyone who is not a teenager or teacher at the college. As can be expected from the narrative perspective of Pauli, the novel is filled with the concerns of a teenager: sex, relationships, drinking, fashion, and music, and figuring out his place in world. There is thus a deliberately universal quality to Lyberth's novel, which highlights that the life of Greenlandic teenagers in the rebellious era of the 1970s was not that different to that of teenagers elsewhere in the world. However, during the course of the narrative, which is set over the course of a school year, Lyberth simultaneously charts the politicization of the students as they increasingly turn their attention towards Greenland's future.

The fact that the young protagonists are shown to be part of the political vision for a modern Greenland is reflected in the novel's title, which in the Danish edition translates as *godt i vej*, literally meaning 'well on the way', an expression that is used to describe a young person developing or growing up and denotes a sense of hope or promise. The students are regularly reminded that they are the privileged few who are receiving an education with the expectation that they will play leading roles in their country as it develops. The students are encouraged to attend public debates dealing with key questions that relate to the future of the Greenlandic nation. One such debate includes the proposition that a proportion of the Greenlandic population should be relocated to Denmark because

> Den grøndlandske befolkning — især den østgrøndlandske — er vokset så meget, at den ikke kan leve af fangst alene. I kan se, at på bare tyve år er befolkingstallet fordoblet. Og dette skaber et væld af problemer, som vi ikke bare kan løse selv.[40]
>
> [The Greenlandic population — particularly in east Greenland — has grown so much that it is impossible to survive on hunting alone. You can see that in just twenty years the population has doubled, and this creates a wealth of problems that we can't just solve ourselves.]

The debates, Lyberth makes sure to mention, are hosted by the Catholic Church and take place in Danish. This not only shows that questions about Greenland's future are reserved for the educated bilingual Greenlanders under the guidance of Danes in positions of power, but also points to the central role played by language in the Danish administration and control of Greenland in the twentieth century.

However, the students also discuss political issues more informally, amongst themselves, and it is in this space, rather than through the formal debates, that the history of Danish colonialism and the ongoing relationship between the two countries is questioned in greater depth. In one such debate towards the end of the novel, Pauli listens intently as his two classmates discuss the impact of Danish colonial rule. His friend Hinnarik claims that the Danish society is the fairest in the world, with free education, healthcare and help for the unemployed. He also suggests that

> Hvordan i så end ser på det, så er vores tilknytning til Danmark en fordel for os. Og vi bliver ikke behandlet som koloniserede indfødte som indianerne i Amerika eller negerene i Afrika. Vi skylder Danmark en stor tak, det må vi åbent indrømme.[41]
>
> [Whichever way one looks at it, our connection to Denmark is an advantage to us. We don't get treated as colonized natives like the Indians in America or the negroes in Africa. We have to admit that we owe Denmark thanks.]

This view is countered by Pauli's friend Jerimi, who argues that Greenland is 'en dansk koloni, og de tog vores gamle tro fra os og gjorde os kristne' [a Danish colony; they took our ancient faith from us and made us Christian], thereby aligning their struggle for independence with that of colonized people elsewhere.[42] With this discussion Lyberth sketches out the broad positions still dominant in the debate about Greenlandic independence, illustrating both the internalization of the narrative of a benign colonialism, which has been the dominant view of Danish rule in Greenland within Denmark, and, on the other hand, the anti-colonialist stance of those who want full independence and secession from Denmark.

Pauli is less opinionated than his friends and finds Jerimi's passion hard to tolerate, but despite this, he becomes increasingly aware of the daily inequalities between the Greenlanders and the Danes in Nuuk, who are there both as manual workers to support the development of infrastructure, mining, and the fishing industry, and as members of the elite, 'de høje herrer' [the overlords], with leading positions in the administration.[43] One episode in particular exposes Pauli to the unfair treatment of Greenlanders and makes him aware of the fact that the Danish-led modernization and urbanization of Greenland hasn't always had a positive impact. Pauli has been admitted to hospital due to an ear infection and while there he befriends a Greenlander called Veerti. In a monologue, Veerti gives Pauli a detailed description of his life, including the changes he has seen since the Second World War and his experiences working as a painter and construction worker in Nuuk. He tells Pauli about growing up in a small community of hunters; about the changes to his village when the seal population began to diminish; and how people had to find new means to survive. Like many former hunters, Veerti ended up working on the construction sites of Nuuk and he has witnessed the social problems, including violence, alcoholism and suicide, that became common place amongst the Greenlanders who had relocated to the city to work in construction or the new fish processing factory. He also complains about the different treatment of his Danish co-workers, who he claims are often drunk at work and yet are treated favourably, while Greenlanders are given the harder jobs or even get fired so their positions can be filled by Danes.

Veerti explains that he has been hospitalized due to feeling dizzy at work, the result of repeated exposure to toxic fumes from the paint used in the building of the controversial Block P. Once the biggest construction project in the Danish realm, Block P was an apartment complex built in central Nuuk as part of the urbanization programme of the 1960s. It was famously inadequate for the Inuit population of Greenland as the corridors were too narrow to accommodate the traditional winter clothing and, as Veerti recalls, the toilets where always blocked because 'dumme grønlændere, [...] smed fjerene ned I dem, når de plukkede alke' [the stupid Greenlanders flushed the feathers down them when they plucked the razorbills].[44] While Block P certainly epitomizes the underlying violence in the drive to modernize and 'develop' Greenland, it also provides an illustration of the complex and uneven experience of modernity in the colonial peripheries, which can be characterized by the 'coexistence of the past and the contemporary' as the result of the uneven process of capitalist modernization.[45] Lyberth's depiction of Nuuk, especially through Veerti's story, encapsulates this experience: the industrialization of the fishing industry means more workers are needed in Nuuk to work in the fish processing factory, and the Greenlanders who relocate from the villages to the city bring with them their traditional culture and way of life, which is inadequately housed in modern buildings such as Block P. Indeed, the complex interconnectedness of the modern and the traditional is an overarching theme in Lyberth's novel and central to his representation of Greenland in the 1970s. Thus, although the novel is primarily about the daily life of high school students during a turbulent moment in Greenlandic history, it provides a valuable insight into how Greenland was administered by the Danish state in the years between the official end of colonial rule in 1953 and Home Rule in 1979.

Lyberth's combination of a semi-autobiographical coming-of-age narrative with questions about the relationship between Denmark and Greenland, national identity, and independence gives the novel a clear national allegorical register, which has been a common feature of much Greenlandic writing in the twentieth century. Karen Langgård explains that along with the national newspapers, which began to be published in the late nineteenth century, literature played a vital role in 'the process of nation building' in twentieth-century Greenland, and that writers such as Mathias Storch (1883–1957), who wrote the first Greenlandic novel, *Singnagtugaq* [*A Greenlander's Dream*] (1915), and Augo Lynge (1899–1959), the first Greenlandic representative in the Danish Parliament and author of the novel *Ukiut 300-nngornerat* [*Three Hundred Years After*] (1931), used literature to imagine a future Greenland without colonial domination.[46] Others, such as the songwriter Moses Olsen (1928–2008), who drew on the Inuit roots of Greenlandic culture and images of Artic wilderness in his articulation of Greenlandic identity, and the novelist Hans Anton Lynge (1945–), Nordic literature prize nominee in 1991, have continued to explore national questions in the context of modern Greenlandic society.[47] Indeed, Langgård summarizes Greenlandic literature in the twentieth century as 'a postcolonial literature that deals with nation building', but she also draws attention the fact that 'from the late 1980s younger readers began to complain that Greenlandic literature did not address their lives'.[48] Where Lyberth's *Godt I Vej* can be seen as continuing in the tradition of the 'ethnic-national perspective' dominant in Greenlandic writing, young Greenlandic authors such as Niviaq Korneliussen are increasingly distancing themselves from the national-political novel tradition of the past, and instead focus on 'individuality' and non-national forms of belonging in Greenlandic identity.[49]

Korneliussen has recently gained attention in the Nordic region and beyond with her debut novel *HOMO Sapienne*, which was nominated for the Nordic Council's Literature Prize in 2015 and has since been translated into eight languages.[50] The novel was first published in Greenlandic in 2014 and then translated to Danish by the author; it tells the stories of five young people from Greenland, Fia, Inuk, Arnaq, Inuk/Ivik and Sara, and introduces the reader to Nuuk through its queer topography (the novel's characters are gay, bisexual and transgender). In her foreword to the novel Mette Moestrup observes that 'just because the novel is set in Greenland doesn't mean it is full of endless descriptions of nature, rather it is the subjective experience and communal dramas which are focused on'.[51] However, despite moving away from the traditional themes associated with Greenlandic writing, what it means to be a Greenlander in the twenty-first century remains a key question for Korneliussen.

Written in a stream of consciousness narrative style, the opening chapter, titled 'Crimson and Clover', tells the story of Fia's breakup with her boyfriend of three years, Peter, and her realization that she is gay after meeting and falling in love with Sara. The chapter starts with a list of Peter and Fia's life plans:

1. Når jeg er færdig med min uddannelse og pengene er på plads, køber vi et hus med mange værelser og en altan.
2. Vi gifter os.
3. Vi for tre/fire børn.
4. Dag efter dag efter dag køber vi ind efter arbejde og kører hjem i vores bil.
5. Vi bliver gamle og dør.[52]

[1. When I am finished with my education and our finances are in order, we'll buy a house with many rooms and a balcony.
2. We'll get married.
3. We'll have three or four children.
4. Day in and day out we'll go shopping after work and drive home in our car.
5. We'll grow old and die.]

The list expresses the sense of banality felt by Fia towards the routines prescribed by society for a heterosexual relationship. On the very next page Korneliussen adds a stirring sense of rebellion as Fia describes her realization that the relationship is coming to an end: 'Tak fordi du elsker mig, mig som begår fejl. Men nej, jeg takker nej, siger jeg!' [Thank you for loving me even though I make mistakes. But no, I'm saying no!].[53] Fia moves out of the flat she shares with Peter to live with a friend, Arnaq, who introduces her to the queer subculture of Nuuk. Fia's chapter thus sets the tone for the novel's rejection of normative sexual and social relationships, which is echoed in the novel's title and cover image, but through the use of lists and stream of consciousness narration it also introduces Korneliussen's experimentation with the novel form.[54]

In chapter 2, titled 'Home', Korneliussen moves deftly from Fia's stream of consciousness to the narrative perspective of her brother Inuk, which is comprised of a combination of diary entries, notes, lists and fragments, and illustrates the way Korneliussen complicates essentialist notions of Greenlandic identity by showing it to intersect with gender and sexual identity. Inuk, we soon realize, has left Greenland suddenly due to a rumour that he has had an affair with a married member of the Greenlandic parliament called Miki Løvstrøm. In the first few paragraphs of the chapter, Inuk describes feeling 'fængslet' [imprisoned] and 'muret ind bag høje fjelde' [trapped behind the tall mountains] of Greenland, and he leaves suddenly to 'flygte' [escape] to Copenhagen.[55] Once in Copenhagen he writes a letter to Fia, explaining where he is and telling her not to worry. He begs her to avoid Arnaq, who he claims is 'djævlen selv' [the devil], as she revealed the secret of his affair with Løvstrøm at a party.[56] Inuk denies the affair to his sister but confesses his disappointment and anger at having seen Fia kiss Sara. He blames Arnaq, who is bisexual, for corrupting Fia and describes homosexuals as evil and in need of treatment to be 'cured'. The homophobic rants and fragmentary nature of the chapter emphasize Inuk's psychological breakdown as he comes to terms with being transgender, and it eventually becomes clear that the need to escape from Greenland is as much an attempt to avoid confronting his own sexual and gender identity as it is to escape the unfolding scandal surrounding him and Løvstrøm. Just as Inuk directs anger at Arnaq and Fia, he is angry at Greenland and at himself for being Greenlandic. In one entry for instance, he writes a list of positive and negative aspects of being Greenlandic,

> Man er Grønlænder når man er med til at udvikle sit land.
> Man er Grønlænder når man taler sit sprog.
> [...]
> Man er Grønlænder når man er alkoholiker.
> Man er Grønlænder når man banker sin partner.
> [...]
> Man er Grønlænder når man er homo.[57]
>
> [You're a Greenlander when you contribute to developing your country.
> You're a Greenlander when you speak your language.
> [...]
> You're a Greenlander when you're an alcoholic.
> You're a Greenlander when you beat your partner.
> [...]
> You're a Greenlander when you're a homo.]

However, despite the initial relief at having 'escaped', Inuk does not feel at home in Copenhagen, but instead feels isolated amongst the Danes, unable to 'grine med danskerne' and 'deltage i en samtale med danskerne' [laugh with the Danes and contribute to a conversation with the Danes].[58] Towards the end of the chapter the anger towards Fia and Arnaq dissipates, and Inuk comes out as transgender, writing that Inuk has 'forsvundet' [disappeared], and instead 'kommer Ivik frem' [Ivik has appeared]. With coming out as transgender, the hatred for Greenland also disappears and in the final diary entry and letter Ivik writes about feeling homesick, claiming, in English, that '[h]ome is in me. Home is me. I am home'.[59] The feeling of being 'at home' in Greenland is thus fundamentally subjective and tied to feeling at home in yourself; as much an internal, subjective experience, as a national identity defined by an external set of criteria around language, culture, and geography.

Korneliussen does not just challenge the established portrayals of life in Greenland associated with both Greenlandic and Danish-Greenlandic literature, but, as we have seen in the quotes above, she also challenges the established conventions of the novel form to create a 'hybridt litterært værk der går på tværs af forskellige mediegenrer, skriver sig ind i en mere transnational kontekst' [hybrid literary work that crosses the lines of several different forms of media and writes itself into a more transnational context].[60] The form of her novel can itself be read as a form of protest to the image of Greenland presented in both *Smilla* and *Kalak*, and the inclusion of song lyrics and text messages make it clear that this is neither the deprived Nuuk of Leine's *Kalak* nor the traditional image of Greenland that Smilla remembers in Høeg's novel. Furthermore, the fact that Korneliussen translated the novel into Danish herself might be worth considering in light of the minority status of the Greenlandic language and literature. Also encountered in literature of the Iberian peninsula, where Catalan, Basque and Galician writers are translating their work into Castilian,[61] and in some postcolonial writing, notably by Kenyan writer Ngũgĩ wa Thiong'o who has translated his later works from Gikuyu to English, self-translation can be seen as a direct attempt to challenge the hegemony of dominant languages in a given region by asserting and maintaining control of the text after publication. From this perspective the act of self-translation resists the colonial hierarchies still in place within the Nordic region, which are often played out at the level of culture.

Finally, by writing about the queer community in Greenland, Korneliussen consciously aligns herself with an international LGBTQ+ community and literary tradition, exploring the complexity of identity from an entirely different perspective. In her depiction of the lives of Fia, Inuk, Arnaq, Ivik and Sara she articulates a Greenlandic identity which is distinctly rooted in the present and thereby claims the representation of Greenlandic identity for her own generation. Read in tandem with Lyberth's *Godt i Vej*, the two novels mark a generational shift from a focus on postcolonial nation-building to Greenland's place within the late capitalist, globalized world.

Conclusion: Greenlandic Literature and the Postcolonial Canon

This chapter has provided an introduction to Greenlandic literature and has endeavoured to think through some of the issues contributing to Greenlandic literature's minority status. Through comparison of recent Greenlandic and Danish Greenland novels, it has shown that although the history and legacies of Danish colonialism are still not widely discussed in Danish society, the complex relationship between Denmark and Greenland is an important feature in the literary cultures of both countries. In the Danish Greenland literature canon, as illustrated in the novels by Kim Leine and Peter Høeg, Greenland continues to be a space for exploration, adventure, exoticism — an 'arktisk version af den gamle drøm om Afrika' [arctic version of the old dream of Africa], and Greenlanders tend to be represented using negative stereotypes, despite the fact that for instance the two Danish authors considered here are broadly critical of Danish colonialism and imperialism. The Greenlandic novels, *Godt i Vej* and *HOMO Sapienne*, on the other hand, both offer very different insights into Greenlandic life and culture. In *Godt i Vej*, Lyberth pairs a coming-of-age narrative with the burgeoning independence of the Greenlandic nation and shows the impact of rapid modernization of Greenlandic society in a way that highlights the ongoing influence of Danish political and cultural hegemony. Finally, in *HOMO Sapienne* Korneliussen makes a move away from the national themes of the past in her conception of Greenlandic identity, aligning her queer characters with an international LGBTQ+ community instead. By outlining some features of Greenlandic literature in relation to its status as minority and postcolonial literature, this chapter has contributed both to current attempts to configure and analyse the contemporary 'power paradigm'[62] of the Danish state in relation to its former colonies, and to the ongoing efforts to expand the geographical and temporal reach of postcolonial studies.

Notes to Chapter 5

1. Axel Kjær Sørensen, *Denmark- Greenland in the Twentieth Century* (Copenhagen: Museum Tusculanum Press, 2007).
2. Magdalena Naum and Jonas Nordin, *Scandinavian Colonialism and the Rise of Modernity: Small Time Agents in a Global Arena* (New York: Springer, 2013).
3. Kristian H. Nielsen, 'Transforming Greenland: Imperial Formations in the Cold War', *New Global Studies* 7.2 (2013), 129–54.
4. Kirsten Thisted, 'Emotions, Finances and Independence: Uranium as a "happy object" in the Greenlandic Debate on Secession from Denmark,' *Polar Record*, 56.1(2020), 1–12.
5. See Thisted, 'Emotions, Finances and Independence'.
6. Adam Grydehøj notes that Greenland was 'never a site of settler colonialism', instead being administered by Denmark 'to maximize resource extraction', primarily seal skins and commercial fishing. 'Unravelling Economic Dependence and Independence in Relation to Island Sovereignty: The Case of Kalaallit Nunaat (Greenland)', *Island Studies Journal*, 15.1 (2020), 89–112 (p. 95).
7. Karen Langgård, 'Greenlandic Writers', in *A Historical Companion to Postcolonial Literature: Continental Europe and its Empires*, ed. by Prem Poddar, Rajeev S. Patke and Lars Jensen (Edinburgh: Edinburgh University Press, 2008), pp. 71–72.
8. Christian Berthelsen, 'Greenlandic Literature: Its Traditions, Changes, and Trends', *Arctic Anthropology*, 23 (1986), 339–45.
9. See Berthelsen, 'Greenlandic Literature'.
10. See Langgård, 'Greenlandic Writers'.
11. Kirsten Thisted, 'Imperiets Genfærd- *Profeterne I Evighedsfjorden* og den Dansk-Grøndlandske Historieskivning', *Nordlit*, 35 (2015), 105–21.
12. Lyberth's novel was originally published in Greenlandic as *Naleqqusseruttortut* in 2012, and subsequently translated into Danish by Lars Wind in 2014. The title of the novel in Danish translates as *Well on the Way*. HOMO Sapienne was published simultaneously in Danish and Greenlandic. As my Greenlandic is limited, I will be relying on the Danish translations of both novels and provide a brief translation of quotes for the readers.
13. Thisted, 'Emotions, Finance and Uranium', p. 2.
14. See Lars Jensen and Kristín Loftsdóttir, *Whiteness and Postcolonialism in the Nordic Region: Exceptionalism, Migrant Others and National Identities* (Farnham, Surrey: Ashgate, 2012) on Nordic exceptionalism.
15. Thisted, 'Emotions, Finance and Uranium', p. 2.
16. In 'Introduction: Denmark and its Colonies', *A Historical Companion to Postcolonial Literature: Continental Europe and its Empire*, ed. by Prem Poddar, Rajeev S. Patke and Lars Jensen (Edinburgh: Edinburgh University Press, 2008), Lars Jensen describes Greenland and the Faroe Islands as 'reluctant members of the Danish Commonwealth (*Rigsfællesskabet*)', p. 59.
17. Ibid.
18. Ibid.
19. Bolette Blaagaard, 'Remembering Nordic Colonialism: Danish Cultural Memory in Journalistic Practice', *KULT-Postkolonial Temaserie*, 7 (2010), 101–21 (p. 102).
20. The controversial experiment, which sought to make the Greenlandic children into model Danish citizens, has been criticized as an act of cultural genocide, and came to public attention again recently after the current Danish Prime Minister, Mette Frederiksen, gave an official apology to the remaining six survivors, following the publication of a report investigating the event coordinated by the Danish government and the Greenlandic *landsstyre* [national government]. See Emma Qvirin Holst, 'Frederiksen siger undskyld til grønlandske eksperimentbørn', *Altinget*, (2020) <https://www.altinget.dk/artikel/frederiksen-siger-undskyld-til-groenlandske-eksperimentboern> [accessed 4 January 2021].
21. Prem Poddar and Cheralyn Mealor, 'Danish Imperial Fantasies: Peter Høeg's *Miss Smilla's Feeling for Snow*', in *Translating Nations*, ed. by Prem Poddar (Aarhus: Aarhus University Press, 2000), pp. 161–202 (p. 176).

22. Poddar and Mealor, 'Danish Imperial Fantasies,' p. 177.
23. Poddar and Mealor, 'Danish Imperial Fantasies,' p. 177.
24. Poddar and Mealor, 'Danish Imperial Fantasies,' p. 194.
25. Peter Høeg, *Frøken Smillas Fornemmelse for Sne* (Copenhagen: Rosinante, 2010), p. 336.
26. Høeg, p. 335.
27. See David Harvey, *The New Imperialism* (Oxford: Oxford University Press, 2003).
28. Peter Bjerregaard, Christina V. L. Larsen, Ivalu K. Sørensen and Janne S. Tolstrup, 'Alcohol in Greenland 1950–2018: Consumption, Drinking Patterns, and Consequences', *International Journal of Circumpolar Health*, 79 (2020), 1–11.
29. Thisted, 'Imperiets Genfærd-'.
30. Kim Leine, *Kalak* (Nørhaven: Gyldendal, 2007), p. 137.
31. Leine, *Kalak*, p. 88.
32. Leine, *Kalak*, pp. 81–82.
33. Leine, *Kalak*, p. 80.
34. Leine, *Kalak*, p. 89.
35. Leine, *Kalak*, pp. 88–89.
36. Leine, *Kalak*, p. 87.
37. Leine, *Kalak*, p. 88.
38. Hans A. Lynge, 'Juaaka Lyberth', (2014) <https://www.norden.org/en/nominee/juaaka-lyberth> [accessed 4 January 2021].
39. Juaaka Lyberth is well known in the Greenlandic cultural scene, having served as the director of *Kulturhuset* [The Culture House] in Nuuk, and is an actor and writer of songs and poems as well as novels.
40. Juaaka Lyberth, *Godt i Vej* (Nuuk: Milik, 2014), p. 277.
41. Lyberth, *Godt I Vej*, p. 279.
42. Lyberth, *Godt I Vej*, p. 279.
43. Lyberth, *Godt I Vej*, p. 273.
44. Lyberth, *Godt I Vej*, p. 249. Blok P was demolished in 2012 and there are plans to demolish similar apartment blocks in central Nuuk.
45. Benita Parry, 'Aspects of Peripheral Modernism', *Ariel: A Review of International Literature in English*, 40.1 (2009), 27–55 (p. 32).
46. Karen Langgård, 'Oral/Past Culture and Modern Technical Means in the Literature of the Twentieth Century in Greenland', *Acta Borealia: A Nordic Journal of Circumpolar Societies*, 25.1 (2008), 45–57 (p. 48).
47. Langgård, 'Oral/Past Culture', p. 53.
48. Langgård, 'Greenlandic Writers', p. 72.
49. Langgård, 'Greenlandic Writers', p. 72.
50. *HOMO Sapienne* was published as *Crimson* in English, translated from the Danish version by Anna Halager. Korneliussen's second novel, *Naasuliardarpi* (2020), has also been nominated for the 2021 Nordic Council Literature Prize.
51. Mette Moestrup, 'Forord', in *HOMO Sapienne* by Niviaq Korneliussen (Nuuk: Milik, 2014), p. 11.
52. Niviaq Korneliussen, *HOMO Sapienne* (Nuuk: Milik, 2014), p. 17.
53. Korneliussen, *HOMO Sapienne*, p. 18.
54. The Greenlandic cover has a picture of a naked woman eating a banana, which Agata Lubowicka suggests along with the novel's title, 'artikulerer en antidiskurs mod normative opfattelser af køn — og menneskelighed' [articulates a counter-discourse against normative understandings of gender and humanity]. See Agata Lubowicka, 'Mellem det (post)koloniale, det (post)nationale og det globale: en analyse af Niviaq Korneliussens *HOMO Sapienne*', *Folia Scandinavica*, 24 (2018), 39–55 (p. 43).
55. Korneliussen, *HOMO Sapienne*, p. 51 and p. 56.
56. Korneliussen, *HOMO Sapienne*, p. 50.
57. Korneliussen, *HOMO Sapienne*, p. 65.
58. Korneliussen, *HOMO Sapienne*, p. 66.

59. Korneliussen, *HOMO Sapienne*, p. 73.
60. Lubowicka, 'Mellem det (post)koloniale, det (post)nationale og det globale', p. 41.
61. See the contribution by Mari Jose Olaziregi in this volume.
62. Jensen, 'Introduction: Denmark and its Colonies', p. 62.

PART II

Circulation and Readership

CHAPTER 6

A Move Towards the Mainstream? New Perspectives on the Public Reading of Minority Writing in the UK

Briony Birdi

Introduction, Context and Terminology

The subject of this chapter is the *public* reading of minority writing, focusing in particular on the UK public library user, and on works of fiction written by Black British and British Asian authors, in the English language. Drawing on research methods and theoretical approaches from the Social Sciences, this chapter triangulates selected findings from two broader, empirical studies of the readership of different fiction genres. (Working with typical genre classifications used by public libraries, Black British fiction and British Asian fiction are referred to here as fictional genres in their own right.)[1] The first study regards the fiction reading choices and attitudes of a large population of UK public library users, and the second investigates the perceived profile and characteristics of the readers of different genres among library employees. Bringing together elements of each of these datasets, the aim of this chapter is to investigate the UK public library user's engagement with Black British and British Asian fiction.

Five decades since the main waves of immigration to the UK from countries in (for example) the West Indies and Indian subcontinent, is it commonplace to regard the fiction written by members (and descendants) of these often long-settled populations as removed from the mainstream? In 2013, Afua Hirsch asked, 'Why does it take a white face to keep us interested in African stories?', observing that Hollywood films set in Africa will always feature white Americans in the leading roles.[2] Similarly, in 2011 Catherine Johnson asked where Britain's black writers could be found, suggesting 'It seems our stories are truly acknowledged only when coming from the pen of white writers'.[3] There is still perceived to be a white bias in mainstream popular culture, and a reluctance to raise the status of works of fiction by black authors to equal that of white authors. This perspective was similarly described by Pauwke Berkers et al. (2013) in a comparative study of the classification of Dutch, German and American minority ethnic authors in newspaper reviews: 'ethnic minority authors themselves have few options to facilitate their entry into the literary mainstream since writing about majority themes, having their publisher classify them as mainstream authors or publishing with a mainstream publisher seem to have little effect'.[4]

Indeed, despite the recent success of a relatively small number of Black British authors in the bestselling fiction, non-fiction and book awards lists — for example with Bernardine Evaristo and Candice Carty-Williams becoming in 2020 the first black authors to win the Book of the Year and Author of the Year prizes respectively at the British Book Awards — it would be naïve to assume that such authors can now enjoy a mainstream publishing space equal to their white counterparts.[5] And as Evaristo has reportedly commented, the success of her prizewinning novel *Girl, Woman, Other* 'stems from the fact that "we black British women know that if we don't write ourselves into literature, no one else will" '.[6]

Despite (or perhaps because of) these continued concerns, it is relatively common for the key stakeholders in the provision of 'minority writing' — publishers, booksellers, library suppliers and public libraries — to use certain grouped terms in promoting it to the reading public. As the context for the findings presented here is the public library, the research design separated Black British and British Asian fiction from other works of popular fiction perhaps more traditionally associated with a public library collection and classified by genres. To an extent this was an artificial separation, as a title by a Black British or British Asian author could also be classified as 'Crime fiction' or 'Literary fiction' (for example), and arguably any of the books perceived by the research participants — all users of public libraries and readers of fiction — could be classified in a number of different ways. However, in making this deliberate separation we can examine readers' interpretations and perceptions of terms such as Black British fiction and British Asian fiction, which for similarly pragmatic reasons can be fitted within a broader category of 'minority writing'. Whichever term one chooses to describe this significant body of literature in the English language, the problematic nature of labels used to describe such a complex and diverse range of books should be acknowledged.

Directly related to their socio-political context, Black British and British Asian fiction emerge both directly and indirectly from a long tradition of British literature. Sara Upstone contends that British Asian authors 'who have emerged only in notable numbers in the late twentieth and early twenty-first centuries, mark the establishment of a definitive genre of British Asian literature deserving recognition in its own right'.[7] Similarly, Kadija Sesay argues that the absorption of Black British into mainstream British literature should only go so far, as 'laying claim to a [... distinct] literary tradition is particularly important for us [Black British people] in racially stratified societies where the acquisition of a certain kind of skill with the written word and an identifiable intellectual progression are seen as key markers of a civilised culture'.[8] However, certain authors — generally those who are living in Britain but have a South Asian or African heritage — have chosen to identify themselves as 'British writers', and deliberately not 'British Asian' or 'Black British' writers respectively, in part as a political statement. Bronwyn T. Williams cites Hanif Kureishi and Caryl Phillips as two such examples, explaining that, for

Phillips, the use of the term 'Black writer' or 'Caribbean writer 'lets people off the hook, because they don't want to then reconsider, to reconfigure, Britain in their minds'.[9] Related to this point, others have argued that the labels 'Black British' or 'British Asian' are too 'homogenizing', convenient terms which ignore the plurality of nationalities and cultures within the apparent group.[10] This plurality could also stem from the fact that second or third generation Black British and British Asian authors' works 'can be compared to neither the postcolonial writing of their parents' generation nor an earlier British literature written from a predominantly white, predominantly Christian, perspective'.[11]

The question of the readership of Black British and British Asian fiction arguably raises more issues than it resolves. One underlying issue is whether or not members of minority ethnic communities are themselves the main readers of titles by authors from these communities. It has been commented that publishers often consider the reader's cultural background when devising book marketing strategies.[12] This supports the argument of reader response theorists that readers are more likely to respond to a text they can relate to.[13] For Wolfgang Iser each author has a particular reader in mind, in the form of a 'textual structure anticipating the presence of a recipient without necessarily defining him'.[14] In this way, the reader brings their own historical reality and experience to their reading of a title, producing an energy, a tension that inevitably results in different connections and interpretations. Interestingly, however, a 2020 investigation of diversity within the UK publishing industry found that these potential differences were largely ignored, and that the industry is 'set up to cater for just one white, middle-class audience'. Furthermore, the findings indicated that when the works of writers of colour are promoted to this core white audience, this leads to their 'exoticisation and marginalisation'.[15]

The Public Library Service and its Provision of Culturally Diverse Materials

Liz Greenhalgh and Ken Worpole posit that the public library represents 'the inherited culture of rational thought, self-education and individual enlightenment', having sustained 'an enviable tradition — unlike many other institutions — of non-sectarianism and secularism'.[16] Within the Library and Information profession, this tradition is also applied to the process of selecting reading materials for public use, whereby such a collection should contribute to an environment which 'truly represents and achieves diversity and celebrates and encourages it in others'.[17] These two objectives of the public library service map neatly onto the 1970s ideal of the former UK Library Advisory Council, for whom the provision of materials for 'diverse communities' could be divided into two categories, 'those which are aimed at meeting the needs of minority groups and those consciously designed to reflect a multi-cultural society'.[18] In line with the theory of multiculturalism that society becomes richer as the cultural horizons of its inhabitants are expanded,[19] it has also been suggested[20] that readers of all ages who regularly engage with texts written by those from cultural backgrounds other than their own may experience a stronger sense of 'social capital'.[21] Indeed, during the past three decades the perception that reading fiction can challenge, and even change a reader's inaccurate or stereotypical views of other ethnic cultures, has repeatedly been linked to a call for public libraries to promote minority ethnic fiction to all their users.[22] There is evidence to suggest that many library services have made a sustained effort to develop substantial collections of books by (for example) Black British, Black American, Asian and South Asian authors, promoting them beyond the minority ethnic communities they will often depict.[23]

Referring in particular to the South Asian communities, Parveen Akhtar proposes that those books which are 'aimed at acquainting the host population with the cultural, religious and historical backgrounds of ethnic minorities, have the potential to enable libraries to succeed where others have not made much headway'. Such material, she argues, has the capacity not only to build 'a bridge of understanding between different communities' but has also 'given Asian readers a sense of pride and security'.[24] Simsova similarly refers to the capacity of material 'about the old country in the new language' to form 'a kind of bridge',[25] or, as termed by Lambert, a 'psychological continuity'.[26]

In recent years my own empirical research within the Social Sciences has included a number of related studies of readers' attitudes towards, and engagement with, fiction and selected fiction genres. This work has resulted in a new, sociological model of fiction reading.[27] This chapter presents findings relating to readers' attitudes towards minority writing, which emerged through two related studies using personal construct theory and the repertory grid method, the first a large-scale quantitative survey of the reading habits and attitudes of public library users in the East Midlands region of England, and the second a study of the perceived characteristics of fiction readers and their associated genres.

Study 1: The Reading Habits and Attitudes of Public Library Users

For this study, which is embedded in the idea of fiction as a means of achieving attitudinal change,[28] a general survey was conducted of the reading habits and attitudes of public library users within nine local authorities in the UK East Midlands, with a particular focus on Black British and British Asian books. This was conducted as part of an evaluation of *black bytes*, a public library fiction promotion of fifty fiction titles written in the English language by Black British authors. The original book list for the promotion was devised for a three-year East Midlands Reader and Library Development initiative, funded by each of the nine East Midlands public library authorities and Arts Council East Midlands, and managed by Opening the Book Limited, a UK-based reader development agency. As an intervention it aimed to increase the readership of Black British fiction by both minority and majority ethnic communities. Although the titles within the promotion itself were all written by Black British authors, the focus of the study was expanded to include British Asian authors writing in English, in order to broaden the investigation of attitudes towards British minority ethnic fiction.

The survey was methodologically interesting in its focus on both positive and negative reading choices. A brief, quantitative reading habit survey was devised, and distributed by library staff at issue points in sixteen libraries in the nine participating local authorities. This consisted of five simple questions, asking readers which genres they were borrowing from today and would usually borrow from, which genres they would not consider reading, and which factors would influence them in choosing their books. The survey was designed to be distributed at library issue points at two separate time-points, i.e. prior to, and towards the end of, the installation of the *black bytes* promotion.[29] (A key aspect of the longitudinal evaluation was the inclusion of five 'control' libraries in addition to the sixteen, i.e. libraries in which the *black bytes* promotion would not be installed.) In combination, these two measures enabled an investigation as to whether *black bytes* had a noticeable impact on the fiction borrowing habits of the library user.

The data for this study have revealed an openness on the part of many respondents to read from a wide range of genres, and to try new material. Statistical (chi-square) tests showed that there was a significant increase in respondents from experimental libraries (i.e. those with the promotion) reporting that they were 'usual' readers of Black British fiction after the intervention had taken place (chi-square = 7.37, $p < 0.01$), whereas the control group (those from libraries without the promotion) showed no significant change between the two time points (chi-square = 0.27, ns).

Interestingly, the number of respondents who listed no particular genre that they would not consider reading slightly increased from the first to the second distribution, suggesting that there had been a positive change in attitudes towards minority fiction reading as a result of the *black bytes* intervention. Tests showed that there was a reduction (7.8%) between the two time-points in the number of respondents from experimental libraries who actively chose not to read Black British fiction, whereas the proportion of respondents from control libraries who actively avoided Black British fiction had increased slightly (1.0%).

Reader response theory, and the related concept of reader development, can help us to explain this pattern of respondent behaviour; according to reader response theory the reader plays a critical role, participating in a 'triangular relationship' between 'reader, text and the interaction between the two',[30] even acting in some sense as co-author.[31] The term 'reader development' has since the 1990s become an established term in the application of reader response theory to Library and Information Science;[32] in line with reader response theory, the concept of reader development has as its stated objectives to raise the status of reading as a creative act, to increase people's confidence in their reading, and to bring isolated readers together.[33] An accepted definition is that it is an 'active intervention to increase people's reading confidence and enjoyment of reading, open up reading choices, offer opportunities for people to share their reading experience, and raise the status of reading as a creative activity'.[34] It is therefore perhaps unsurprising that this first study revealed an openness on the part of certain survey respondents, who indeed appear to have opened up their reading choices, and perhaps even increased in reading confidence, as a result of the intervention of the *black bytes* fiction reading promotion.

Study 2: The Readership of 'Black British Fiction' and 'British Asian Fiction'

A second study was subsequently designed to collect further data from a group ($n = 15$) consisting of library staff, and Library and Information Science postgraduate students, each of whom had some experience of working with a cross-section of the reading public. The objectives for this new study were firstly to apply personal construct theory and the associated repertory grid technique in order to generate a series of perceived characteristics of the readers of the same ten fiction 'genres' used in the first study, and secondly to explore these characteristics in relation to the readers of Black British and British Asian fiction.

Originally presented by George Kelly[35] and then developed in the context of clinical psychology, the significance of personal construct theory is today widely acknowledged.[36] Defining the term 'construct', Kelly posits that each person's subjective reality is 'based on the meanings we have attached to previous experiences'.[37] The principle underpinning this study is that our own interpretation of these experiences is the influential aspect, and not the event itself. In other words, the clue to understanding an individual 'lies in their particular construction of the world'.[38] Personal construct theory allows us to explore the values of others by recognizing the values present in our own constructs and interpretation of those constructs, in the case of this study an exploration of the diverse perceptions of reader 'types'.

The repertory grid is the most well-known aspect of Kelly's personal construct theory. In brief, this method is based on three interlinked processes, conducted in the order as stated below.

1. The definition of a set of elements

For the broader attitudinal investigation of fiction reading from which this study is taken, eleven elements were used for the repertory grid, namely the 'Reader of ...' ten fiction genres (Reader of Romance fiction, Reader of War & Spy fiction, etc.) and 'Myself as reader' for the final element, which was used for rating purposes only (see below) and not within the triads.[39] Using an identical list of elements for each participant increased the generalizability of the data collected.

2. The eliciting of a set of constructs to differentiate between these elements

Repertory grids are generally administered using either dyads (pairs of elements) or triads (groups of three elements), and the participant is asked to describe either a perceived difference between, or the perceived opposite of, combinations of elements. (It was Kelly's contention that all constructs are bipolar, in other words that an individual never affirms something without simultaneously denying something else.) The stated difference, or opposite, is then the construct. All participants were given the same set of ten triads.[40] As each triad was presented to the participant, he or she was asked to describe a way in which two of the three elements were alike in some way, but different from the third. Having elicited this construct (the implicit construct), the polar construct was then requested, in other words a way in which the third element is perceived to be different from the other two.

3. The relating of the elements to the constructs

During the elicitation process (described above), the implicit and polar constructs were recorded in the repertory grid template by the researcher, and when all triads had been presented and all constructs noted down, the grid was passed to the participant so that each construct could be rated. Participants were asked to allocate a number within a stated range to each element in order to indicate strength of feeling (e.g. from 1 to 10 if there were ten elements in the grid).

Participants elicited new constructs regarding the perceived characteristics of the reader, for example that neither Black British nor Asian fiction readers were drawn to 'mainstream' fiction, whether the term was interpreted as 'non-serious' fiction such as the more established genres Romance fiction or Crime fiction, or as 'majority' fiction, enjoyed by the reading public as a whole.

Participants regarded neither Black British fiction nor British Asian fiction as 'mainstream' fiction, yet what is 'mainstream', in this context? Two not entirely unrelated interpretations emerge from this study. Firstly, that 'mainstream' describes a novel more concerned with plot and entertainment than literary style — more in line, perhaps, with the traditional genres of Romance fiction, Crime fiction, War & Spy fiction, etc. Certainly, Nicholls would agree that mainstream fiction can be distinguished from other fiction of 'seriousness',[41] although Pearl gives an alternative name for 'mainstream fiction' as 'literary fiction', which 'may have genre elements (e.g. historical, adventure)', but may equally be more complex in terms of plot and/or style.[42] The second interpretation is that 'mainstream' refers to the reading material of the 'majority', whether in terms of an ethnic majority or its overall popularity with the reading public.

New themes emerged from the second study regarding the perceived social and reading interests, preferred plot and wider reading choices of the reader of genre fiction, thereby starting to build a more detailed profile than the first study. For example, in exploring the readers' preferred plots it can be inferred that, given the similar ratings frequently made across the constructs to 'Black British fiction', 'British Asian fiction' and 'Literary fiction', the first two are perceived as sharing similar characteristics to a more established, perhaps culturally broader genre which includes both classic (older) and contemporary novels. Readers of all three were felt to be likely to be looking for a more 'challenging', 'mind-exercising' reading experience, and to be generally more interested in literary style than the plot itself.

Although not inevitably the case, the readers of Black British fiction and British Asian fiction were generally perceived as sharing similar characteristics. A quantitative analysis was conducted of the total number of shared (perceived) characteristics across the readers of the ten fiction 'genres' selected for this research, using constructs grouped under five main themes,[43] and the readers of Black British fiction and British Asian fiction were the most strongly related pair within the ten. However, they are by no means perceived by the participants as an identical pair. For example, according to the quantitative and qualitative data each reader could be either male or female, or younger or older, but the Black British fiction reader is regarded as slightly more likely to be female than male, and the British Asian fiction reader as slightly more likely to be younger than older. In terms of the perceived nature of plot in the books chosen by the readers of Black British and/or British Asian fiction, the British Asian fiction reader is regarded as just as likely to look for a happy ending as not, whereas the Black British fiction reader is felt to be more likely *not* to look for a happy ending. Statistical intraclass correlations[44] revealed very little agreement among participants regarding the nature of the readers of British Asian fiction and, to a slightly less extent, the readers of Black British fiction. There would appear to be two possible explanations for this lack of generalizability for each of the minority fiction genres, namely:

1) That it is very difficult to 'define' the reader of Black British fiction or British Asian fiction, as he/she could have any of a wide range of characteristics.

2) That participants are simply unfamiliar with titles within such groupings, and therefore have no stereotypical view of the reader(s) in question.

Both arguments are plausible, although given the significant levels of agreement across participants regarding the more 'established', traditional genres (Crime fiction, Romance fiction, Science fiction/Fantasy, War & Spy fiction) which would be given a clear section within any public library collection, there appears to be considerable evidence to support the second argument in particular. It is easier to stereotype the readers of more established genres, as they are well-known to us, frequently read by the general public and some participants could clearly imagine a 'typical' reader of those genres without difficulty:

> [...] funnily enough that's what was going through my head, at [name] public library, my first library where I grew up, walking round the shelves, and I remember the War and Spy thriller sections, and seeing the old boys there, and I think it was near the Westerns, and the non-fiction war books, and I sort of associate it with that.

> If there's a sole reader of that type of 'Literary fiction', he's not really interested in Science fiction, but they would on occasion take out Black British fiction... It's quite interesting, trying to going back through my mind about what people take out.

However, public libraries would not inevitably have a separate section for 'Black British fiction' or 'British Asian fiction', and their popularity with the reading public is arguably less. This was illustrated in the findings of the first study presented in this chapter, wherein a sample population of 1,047 library users contained just twenty-nine (2.8%) readers of British Asian fiction and thirty-six (3.4%) readers of Black British fiction.

Through the application of personal construct theory and the associated repertory grid technique, this second study has generated a series of perceived characteristics of fiction readers and their associated genres, expanding upon these characteristics in relation to the readers of Black British fiction and British Asian fiction.

Conclusions

The most well-known aspect of personal construct theory as presented by Kelly in 1955, the repertory grid technique used in the second study, has been an appropriate method to employ for research into the nature of fiction reading.[45] The essential aspect of personal construct theory is its reflexivity, in other words that it requires reflection, interaction and construction on the part of both researcher and participant, with the elicited constructs forming part of a new framework. This research has indicated that this participative, democratic approach could also be related to reader response theory, which helps us to understand the active role a reader plays in interpreting a text, in the same way creating a new narrative from the interaction between the individual reader and the text.

Both theoretical approaches place the individual at the centre, contributing to the creation of a new 'subjective reality', and bringing them together in the empirical research has helped to develop an understanding of the characteristics of the readers of (in this case) Black British and British Asian fiction.

Previous research had indicated that the public library is still regarded by many as a white institution whose services do not fully reflect the interests of all members of its local community. Certainly the empirical research presented in this chapter does not contradict this in terms of its provision of Black British or British Asian fiction. Such titles do not have a large readership in public libraries because readers do not generally choose books outside the 'mainstream' collection, and library staff do not have a clear profile of the readers of these genres.

Encouragingly, however, the research also indicates that a deliberate attempt to promote minority ethnic fiction titles can be successful in developing its readership, with both white and minority ethnic communities. It is therefore recommended that public library staff ensure that books written by minority ethnic authors are regularly included in stock promotions, not only those specifically related to ethnicity (e.g. Black History Month), but also in the overall programme of promotions for the library service as a whole. At the time of writing there is increased interest across the book trade in the works of authors of colour because, as Evaristo argues, the Black Lives Matter movement has generated an unprecedented amount of interest and 'self-interrogating' in the publishing industry. Whether or not this interest will be sustained is a moot point; as Evaristo continues, 'I hope they don't revert back to the status quo once the heat has left the conversation around racism, as will inevitably be the case.'[46]

Having recommended that the visibility of Black British and British Asian fiction to all readers be enhanced and sustained, and that the range of stock collections provided within the book trade and public library service be broadened on an ongoing basis, it seems appropriate to conclude with an insight from one of the authors themselves:

> There's a beautiful image in Saul Bellow's latest novel, *The Dean's December*. The central character, the Dean, Corde, hears a dog barking wildly somewhere. He imagines that the barking is the dog's protest against the limit of dog experience. "For God's sake", the dog is saying, 'open the universe a little

more!' And because Bellow is, of course, not really talking about dogs, I have the feeling that the dog's rage, and its desire, is also mine, ours, everyone's. 'For God's sake, open the universe a little more!'[47]

Although the book to which Rushdie refers in the above comment was written neither by a 'Black British' nor an 'Asian' author, it is included here for two reasons. Firstly, because Rushdie regards a work of fiction by a white, Canadian-born American author as important and highly relevant to his own position as an Indian-born British writer, and secondly because it could very easily represent the voices of other authors from minority ethnic communities whose work has been the subject of this chapter: a plea to publishers, booksellers, library suppliers, library staff and readers, to open their collective universes and to ensure that their interpretation of terms such as 'fiction' and 'literature' are as broad and all-encompassing as they could be.

Notes to Chapter 6

1. Other genres considered here included LGBT fiction, Sciene fiction/Fantasy fiction, Romance fiction, Lad Lit fiction, Crime fiction, Chick Lit fiction, War & Spy fiction and Literary fiction.
2. Afua Hirsch, 'Why does it take a white face to keep us interested in African stories?', *The Guardian*, 4 October 2013, p. 35.
3. Catherine Johnson, 'Where are Britain's black writers?', *The Guardian*, 5 December 2011 <http://www.theguardian.com/commentisfree/2011/dec/05/where-are-britains-black-writers> [accessed 8 September 2020].
4. Pauwke Berkers, Susanne Janssen and Marc Verboord, 'Assimilation into the Literary Mainstream? The Classification of Ethnic Minority Authors in Newspaper Reviews in the United States, the Netherlands and Germany', *Cultural Sociology*, 8.1 (2013), 25–44 <https://doi.org/10.1177%2F1749975513480960>, p. 37.
5. Alison Flood, 'Evaristo and Carty-Williams become first black authors to win top British Book awards', *Guardian*, 29 June 2020 <https://www.theguardian.com/books/2020/jun/29/candice-carty-williams-bernardine-evaristo-first-black-authors-to-win-top-british-book-awards> [accessed 8 September 2020].
6. Evaristo quoted in Alison Flood, 'Backlash after Booker awards prize to two authors', *The Guardian*, 15 October 2019 <https://www.theguardian.com/books/2019/oct/15/bernardine-evaristo-margaret-atwood-share-booker-prize-award> [accessed 8 September 2020].
7. Sara Upstone, 'Introduction', in *British Asian Fiction* (Manchester: Manchester University Press, 2013), <https://doi-org.sheffield.idm.oclc.org/10.7765/9781847793539.00004>.
8. Kadija Sesay (ed.), *Write Black, Write British: From Post Colonial to Black British Literature* (Hertford: Hansib Publications, 2005), p. 14.
9. Bronwyn T. Williams, 'A State of Perpetual Wandering: Diaspora and Black British writers', *Jouvert: A Journal of Postcolonial Studies*, 3.3 (1999), para. 11.
10. Okwui Enwezor, 'A Question of Place: Revisions, Reassessment, Diaspora', in *Transforming the Crown: African, Asian and Caribbean Artists in Britain, 1996–1996*, ed. by Mora Beauchamp-Byrd and M. Franklin Sirmans (New York: Caribbean Cultural Center, 1997), p. 87; David Dabydeen and Nana Wilson-Tagoe, *A Reader's Guide to Westindian and Black British Literature* (London: Hansib Publications, 1997).
11. Upstone, 'Introduction', p. 209.
12. Sunny Hundal, 'Why multiculturalism matters', *Guardian*, 19 March 2007 <http://www.theguardian.com/media/2007/mar/19/mondaymediasection8> [accessed 8 September 2020]; Marie F. Zielinska and Francis T. Kirkwood (eds), *Multicultural Librarianship: An International Handbook*, IFLA Publications, 59 (Munich: K. G. Saur, 1992).

13. J. A. Appleyard, *Becoming a Reader* (Cambridge: Cambridge University Press, 1994); Louise Rosenblatt, *Literature as Exploration*, 4th edn (New York: Modern Language Association, 1983).
14. Wolfgang Iser, *The Act of Reading: A Theory of Aesthetic Response* (Baltimore, MD: Johns Hopkins University Press, 1978), p. 34.
15. Anamik Saha and Sandra van Lente, *Rethinking 'Diversity' in Publishing* (London: Goldsmiths Press, 2020), p. 23 <https://www.spreadtheword.org.uk/wp-content/uploads/2020/06/Rethinking_diversity_in-publishing_WEB.pdf> [accessed 8 September 2020].
16. Liz Greenhalgh and Ken Worpole, *Libraries in a World of Cultural Change* (London: UCL Press, 1995), p. 24.
17. CILIP, 'Equalities and Diversity Action Plan', *CILIP — The Library and Information Association*, 2017 <https://www.cilip.org.uk/page/EqualitiesandDiversityAction> [accessed 8 September 2020].
18. Library Advisory Council, *Public Library Services for a Multi-Cultural Society*, 2nd edn (London: Commission for Racial Equality, 1997), p. 3.
19. Bhikhu Parekh, *Rethinking Multiculturalism: Cultural Diversity and Political Theory* (London: Macmillan, 2000); Paul Sturges, 'Understanding Cultures and IFLA's Freedom of Access to Information and Freedom of Expression (FAIFE) Core Activity', *Journal of Documentation*, 61.2 (2004), 296–305.
20. Briony Birdi, Kerry Wilson and Sami Mansoor, '"What we should strive for is Britishness": An Attitudinal Investigation of Ethnic Diversity and the Public Library', *Journal of Librarianship and Information Science*, 44.2 (2012), 118–28 <https://doi.org/10.1177%2F0961000611426299>; Salvador Guerena and Edward Erazo, 'Latinos and Librarianship', *Library Trends*, 49.1 (2000), 138–82.
21. Putnam defines 'social capital' as a 'citizen's feelings of trust in other members of society, social norms supportive of cooperation, and networks of civic engagement'; Robert D. Putnam, *Bowling Alone* (New York: Simon & Schuster, 2000), p. 447.
22. Margaret Kendall, 'Keeping Multiculturalism on the Agenda: Strategies for Actions in Public Libraries', *Library Review*, 41.1 (1992), 25–33.
23. Neil Denny, 'The Importance of Ethnic Inclusion', in *Books for All: A 16-page special on books, diversity and your business* (London: The Bookseller, May 2006), p. 3; Hans Elbeshausen and Peter Skov, 'Public Libraries in a Multicultural Space: A Case Study of Integration Processes in Local Communities', *New Library World*, 105.3/4 (2004), 131–41 <https://doi.org/10.1108/03074800410526767>
24. Parveen Akhtar, 'Meeting Ethnic Minorities' Needs', *Assistant Librarian*, 77.9 (1984), pp. 120–22 (p. 120).
25. Simsova, in Zielinska and Kirkwood, *Multicultural Librarianship*, p. 31.
26. Claire M. Lambert, 'Library Provision for the Indian and Pakistani Communities in Britain', *Journal of Librarianship and Information Science*, 1 (1969), 41–61 (p. 52).
27. Briony Birdi and Nigel Ford, 'Towards a New Sociological Model of Fiction Reading', *Journal of the Association for Information Science and Technology*, 69.11 (2018), 1291–1303.
28. See Briony Birdi and Mostafa Syed, 'Exploring Reader Response to Minority Ethnic Fiction', *Library Review*, 60.9 (2011), 816–31 <https://doi.org/10.1108/00242531111176826>.
29. 552 questionnaires were collected prior to the promotion (428 experimental, 124 control), and 495 afterwards (377 experimental, 118 control).
30. Appleyard, *Becoming a Reader*, p. 6.
31. Iser, *The Act of Reading: A Theory of Aesthetic Response*.
32. Briony Train, 'Reader Development', in *Reading and Reader Development: The Pleasure of Reading*, ed. by Judith Elkin and others (London: Facet Publishing, 2003), pp. 30–58.
33. Rachel van Riel, *Report to Arts Council Literature Department on Creative Reading Training in Libraries* (London: The Arts Council of England, 1992), p. 4.
34. Opening the Book, 'Reader-Centred Approach', *Opening the Book*, 2013 <http://web.archive.org/web/20150315230244/http://openingthebook.com/reader-centred-library> [accessed 8 September 2020].
35. George A. Kelly, *The Psychology of Personal Constructs* (New York: W. W. Norton, 1955).

36. Fay Fransella (ed.), *The Essential Practitioner's Handbook of Personal Construct Psychology* (Chichester: John Wiley & Sons, 2005).
37. Peter Banister, Erica Burman and Ian Parker, *Qualitative Methods in Psychology: A Research Guide* (Buckingham: Open University Press, 1994), p. 73.
38. Trevor Butt and Vivian Burr, *Invitation to Personal Construct Psychology* (London: Whurr Publishers, 1992), p. 3.
39. Reader of LGBT fiction, War & Spy fiction, Romance fiction, Lad Lit fiction, Crime fiction, Chick Lit fiction, British Asian fiction, Literary fiction, Black British fiction, Science fiction/Fantasy fiction.
40. Triads in the order that they were presented to participants: 'Reader of ...' Crime/Black British/Romance fiction, Black British/British Asian fiction/Literary fiction, Lad Lit/War & Spy/Crime fiction, British Asian/Black British/LGBT fiction, Black British/Literary/Science fiction & Fantasy fiction, Science fiction & Fantasy/British Asian/Lad Lit, LGBT/Romance/War & Spy fiction, British Asian/Black British/Science fiction & Fantasy fiction, LGBT/Chick Lit/Romance fiction.
41. Peter Nicholls, 'Introduction', *Critical Quarterly*, 37.4 (1995), 1–3 (p. 2).
42. Nancy Pearl, *Now Read This II: A Guide to Mainstream Fiction, 1990–2001* (Santa Barbara, CA: Libraries Unlimited, 2002), p. ix.
43. Perceived demographic profile of the reader, Perceived approach to reading, Preferred Nature of Plot, Subject Interests, Preferred Genres. For a full description of these themes and how they were arrived at, see Briony Birdi and Mostafa Syed, 'Exploring Reader Response to Minority Ethnic Fiction'.
44. The means of construct ratings for fiction variables are useful in telling us whether, on average, there tends to be participant agreement across the constructs. Although this is useful in itself, mean scores can conceal great variation in rating, whereas a second test — the intraclass correlation (ICC) — can be conducted to overcome this. A descriptive statistic, the ICC is a measure of the reliability of ratings, so can be used to take into account any such variation in ratings, enabling a more precise measurement of agreement (i.e. the extent to which participants rated each construct similarly) than would have been possible with only the means of construct ratings.
45. Kelly, *The Psychology of Personal Constructs*.
46. Flood, 'Backlash after Booker awards prize to two authors'.
47. Salman Rushdie, *Imaginary Homelands: Essays and Criticism, 1981–91*, 2nd edn (London: Granta Books, 1992), p. 21.

CHAPTER 7

Small Literature, Big Ambition: Basque Literature of the Present

Mari Jose Olaziregi

> Kultur alorrean zerbait sortzen duen herriak beretzat eta besterentzat sortzen du eta, orobat, besterentzat sortzen ez duenak ez du beretzat ere sortzen
>
> [People create something in the field of culture, they do it for themselves and for everyone else]
>
> — Koldo Mitxelena

Can a writer in a minority language such as Basque resist the need/temptation to be translated into a hegemonic language like Spanish? Can we say that a writer in a minority language writes in order to be translated? Can new translation strategies serve to counteract the hegemony of Spanish? These are some of the questions that are addressed in this chapter. In order to do so, the analysis is organized into three sections that seek to explore the tensions provoked by the multilingual reality of Basque writers within and outside their literary environment. First, I discuss the debate that has dominated literary historiography in the Iberian context. Recent critiques of histories of Spanish literature, which ignore so-called 'peripheral' literatures like those in Catalan, Galician and Basque, have led to a reformulation of the comparative frame, from which to address and understand that pluriliterary reality. I then move on to emphasize the advantages of applying a 'distant reading' (Moretti)[1] to the multilingual and plurinational reality of the Iberian context, an approach that highlights the asymmetric relations between literatures such as that in Basque and Spanish literature. Finally, I explore the systematic invisibility of Basque-language writers and how this generates tensions and resistance among the writers themselves.[2]

Basque Literature in the Iberian Context and the Politics of Spanish Literary Historiography

The notion of a small literature with a big ambition has been mooted by the celebrated philologist and architect of Basque-language standardization, Koldo Mitxelena (1915–1987). As it captures the situation succinctly, the notion serves as inspiration for the reflections that follow here and that focus on the strategic importance that translation into/from Basque has had and continues to have for this minoritized language, with at present 900,000 speakers on both sides of the Pyrenees. Legally, it is a co-official language, alongside Spanish, within Spain (in the Basque Autonomous Community and the Community of Navarre), and a non-official language in France (in the three Basque provinces that are part of the Département des Pyrénées Atlantiques). This results in a diverse sociolinguistic reality that, according to UNESCO, would categorize the language as weak or at risk in areas like Navarre and the French Basque Country.[3] In the Basque Autonomous Community, however, the situation is better and Basque enjoys a healthier status. Here, 59% of parents, whether they speak Basque or not, choose it as the language of instruction for their children,[4] with the result that there is a significantly different reality to that of the other aforementioned areas.

When discussing the status of Basque, one must bear in mind the multilingual and plurinational reality of the Spanish state. Indeed, multilingualism, as Olga Anokhina and Emilio Sciarrino emphasize in a recent edition of the journal *Genesis*,[5] affects 90% of the global population and therefore conditions much of world literature. Anokhina and Sciarrino go on to contend that Nabokov, for example, became one of the 'greats' of American literature due, precisely, to his mastery of the Russian language.[6] Nabokov was perfectly trilingual in Russian, French and English, and the presence and interactions of all three languages can be found in his drafts, letters and published works. For example, a close inspection of the neologisms and the omnipresent play on words in his English-language works reveals that this linguistic creativity is often motivated by Russian and French influences.[7]

Another question is that of the challenges posed for scholars of literature by a multilingual reality as literatures created in multilingual environments have been and are subject to particular interpretations and treatment. In his study of languages in the Iberian context and Spanish nationalism, for instance, Xosé María Núñez Seixas contends that, around the 1880s, language as a mark of national identity coincided with diverse 'renaissances' of the *other* literatures in the Spanish state.[8] The re-emergence of the Catalan, Galician and Basque languages within the late nineteenth-century Cultural and National Renaissance movements in Spain was an attempt to respond to the political, administrative and educational centralization that the Spanish government had initiated in the eighteenth and continued during the nineteenth century.

There is, moreover, the question of the strategic value that may be granted to language as an identity marker when it comes to projecting the image of a nation state abroad. I have commented elsewhere on the restricted value that literature in Basque had within the strategy of the Basque Government's 'Euskadi. Basque Country' branding , where I noted that successive Basque nationalist governments have been more interested in Basque economic data (which resemble those of countries like Luxemburg) and the cultural industries (film, the audio-visual sector, and so on) than Basque literary production.[9] In contrast, Elena Delgado observes the strategic importance that Spain's government has given to Spanish culture and the Spanish language as its greatest exportable asset and the main element of national cohesion.[10]

Yet it is not the current marginalization of the Basque language — the result, clearly, of its lack of official status until the 1980s — but its specific nature, its *difference* within the Iberian context due to the fact that it is not a Romance language (unlike the other non-Spanish languages), which has conditioned many of the historiographical reflections on Basque literature, including comparative studies. In effect, the fact that Basque is a language *isolate,* with no known relatives, has led historically to the creation of an aura of mystery and exoticism surrounding it. This exoticization has been used by both its supporters (like the Basque institutions) and its detractors to praise or criticize its virtues. One prominent detractor was the Basque writer and philosopher Miguel de Unamuno (1864–1936), who in 1901, during the Floral Games in Bilbao, expressed his doubts about the value of Basque in the modern world. Yet the same notion of difference, or uniqueness, underpins the perception that writers themselves have of the language.

Beyond questions of language, though, what is more interesting for the argument here is the view of Basque-language literature as unique within the realm of Iberian literary criticism. This specificity, symbolized very expressively by the geo-mytheme of the term language *island* and the sense of solitude that has stalked Basque writers and literary historiography, has been explained clearly by César Domínguez[11] and by Fernando Cabo Aseguinolaza[12] in their analysis of the peculiarities of Iberian literary history. As Cabo concludes, peninsular literary criticism has in general viewed literature in Basque negatively, to the point of suffocating it.

However, it could be pointed out that one of the most prominent developments in recent decades has been the profusion of publications that attempt to approach the study of the pluriliterary reality of the Iberian context by underscoring the need to overcome monological Spanish literary historiography. The importance of the spatial turn, the postnational impulse, the rejection of a monological concept of culture and an emphasis on interferences, transmissions and convergences has been underlined in efforts to decentralize the historiography of Spanish literature and to foster a multipolar approach, without renouncing the analysis of relations with European and global literatures. Publications like *Spain Beyond Spain,*[13] or *Iberian Modalities,*[14] to mention only two, are good examples of recent works that have provided insightful reflection on the limitations of the traditional Spanish literature historiography.

The problem is quite obvious: although in theory we may support the idea of a new historiography that seeks to present the plurilingual literary reality of the Iberian context, how are we going to create this in practice? How many of the literary languages of Spain does the historian need to know in order to become an expert in Iberian literatures? The issue clearly resides, as I emphasize in a previous study of the university-level teaching of Basque outside the Basque Country,[15] in the real possibilities offered by the comparative study of literatures in the Iberian context. Such an approach obliges the Iberian comparative scholar to transcend their monolingualism and embrace, as Gayatri Chakravorty Spivak terms it, the language of the Other.[16] Put another way, thinking that literature in Basque, Catalan or Galician can be addressed only through their translations into Spanish is, without any doubt, practising a very limited comparative approach.

The Need for a Distant Gaze

Although Umberto Eco has characterized translation as the language of Europe,[17] I would argue that it is actually the world's language, in the sense that most literatures address readers in multiple languages, and plurilingualism is the norm, not the exception. Indeed, comparative scholars like David Damrosch have had no hesitation in granting translation the centrality it deserves in publications such as *What is World Literature?*[18] Therein, he argues that world literature is: a) an elliptical refraction of national literatures; b) writing that gains in translation; and c) a new form of reading that we could describe as an affinity with worlds beyond our own in place and time, and not a set canon of texts. In his essay *Moroak gara behelaino artean? [Are We Moors in the Mist?]*, winner of the Euskadi Prize for Essays in 2011, the Basque writer Joseba Sarrionandia alludes to Damrosch when he pleads for translations from Basque into other languages, precisely in order to change that rather uneven field of world literature in which minority languages are invisible.[19] A more sceptical stance is taken in the provocative arguments of Andrea Pisac, proposed at the well-known festival World Voices, organized by the American PEN. Pisac contends that, in reality, world literature is 'the literature of the small nations available in English translation. It is most often written by exiled, migrant or otherwise displaced writers — cultural brokers — who 'speak the dominant language' and offer a view into their 'culture'.[20] Whatever the case, it has been some time since Pascale Casanova granted translation a strategic value with regard to the construction of literary capital in the face of legitimizing institutions. Put another way, translation is equivalent to *littérarisation* or its own reaffirmation as literature, and therefore translation is crucial for minority and lesser-known literatures like that of Basque if it aims to be visible and valuable in the global arena.[21]

It is for this reason that approaching peninsular literatures from 'afar', through *distant reading* (in accordance with the vision of Franco Moretti) would contribute significantly to their comparative study and to a greater understanding of the relations that small literatures, like Basque literature, establish with hegemonic literatures, like Spanish literature, or with other peripheral literatures like those of Catalan and Galician. I am not referring merely to the flow and exchange of translations amongst literatures, but also to the analysis of how these literatures are received, to the tensions which translations generate intra- and intersystematically, to institutional influence, through translation promotion policies, and to the influence of historiographical discourse, for instance. I argue for the need to incorporate or benefit from many of the aspects which translation studies already explore in the comparative analysis of literatures. This would call for a more quantitative, sociological and political approach in addition to a focus on the textual strategies of translation.

Some experts like Mario Santana have already reclaimed the importance of such distant reading,[22] and have presented results that underscore the centrality that literary translation has in the Iberian frame. The fact that 36% of literature published in Spain between 2003 and 2012 was translated from other languages is significant. Moreover, this translated literature, translated mostly into Spanish from English — with only 2% translated from the other peninsular literatures — is, de facto, Spanish literature, if we understand the latter as 'the site where the various literatures of the world find expression in that language'.[23] The picture is completed with data on the rate of translation into other peninsular languages: of the literature published in Catalan, 27% is translated, only 0.5% of which is translated from the other peninsular languages (except from Spanish, which corresponds to 10.3% of the translations); of the literature published in Galician, 16% is translated literature, of which only 4.2% are translations from the other peninsular literatures (except from Spanish, which corresponds to 19.2% of the translations); of the literature published in Basque, 22.2% is translated literature, of which 27.6% are translations from Spanish and 8% translations from the other peninsular literatures (Catalan and Galician). Proportionately, the Basque-language literary system is that which translates most peninsular literature into Basque, especially from Spanish, on which it is very dependent and with which it establishes clear asymmetries. The percentage of self-translated texts and allographic translations (those done by professional translators) is similar in the Basque language, although it is also true that 86% of self-translations, almost always supra-self-translations or translations from a subordinate into a hegemonic language, are done in Spanish, and those in French only account for 11%. Self-translation, experienced by most Basque writers as a space of freedom, has been, also, a fundamental aspect of the autonomization process within the sub-field of literary translation in Basque.[24]

In the 1990s a policy of translating and internationalizing literature in Basque began to take shape, with the goal of 'standardizing' it in line with the rest of the adjacent literatures. This began with translations by Basque authors on the part of Basque publishing houses like Erein, Elkar, Pamiela and Alberdania, which, until then, had only published in Basque. The goal was to seek a wider Basque readership that incorporated monolingual Spanish-speakers. But it was also an era in which there was much social debate between those who eulogized the advantages (such as professionalization and promotion) of translation into other languages for a minoritized language like Basque, and those that believed that translations and market pressures reduced the freedom of Basque writers and did not contribute great benefits to the system.[25] Writers like Ramon Saizarbitoria, for example, underscored the advantages of a small publishing market such as that in Basque for experimenting outside the pressure of the market. Saizarbitoria has stated that the fact he knows the text he is writing will soon be translated into Spanish affects his own writing process. It obliges him, in some way, to think about that future translation.[26]

I have commented in previous publications on the unequal asymmetrical reality revealed by Elizabete Manterola's analysis[27] of the catalogue of translations from

Basque-language literature into other languages.[28] With 480 titles translated from Basque into thirty-eight languages up to 2010, translations into Spanish constitute almost half the entire production; this is clear proof, as I have emphasized in the above paragraphs, of the Basque literary system's dependency on its Spanish counterpart; and a greater dependency, according to Mario Santana,[29] than that experienced by other literary systems on the peninsula. Translations into Catalan and into English are, followed by Galician, the next most popular target languages in the Basque literary system. This, and the fact that the success of Atxaga's *Obabakoak*[30] was based on his winning of the National Literary Prize for Narrative in 1989, awarded by the Spanish Ministry of Culture, generated criticism among some members of the Basque literary field. In effect, the fact that it was this, the most prestigious award in Spain, which catapulted a Basque work, *Obabakoak*, to international renown, came in for criticism on the grounds that it took a Spanish institution to grant legitimacy to a Basque work. Furthermore, translations of Atxaga's work into other international languages are done not from Basque, but from Spanish, which some interpret as a dual form of Spanishization, subordination and minoritization.[31]

Bernardo Atxaga's unquestionable international success, with a total of thirty-five of his titles translated into thirty-three languages, was followed, in terms of both a national and international repercussion, by Kirmen Uribe's professional trajectory. Kirmen Uribe was awarded the National Literary Prize for Narrative in 2009 for his novel *Bilbao-New York-Bilbao*,[32] which has been translated into fourteen languages to date. Between *Obabakoak* and *Bilbao-New York-Bilbao*, then, twenty years passed that were absolutely fundamental in the autonomization process within the sub-field of Basque literary translation. Spanish is no longer necessarily the bridge language for translation into international languages. Kirmen Uribe's case is revealing in this regard: of the fifteen translations produced of *Bilbao-New York-Bilbao*, seven were done directly from Basque, including the translation into Japanese by Nami Kaneko. Kaneko also received the 2016 Grand Prix Translation in Japan (Nihon Hon'yaku Taishō) for the best translation of a foreign work for her translation into Japanese of another of Uribe's novels, *Mussche*,[33] in 2016. And it was Kaneko, too, who translated the novel *Soinujolearen semea* [*The Accordionist's Son*] (2003)[34] by Bernardo Atxaga; the Japanese translation was published in 2020.

Translating (into) the Language of the Enemy

Echoing the bypassing of the hegemonic Spanish language in Kaneko's translations of Uribe and Atxaga's works, some recent conferences, courses and publications have addressed the multilingual reality in the diverse literatures of the Spanish state, such as that held in 2008 at the Center for Basque Studies at the University of Nevada, Reno, in the United States titled 'Writers in Between Languages: Minority Languages in the Global Scene', selected papers of which were published a year later in a book with the same title;[35] and international courses like that held between 18 and 28 September 2017 at the Universität Konstanz, Germany, 'Plurilinguisme en

Europe Occidentale: La France et L'Espagne'.[36] Both events addressed the different views put forward by Basque-language authors on their choice of writing language; views which, amongst the six Basque writers that attended the Reno conference (Arkotxa, Arregi, Atxaga, Landa, Meabe and Zaldua), ranged from seeing writing in Basque as a logical and natural option (Atxaga, Arregi), as related to context, tradition and community (Meabe), and as a tool for the promotion of writing in Basque and Spanish as well as French (Arkotxa, Zaldua, Landa), and thus making use of the diverse languages the authors use in their daily lives. Whatever the case, it is undeniable that all writers in a minoritized language like Basque will, in the course of their career, come up against the question of whether they want to or should be translated into a hegemonic language like Spanish.

Herein reside the importance and the strategic value that translation and translators acquire in contexts like that of Basque literature. It is for that reason that contemporary fiction in Basque incorporates more and more characters and protagonists who are translators; and it has done so, moreover, by granting them an additional function, above all in the 'trend topic' of the most recent Basque writing, which is the remembering of the conflict generated by the terrorism of ETA. Novels that have received the Euskadi Prize for Literature, like *Twist* (2011)[37] by Harkaitz Cano and *Martutene* (2012)[38] by Ramón Saizarbitoria, are examples of the importance of the translator as a fictional character when it comes to 'translating' or 'narrating' the Basque conflict. It is clear that in this case, Basque literature on ETA terrorism does not just have, according to Basque writers such as Iban Zaldua, a homeopathic function, that is, it does not just attempt to contribute to healing the suffering through non-invasive and nonconventional methods,[39] but it also contributes to recognizing the harm caused by terrorism and encourages a process of reconciliation. Illustrative of this trend are the more than seventy novels on terrorism that have been written in Basque, novels in which it is often a fictitious writer or translator that describes the conflict.

Yet the commemoration of the conflictive past in the Basque Country is not the subject of interest here, but rather the pressure, almost alienation, to which writers in Basque are subject for the *duty* of translation.[40] At some point, every single one of the approximately 300 Basque literary writers has commented on the experiences resulting from the consecutive translation of their work, or even on simultaneous translation during the process of creation. These experiences can be grouped into the dynamic of domestication and resistance that any act of translation involves, as highlighted by Venuti.[41] There are authors, like the aforementioned Saizarbitoria, who denounce the alienation imposed by knowing their work in Basque will be translated, and thereby exported to a non-Basque-speaking public,[42] and there are others, like Eider Rodriguez, who contend that self-translation allows them to have a kind of communion between the languages they inhabit, namely Basque, Spanish and French.[43] A more extreme example can be found in the French Basque writer, Itxaro Borda, who argues that it has taken her many years to accept that she can self-translate into French and not feel like she is collaborating with the enemy. As the author herself said,[44] her attitude was befitting of the alienating socio-political ideology which had oppressed her for years, and which constrained her 'outing' in the French market. These are statements that demonstrate, clearly, the limitations that a small literature has on account of its high level of politicization. 'Loyalty to the tribe', in the words of Kundera in *Les Testaments trahis*,[45] obliges writers in a minoritized language like Basque to pay certain tolls. The analysis of the market strategies that have been followed in order to 'situate' Basque-language writers in the Spanish market (the almost simultaneous publication of the original alongside a translation into all the other peninsular languages), and of the assimilation processes that these translations activate that may lead to the disappearance of the original in Basque from the ISBN database or well-known Spanish government websites dedicated to foreign promotion (www.espanaescultura.es), shows a reality that is conditioned by the centralizing dynamics of the Spanish system. In resistance to this reality, Basque writers deploy textual strategies, such as the introduction of footnotes in order to explain terms, the insertion of non-translated words and terms in Basque in novels like the abovementioned *The Accordionist's Son*, by Atxaga, or the use of appendices which explain vocabulary and terms in Basque, amongst others. Comparing the similarities of this reality with translations of literature in Basque into French, would demonstrate, moreover, a necessarily more complete picture of the Basque literary system, on account of its cross-border reality.

The assimilating and centralizing forces that the Spanish system exerts on its Basque counterpart become even more evident if we compare them to the casuistry which is established in translations from Basque into other languages. For example, Bernardo Atxaga is marketed as a 'Basque writer' in Britain. This assumption implies a widespread belief in Britain that his translations into English have been done directly from Basque and not from the Spanish versions of his work, as is actually the case. For the British market, it is of little importance whether they have been done from Basque or from Spanish, as both are peripheral languages in the eyes of the English-language literary system.

A comparison might be made between the policy of translation strategies of literature published in English in Britain with literature published in French in France in recent years. In this market, publications like the well-known *Translatio* (2008) by Gisèle Sapiro[46] show the growing number of translations of French literature into hitherto less explored languages and markets (such as Arabic, Dutch, Hebrew, and Finnish) with the objective of resisting the hegemony of English. Literature in Basque has followed the same strategy with the aim of resisting the hegemony of Spanish and of opening up new markets with translations of texts originally written in Basque into Bulgarian, Serbian, and Slovenian. Since 2016 the Etxepare Basque Institute, moreover, has promoted the training of translators into foreign languages with courses in the Basque language in programmes like 'Itzultzaile berriak' [New translators].[47]

Conclusion

As mentioned at this chapter's outset, multilingualism is a (happy) reality which affects 90% of the world's people and which, as I have tried to demonstrate here, generates debates and controversy within the Iberian setting. While there are recent publications that employ a comparative and historiographical study of the different peninsular literatures which overcome the monological focus that used to predominate in the historiography of Spanish literature, it is also true that such approaches are still in the minority. This is due, in great part, to the belief that the *other* literatures in the Iberian context can only be studied on the basis of their translations into Spanish. This is a belief which demonstrates the persistence of a hegemonic language ideology among some scholars in the field. In addition, I have reflected here on the consequences of the asymmetric relations established by the Basque literary system with its Castilian counterpart. However, foreignizing translation strategies can work to counteract the invisibility of Basque: strategies such as inserting terms and expressions in Basque, not translating sections of text, or adding commentaries and footnotes are used repeatedly in order to resist the domestication that all translation activity involves. Although nowadays nobody doubts the importance and strategic value of translation into other languages for literature in Basque, its dependency with regard to Spanish in the field of translation and promotion continues to generate resistance amongst some Basque writers.

Notes to Chapter 7

1. Franco Moretti, *Distant Reading* (London and New York: Verso Books, 2013).
2. This paper was written as part of the research projects undertaken by the Consolidated Research Group MHLI (Memoria Histórica en las Literaturas Ibéricas, Historical Memory in Iberian Literatures), financed by the Basque Government (IT 1579-22) and the MINECO (PID2021-125952NB-I00). It was translated from Spanish by Cameron Watson.
3. Ivan Igartua and Xabier Zabalza, *Euskararen historia laburra. Breve historia de la lengua vasca. A Brief History of the Basque Language* (Donostia: Etxepare Basque Institute, 2012), p. 72.
4. Igartua and Zabalza, *Euskararen historia laburra*, p. 81.
5. Olga Anokhina and Emilio Sciarrino, 'Présentation', *Genesis*, 46 (2018), 7–10 (p. 7).
6. Olga Anokhina and Emilio Sciarrino, 'Plurilinguisme littéraire: de la théorie à la genèse', *Genesis*, 46 (2018), 11–33 (p. 25).
7. Olga Anokhina and Emilio Sciarrino, 'Plurilinguisme littéraire: de la théorie à la genèse', *Genesis*, 46 (2018), 11–33 (pp. 24–25).
8. Xosé María Núñez Seixas, 'La(s) lengua(s) de la nación', in *Ser españoles: imaginarios nacionalistas en el siglo XX*, ed. by Javier Moreno Luzón and Xosé María Núñez Seixas (Barcelona: RBA, 2013), pp. 246–86 (p. 274).
9. Mari Jose Olaziregi, 'Going Global: The International Journey of Basque Culture and Literature', in *The Routledge Companion to Iberian Studies*, ed. by Laura Lonsdale and Manuel Delgado Morales (London: Routledge, 2017), pp. 547–57.
10. Luisa Elena Delgado, *La nación singular: fantasías de la normalidad democrática española (1996–2011)* (Madrid: Siglo XXI, 2014).
11. César Domínguez, 'Historiography and the Geo-literary Imaginery: The Iberian Peninsula: Between *Lebensraum* and *espace vécu*', in *A Comparative History of Literatures in the Iberian Peninsula*, vol. I, ed. by Fernando Cabo Aseguinolaza, Anxo Abuín González and César Domínguez (Amsterdam and Philadelphia: John Benjamins, 2010), pp. 53–132.
12. Fernando Cabo Aseguinolaza, 'The European Horizon of Peninsular Literary Historiographical Discourses', in *A Comparative History of Literatures in the Iberian Peninsula*, vol. I, pp. 1–52.

13. Bradley S. Epps and Luis Fernández Cifuentes, *Spain beyond Spain: Modernity, Literary History, and National Identity* (Lewisburg, PA: Bucknell University Press, 2005).
14. Joan Ramon Resina (ed.), *Iberian Modalities* (Liverpool: Liverpool University Press, 2013).
15. Mari Jose Olaziregi, 'Going Global'.
16. Gayatri Chakravorty Spivak, *Death of a Discipline* (New York: Columbia University Press, 2003), p. 9.
17. Umberto Eco, 'The Language of Europe is Translation'. Lecture given at the conference of ATLAS *Assises de la traduction littéraire* in Arles, 14 November 1993.
18. David Damrosch, *What Is World Literature?* (Princeton, NJ: Princeton University Press, 2003).
19. See Joseba Sarrionandia, *Moroak gara behelaino artean?* (Iruña: Pamiela, 2010).
20. Andrea Pisac, 'Big Nations' Literature and Small Nations' Sociology', *Etnološka tribina*, 35, vol. 42 (2012), 187–206 (p. 188).
21. Pascale Casanova, *The World Republic of Letters* (Cambridge, MA: Harvard University Press, 2004).
22. Mario Santana, 'Translation and Literatures in Spain (2003–2012)', *Revista de Historia de la Traducción*, 9 (2015), 1–13 (p. 3) <http://www.traduccionliteraria.org/1611/art/santana.htm> [accessed 8 February 2020].
23. Ibid, p. 5.
24. Miren Ibarluzea, 'Itzulpengintzaren errepresentazioak euskal literatura garaikidean: eremuaren autonomizazioa, euskal historiografiak eta eta itzultzaileak fikzioan' [Representations of translation in contemporary Basque literature: the process of autonomy of the field, literary historiographies and translators in fiction]. (Unpublished doctoral dissertation, University of the Basque Country, 2017).
25. Mari Jose Olaziregi, 'La literatura vasca y sus ansiedades', in *Interacciones entre las literaturas ibéricas*, ed. by Francisco Lafarga, Luis Pegenaute and Enric Gallén (Bern: Peter Lang, 2010), pp. 345–52 (p. 347).
26. Ramon Saizarbitoria, *Aberriaren alde eta kontra* (Irun: Alberdania, 1999).
27. Elizabete Manterola, *La literatura vasca traducida* (Bern: Peter Lang, 2014).
28. Miren Ibarluzea and Mari Jose Olaziregi, 'Autonomización y funciones del subcampo de la traducción literaria vasca contemporánea: una aproximación sociológica', *Pasavento*, 4.2 (2016), 293–313 (pp. 304–06).
29. Mario Santana, 'Translation and Literatures in Spain (2003–2012)', p. 235.
30. Bernardo Atxaga, *Obabakoak* (Donostia: Erein, 1998). Translated into English by Margaret Jull Costa as *Obabakoak* (London: Vintage, 2007).
31. María José Olaziregi and Lourdes Otaegi, 'Pensamiento y crítica literaria en euskera en el siglo XX', in *Pensamiento y crítica literaria en el siglo XX (Castellano, Catalán, Euskara, Gallego)*, ed. by José María Pozuelo Yvancos et al. (Madrid: Cátedra, 2019), pp. 417–604 (p. 561).
32. Kirmen Uribe, *Bilbao, New York, Bilbao* (Donostia: Elkar, 2008). Translated into English by Elizabeth Maclin as *Bilbao, New York, Bilbao* (London: Seren Books, 2014).
33. Kirmen Uribe, *Mussche* (Zarautz: Susa, 2012). Translated into Spanish by Gerardo Markuleta as *Lo que mueve el mundo* (Barcelona: Seix Barral, 2013).
34. Bernardo Atxaga, *Soinujolearen semea* (Iruña: Pamiela, 2003). Translated into English by Margaret Jull Costa as *The Accordionist's Son* (London: Vintage, 2008).
35. See Mari Jose Olaziregi (ed.), *Writers in Between Languages: Minority Literatures in the Global Scene* (Reno: Center for Basque Studies, 2009).
36. See <https://www.uni-konstanz.de/fr/international-participation/partner-und-kooperationen/dfh/> [accessed 3 May 2020].
37. Harkaitz Cano, *Twist* (Zarautz: Susa, 2012). Translated into English by Amaia Gabantxo as *Twist* (New York: Archipelago Books, 2018).
38. Ramon Saizarbitoria, *Martutene* (Donostia: Erein, 2012). Translated into English by Aritz Brandon as *Martutene* (Madrid: Hispabooks, 2016).
39. Iban Zaldua, *Ese idioma raro y poderoso* (Madrid: Lengua de Trapo, 2012). Translated into English by Mariann Vaczi as *This Strange and Powerful Language: Eleven Crucial Decisions a Basque Writer is Obliged to Face* (Reno: Center for Basque Studies, 2016).

40. The statements of the writer Harkaitz Cano are eloquent in this sense: 'Gaztelaniaz argitaratzean, badago idazle subordinatu sentiarazten zaituen dinamika nahiko perbertso eta sotil bat. Eta ez dakit prest nagoen dinamika horretan jokatzeko' [When we publish in Spanish there is a somewhat perverse and subtle dynamic which makes you feel like a subordinate writer. I don't know if I'm ready to take part in that dynamic] (ARGIA, 13 January 2019).
41. Lawrence Venuti, *The Translator's Invisibility: A History of Translation* (London and New York: Routledge, 2004).
42. Ramon Saizarbitoria, *Aberriaren alde eta kontra*.
43. Eider Rodríguez, 'Los premios harán un favor a los relatos y al cómic', *El Diario Vasco*, 18 October 2018 <https://www.diariovasco.com/culturas/libros/eider-rodriguez-literatura-20181018001126-ntvo.html> [accessed 8 February 2020].
44. Frederik Verbeke, 'Paris and the Worlding of Minor/Small Literatures: The Case of Basque Literature', *TSLA: Theoretical Studies in Literature and Art*, 39.1 (2019), 1–14 (p. 8).
45. Milan Kundera, *Les Testaments trahis* (Paris: Gallimard, 1995), p. 56.
46. Gisèle Sapiro (ed.), *Translatio: le marché de la traduction en France à l'heure de la mondialisation* (Paris: CNRS, 2008).
47. The list of translations from Basque into other languages in the period 2014–18 would include: 2014: Spanish (11), Bulgarian, Catalan, English, Slovenian; 2015: Spanish (2), Japanese, Bulgarian (2), Ukrainian, Serbian, Chinese, Italian (3), Amharic; 2016: Spanish (7), Macedonian, Bulgarian, Slovenian (2) Catalan, Italian (3), German; 2017: Spanish (5), Slovenian, French, Catalan, Macedonian, English, Italian (4); 2018: Spanish (6), Catalan, Serbian, Greek, Slovenian, Albanian, Bulgarian, Danish.

CHAPTER 8

Land un Lü: Low German Diversities

Stefan Willer

This chapter examines current interactions between extra-textual factors and textual production in Low German literature. Low German ('Niederdeutsch', 'Plattdeutsch', or 'Platt'), the idiom of the Northern German 'lowlands', used to be a language of government and of poetry in the Middle Ages and continued to be the native tongue of North Germans over centuries. Today it is one of Germany's officially protected minority or regional languages, according to the combination of both categories in the 'European Charter for Regional or Minority Languages'. In the first part of the chapter I discuss some implications and consequences of language preservation, highlighting concepts of linguistic and cultural diversity. The question is how such concepts affect literary production itself, given the problem that the policy of safeguarding 'small' language cultures seems to encourage territorial restriction and the isolation of regional language communities. The title of this chapter, the common Low German formula 'Land un Lü' [Land and People], is meant to indicate both the idea of diversification and the risk of provincial territorialism.

In the second part I examine two literary examples in which the regionality of Low German is at the same time questioned and affirmed. Dörte Hansen, in her successful novel *Altes Land* [*Old Land*] (2015), uses the setting of the North German countryside to juxtapose the life stories of two women, one of which is situated in the post-war decades whereas the other takes place in the present. Both are characterized by flight and refuge. Within the High German text of the novel, Low German phrases serve as a means of locating the text in its regional setting, but at the same time they are used to represent the experience of being 'out of place' which is topical for the novel. Then I turn to Yared Dibaba, currently one of the most prolific protagonists of Low German culture. Born in 1969 in Southwest Ethiopia, he came to Germany first as a small child and learned Low German out of fondness for its regionality. In his essays and short narratives, published under the title *Ünnerwegens* [*On the Way*] (2016), he uses his own biography as an argument against the myth of the autochthonous essence of language, speakers, and territory, while he still seems to indicate that Low German is somehow appropriate for the land and for the people of the North.

Diversity through Low German

'Plattdeutsch ist eine Sprache unserer Zeit' [Low German is a language of our time]. So begins the preface — written in High German — of *Platt: Dat Lehrbook* [*Low German: The Textbook*], published in 2016 by the Institute for Low German Language in Bremen. Efforts are also being made elsewhere to disseminate Low German in a contemporary way, on websites such as 'www.plattnet.de' and 'www.plattdeutsch.net', at festivals and competitions such as 'Plattart', 'Plattsounds' or 'Platt is cool', or in the design of elementary school curricula in the northern German states. What is striking in all of this is the proximity of current Low German education to programmes of linguistic and cultural diversity. At the launch of Plattart in March 2017, the festival director, author and actress Annie Heger, wrote:

> Unser Motto: WI KRIEGT DAT HEN! Wi Plattdüütschen, wi seggen dat nich blot so, wi meent dat ook. Wi packen an. Wi sünd dat leed un dat verdrütt us, dat de Lüüd jümmer blot över dat Starven van Platt snackt. Us Spraak is mehr as lebennig. Se is bunt, upregend, entwickelt sik jümmers wieter, Platt hett so vööl to seggen un doch kannst op Platt ook an'n besten swiegen. Jo, us Spraak is so kakelbunt as de Regenboog, een Blomenstruuß un de Minschen, de Platt snacken, prooten oder küren. Wi maaken us Spraak lebennig, denn wi sünd doch al so verscheden.[1]

> [Our motto: WE CAN DO IT! We Low Germans don't just say it, we mean it. We are getting down to work. We are tired and it annoys us that there is always talk of the dying of Low German. Our language is more than alive. It is colourful, exciting, always evolving; Platt has so much to say, and yet Platt is also the best way to keep silent. Yes, our language is as motley as the rainbow, a bouquet of flowers and the people who speak Platt. We make our language alive, because we are all so different.]

Obviously alluding to Angela Merkel's famous dictum 'Wir schaffen das', Annie Heger emphasizes the competencies of 'us Low Germans'. Low German language and culture is in no way described as in need of protection or care, but as strong, lively and changeable. The language is said to be suitable for saying a lot (emphasized by having three verbs for 'to speak': *snacken, prooten, küren*), but it is also expressive when saying nothing. According to Heger, Low German is 'as' motley 'as' other colourful things: the rainbow, flowers, and Low German speakers. The phrase 'as... as' suggests a continuity between these three entities, but on closer inspection, the first two are used as similes, while the third names a basic condition of language: the fact that it is being spoken. In Heger's view, this turns out to be the epitome of linguistic liveliness. It is only the speakers who generate and keep up the life of language, and this because they are heterogeneous as a group: 'because we are all so different.'

This declaration combines the self-statement in the plural ('we') in a comprehensive way ('all') with the emphasis on heterogeneity ('different'). If all are different, then their difference escapes relational determination by a counter-concept (classically 'identity') and becomes an absolute category. One might say that this is precisely the way in which *diversity* can be defined and that Heger's sentence, 'because we are all so different', provides an exemplary formula for the logic of diversity.² But it also shows that this logic can only be understood in terms of its political use. It is no coincidence that the text at this point mentions the rainbow, the symbol of LGBTQ pride, as the epitome of colourfulness. Annie Heger, who not only advocates Platt but is also a queer activist, understands the 'motley', but dismissed, minoritarian, even marginalized Low German idiom as a language *in* change and *for* change. Diversity as a cultural-political concern affects the themes and content of what can be said in Low German. Heger bids farewell to the affirmative folk and regional culture to which Low German was long confined, and calls instead for a reference to the 'world':

> De Spraak dürft nich instuven un blot för Döntjes van verleden Tieden herhollen. Se muss sik mitentwickeln, mit us Minschen un de Welt wassen. So warrd se doch blot noch bunter.³

> [Language must not gather dust and be used only for anecdotes from old times. It must evolve with us, grow with us and the world. That way, it will only become more colourful.]

These announcements are encouragingly clear, but not without problems. For if Low German has to be 'motley' by definition, in order to model the diversity discourse, there is the danger of making it serviceable again for cultural affirmation. Can one really escape homogenization with the argument of 'colourfulness'? And does Low German not remain a language in need of care even under the sign of diversity? In order to examine these questions more closely, it is advisable to take a look at official German and European policy with regard to minority languages.

In 1992, the Council of Europe adopted the European Charter for Regional or Minority Languages. With this, linguistic diversity became an official concern of European politics. Since Germany ratified the treaty in 1999, five minority languages have been recognized here, one of which — Sorbian — is Slavic and a second — Romany — belongs to the Indo-Aryan languages. The remaining three are North or West Germanic: Danish, Frisian and Low German. The fact that in a German-speaking country a Germanic language is marked as minor may seem strange. Strictly speaking, Low German is not a minority language, but a regional language. However, the concern of European language policy is precisely to avoid this strict distinction and to combine the protection of regional and minority languages in the same programme of language policy. By definition in article 1 of the Charter,

> 'Regional or minority languages' means languages that are:
> i. traditionally used within a given territory of a State by nationals of that State who form a group numerically smaller than the rest of the State's population; and
> ii. different from the official language(s) of that State.⁴

Since the words 'traditionally' and 'nationals of that State' are used, it becomes clear that linguistic diversity due to historically recent migration movements (in the case of German, for example, through immigration of 'guest workers' since the 1950s) is thus not the subject of the Charter. Furthermore, it is noticeable that in the cited article the minority status of a language is closely linked to its regionality. The language community or 'group' is understood as a spatially situated entity that can be located in a 'given territory'. It should be noted, however, that 'non-territorial languages' are explicitly mentioned in article 1 of the Charter, which is of particular importance for Romany among the minority languages in Germany. Danish, Frisian and Sorbian, on the other hand, are limited to small regions in Schleswig-Holstein and Brandenburg, respectively, outside of which they virtually do not exist as languages in Germany. (Yet this raises the question of what kinds of minority language would emerge if small population groups spoke Sorbian in Saarbrücken or Frisian in Frankfurt.)

By contrast, the territory of Low German is much more extensive, which can be seen in language atlases, one of the most common media for spatial mapping of languages and territories.[5] According to these maps, Low German encompasses the entire region north of the so-called Benrath Line: everything that is not High German in historical terms, i.e., that has not undergone the second sound shift since the middle of the first millennium AD.[6] Yet Low German was a complete written, official and literary language only until the beginning of the early modern period; from then on, High German increasingly took over these functions for the entire German-speaking area. The distinction between Low and High German therefore concerns not only the geographical distribution between the North German lowlands and the Middle and Upper German highlands, but also aspects of sociolect and the attitude of the speakers to their language. According to this notion, Low German, especially evident in the designation 'Platt', is a simple, plain language in which people speak straightforwardly. The same applies to the various attempts at reliterarization, which from the eighteenth to the middle of the twentieth century almost always emphasized the vernacular and popular, for example, in Johann Heinrich Voß's Low German idylls of the 1770s, or, about one century later, in Klaus Groth's folksong-like poems and Fritz Reuter's realistic-autobiographical novels.

Such a reduction to the supposed simplicity and expressiveness of the vernacular is no longer found in today's language policy. Instead, the European Language Charter names as its goal 'the recognition of the regional or minority languages as an expression of cultural wealth'.[7] This means first of all a prohibition of discrimination: the contracting states undertake 'to eliminate, if they have not yet done so, any unjustified distinction, exclusion, restriction or preference relating to the use of a regional or minority language and intended to discourage or endanger the maintenance or development of it'.[8] Yet the main part of the Charter also lists a large number of proactive measures in the fields of education, law, public service, media, culture, economy and cross-border exchange, by which the recognition of minority languages is to be implemented.

Implementation is not easy, though. In Germany, this is especially true because of the federal structure, which is always dominant in cultural matters. The measures taken in the participating federal states were and are correspondingly different. (Incidentally, these are not only the northern German states in the narrow sense, but also North Rhine-Westphalia, Brandenburg and Saxony-Anhalt; in other words, a total of eight of the sixteen federal states.) In a 2014 report, the Bundesraat för Nedderdüütsch [Federal Council for Low German], as the most important monitoring and advisory body in matters of Low German, criticized the fact that even fifteen years after ratification too little progress was discernible, especially in media policy, translation funding, and foreign cultural policy. Low German instruction in schools also left much to be desired.[9] From this finding, one may derive fundamental questions: did the responsible politicians and administrators fail? Were the goals too ambitious? Are they even feasible within the planned implementations? And is language culture in practice not entirely independent of such agreements and guidelines?

To answer such questions, it would be necessary to consider and research more closely how the official inclusion of Low German among the minority and regional languages has actually had an impact in practice. Empirical studies have indeed shown that speakers' attitudes toward Low German are currently changing. Apparently, Platt is gaining in esteem as an expression of linguistic and cultural diversity.[10] Certainly, the associations, initiatives and series of events mentioned at the outset have received considerable impetus as a result of the European Language Charter or have only been founded since then. Considering Low German as an integral part of European linguistic diversity is an innovative outlook. In literature, the relationship between linguistic regionality and linguistic minority is again given a different perspective. In what follows, I would like to use two current examples to show what possibilities for mapping languages and cultures emerge from this policy landscape.

'On the Way' to the 'Old Land': Dörte Hansen and Yared Dibaba

One of the great literary successes of the 2010s in Germany was Dörte Hansen's novel *Altes Land*, published in 2015. 'Altes Land' [old land] is the name of a marshland at the side of the River Elbe, near Hamburg. It is an important cultural landscape, interesting for certain techniques of land reclamation and of fruit production, as well as for the ancient rural half-timbered houses. Dörte Hansen situates her novel in one of these houses. This is the setting for a multi-generational story, focusing on two female figures: one is Vera, who has been living in this place ever since she came here as a small girl after the Second World War, fleeing with her mother from East Prussia; the other is Anne, Vera's niece, who comes to live with her aunt after splitting up with her partner. The two stories, of the two women getting together and of Vera's earlier life, are constantly intertwined, as are their narratives of flight and displacement: Vera's post-war situation and Anne's private unhappiness. This does not mean that the obvious historical differences are levelled, but nonetheless the novel suggests certain parallels of female destinies and of coping with them.

The novel is written in High German; otherwise it could not have sold tens of thousands of copies. But there are a significant number of Low German phrases in the text, starting on the very first page with the description of the house. On the gable there is an inscription which says: 'Dit Huus is mien un doch nich mien, de no mi kummt, nennt't ook noch sien' [This house is mine and isn't mine, he who succeeds me will call it his]'.[11] This chronotopical motto — which turns out to be a leitmotif in the novel — is said to be the first Low German phrase that the little Vera had learned as a displaced child; the second one (still on the first page) is the aggressive question raised by the landlady, 'Woveel koomt denn noch vun jau Polacken?' [How many of you Polacks are going to follow?].[12] These two initial Low German phrases are followed by many others, especially in those parts where Vera's life story is narrated. This is plausible in the realistic context of the novel, since in the 1950s, '60s and '70s there were many native speakers remaining in the countryside. Interestingly, however, Low German is also used within the present setting, which often deals with the fashion for country manners among townspeople, resulting in certain acts of what might almost be called cultural appropriation. There is one particularly narcissistic character who comes to the Altes Land from Hamburg, just like Anne, but for different reasons, namely, to write 'books on the country life and articles for a slow food magazine'.[13] He loves to be photographed in rural clothing by his fellow journalists and is fond of his own authentic appearance: 'Er streute kleine plattdeutsche Brocken in seine Sätze, er sagte "kiek mol an!" oder "dat segg man!", und zum Abschied rief er, kurz und kernig, "seh to!"' [He interspersed small fragments of Low German into his phrases, he said 'Kiek mol an' [expression of slight surprise] 'Dat segg man!' [expression of affirmation], and for goodbye he curtly said, 'seh to!'].[14]

A High German reader can easily understand these short expressions and exclamations from their contexts. They do not affect the readability of the High German text (although the novel probably sold better in the Northern parts of Germany than in the South). However, there exists a version with a bigger share of Low German, namely, a radio play which was co-produced promptly after the novel's publication by two public broadcasting stations (Radio Bremen and Northern German Broadcasting). The genre of the radio play has been a very important part of Low German literary life since the post-war period, and still is to date, with regular productions being broadcast on an almost weekly basis.[15] The audio version of *Altes Land*, written and directed by Wolfgang Seeskow, translates the complex temporal structure of the novel by using overlaying voices, such as the narrator describing a situation which is simultaneously performed by the actresses and actors (using different auditive spaces to create distinctions between foreground and background). This procedure leads to an intertwining of languages, the narrator's High German contrasting with some of the characters' Low German, the latter being considerably more frequent than in the original text of the novel. Thus, the technical skills of the radio play are being used to stage phenomena of language contact and of diglossia.

Incidentally, Dörte Hansen herself is not only a bilingual High and Low German speaker but also a trained linguist who wrote her PhD dissertation on language contacts between High and Low German.[16] According to this thesis, the differences between the two German languages are to a certain extent levelled, in bilingual speakers. As for grammar and lexis, these speakers tend to speak Low German 'like' High German, practising linguistic analogies and parallel connections. Ironically, Low German native speakers often seem to be least capable of recognizing it as a genuine language and, given that High German will always be their language of education, understand Low German as a dialect.[17] Diglossia thus produces interesting effects of hybridity and impurity that are sometimes understood as a threat to linguistic purity. This is not so much a problem for the standard language, which will always be robust enough to cope with such effects, but it is often condemned by the advocates of minority or regional language, who insist that the task of minority or regional literature — and culture, more generally — is to partake in the project of safeguarding that language.

This brings me to my second example. Hamburg-based Yared Dibaba is a prolific Low German author, as well as an actor, presenter and singer. He was born in 1969 in southwestern Ethiopia and first came to Germany at the age of four, when his father was studying for a time in Osnabrück. He learned High German in kindergarten through 'immersion', as he stated in an interview 2016.[18] The family returned to Ethiopia, but had to flee the civil war in 1976, moving to Germany again and settling in a village near Oldenburg, where a relatively large amount of Low German was still spoken. In this interview, Dibaba recalls that he was immediately taken with the language, which he refers to as his 'home language', in addition to the 'mother tongue', Oromo, which, however, as he recounts in the interview, he forgot during the childlike, immersive reception of German and had to reacquire in Ethiopia. In this complex back and forth of language acquisition, he sees Oromo and Platt as closely connected, even as equals — through their regionality, which has as much to do with limitation and peripherality as with rootedness.

Yared Dibaba has been appearing in various TV formats for about fifteen years, many of them on Norddeutscher Rundfunk's Third Television Programme. In programmes like *De Welt op Platt* ['The World in Low German'] (2006–07), broadcast in High German but with interviews and other interjections in Low German, he has positioned himself as a cosmopolitan North German. A series of tutorials can be found on YouTube in which Dibaba, sitting in front of a fireplace background and using witty didactics in the style of 'Sesame Street', introduces the basics of Low German.[19] The North German regional language is presented by someone who is clearly 'from here' in terms of language and cultural affiliation, but who just as obviously does not look 'North German' by traditional standards. In such performances, the crossing of attributions — Low German, Afro-German — is likely to produce an eye-opening effect in many viewers. In contrast to the usual interweaving of linguistic and regional affiliation in the discourse on Low German, here one learns that linguistic competence has nothing to do with autochthony.

As an author, Dibaba contributes to a Low German radio programme that has been established for decades (*Hör mal'n beten to* [*Listen a While*]). He has published the short stories presented there and elsewhere in several books, including *Ünnerwegens* in 2016.[20] This book with its programmatic title (*On the Way*) contains several texts with which Dibaba participates in current discussions about migration, belonging, majority and minority culture, foreign and self-attribution. What he expresses there combines political (perhaps, even, 'politically correct') statements with problems of linguistic marking that appear overdetermined in regional and minority language discourse in interesting ways. Thus, under the heading 'Flüchtling langt nich' [Refugee is not enough], he criticizes the imprecise use of this word in current migration debates. According to Dibaba, the German word 'Flüchtling' sounds 'as if someone just made for the other side',[21] so it would be more suitable for stress-ridden vacationers or tax evaders. On the other hand, the people who are mostly called refugees today should better be called displaced persons: 'Dat sünd Verdrevene — de hebbt se vun ehr Heimat verjoogt' [These are displaced persons — they chased them out of their homeland].[22]

In another text, entitled 'Wo fangt de Süden an?' [Where does the South begin?], Dibaba addresses typical prejudices against people in the European or global South. He asks, with deliberate naiveté, where the South begins: south of the Elbe in Hamburg-Harburg? In Cologne? In southern Germany? Or only south of Germany, in Austria? He thus sets the relativity of the term 'South' against essentialist determinations and thus also brings up his own status as a 'southerner', which he then relates to his Ethiopian origin:

> Bün ik een Südlänner? Vertell mol een Südafrikoner de Dibaba ut Oromia in Äthiopien is een Südlänner, he kümmt ut den Süden — tja, dor passt dat denn ok nich. Büst du Südlänner wenn du blots swatte Hoor hest? Denn bün ik definitiv keen Südlänner — ik heff keen Hoor. Dorför heff ik een Seemannspulli un een Freesennerz und schnack gern Platt, also bün ik definitiv Nordlänner.[23]
>
> [Am I a southerner? Tell a South African that the Dibaba from Oromia in Ethiopia is a southerner, that he comes from the south — well, that doesn't fit there. Are you a southerner if you have black hair? Then I am definitely not a southerner — I have no hair. But I have a sailor sweater and a Friesennerz [raincoat] and I like to speak Platt, so I'm definitely a northerner.]

In this witty way, Yared Dibaba treats the sensitive topic of belonging, so often discussed when it is about Low German culture. Under the heading 'Dat is een vun uns' [That's one of us] he writes a tribute to German rock singer Udo Lindenberg on the occasion of his seventieth birthday. Since Lindenberg is known to live in Hamburg, Yared states, he is often mistaken for a 'real North German', even though he comes from Gronau near the German-Dutch border.[24] Dibaba ironically calls this the singer's 'migration background', adding that some of Lindenberg's ancestors supposedly came from a former Dutch colony, the Indonesian Moluccas. The implication is: 'Molukken — Holland — Gronau — Hamborg — ik segg doch, Udo Lindenbarg — dat is een von uns! [Moluccas — Holland — Gronau — Hamburg — I already told you, Udo Lindenberg — that's one of us!].[25]

Conclusions

The finding that all 'of us', depending on the context, are not 'from here' but from elsewhere, consequently predominantly different, might seem trivial — but only in the linguistic-literary environment of the majority culture. In Low German, on the other hand, the concept of belonging still requires fundamental reflection, because it is usually related entirely to the affirmation of regional identity. In this sense, the 'small' Low German literature is probably truly capable of contributing to the representation, reconstruction and reshaping of a cultural community understood as 'threatened'. So the argument can be raised — and is being raised in more essentialist approaches — that as a minority and regional literature it should be as pure as possible, in order to fulfil the imperative of safeguarding. In this vein, regionalism and provincialism continue to be promoted in Low German, as they are in many other 'small' literatures. As for the broader literary market, the 'pure' Low German literature does not appear there at all. It is hardly ever translated into High German or other languages.

This is not a problem specific to Low German literature, but is equally found in the 'small literatures' of other European minority languages. Basque, Sardinian, or Scottish Gaelic literatures are also claimed for the (re)formation of linguistic-cultural communities that have to assert themselves in a majority culture, often explicitly against it. Such literatures are therefore required to adopt a strategy of linguistic demarcation in order to maintain a clear difference from the main and official language, and not to be influenced by them, for example, in grammar and lexis. The tendency toward isolationism has its price. The small literatures are perceived almost exclusively within the respective minority language, hardly ever translated into the majority language or even transnationally. It would be interesting, however, to imagine that the European regional and minority languages would increasingly establish contact with each other — in translations from Catalan into Sorbian, from Romany into Sicilian, etc.

Compared to such utopian visions of translation, both Dörte Hansen's restrained bilingualism in High and Low German, used only situatively, and Yared Dibaba's contributions to Low German literature seem to remain more connected to an attitude that seeks to protect the inviolability of the minority culture. This is noticeable when Dibaba makes the Low German language itself the subject of his reflexions. Here the argumentation sometimes seems astonishingly restrictive, for example when he argues for a decidedly Low German stance and against the use of Anglicisms. Hence the title of one of his texts: 'Lever een Platt-Attitüde as jümmers Anglizissmen' [Rather a Low German Attitude than always Anglicisms].[26] But in truth both examples that I have introduced open up a non-purist argument in the debate about regional and minority literature. They do so in their respective ways of using Low German: in re-arrangements of 'self' and 'other', in effects of language shift and linguistic migration, in crossover phenomena between German and other languages, all of which question the nativeness and naturalness of the regional language in its very ties to the territory and to the speakers.

Within this argument there is still enough space for negotiating questions of community. In Dibaba this leads to particularly interesting contradictions, as he puts the regional bond, the naturalness and immediacy — in short, the nativeness — of Low German up for discussion by simultaneously affirming and doubting it. On the one hand, he seems to insist again and again that Low German is somehow appropriate to Northern Germany: both to the land and to the people, *Land und Lü*. On the other hand, he uses his own biography as an argument against the myth of the autochthonous interrelationship of language, speakers, and region. The resulting concept of speaker community and language territoriality is inclusive; it is based on encounter, curiosity, and mutual willingness to learn. That is what Dibaba's experiences with learning High and Low German as well as with learning and relearning his mother tongue Oromo stand for. His story is about ever new linguistic immersions and how languages themselves diversify — within those who speak them.

Notes to Chapter 8

1. Annie Heger, 'Editorial', *Plattart. Festival Neue Niederdeutsche Kultur 10. bis 19. März 2017* [programme], p. 1 <https://oldenburgische-landschaft.de/uploads/live/aktuelles/103/programmheft2017.pdf> [accessed 23 March 2021]. All translations in this chapter are mine.
2. Cf. Nicolai Scherle, *Kulturelle Geographien der Vielfalt: Von der Macht der Differenzen zu einer Logik der Diversität* (Bielefeld: Transcript, 2016).
3. Heger, p. 1.
4. Council of Europe, *European Charter for Regional or Minority Languages. Strasbourg, 5.XI.1992*, article 1 <https://www.coe.int/en/web/conventions/full-list/-/conventions/rms/0900001680695175> [accessed 23 March 2021].
5. Susanne Gal calls the geopolitics of language as such a 'project of mapping'. The actual language maps then 'represent this conception iconically with solid lines marking boundaries and spaces within these lines'. Susanne Gal, 'Language and Political Spaces', in *Language and Space: An International Handbook of Linguistic Variation*, ed. by Peter Auer and Jürgen Erich Schmidt (Berlin and New York: De Gruyter Mouton 2010), pp. 33–49 (p. 35–36).
6. For historical and regional distinctions, cf. *Niederdeutsch: Grenzen, Strukturen, Variation*, ed. by Helmut H. Spiekermann and others (Vienna, Cologne and Weimar: Böhlau, 2016).
7. *European Charter for Regional or Minority Languages*, article 7.1.a.
8. Ibid., article 7.2.
9. Cf. *Chartasprache Niederdeutsch: Rechtliche Verpflichtungen, Umsetzungen und Perspektiven*, ed. by Christiane Ehlers (Bremen: Bundesraat för Nedderdüütsch, 2014).
10. Cf. Birte Arendt, *Niederdeutschdiskurse: Spracheinstellungen im Kontext von Laien, Printmedien und Politik* (Berlin: Schmidt, 2010); Carolin Jürgens, *Niederdeutsch im Wandel: Sprachgebrauchswandel und Sprachwahrnehmung in Hamburg* (Hildesheim: Olms, 2015).
11. Dörte Hansen, *Altes Land. Roman* (Munich: Knaus, 2015), p. 7.
12. Ibid.
13. Ibid., p. 90. 'Jetzt schrieb er Bücher über das Landleben und Kolumnen für ein Slow-Food-Magazin'.
14. Ibid.
15. Cf. Cornelia Fieker, *Das literarisch ambitionierte niederdeutsche Hörspiel* (Leer: Schuster, 1985); Ingrid Straumer, 'Plattdeutsches Hörspiel im Aufwind?', *Quickborn*, 93 (2003), 33–35.
16. Cf. Dörte Hansen, *Transfer bei Diglossie: Synchrone Sprachkontaktphänomene im Niederdeutschen* (Hamburg: Kovač, 1995).
17. In the 1970s, linguist Heinz Kloss termed this phenomenon of language attitude 'pseudo-dialect': Heinz Kloss, 'Abstandsprachen und Ausbausprachen', in *Zur Theorie des Dialekts*, ed. by Joachim Göschel and others (Wiesbaden: Steiner, 1976), pp. 301–22 (pp. 303, 305).

18. '"Ich bin mit allen Sinnen in die Sprache und Kultur eingetaucht". Interview mit Yared Dibaba', *Bildungsthemen*, 1 (2016), 12–14.
19. Cf. <https://www.youtube.com/watch?v=rb3P2hv8aP8> [accessed 23 March 2021].
20. Yared Dibaba, *Ünnerwegens* (Hamburg: Quickborn, 2016). Other titles (all Hamburg, Quickborn): *Platt is mien Welt* (2009), *Mien Welt blifft Platt* (2011), *Moin tosomen!* (2014).
21. '[...] as wenn sik een vun Acker mookt hett' (Dibaba, *Ünnerwegens*, p. 29). Literally translated: 'as if someone got off the field' (i.e., in order to take an undeserved break).
22. Ibid., p. 31.
23. Ibid., p. 33.
24. Ibid., p. 27. 'Udo Lindenbarg — veele Lüüd hebbt ja dat Geföhl — Udo, dat is een echten Noorddüütschen — dorbi is he in Gronau op de Welt komen [...] avers da is nicht de eenzige Migratschoonsachtergrund, den he hett' [Udo Lindenberg — many people feel — Udo, that's a true North German — but he was born in Gronau [...] and that's not the only migration background he has].
25. Ibid., p. 28.
26. Ibid., p. 44.

CHAPTER 9

Lontano da Mogadiscio and *Nuvole sull'equatore*: Belonging, Language and the Market[1]

Simone Brioni and Shirin Ramzanali Fazel

According to Donald Pease, the relationship between novelists and critics has often been imagined 'in such a way that the author seemed an effect of the critic's interpretation rather than a cause of the work'.[2] It is possible to rethink this relationship by looking at novels as a dialogue between different parts — the author, the market, the critics, and the readers, among others — rather than simply a reflection of the author's thoughts that needs to be deciphered by the critics. The author is not a prophet and his or her text is not holy, but he or she is part of a constant interpretative and discursive process that involves many people who share their agency, creativity and competence. To look at the text as the result of such dialogue does not only mean to change the way we understand reading and writing practices, but to rethink the notion of *impegno* [commitment] beyond the top-down approach of cultural formation.[3] In other words, to show that the dialogue from which a text originated has political implications and aims to locate the activity of professional readers and writers within a broader set of power relationships.

The aim of this chapter is to expand on a dialogue that started in 2012 and led to the publication of Shirin Ramzanali Fazel's own translation into English of two texts she originally published in Italian. The first was her 1994 autobiographically inspired novel *Lontano da Mogadiscio* [Far from Mogadishu],[4] which was republished in Italy in 2013 by Laurana as a bilingual e-book called *Lontano da Mogadiscio/Far from Mogadishu*,[5] and again in 2016 as an English translation of the novel in printed form, through a print-on-demand service by Amazon.com, CreateSpace. The second was her *Nuvole sull'equatore: gli italiani dimenticati. Una storia* [Clouds over the Equator: The Forgotten Italians. A Story],[6] whose English translation was released in 2017 in printed form, again through CreateSpace.[7] Referring to the many articles that have been dedicated to Shirin's first novel, the introduction to *Lontano da Mogadiscio* maintains that it 'is crucial in the contemporary literary panorama for at least three reasons: the contribution to decolonizing Italian memory, the testimony of a black person's experience living in Italy from the 1970s to the 1990s, and in the present version, to the 2000s, and the memory of a Mogadishu destroyed by a devastating Civil War beginning in 1991, in view of a possible reconstruction of Somalia'.[8] These features perhaps explain why Datanews reprinted this text twice, in 1994 and 1997, and a third edition of the novel was released in 1999. Simone described the process of collaboration that led to the publication of the fourth edition of *Lontano da Mogadiscio* in these terms:

> In synergy and in a desire to bring her text to a larger audience, Shirin and I found a publisher and proposed a bilingual edition. Throughout the process our goal was to deliver the best product in the time available and with the resources available. This also meant discussing with Shirin some solutions that could mediate the suggestions of the proof-readers and her original translation, in order to retain the authenticity of Shirin's voice and the complexity of her writing but at the same time provide to the English reader a fluid text, which could be also used as didactic material in courses of Italian Studies, Somali Studies, Diaspora Studies, and Transnational Feminist Studies.[9]

Shirin's second novel, *Nuvole*, was originally published by a 'minor' Italian publisher based in Cuneo, Italy: Nerosubianco.[10] Set during the period of the Italian trusteeship of Somalia, the key themes of the novel are the protagonist Amina's agency and the emancipation from male authority,[11] and the discrimination against her daughter Giulia, because she is a *meticcia* [mixed-race] person. This novel investigates the legacy of the Italian racial laws in Somalia, such as Law 1019 of 1936, which denied *meticci* their Italian citizenship, and law 880 of 1937 that punished interracial unions with five years of imprisonment.[12] Italy also enforced apartheid measures through the racial laws of 1938.

This collaborative text shows the difficulties that Shirin has faced in publishing and making her text available. Despite the fact that modern technology has made it easier to publish and circulate literature, this text argues that 'minority' authors still face difficulties in bringing their work to the cultural market. Shirin's novels can be considered as an example of 'minority literature' because migration literature 'has a minor status with respect to the culture and the language in which it has been produced' and 'it provides a representation of the minor condition of subjects who are discriminated in terms of race, class, religion, and gender'.[13] Shirin is an Italian woman of Pakistani and Somali origins who wears a *hijab*, and she recounts her autobiographically inspired experiences of discrimination and marginalization. Moreover, Shirin's works were mostly published by publishers that did not have 'strong distribution networks'.[14] Along with noting the limited circulation of these texts within a national context, it is important to acknowledge that postcolonial literature in Italian occupies a minor role in the global context, which is dominated by novels written in French or English.[15] The use of the term 'minor' to identify Shirin's literature refers to Gilles Deleuze and Félix Guattari's concept of 'minor literature'.[16] Simone has argued elsewhere the extent to which Shirin's work and that of other Somali Italian writers relate to the three criteria that characterize this literature according to Deleuze and Guattari,[17] namely 'the deterritorialization of language, the connection of the individual to a political immediacy, and the collective assemblage of enunciation'.[18] What is important to remark in this context is that, despite its '"minor" condition', Shirin's literature might have inspired a major change in Italian literature, given that many novels about colonialism have been published since *Lontano da Mogadiscio* was released, and writers publishing with major Italian publishers like Wu Ming 2[19] and Igiaba Scego[20] have acknowledged Shirin's influence on their works.

Dialogue is intended in this chapter as a methodology that can support and help position our artistic practices and scholarly research, respectively. Our dialogue is structured around three key topics — Belonging, Language, and Market — and it reflects on the challenges we have encountered in our quest to make these books more widely available. An important aim of this text is to identify key themes in literature about migration and suggest new ways of reading texts such as *Lontano da Mogadiscio* and *Nuvole sull'equatore*, rather than approaching them with the same expectations and questions readers would have when reading canonized texts, such as Dante Alighieri's *Commedia*.[21] In other words, a new critical terminology is needed in order to understand the innovative idioms that Shirin and other migrant writers have invented in order to describe a reality that has lacked representation, such as Italian colonialism, or which has frequently been misrepresented, such as contemporary migrations to Italy.

Belonging

My sense of belonging does not confine me into one country, one continent, one ethnic group. I feel comfortable with people of different creed and nationality; maybe it is because I have travelled and lived in different parts of the world, including Italy, Kenya and the UK. Nonetheless, many people keep asking me: 'Where are you from?' The obvious answer is the city where I live, but they are not satisfied by my answer. 'Where are you from *originally*?' 'Where were you born?' 'Where are your parents from?' They always try to strip off all the layers of my identity, and I feel I have to justify my own existence.

My belonging to Italy has deep roots, because I speak and I write in Italian, which is part of the colonial legacy of the Italian presence in Somalia. I was eighteen years old when I received my Italian passport: I was able to vote and I got involved not only emotionally but also juridically with this country. In that very moment, I felt I belonged to Italian culture. In Italy I have raised my

The term 'immigration' does not account for the many conditions in which a person moves from one country to another. Let me explain this statement by comparing my experience of migration with that of Shirin. Shirin and I have known each other since 2010, when we were both Italian citizens living in the UK. Some would have considered me an 'expat', part of Italy's 'brain drain', and Shirin a Muslim or an 'immigrant' (writer) — as if she had no 'brain' to export, was not residing in a country other than that of her upbringing, and her religion was only important to mention because it emphasizes an irreducible difference between her and those who have other or non-religious beliefs — thus showing the implicit racism that defines the migratory experience of people of European and African origins.[23] The 'brain drain' and 'expat' rhetoric is used to cover the fact that Italy is still a country of emigration, and many of the young people have left the country because of precarious job conditions rather than to fulfil their career aspirations

daughters and buried my parents. My grandchildren are growing up there.

Unfortunately the majority of my fellow citizens do not accept me as an Italian. When I say I am Italian, they say: 'You do not look Italian'. Why is a person of my color always considered an immigrant in my country, and is he/she associated with people who bring criminality, drugs, prostitution and terrorism?

Twenty years back I was travelling to Rome by train. I asked the man sitting in the compartment if the seat next to him was vacant. He looked at me in a judgmental way and replied: 'Yes, it is vacant, but this is the first class!' It hit me to see that this man assumed in his little brain that a person of colour was poor and could not afford a first-class ticket. Calmly, I replied: 'I have a first-class ticket!'

Things have not changed much today in Italy. It annoys me when Italian officers at the custom border give that suspicious look and scrutinize my passport as if I have stolen it. Last summer I went on holidays to Tunisia, and on my way back to the Venice airport, I changed my flight at Rome Fiumicino airport. I was approached by a policewoman who asked me in English: 'Do you speak English?' At my affirmative answer, she intimated: 'Follow me!' It was like receiving a bucket of cold water in my face. I knew where she was taking me, many of my friends told me how embarrassed and humiliated they felt at Fiumicino when they were asked to take off their hijabs. Several times I have wondered how would I react if the same happened to me, and I tried to mentally prepare for this scenario. Nonetheless, everything happened so fast at Fiumicino that I was caught off guard. I was numb. I followed this woman and before entering the searching room I told her in Italian: 'I know. You want me to

or intellectual curiosity.[24] While in Italy, Shirin was often considered a foreigner; in contrast, her Italian-ness was frequently acknowledged by Italians in the United Kingdom. If I had stayed in the UK after the British vote to leave the European Union, I might have shared with Shirin — although with significant differences due to my white-looking appearance — a similar condition of uncertainty and a similar feeling of being unwelcomed that European 'immigrants' may experience in the post-Brexit scenario.

My status as foreigner in the UK and the US was characterized by the experience of teaching Italian Studies, which made me feel like I was functioning as a representative of 'Italian culture' abroad for my students and within the communities in which I lived. How could I explain to my students that when I lived in Rome, Romans frequently asked me where I was from (often implying from which other country), because of my accent? How could I tell them that the food I missed the most from my hometown Brescia was 'kebab'? My way of approaching or taking distance from 'Italian culture' through an ethnic signifier like food was radically different from the one expressed by my parents. While they would identify in 'polenta' the traditional food of our area, my answer would — except for the presence of swear words, which are employed in the song to emphasize the frequent use of imprecations in Brescia — go along the lines of the song 'POTA F**A ALÜRA ENCÜLET' [swear words frequently used in Brescia] (2018) by Ukrainian Italian rapper Slava: 'Sono di Brescia, sono un fottuto polentone | Che mangia il kebab con cipolla a colazione | Che dice *pota encület* a ripetizione | Ti chiamo *vecio* se non mi ricordo il nome | Brescia | Cresciuti in mezzo a queste strade con i *gnari* | Brescia | La capitale dei

take off my hijab!' Her jaw dropped. As I was not prepared to follow her orders, she was surprised that I was defending my dignity. I stripped my headscarf and ran my fingers through my hair before she could touch me. 'I have nothing to hide.' I said. She was embarrassed: '*Signora*, we are no lawmakers.' Showing a fake smile, I put my hijab back on my head: 'Would you be so kind to tell your superiors that Muslim women have a bright brain under the headscarf?' Spontaneously, I kissed her on the cheek and left the room. Until now I do not realize how I came up with that reaction, how these words came out from my mouth. I was very upset, but not at her. She was doing her job. This kind of experience left me feeling violated. It is not easy to explain how I feel about it, I can just say that it stays with me. I wish that the policewoman will remember my words.

I get that same unwanted attention in the UK. In Birmingham, I felt comfortable walking around, since most people accepted my headscarf. However, a lot has changed since the process of withdrawal of the United Kingdom from the European Union has begun. Muslim women wearing the hijab are insulted, spat on, and beaten. Their headscarf is pulled off. Hate crime against people who are not white and carry a different accent is on the rise. Brexit has created an atmosphere of silent terror that is always in the back of my mind. My rationality and my being a positive person give me the strength to live my daily life calmly.

As an African European person, I feel under threat because of racism, but I also feel the urgency to testify to stories that I witnessed and many European and Africans of the diaspora do not know about. In October 2017, I was invited to the Somali week festival in London. It was wonderful to have the hall packed with young Somalis. Normally it is not migliori kebabbari' [I am from Brescia, I am a fucking polenta eater | Who eats kebab with onion at breakfast | Who continuously swears | I call you 'old man' if I don't remember your name | Brescia | Grown up in these streets with the boys | Brescia | The capital of the best kebab shops]. The popularity of kebab in Brescia is the result of the multicultural nature of a city in which the most common surname since 2012 is Singh.[25] I found myself discussing with students how the format of the British documentary program *Make Bradford British* (2012) could be used to highlight the presence in Brescia of two groups who do not feel exclusively or quite Italians: those (mostly dialect speakers) who supported in the 1990s the Lombard League — a separatist party that demanded the independence of Northern Italy[26] — and those who emigrated to Brescia and identify with more than one culture.

Indeed, my identification with symbols of Italianness has been further complicated when I moved to the US. It had been difficult to explain what symbols I associated with Italian culture to most members of the Italian American community, which came from the Southern Italy before I was even born. To keep with examples related to food — an aspect which frequently was used to define Italian identity in the US[27] — most of my students' grandparents probably had their first pizza before my grandparents, who told me with excitement when they ate their first pizza in the late 1960s in Brescia, since they moved to this town from a rural and isolated village named Brandico. As 'Pizza Hawaii' is present in most pizza places of Lake Garda, I perceive this 'foreign' interpretation of a typical Italian pizza as part of my own tradition. Indeed, I spent most of my summers at Lake Garda, where German tourists are

easy to gather all the youth in one place to discuss and share our work and ideas. Generally, we Somalis meet at weddings and funerals. I read some passages from *Far from Mogadishu* and poems from my book *Wings*.²² The majority of these youth have not been in Somalia, they were born and bred in London. Others came from Somalia as infants, when the civil war had already erupted. After the event, many girls bubbling with enthusiasm surrounded me. '*Habo*, you are so cool!' — they told me — 'I have never imagined you were listening to James Brown.' They were surprised that a lady like me, wearing a hijab, could speak so freely of her teenage years, when she was listening to music, dancing and going to the movie theatre. I felt like a survivor from a past that will never come back. I feel that sometimes we do not tell our kids our stories, as if the war has cancelled our history and our lives back in Somalia. Discrimination and the lack of memory are two of the most difficult tasks to overcome to raise our kids as European Muslims. The fact that many think that 'being European' means to be white and Christian shows that Europe is still battling to find its own identity. It saddens and surprises me the fact that I feel less a 'minority' when I travel as a privileged European tourist in Malaysia or in Kenya, because people do not judge me by the way I dress or I look.

so present that some street and shop signs are bilingual.

What some people expect me to talk about as an Italian Studies scholar are topics that promote Italy abroad, without redefining what it means to be Italian or interrogating Italy's national identity. However, the research of those who study migration and mobility crosses disciplinary and linguistic boundaries, therefore it cannot be unequivocally associated with one single Department, Program, or Unit within the Humanities. As a consequence, area studies specialists do not always receive favourably the interdisciplinary dialogue that the study of transnational migration engages with. For instance, in 2014 I received a letter from a professor of Italian Studies who vehemently rejected the edited volumes *Somalitalia: Quattro vie per Mogadiscio | Somalitalia: Four Roads to Mogadishu* and Ribka Sibhatu's *Aulò! Aulò! Aulò! Poesie di nostalgia, d'esilio e d'amore | Aulò! Aulò! Aulò! Poems of Nostalgia, Exile and Love*.²⁸ The letter reads 'Simone, I give you back this material, which does not belong to my field of research which is and remains that of *Italianistica*'. This letter made me interrogate the role of the study of national cultures in the reproduction of social and economic inequalities, which cuts off immigrants from representation, civil rights, and sense of belonging.

Language

Translation and multilingualism are part of my upbringing. I was born in Mogadishu in a mixed family where my parents spoke different languages. My relationship with the Somali language is linked to my land, to my childhood, to my mother. It feels like the sound of a musical instrument that has the magic to bring out my deepest emotions. My schooling followed an Italian curriculum as Somalia was an ex-colony of Italy, but I consider Somali my first language. In later years I spent most of my life travelling around the world where I picked up different dialects. It has always been easy and natural for me to juggle between different languages.

Today I am fortunate to be able to use the Somali language in a cosmopolitan city like Birmingham. I have also maintained friendly relations with old childhood friends and we speak in Somali. Listening to news and talk shows through satellite channels is a constant practice to enrich the language with new words. My decision to self-translate my two novels into English, comes from different needs. One is the fact that I moved to Britain, although I spend short periods in Italy, where I keep my home and family ties. I had two choices; to continue writing in Italian and have no contact with the country that hosts me, or to adapt to the new reality. It is very important to be part of the community where one lives. I love to engage with people, to challenge myself in new projects. Birmingham is a vibrant multi-ethnic city that gives me this opportunity. I was selected to be part of a ground-breaking project run by the United Nations Alliance of Civilizations (UNAOC) and the UK-based partner with the Radical Middle Way Institute of Narrative Growth called 'Storytelling for

> My tongue is like a
> contortionist
> Twisting rolling pulling
> That magic muscle
> — Shirin Ramzanali Fazel,
> extract from 'Stubbornness'[30]

The small Italian publisher Laurana, that specializes in e-books, allowed Shirin's English translation of her first novel *Lontano da Mogadiscio/Far from Mogadishu* to enter the international market through internet-based retailers. Unlike most novels written in Italian, it is striking that Shirin's first novel is available in English, given that — according to a report on all translations recorded in the British National Bibliography, available in the Literature Across Frontiers platform[31] — only 3% of books published in the United Kingdom (and even lower numbers of translations are published in the United States) have been translated from a foreign language on average in the past two decades. Moreover, this novel was included in the 'Reloaded' collection which — as the website of the publisher Laurana puts it — aims to 'recuperare la migliore narrativa italiana comparsa sugli scaffali tra gli anni Novanta e gli anni Duemila e poi scomparsa causa normale ciclo di smaltimento del sistema editoriale' [republishing the best Italian narratives that appeared on bookshelves between the 1990s and the 2000s, and then disappeared because of the short shelf life of books in the editorial system].[32] In other words, the re-print of the book allowed *Lontano da Mogadiscio/Far from Mogadishu* to be acknowledged as one of the best novels of that decade that have gone out of print, rather than as a novel written by an immigrant, as *Lontano da Mogadiscio* was originally presented.

It is interesting to note that *Lontano*

Somalia'. It was a retreat for journalists, change makers and creative people from the Somali Diaspora in Wales. A co-lab on journalism and storytelling with thirty creative change makers from all over the world. It was there, after meeting those very talented young Somali intellectuals, who grew up abroad and had no memories of the homeland except what was passed to them by their parents, that the need to translate my novel *Nuvole sull'equatore* became impelling.

It became clear to me that if I wanted to communicate with the Diaspora and the world I had to use the English language. It has not been an easy choice because English is not like Italian with which I have an intimate relationship. Italian is the language that I love and use every day with my family. My relationship with the English language has been for years a spoken language during my travels and transfers abroad. I have always preferred to watch movies, and read books in the original version. At first I did not feel comfortable translating because I did not have the professional tools; I thought about finding a translator, but it was expensive, and also I knew that with a pure literal translation of the novel a part of it would miss its originality. Self-translating my novels is a journey I took with a lot of humility, and I am aware of my limitations. I feel like a little girl who takes her first steps, and I know I'm not ready to run. I have tried in the new language to rewrite and keep the original voice. In fact, in this new version some words are in Italian. Rewriting and translating helped me to think and write directly in English. Sometimes I feel I am a different person. The publication of my short story, 'Foggy Dreams Under the Sunshine', in the anthology *Moments in Time* by Writers Without Borders Birmingham spurs me to continue.[29]

da Mogadiscio, as well as another key text of Italian literature about migration, Fernanda Farias de Albuquerque and Maurizio Iannelli's *Princesa* [*Princess*],[33] were published as e-books in 2013. This format gives users the opportunity to look up certain words, thus developing alternative paths of reading. Moreover, e-books allow readers to expand their reading online, and have an easy access to additional sources of information such as maps and dictionaries. As Aline Soules argues, 'The biggest advantage the e-book offers [...] is the anytime, anywhere accessibility that users love in the database and Web worlds'.[34] A third opportunity offered by e-books is their close relation with textuality, which gives readers the opportunity to easily re-write the text. To quote Soules again, the chapters of e-books 'may be searchable and navigable in a different way from the print works, but other features, such as the ability to "dog-ear" or "mark" portions or pages, are print concepts and terminology'.[35]

However, selling via online platforms limits the market of plurilingual works by allowing publishers to select just one language for the product description thus penalizing the audience of bilingual novels like *Lontano da Mogadiscio*. This example shows that, along with allowing new forms of publication, e-commerce reinforces the barrier that the cultural market imposes on 'minor' and hybrid products. It should also be noted that, as Elizabeth Kline and Barbara Williams argue, the e-book is still seen as bearing a different cultural value than a printed book.[36] Although new opportunities for publication have proliferated, it seems that the opportunities for 'minor' authors to be read and known by the general audience have remained the same.

Market

In the early 1990s, when the Civil War erupted in Mogadishu, I was very frustrated and felt helpless. My mind could not accept the images of war, destruction and looting I saw on television. The memories I had of my childhood were colliding with the everyday news. The old city had been destroyed, and I was losing my past. I started writing the first pages of my book as a diary. I kept it only for myself. It never crossed my mind to publish my diary. My husband encouraged me to share it with very close friends. They found it very interesting and their support gave me a lot of confidence. They were very surprised to discover the richness and the beauty of my country. They did not know that Italian culture had such a great influence on an entire generation of Somalis. I realized that my story could contribute to remind Italians of their colonial past, and to show a different representation of Somalia, which was not exclusively related to the Civil War.

After two years of hard work, I felt ready to send the manuscript to a couple of publishers. They replied it did not fit for any of their collections because it was a diary, rather than a novel. One early afternoon I was watching Nonsolonero, the first Italian television programme on immigration and racism. I had the idea to call them, and I spoke to the presenter Maria de Lourdes Jesus. She was very enthusiastic about my manuscript and she introduced me to the journalist Alessandra Atti di Sarro. Alessandra put me in contact with Datanews, my first publisher.

Lontano da Mogadiscio was received well, beyond any of my expectations, but the publisher did not support me to promote it. Women's networks, voluntary

The fact that texts by migrant writers have been mostly published by 'minor' publishing companies should not be seen exclusively in negative terms. Some of these publishers encouraged writers to experiment with language, producing texts that cannot be easily categorized within a specific genre, with one or more languages being interspersed. For instance, the publisher Sinnos produced a collection of bilingual books aimed at young readers and called 'I mappamondi'. The authors of these texts are migrant writers, who wrote the text in Italian and in another language they speak. As Graziella Parati argues, 'higher visibility could sensitize readers to important issues about migration, but one could also speculate that a series devoted to migrant writers might set the authors apart in a reductive category marked by isolation'.[37]

Moreover, I believe that these 'minor' publications had an impact in the Italian literary market. When *Lontano da Mogadiscio* came out in 1994, there were only a few contemporary Italian authors writing about colonialism. At present, almost every major Italian publishing house has published a narrative text that deals, although to different extents, with the legacy of Italian colonialism. For example, writer Igiaba Scego, who started her career with an audience that included exclusively readers interested in migration and colonialism, has acquired popularity and writes books and articles for the general public. These facts can arguably show that literature written by authors coming from former Italian colonies had some impact on Italian society and culture.

A proposal for the publication of *Nuvole sull'equatore* and a book chapter

associations working for migrants, friends and word of mouth were my best allies. Within two years, my book was reviewed in newspapers like *La stampa*, *Il corriere di Novara*, *Il gazzettino*, *Il giornale di Vicenza*, *La Gazzetta del Sud*, and magazines such as *Agorà*, *Avvenimenti*, *Internazionale*, and *Rocca*. I presented the book at schools, universities, cultural events, and political debates in Bologna, Brescia, Milano, Modena, Novara, Padova, Torino, and Vicenza. The audience always welcomed my presence very warmly. I was invited as a guest speaker at a panel within the Salone del Libro di Torino, the most important Italian book fair. I was the only woman among male journalists talking about the Somali war. It was not easy for me to be on this spot for the first time, and to speak to a large audience. I have also been invited twice to be member of the jury on the first competition for migrant writers Eks&Tra in Sant'Arcangelo di Romagna. In 1996 my husband and I decided to open a tourism related business in Kenya. We remained there for eight years. I had no idea the book got such a large visibility in academia and influenced other migrant writers. However, I still have no idea of how many copies of my books have been sold. Publishers never got back to me when I asked.

Almost twenty years later, migrant writers seem to have fewer opportunities to publish a book in Italy, since there are fewer small publishing houses specialized in this topic. As a consequence, I have carefully evaluated the choice of self-publishing. I took this decision because I needed physical copies of my book, as I am fond of the materiality of reading and I found it surreal to present an e-book in public, without an actual copy that proved its existence. I am really disappointed by the request for subventions to the authors were presented to four publishers from 2014 to 2016. Three of them, two based in Italy and one based in the United States and specialized in African diasporic literatures, accepted the book with minor revisions, but asked for a contribution towards the cost of publication. One publisher which specialized in translation from Italian rejected it, asking twice whether 'the book was written well in Italian'. This comment is based on a rather outdated idea of translation as a carbon copy of the original. However, I find it interesting, as it shows how the name of the author affects our reading of a novel.[38] If an Italian John Doe, Mario Rossi, had presented them with a novel, I doubt that a publisher would have questioned his proficiency in Italian. A small publisher specialized in e-books accepted the proposal without any cost for the writer, but Shirin decided not to accept their offer, because she preferred to release the book in print. If Marco Belpoliti is right to say that e-books are harder to remember because our memory needs a physical space in order to work,[39] Shirin's choice is justified by the fact that her writing testifies to stories that have already been rescued from oblivion.

Self-publishing seems a very common option for 'minor' writers, although print-on-demand companies extract a very high percentage of the sales proceeds for the services of publishing, printing and distributing. For instance, Laila Wadia — an Indian Italian writer who published some of her works with major publishing companies such as E/O and Laterza — used CreateSpace to publish *Kitchen Sutra. The Love of Language, the Language of Love. L'amore del linguaggio il linguaggio dell'amore*,[40] a bilingual text written in Italian and English. The transformation of these marginal texts into commodities of global exchange through publication by the publishing houses we contacted. I strongly believe that publishers should invest in the product they want to sell and take the risks of publication. I have never paid to publish and I want to stick to my principle.

I have always published with small publishing houses. Although I really respect their mission and I am grateful of the opportunity these publishing houses gave me, my books are really hard to find on the market. Therefore, my main concern in order to publish *Far from Mogadishu* and *Clouds over the Equator* was to enhance the accessibility of my books to the members of the Somali diaspora, given that the political situation in Somalia has still not stabilized.

by Amazon — a corporation whose global cultural influence and ideological homogenization rehearses colonial dynamics — outlines at best the ambiguities of postcolonial literature, which 'enact in an interdependent fashion both complicity with neo-colonial cultural industries and resistance to them'.[41]

Where We Stand

In an article about Italian postcolonial cultures, Roberto Derobertis asks: 'quando parliamo di postcoloniale, da dove parliamo "noi", che con il postcoloniale in Italia ci stiamo confrontando? Da che luogo e in quali condizioni strutturali e lavorative? [...] Su quali confini geografici e storici? Insomma, qual è la nostra *location*?' [When we talk about the postcolonial, from which point do 'we' — who are working on postcolonialism in Italy — speak? From which place and in which structural and working conditions? From which historical and geographical boundaries? In summary, what is our *location*?].[42] As we feel it is key to acknowledge and discuss our positions, we decided that we had to break away from the traditional structure and organization of academic writing in order to reproduce our dynamic conversation across continents, which was held from a distance. We therefore decided to intersperse our voices, producing a fragmented rather than linear text. Writing about migration does not only mean to acknowledge the hybridity, which characterizes the texts produced by migrant authors, but it may also mean to hybridize the ways in which we organize knowledge, to present a linguistic challenge to the reader, by showing the complexity of multicultural encounters, and to account for the fragmented nature of our experiences within a reality increasingly characterized by transnational connections.

An inspiring UK-based project that sparked our interest in sharing our agencies and competences as an activity that could decolonize research and writing practices was called Transnationalizing Modern Languages (2013–16). This project investigated 'practices of linguistic and cultural interchange within communities and individuals and explores the ways in which cultural translation intersects with linguistic translation in the everyday lives of human subjects within mobile and migrant communities'.[43] Shirin was part of the advisory board of this project and she has led a series of creative writing workshops called 'I Write with More than One Voice', which has gathered poets and playwrights from many different ethnic background and countries, such as Nigeria, Sudan, Somalia, Croatia, France, Bulgaria, and Poland. The diversity of the group enriched the understanding of the culture of the people who live in Birmingham, but who often do not have the chance to meet each other. The topics discussed included how to represent one's heritage, where to locate one's home, and how to express one's multilingual identity in English. As the Transnationalizing Modern Languages website points out, these interdisciplinary activities are aimed at facilitating a 'better understanding and communication between and across diverse cultures' and look at the 'role of translation, understood in its broadest sense, in the transmission, interpretation and sharing of languages, values, beliefs, histories and narratives'. These transnational and collaborative research practices — which include writers, scholars and practitioners among other professional figures — offer new resources and theoretical frameworks in order to answer a key question in globalized society: 'how do people respond creatively to living in a bi-lingual or multi-lingual environment and to identifying themselves as mobile individuals or communities?'. Shirin's response to this question was the creation of a poem called 'Afka Hooyo' [mother tongue]:

> The sounds I carry in my memories:
> I live in this bubble of voices –
> The sweet warm milk suckled from *hooyo*'s generous breast,
> My falling into sleep covered in a blanket of words.
>
> My first steps: I wobble, I fall, salty tears ploughing down my face [...]
> I stutter, struggle — a funny sound ...
> *Hooyo* laughs — she giggles ...
> She makes me repeat the same word again and again. [...]
>
> The sound of this language has memories
> Built brick by brick,
> It can move my deepest emotions –
> The hidden ones
> Like pearls buried at the bottom of the sea.
> This language is not always
> Mellow, pure, soft, musical, kind –
> This same language
> Can hurt, curse, wound my heart and leave invisible scars:
> These guttural harsh sounds can heal my soul. [...]
>
> I struggle when I have to read this language I love most,
> Written in an alphabet adopted from a foreign land,
> Signs not strong enough to lift my heavy tongue –
> I feel like a ballerina dancing on a broken toe.
> I abandon this newspaper,
> I refuse to read these words:
> Burcad badeed, burbur, baahi, argagixiso, cadow –
> Pirates, destruction, poverty, terrorism, enemy...

> *Dagaal, dhimasho, dhiig* –
> War, death, blood ...
>
> I treasure the language of poets:
> *Hooyo*'s lullabies,
> Jokes and proverbs ...
> Blessings and goodness –
> *Barako iyo wanaag.*[44]

[Simone] This poem presents some themes that are shared by those who have experienced migration: the struggle to articulate one's thoughts in a new language, the palimpsest of memories and dreams from the past that populates one's lived experience in a new cultural environment, and the multiple languages that are present in his/her/their voices. The text makes its English readership approach Somali words like *Hooyo* [mother] not as a 'foreign' but a 'familiar' linguistic presence, while it simultaneously shows Shirin's sense of estrangement in the pronunciation of words such as *argagixiso* and *burcad badeed*. While critical analysis has the power to conceptualize the experience of proximity or distance that is involved in experiences of migration, poetry has the power to make us feel distant or close to what we are representing. I believe that this interplay of different approaches, styles and points of view is fruitful in order to express in a coherent text an experience that is multilingual, multicultural and transnational.

[Shirin] I left Somalia in 1971, two years before the Somali language had a standardized system of writing. I was not educated to write in Somali, and I perceive Somali as an oral language. I feel like the Latin characters cannot lift my tongue properly when I read a Somali newspaper. It is like borrowing someone else's jacket. Too tight and unfamiliar for me. Hearing Somali takes me back to my childhood, when my mother was holding me in her arms while singing lullabies. The same lullabies that I had sung to my daughters, and now I am singing for my grandchildren. I associate lullabies to that hug, to a physical contact. Many European children that have been raised by a nanny from a different culture have, still vivid in their memories, the tune of a particular lullaby. Maybe they are not able to remember words anymore, but they still remember the sound, the expression of their nanny, her smell, the expression of her eyes, the sweet sensation of being held in her arms or some little fairy tales from the nanny's culture. 'Afka Hooyo' is a lullaby and a prayer for all the children who are growing up surrounded by war and violence, hearing words that I have never heard in my childhood, such as *argagixiso* and *burcad badeed*.

In conclusion, this article shows that despite the presence of new forms of publications such as e-books, there are still many hurdles for migrant authors to access the literary market, and in being recognized as protagonist voices of our contemporaneity. Since literary criticism can have the power — as Shirin maintains — to make 'migrant writers' feel like 'space invaders' of Italian literature,[45] we hope that the collaboration between scholars and writers can challenge the 'minor' role that authors who emigrated to Italy occupy in the present cultural industry.

Subverting the traditional roles of critic and author might be useful to rethink the post- and neo-colonial world we live in, in order to show that literature does not transcend social and economic forces, but it actively participates in social processes and changes.

Notes to Chapter 9

1. A modified and extended version of this text has been previously published in Simone Brioni and Shirin Ramzanali Fazel, *Scrivere di Islam: raccontare la Diaspora* (Venice: Ca' Foscari University Press, 2020).
2. Donald Pease, 'Author', in *Critical Term for Literary Studies*, ed. by Frank Lentricchia and Thomas McLaughlin (Chicago, IL: Chicago University Press, 1995 [1990]), pp. 105–17 (p. 111).
3. Jennifer Burns, *Fragments of Impegno: Interpretations of Commitment in Contemporary Italian Narrative, 1980–2000* (Leeds: Northern University Press, 2001).
4. Shirin Ramzanali Fazel, *Lontano da Mogadiscio* (Rome: Datanews, 1999 [1994]).
5. Shirin Ramzanali Fazel, *Lontano da Mogadiscio / Far from Mogadishu* (Milan: Laurana, 2013). English edition: Shirin Ramzanali Fazel, *Far from Mogadishu* (United Kingdom: CreateSpace, 2016).
6. Shirin Ramzanali Fazel, *Nuvole sull'equatore: gli italiani dimenticati. Una storia* (Cuneo: Nerosubianco, 2010). English edition: Shirin Ramzanali Fazel, *Clouds over the Equator* (United Kingdom: CreateSpace, 2017).
7. Somali proper names are mentioned by referring to the first name, which is the most common practice in African Studies. This choice has been taken to avoid the ambiguity caused by the westernization of these names. For instance, Shirin Ramzanali Fazel is most frequently mentioned in scholarly literature as Fazel, but also as Ramzanali Fazel. However, both of these simplifications lack linguistic legitimacy, and they might create more problems than they solve.
8. Simone Brioni, '"A Dialogue That Knows No Border Between Nationality, Race or Culture": Themes, Impact and the Critical Reception of Far from Mogadishu', in Shirin Ramzanali Fazel, *Lontano da Mogadiscio*, pp. 361–89.
9. Simone Brioni, *The Somali Within: Language, Race and Belonging in 'Minor' Italian Literature* (Cambridge: Legenda, 2015).
10. For a discussion of the 'minor position' of literature by Somali authors in Italy, see Ibid., pp. 145–55.
11. Jennifer Burns, *Migrant Imaginaries: Figures in Italian Migration Literature* (Oxford: Peter Lang, 2013), p. 57.
12. Gaia Giuliani, 'L'italiano negro: la bianchezza degli italiani dall'Unità al Fascismo', in *Bianco e nero: storia dell'identità razziale degli italiani*, ed. by Gaia Giuliani and Cristina Lombardi-Diop (Florence: Le Monnier, 2013), pp. 21–65 (p. 63).
13. Simone Brioni, *The Somali Within*, p. 7.
14. Ibid., p. 8.
15. Sandra Ponzanesi, *Paradoxes of Postcolonial Culture: Contemporary Women Writers of the Indian and Afro-Italian Diaspora* (Albany: State University of New York Press, 2004), p. xiv.
16. Gilles Deleuze and Félix Guattari, *Kafka: Toward a Minor Literature*, trans. by Dana Polan (Minneapolis: University of Minnesota Press, 1986 [1975]).
17. Simone Brioni, *The Somali Within*.
18. Gilles Deleuze and Félix Guattari, *Kafka*, p. 18.
19. Wu Ming 2 and Antar Mohamed, *Timira. Romanzo meticcio* (Turin: Einaudi, 2012), p. 516.
20. Igiaba Scego and Shirin Ramzanali Fazel, 'Scrittrice Nomade', *Internazionale*, 22 February 2008, p. 60.
21. Dante Alighieri, *The Divine Comedy*, ed. and trans. by Robert M. Durling, 3 vols (Oxford: Oxford University Press, 2007 [1321]).
22. Shirin Ramzanali Fazel, *Wings* (United Kingdom: CreateSpace, 2017).
23. On this concern, see Mawuna Remarque Koutonin, 'Why are white people expats when the

rest of us are immigrants?', *The Guardian*, 13 March 2015 <https://www.theguardian.com/global-development-professionals-network/2015/mar/13/white-people-expats-immigrants-migration>. On the criticism of the 'brain drain' rhetoric in Italy, see Alberto Prunetti, 'Per una critica del cervellone in fuga', *Il lavoro culturale*, 1 April 2016, <http://www.lavoroculturale.org/critica-del-cervellone-fuga-un-punto-vista-working-class/>.

24. On the data about migrations to Italy, see Caritas and Migrantes, *XXIX Rapporto Immigrazione 2020* (Rome: Caritas, 2021). On Italian emigration in the twenty-first century, see Maddalena Tirabassi and Alvise Del Prà, *La meglio Italia: le mobilità italiane nel XXI secolo* (Turin: Accademia University Press, 2014).
25. 'Cognomi più diffusi? A Brescia Singh batte Ferrari', *Giornale di Brescia*, 17 April 2012, <https://www.giornaledibrescia.it/brescia-e-hinterland/cognomi-pi%C3%B9-diffusi-a-brescia-singh-batte-ferrari-1.1164440>.
26. Anna Cento Bull and Mark Gilbert, *The Lega Nord and the Politics of Secession in Italy* (Basingstoke: Palgrave, 2001).
27. Simone Cinotto, *The Italian American Table: Food, Family, and Community in New York City* (Urbana, Chicago and Springfield: University of Illinois Press, 2013).
28. Ribka Sibhatu, *Aulò! Aulò! Aulò! Poesie di nostalgia, d'esilio e d'amore / Aulò! Aulò! Aulò! Poems of Nostalgia, Exile and Love*, ed. by Simone Brioni, trans. by André Naffis-Sahely (Rome: Kimerafilm, 2012).
29. Shirin Ramzanali Fazel, 'Foggy Dreams Under the Sun Sunshine', in *Moments in Time*, ed. by Writers Without Borders Birmingham (New York: Lulu, 2015), p. 56.
30. Shirin Ramzanali Fazel, *Wings*, p. 34.
31. Literatures Across Frontiers, 'Translation Statistics from LAF', 13 April 2015, <http://www.lit-across-frontiers.org/new-translation-statistics-from-laf/>.
32. Laurana, 'Reloaded', <http://www.laurana.it/index.php>.
33. Fernanda Farias de Albuquerque and Maurizio Iannelli, *Princesa*, 2013 [1994], <http://www.princesa20.it/>.
34. Aline Soules, 'New Types of E-books, E-book Issues and Implications for the Future', in *Adapting to E-books*, ed. by William Miller and Rita M. Pellen (London: Routledge, 2013), pp. 207–28 (p. 209).
35. Ibid., p. 207.
36. Elizabeth Kline and Barbara Williams, 'Managing Users' Expectations of E-books', in *Adapting to E-books* (London: Routledge, 2009), pp. 249–55 (p. 250).
37. Graziella Parati, *Migration Italy: The Art of Talking Back in a Destination Culture* (Toronto: University of Toronto Press, 2005), p. 100.
38. On this regard, see Catherine Nichols, 'Homme de Plume: What I Learned Sending My Novel Out Under a Male Name', *Jezebel*, 4 August 2015 <http://jezebel.com/homme-de-plume-what-i-learned-sending-my-novel-out-und-1720637627?utm>.
39. Marco Belpoliti, 'Perché non ricordo gli ebook?', *doppiozero.it*, 9 July 2012, <http://www.doppiozero.com/materiali/fuori-busta/perche-non-ricordo-gli-ebook>.
40. Laila Wadia, *Kitchen Sutra. The Love of Language, the Language of Love. L'amore del linguaggio il linguaggio dell'amore* (United Kingdom: Amazon, 2016).
41. Sandra Ponzanesi, *The Postcolonial Cultural Industry: Icons, Markets, Mythologies* (Basingstoke: Palgrave Macmillan, 2014), p. 48.
42. Roberto Derobertis, 'Da dove facciamo il postcoloniale? Appunti per una genealogia della ricezione degli studi postcoloniali nell'italianistica italiana', *Postcolonialitalia.it*, 17 February 2014, <https://www.postcolonialitalia.it/indexbb11.html?option=com_content&view=article&id=56:da-dove-facciamo-il-postcoloniale&catid=27:interventi&Itemid=101>.
43. See the website <https://www.transnationalmodernlanguages.ac.uk/>.
44. Shirin Ramzanali Fazel, *Wings*, pp. 16–17.
45. Simone Brioni, 'Orientalism and Former Italian Colonies: An Interview with Shirin Ramzanali Fazel', in *Orientalismi italiani*, ed. by Gabriele Proglio, vol. 1 (Turin: Antares, 2012), pp. 215–25 (p. 223).

PART III

Emergent Communities

CHAPTER 10

Translating the Dead Other? The Politics of Minority Writing, Non-Identity and the Inoperative in Terézia Mora's *Das Ungeheuer*

Teresa Ludden

Introduction

The first part of this chapter brings together Deleuze & Guattari's concept of minor literature with aspects of Jean-Luc Nancy's 1986 essay *The Inoperative Community* to explore non-identitarian writing and politics. These philosophies open up alternative senses of the political which counter and challenge the conceptualization of 'minority writing' in terms of identity and humanism. The purpose of tracing these philosophers' ideas together is to think what 'difference' can mean and do beyond its use in today's publishing industry to promote literature 'by minorities' as an enrichment of mainstream culture. Such marketization of 'minor writers' defines the 'minority' in the terms of the majority, tending to instrumentalize minority literature and essentialize difference while serving to confirm and re-invigorate the 'norm' or 'majority'. As I argue below, Deleuze's mode of thinking the minoritarian is not just at odds with, but completely opposed to, the ways in which 'minority writers' are mediatized and represented in the contemporary discourse of marketing and publishing. What is very clear from Deleuze & Guattari is that minor writing effects deterritorializations of the majority language; that is, the agency lies with the minoritarian and not with a majority culture that utilizes marginal perspectives. Nowhere do Deleuze & Guattari suggest that 'the minor' is put to work for the 'majority'. Deterritorialization is not a service provided by 'minority literature' but a freeing from fixed relations such as those supposed to exist between language, territory and identity, or the possibility of change immanent to such relations. In what follows I trace Deleuze & Guattari's key points to emphasize a reading of minor literature as a groundless ground, and then read this affirmation of dispossession alongside Jean-Luc Nancy's understanding of the self and the political by focusing on the opacity of the other and on death which cannot be appropriated. I will bring the philosophies together in a reading of a novel, *Das Ungeheuer* (2015), by the German-Hungarian writer Terézia Mora. This novel is part of a trilogy which could be said to thematize the relation between majority and minority insofar as the protagonist is a German 'Everyman' figure in a relationship with a Hungarian female migrant. The trilogy has been interpreted as a journey of discovery for the German who is enlightened about his privileged position as a German (albeit one with an *East* German background), and who learns from his encounters with East Europeans to appreciate the precarity of the notion of majoritarian self-autonomy. Scholarship on the trilogy overwhelmingly concentrates on the German protagonist. In this chapter, however, I argue that in the second novel, *Das Ungeheuer* (2015), we need to switch perspective to the Hungarian migrant. This is important for the discussion of minor literature because to unsettle the focus on the German is also to disrupt the discourse of the improvement of the majority through the relation with 'the minor' which involves incorporating the 'exotic difference' of the minority. By foregrounding the themes of translation and the death of the other which are prominent in this novel but have not yet received critical attention, a different understanding of minority agency and the political may emerge.

Terézia Mora has been marketed as a minority writer and came to be well known in Germany when her first book *Seltsame Materie* [*Strange Matter*] won the Adelbert von Chamisso Prize in 1999. This literary prize (1985–2017) was awarded to writers who, according to the Stiftung's website, were 'writing in the German language to which they have migrated and which has become part of themselves'.[1] All the award winners were 'united through the unusual way of using the language in a manner that enriches German literature'.[2] As these quotations show, the emphasis lay on integration into the majority language in order to effect an 'enrichment of the German language' through the incorporation of the marginal voices of migration. To date Mora's novel, *Das Ungeheuer* [*The Monster*] (2015), has mainly been interpreted in the scholarship through the paradigm of transnational literature which not only tends to consolidate the major/minor divide but also perpetuates the dominant narrative of how the majority is enriched through an appreciation of the minor.[3] My reading of the novel stresses the role of the opacity of the dead lover, linguistic experimentation, the theme of translation, and an attunement to alterity as constitutive, aspects which can be understood through philosophies of difference.

Deleuze & Guattari: Minor Literature, Aporia and Dispossession

In *Kafka: pour une littérature mineure*, Deleuze & Guattari famously extrapolate from the historical, cultural and linguistic specificity of Franz Kafka's literary writing, a formulation of minor literature which can potentially be transferred more generally to relations of power between minority and majority culture in different socio-political moments.[4] For Deleuze & Guattari, minor literature is a delicate balancing act, which Kafka exemplified, the key point being that minor literature is not written in a minor language but is written by a minority in a major language.[5] The emphasis on a majority language which is deterritorialized by minorities rather than an affirmation of minor languages is important for several reasons which will be unpacked here. First, the danger of using what Deleuze & Guattari call patois is that it can lead to reactionary reterritorialization, reinforcing the grounding of identity in a recognizable variety of language. Second, the insistence is on 'minorities' as different from a norm or majority society/culture at any given time. The example of Kafka underlines the cultural, ethnic and linguistic positioning of the Jews of Prague at the turn of the twentieth century, but the point is wider. Blacks in America, write Deleuze & Guattari, are also confronted with the same questions with regards to finding a language within American English. This emphasis is crucial because it evokes the lived experience of real power relations, discrimination and inequality, what Christina Sharpe calls the 'monstrous intimacy' of subjection.[6] It stresses the material difference of 'minority communities' as a plurality which fractures the mythical notion of a whole, self-enclosed majority culture. Minority reality is to be understood as a different inhabitation of majority culture and this involves resisting affirming a 'minority' identity in the terms of the majority culture. As Lyotard states in his comments on Deleuze's concept of minorities, 'it is necessary to insist that the struggles of minorities do not gain their force from any critique, from being placed in relation to the center'.[7] Indeed, it is the rejection of identities constructed by means of an oppositional relation with the majority that is key in understanding non-identitarian politics. As Lyotard also points out, however, such minoritarian politics should not be seen as less real than consolidated and established forms of majority political power.[8] This, of course, signals the political importance of Deleuze & Guattari's essay which is oriented towards questions of normativity, diversity, exclusion, assimilation and hybridity. Crucially, the theory is not to be understood as a lament about the alienation of minorities vis-à-vis majority language and culture. Such a formulation would suggest that there is a prior essential underlying knowable identity which is impinged upon by a distorting language as convention or code exterior to an essential self. The point is rather more paradoxical and to do with the emergence of singularity through a constitutive relationality with exteriority. This brings us to the third point to be made in relation to Deleuze & Guattari's central formulation above: they avoid locating differences in a space 'beyond' the majority and conjure up instead the impasse which confronts minorities in their attempt to express, in the language of the dominant culture, the singularities and specificities of their positioning. Deleuze & Guattari ventriloquize at this point Kafka's own reflections to express the abyss of the impossibility of writing in German; they use Kafka's own metaphor of the tightrope balancing act, of the purloining of the German language that is required for a Prague Jew to write. By using Kafka's own words from a letter to Max Brod in 1921 they stress the impossible possibility that is minor literature: Kafka writes of 'the impossibility of not writing, the impossibility of writing German, the impossibility of writing differently'.[9] Since there is no recourse to alternative or originary languages, since minor literature cannot be written in any other language than that of the majority culture, Kafka writes of the dilemma and despair of his generation and milieu wanting to write in German: 'With their posterior legs they were still glued to their father's Jewishness and with the waving anterior legs they found no new ground.'[10] It is this groundless ground which needs to be thought to understand Deleuze & Guattari's formulation of minor literature. This is not a hybridity as a new certainty formed by conjoining two distinct identities (Jewishness and German). Rather it is about the undecidability and incompletion of non-identity founded on absence which engenders undecided affiliations that undermine usual modes of identity formation in sameness. I link this notion to what Deleuze & Guattari theorize later in their essay as a 'maximum of difference' or 'difference in intensity' in which there is no longer a subject (of a statement).[11] This can be paraphrased as a continual self-differing and deferral, as an affirmation of the uninterpretable, that which does not crystallize into unifying form. Majority language is opened up to deterritorialization which means its function as producing determinations or codes is suspended allowing for expressions of singularities which cannot be subsumed in the general or compared with reference to 'the same': 'The animal does not speak "like" a human but extracts tonalities without signification from language'.[12] The idea here is of the incommensurable, the blocking of the notion of comparing like with like, which has severely disruptive implications for the signifying system.

To think minor literature, then, is to be attuned to Deleuze & Guattari's challenge of a maximum difference (self-differing difference), which cannot be co-opted into an identity to be asserted positively. The question is: how does this minoritarian self-differing difference also speak for, or on behalf of, a community? For Deleuze & Guattari are equally clear that minority writing cannot *not* speak of the political, the cultural and historical. How is maximum difference linked to the communication of the political? An answer to this question would be to read Deleuze & Guattari's predilection for experimental writing (and Kafka in particular as exemplary in this regard) as a way of making the plurality of interpretation the key theme and political strategy. Politics can be found in the rejection of a single way of reading, and in the process of reading the work itself as the reader participates in the work as rhizome, that is, a non-hierarchical absence of crystallization into a unifying whole. Hence the idea of experimentation is important for minorities where deterritorialization might be linked to the desire to 'affirm perspectives that are not those of the culture they inhabit'.[13] What is affirmed in experimentation, however, is not positive, self-identical identities but the 'movement of language towards its extremes' and this means there comes a point where language ceases to be representation.[14] Hence there is a tension in the minoritarian between communicability and untranslatability. Deleuze & Guattari suggest interpretation is a kind of violence that closes down 'entry points'; the desire to evade interpretation is not to negate interpretation but to affirm an alternative that is uninterpretable. This is not a point about arbitrariness or the impossibility of differentiating between different interpretations.[15] Rather it highlights how any one particular mode of access to Kafka's texts necessarily excludes other possibilities which means that every kind of access is limited and incomplete (which is not to claim that all access points are equally valid).

The link between language and non-identitarian politics can be seen in Deleuze & Guattari's formulation of Kafka's 'Prague German' as both a singular 'new intensity' or 'sober line of revolution' and a material result of the socio-political realities of the criss-crossing conglomerate of languages in the multi-ethnic, multi-lingual Austro-Hungarian culture.[16] It is the *type* of the German that Kafka uses that is key. Strictly speaking he does not deterritorialize German but he deterritorializes an already deterritorialized German. As a Czech Jew who belonged to a German-speaking urban elite in Bohemia, the everyday German he used was removed geographically from the German nation; further, it was an urban public language of commerce and bureaucracy, a 'paper German' which reinforces the sense of distance from the mythic, organic community of native speakers.

While Deleuze & Guattari link Kafka's deterritorialization of this 'artificial' language to the idea of a 'maximum of difference',[17] it is difficult to see, given the cultural, historical and personal specificity of Kafka's case, how his writing could be used as an exemplar for all minor literature. But to read Deleuze & Guattari in this narrow way would be to misunderstand the overall trajectory of the argument as a philosophy of literary language and the minoritarian. What is of interest here — and will become relevant in the interpretation of Terézia Mora's novel below — is their use of Henri Gobard's tetralinguistic model of language functions as a way to think a relationality between different modes of languages. The 'mythic mode' of Yiddish for Kafka was not a linguistic territoriality, they assert, but a 'movement of nomadic deterritorialization for German'.[18] That is, Kafka did not utilize the vernacular (Yiddish) as a means of reterritorialization (Hebrew, as mythic tongue, was incidentally even less of a resource) but used it to burrow into German, which is seen in political terms as a deliberate ungrounding of the majority language. This does not amount to his utilizing Yiddish to affirm difference; the emphasis is on the *differential between* Yiddish and German as a movement of difference through which dispossession may be expressed in a language he does not own.

Nancy and the Self–Other Relation

For Jean-Luc Nancy, literature plays an important role in undoing or 'incompleting' myth in ways that are broadly analogous to Deleuze & Guattari's movement of deterritorialization as deferral of stable ground (of identity or belonging). We will turn now to Nancy's concept of the inoperative which expands Deleuze & Guattari's discussion of the 'maximum of difference as difference in intensity'. Like Deleuze & Guattari, Nancy takes issue with the notions of organic totality and is critical of 'the fusional self-perception of societies, nations, or communities'.[19] What Nancy calls immanence or communion expresses the idea of transparent self-identity and the complete 'self-presence of individuals to one another in and by their community'.[20] Individuals are properly exposed to the impossibility of immanence when they are confronted with the death of the other. That is, the death of the other is a limit which undoes the notion of a self which coincides with itself because in this death we are exposed to the limits of recognition. There is no discovery of the self in the other but an encounter with the other's alterity or the alterity of death. This experience 'sets my singularity outside me and indefinitely delimits it'.[21] Where Deleuze & Guattari focus on an intensive use of language and linguistic plurality as an instance of becoming in their formulation of minoritarian singularity as groundless ground, Nancy foregrounds ontological questions that centre on the relation between self-presence and otherness. Here Heidegger's influence is crucial as Nancy emphasizes the role of absence in the formation of the self. In *Being and Time*, Heidegger showed how death is most our own (no one can die our deaths for us), but that death is also nothing we possess (when it is here, we are gone, and when we are here, it is not). To be mortal is to be defined by just such a dispossession, by a death we can never have. 'What is most my own remains outside of me, and this fact draws me out of myself, and is thus my fundamental opening to world. Mortals exist as members of a community that participates in world.'[22] For Nancy, closely reading Bataille, it is the experience of the mortality *of the other*, not our 'own', which is the key limit experience.[23] When death presents itself as *not ours* the very impossibility of representing its meaning suspends the possibility of self-presentation and exposes us to our finitude.[24] There can be no complacent self-discovery but only at best an affirmation of dispossession.

For Deleuze & Guattari, minor literature expresses the state of homelessness or impasse that was key for thinking non-identity. Nancy argues that a pure collective totality is impossible since the fusional self-other model is replaced with a relationality with the alterity or opacity of the other. Further, if the self is an event that takes place outside itself (something which is acutely felt when we witness the death of a fellow human being), then the notion of individuality as absolute immanence is shown to be mythical.[25] Thinking the subject in terms of identity does not allow for the difference of the other,[26] because 'otherness' becomes merely an object of a subject's representation. In other words, Nancy is critical of instrumentalizing alterity as this blocks communication of and with difference. To have communication there needs to be a relational movement between and with an other that is different and external to the self. The terms 'being-communication' and 'being-outside-itself' stress the difference between his notion of selfhood and the metaphysical subject for whom:

> its outside and all its 'alienations' or 'extraneousness' should in the end be suppressed by and *sublated* in it. It is altogether different with the being of communication. The being-communicating (and not the subject-representing), or if one wants to risk saying it, communication as the predicament of being, as 'transcendental' is above all *being-outside-itself*.[27]

Reading between Nancy and Deleuze & Guattari

We can relate Deleuze & Guattari's non-identitarian politics to Nancy's 'being-outside-itself' through the common idea of the groundless ground where the self never comes to rest finally once and for all. Deleuze & Guattari's notion of minor literature as impasse or impossibility evokes perpetual non-consolidation as the central characteristic of the minor(itarian), while Nancy's concept of being-outside-itself appears as a general ontological category. For Deleuze & Guattari the stress is on non-foundational minoritarian agencies as already existing within majority culture which opens this majority culture up to difference. 'Difference in intensity'[28] is linked both to actual Prague German as a 'desiccated language intermixed with Czech or Yiddish' and to the wider notion of a non-identitarian agency. The emphasis is on what minor literature (at specific historical moments) can *do* in its state of impossibility, and via its specific positionings vis-à-vis the majority. Nancy, on the other hand, emphasizes the moment of breach or interruption, the limit experience as the shock of the encounter with (the death of) the other. Being-outside-itself comes about through an exposure to another singular being so the mutual unsettlement of the self-other relationship is foregrounded as a mode of resisting the myth of self-presence or fusional wholeness. Reading between Deleuze & Guattari and Nancy, we could see Kafka, who was bilingual in Czech and German and knew Yiddish and Hebrew, as being between and outside these languages as opposed to fused together with them as a subject. This means that he created a solitary and unique voice not by writing in patois or a religious/mythical tongue but precisely by bending the German language, appropriating a 'foreign' language, not to make it a home, but to make its foreign-ness more visible. This is the condition of all migrants and their descendants, according to Deleuze & Guattari. The condition of not owning one's 'own' language and yet having an ongoing living relation with it finds resonance in Terézia Mora's novel which is discussed below. Deleuze & Guattari touch on phenomena such as multilingualism and translation in ways that suggest an alignment of the minoritarian with a movement between languages. While it does not necessarily follow that you belong to a minority group if you are multilingual, in Kafka's case his multilingualism draws attention to how the myth of the monolingual nation of 'native speakers' cedes to the idea and reality of plurality. Being-outside several different languages meant that none of his languages served as territory for Kafka, Deleuze & Guattari argue, although they stress that his knowledge of Czech and Yiddish influenced his style. We can perhaps link Nancy's articulation of the sense of a limit which the self encounters in the other, to the relationality between different languages where the condition of multilingualism is understood as one (mode of) language delimiting another. Translation and existing in-between languages, then, are implicitly important to the concept of minor literature, whereby what is at stake is not so much the foreignization of the mother tongue as the acknowledgement of the impossibility of finding a 'native' stability in the first place.

Minority Writing, Absence and Alterity in Terézia Mora's *Das Ungeheuer* (2015)

Terézia Mora (b. 1971) is a well-known writer in Germany; she grew up in Sopron, a village on the Hungarian-Austrian border and is bi-lingual in Hungarian and German. Since the early 1990s she has lived in Berlin. She won acclaim for her debut collection of short stories *Seltsame Materie* (1999) which was celebrated for its experimentation and for 'hybridity', creating in the German language the atmosphere and milieu of a small Hungarian community. More recently she has written a trilogy with the central character, Darius Kopp, a kind of hapless 'German Everyman' who falls in love with Flora, a Hungarian migrant working as a waitress in Germany, whom he marries. At the end of the first book, *Der einzige Mann auf dem Kontinent* [*The Only Man on the Continent*], Kopp, after being made redundant, has an epiphany about how the love relationship with his wife is the only aspect of his existence which gives him a sense of being. There is clearly a power relation between the German male subject and Hungarian female other and it is as if Mora is using the Hungarian other to dismantle the notion of a fusional, united German norm. In Nancy's terms Mora is critiquing immanentism. Through the experience of falling in love with Flora, Kopp learns that he is not a solipsistic isolated individual but a being-outside-itself who 'finds himself' in the love relationship. The first part in the trilogy finishes here and in between the first and second book Flora commits suicide, so the potential for Kopp to develop a relation with the alterity of the *living* other is not realized. In the second book, *Das Ungeheuer* (2015), Kopp's relationality is re-figured as a connection to the dead other, his dead wife, through her words contained in her diaries which she left behind, translated from Hungarian into German, and which are printed on the page underneath Kopp's narrative.

Das Ungeheuer (2015) starts a year after Flora's suicide with Kopp struggling with debilitating grief and guilt. He has yet to find a resting place for the urn containing his wife's ashes and decides to take a road trip through central and Eastern Europe, partly to see for himself the village where Flora grew up and to arrange burial of her remains. With Flora dead, the Hungarian-German relation has changed and become ostensibly even more unequal as we are now dealing with an absent dead female East European other and an 'active' German male on an epic journey who thinks of his car (a wonderful German machine) as a kind of alter ego, a home or protective shell which shields him from potentially annihilating encounters with East European Others. Of course, as the narrative progresses his car suffers all kinds of breakdowns, sometimes necessitating long periods when he is unable to travel and becomes embroiled in local relationships and cultural differences. Scholars concur that Mora's Darius Kopp novels are to be read as a form of *Gesellschaftskritik* [cultural criticism]. Katharina Gerstenberger thinks that Kopp becomes a better person after losing job and wife. In his former job in IT he had dealings with Armenians online but this remote 'imagined territory' of Armenia becomes concrete when he gets trapped there. Gerstenberger links the insight Kopp gains into the reality of the local to a wider reading of 'transnational literature which reflects contemporary German responses to a global economy'[29] with the overall point being that Kopp comes to terms with power imbalances and his relative superiority as a German in the European hierarchy.[30] Bohn Case links the text to Mora's own biography and agenda which is perceived to be calling for an understanding of German culture that can and must integrate transnational voices like hers. Integration of 'difference' which expands national identity and language is stressed with the upshot that German interactions with Hungarian otherness (which mirrors Mora's own hybridity) results in renewal, augmentation, re-negotiation of the German nation and culture.[31] The emphasis, then, is on the nation as a substantiality which endures, transnational movement notwithstanding. German (national) identity may be changed by incorporating different voices but is preserved just as, according to

Gerstenberger, Kopp 'regains equilibrium at the end of his journey' (p. 302). In what follows I argue against this interpretation because it effaces the difference that is Flora. Gerstenberger concentrates on Kopp and forgets the difficult words of the dead other which are brought inside the text in the form of extracts from her diaries which are printed underneath a line dividing them from Kopp's story. Bohn Case's argument rightly focuses on the role of relations between subjects, languages and nations, but similarly does not give enough attention to what is after all the key relation in the text — that between Kopp and the radical withdrawal of the dead Hungarian other. The text requires us to think the more probing question of a relationality with what is missing. Flora's written words are present in the text to refer to her absence but equally her absence has agency in the text in their disruptive visual presence on the page. While this textual strategy could be read as a reference to Kopp's inability to come to terms with his loss and to his melancholy predilections, as Mary Cosgrove's reading suggests, this interpretation retains Kopp and his pathologies as central.[32]

By shifting attention to Flora and the role of absence my reading here attempts to read *Das Ungeheuer* in ways that see the text as striving to hold open a space of irreducibility. The title, I would argue, could refer to exactly that: the monstrous as the incommensurable, that which resists signification. The idea of 'the monster' suggests a threat directed towards a person or community, as in mythic tales such as St George and the Dragon.[33] Perhaps 'the monster' could be Flora herself, as 'the East European Other', in relation to a 'German self'. More precisely it could refer to the depression which led to Flora taking her own life. However we interpret it, what is clear is that Mora wanted a voice for 'the monstrous' in her book. She was concerned that given the plot twist, the dead wife would only ever appear as an object of Kopp's narration so she devised a way that her voice could be heard in the form of her diaries which Kopp finds after her suicide. When he discovers that these are written in Hungarian he feels betrayed because Flora had told him she had ceased to use the Hungarian language, and this revelation is as if he had discovered she had been having an affair. This evokes language — specifically here Hungarian — as a secret lover; Hungarian, the language itself, is positioned as the clandestine 'unknown other', the dark language she kept hidden while speaking Kopp's native German language. This of course establishes the power relation between the languages with the East European language, now that Flora is dead, literally haunting German. Indeed given the author's own bilingualism in these languages, it is tempting to read the relation between German and Hungarian as the author's metaphor for her own assimilation into the German literary establishment which appears to have been accomplished by relegating Hungarian to an exotic supporting role.

Flora's diaries appear at intervals throughout the novel underneath Kopp's journey narrative. The most striking aspect of the text is the visual typographical feature of a thick horizontal black dividing line which runs across every page with Kopp's narrative above and Flora's words below. When Kopp sets off from Berlin on his journey to Hungary then (via a detour into Austria to repair a tyre) into

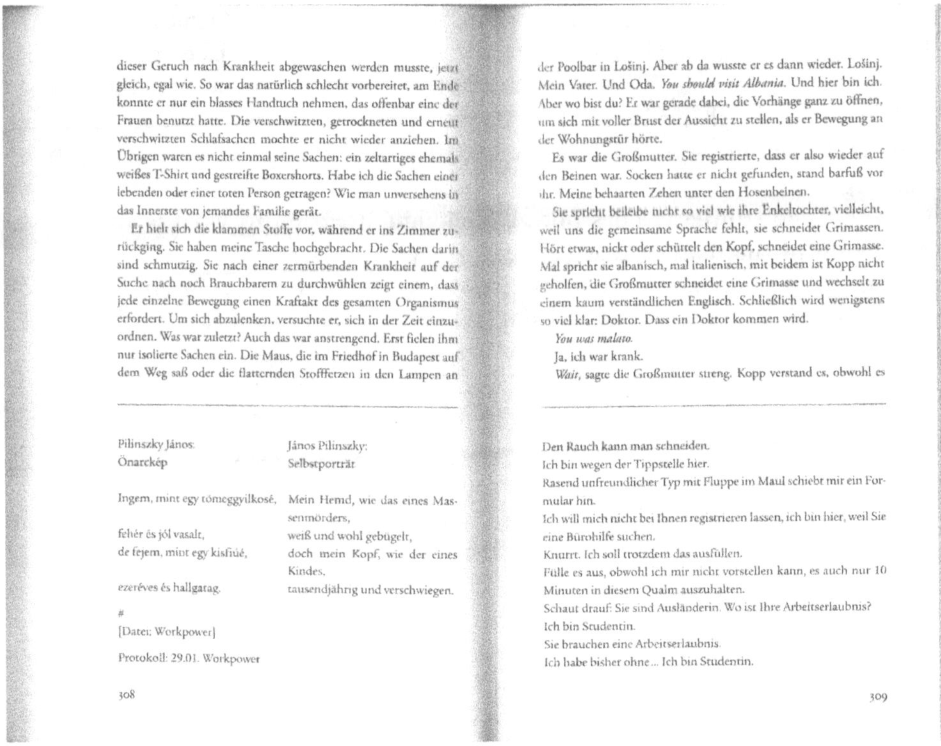

Fig. 1 Double page from the novel *Das Ungeheuer* showing the page layout
and use of Hungarian in Flora's diaries underneath the line.
Kopp's narrative of his East European journey is above the line.

former Yugoslavia, Albania, Bulgaria, Istanbul, Armenia and finally to Athens, he takes Flora's diaries to read on the way. When Kopp breaks his journey, he reads Flora's diaries in stages, and the reader is directed towards the text (that Kopp is also reading) underneath the line. While this aligns the reader with Kopp's temporality, it also means that we read Flora's words 'directly' without Kopp's mediation. For large sections there is nothing underneath the line and this itself makes a striking visual impact as if the silence or the unsaid may be seen beneath Kopp's words. The visual separation has the further effect of alluding through the spatial layout to the difference between the mental states of the husband and wife. Kopp is melancholic as the grieving husband but his story continues above the line while below the line the words bear witness to the ultimately fatal depression of Flora where narrative has ceased. While melancholia helps the individual to face the truth and to create order, depression, by contrast, destroys structure and leads to death.[34] Hence the fragmentary texts from Flora's diaries underneath the line are aligned with the limits of language, the impossible non-narrative language of depression. Close attention to her words in her diary reveals references to trauma, her bi-polar disorder, the childhood abuse she suffered when she was growing up in Hungary, and the experience of a female migrant (she writes of what appears to be a racist attack while waiting at a bus stop). Many sections are not diary entries at all but fragments written at the very limit of understanding, on the point of breakdown of language. Several entries do not yield obvious sense; some are series of letters apparently expressing breakdown.

The experimentation and difficulty of these sections have been understood as indirectly commenting on Kopp and his story, contributing to the notion of male Enlightenment through learning from a sensitive female foreign other. Sarah-Christina Henze argues that the radical nature of the form and content of Flora's writing below the line penetrates and explodes Kopp's narrative above the line.[35] Her reading of the relation between the two texts attributes a disruptive agency to Flora's writing which affects the language of Kopp's narrative above the line by starting to make it less a tool of representation. Her reading echoes Deleuze & Guattari's deterritorialization of the major by the minor. While I agree that we are not supposed to conceive of the two texts as separate (and I also read the dividing line as a boundary which connects as much as separates), Henze's reading utilizes Flora's writing as that which 'infects' and breaks down the still too coherent narrative above the line. The focus is again on Kopp and his process of 'becoming other'. What a reading of the text as male Enlightenment leaves aside are the political and philosophical implications of the opacity of the Flora diaries which resist instrumentalization in their untranslatability. It is as if grief for the dead other is incommensurate with narrative and the Flora fragments serve as a reminder of this unavailability. In terms of Nancy's theory, what Kopp encounters in Flora's words is the otherness of the dead other in which he cannot recognize himself and thus encounters difference. In the text this is underscored through the use of Hungarian words left untranslated. The words left behind by the dead other, however, foreground the female as unavailable other and thus stress the unequal access to the position of the ec-static subject.

Translation, the possibility and impossibility of translation, is a crucial theme of the novel which has not been fully addressed to date in the scholarship. It is an important facet of the central theme of absence and the conjunction of the dead other/lover (as untranslatable) and the theme of textual/linguistic translation itself links back to the ideas of both Deleuze & Guattari and Nancy discussed above. Flora has been dead a year before we and Kopp read her words which have been translated from the Hungarian into German. The activity of translating from one language to another is linked to the idea of translating the voice from the dead and highlights the text's attunement to an alterity that is unpresentable and yet gestured towards through the notion of translation as a concept and praxis. Flora's texts (supposedly diary entries) are translated into German and read by Kopp and the reader in between and at the same time as the narrative of Kopp's journey above the dividing line on the page.

For Deleuze & Guattari the minor is untranslatable into the terms of the same and yet it asserts itself in its groundlessness, while for Nancy the experience of (the death of) the other is what triggers the realization that being and community must be understood in terms of that which cannot be appropriated. As we have seen,

Deleuze & Guattari explicitly reference translation in the conception of 'Minor Literature' when they write of the impossibility of translating Yiddish into German. The impossibility lies in the way Yiddish is totally enmeshed in the German language and vice versa so that to use 'German' and 'Yiddish' as separate codes would be to disregard the interpenetrating inter- and intra-linguistic intensive vectors of forces. Yiddish is itself 'an intensive tongue or an intensive use of German' and is 'grafted onto High German that works so much from within it that it cannot be translated into German without being abolished'.[36] In Mora's novel the translations of Flora's diary entries below the line are figured as such 'minor writing'. Fragmentary, including Hungarian words and phrases, sometimes translated passages and other passages which purport to be Flora's own translations of Hungarian poetry, elliptical and esoteric, they display themselves as difficult, if not impossible, to translate. Even where the German translations are grammatically and syntactically correct, they are often resistant to meaning. These texts, associated with the voice from the dead, are also brought into a connection with mourning as Kopp reads them as a way to be closer to Flora but also as part of the process of leave-taking.[37] The typography of the line separating the Flora texts from the more straightforwardly representational language describing Kopp's travels in Eastern Europe creates a specific sense of space visually on the pages of the novel. This space is the locus of difference which figures death as completely irreversible (because the bottom part of the page is separated from the top) and yet suggests the possibility of 'carrying over' the line by virtue of the fact that the texts have been translated into German and that Kopp reads and interacts with the translations. Translation seems to permit an 'after-life' for the Flora texts, allowing them to live on yet emphasizes the absence of the writer. The page layout visually alludes to a proximity of distance whereby the death of the other appears as the limit or horizon in relation to which life (in the form of Kopp's journey) continues. When there are no words under the line, the line remains as a visible presence of the incommensurate that draws attention not just to Flora's disappearance but to the dimension of life that Heidegger expresses as acknowledgement of finitude — an awareness of the unknowability of one's own death as an otherness that is ungraspable yet also the condition of possibility of life. That is, the impossibility of translating (death) is figured in the text, as that which makes translation possible. We have multiple translator figures (both literal and figurative). I have already mentioned Kopp as a reader of Flora's words, and he is of course mirrored by the extra-textual reader herself; but Kopp is not the first reader-translator of Flora's diaries. Flora herself worked as a freelance translator and many of her fragments are versions of her translations of Hungarian poetry. Some sentences and poems are left in Hungarian which suggests that the Hungarian language is being used to gesture towards that which eludes understanding as most German speakers would not be able to read Hungarian. In the first chapter, the student, Judit, is a key but very minor character, for it is she whom Kopp pays to translate his wife's writing into German. Hers is a very shadowy role appearing in only one scene but she is a cipher for the author who herself wrote the Flora fragments in Hungarian and translated them herself into

German. The Hungarian texts that Mora wrote can be found on the author's website as absent-present 'originals' of the translated texts that comprise Flora's diary entries under the line.[38] This situation, where texts written in one language (Hungarian) exist outside (as originals of translations within the novel) the main German text, recalls relationality between the major and the minor as well as suggesting that the novel, *Das Ungeheuer*, gestures beyond its own boundaries, displaying its incompletion and ec-stasis. In this permutation, 'being-outside-itself' is symbolized by the use of the Hungarian and German languages as delimiting each other, while the relation between the present German text (the book we read) and the absent Hungarian alludes to a differential within and between both languages whereby language is shown to fall short of full presence. The Hungarian in its ostensible externality (outside the German text) is linked via Flora to the latent underside of language as well as to the opacity of death. The impossible possibility of minor writing is connected to the situation where the impossibility of bringing Flora back acts as a spur to translate her words. The translation of the Hungarian into German permits a kind of 'after-life' for the texts and means that Kopp and the reader can partially access Flora's thoughts, but because her words exist only in translation their concealment is underlined again. As Derrida has argued, texts are 'at once translatable and untranslatable (always "*at once ... and ...*") *hama*, at the same time'.[39] Thus the experience of a sign necessarily implies *lack* of full presence of self to self. Signs/words stand for and point towards something other than themselves. Further, words are supplementary, they 'supplement the absence of what they point towards; they make what is absent present while at the same time maintaining it as absent'.[40] In this way the theme of translation in *Das Ungeheuer* emphasizes absence and dispossession to suggest that selves and languages are open to, and affected by, difference in ways that fundamentally question notions of internal cohesion and unity. Relationality and movements across boundaries are of course intrinsic to translation, as well as the notion of multiplicity since the translated text exists in multiple forms. Translation cannot *not* be anything other than relational. It is important to read the German language in the Flora fragments as 'haunted' by Hungarian, as having arrived on the page via a detour through both fictional and actual translation and marked by these migratory alterations. Moreover, we must understand the author's decision to make the Hungarian texts available elsewhere, outside and alongside her German text, not as a harking back to the 'original purity' of the Hungarian as *Urtext*. Rather it signals an awareness of the activity of translation itself as characterized by absence and presence at the source of creation/writing. That is, while the translator makes available in one language words and meanings from a different language, they can disclose meanings only by virtue of concealing the original words/meanings. To translate is to necessarily allude to an absent text and to the inevitable remainder of the work of translation when a text carries across (the German verb for 'to translate' is *über-setzen*) words from one language to another. Mora uses Hungarian in her novel to underscore the theme of translation as presentation of wordlessness which is closely associated with Flora's depression and Flora as the dead other. These aspects are not nothingness, however, but are made to resonate through the various traversals, movement across the line, and movement between translated texts, and between readers and translator-writers. The type of language that appears in Flora's diaries chimes with Deleuze & Guattari's non-foundationalism. By leaving semantically challenging fragments and excerpts of Hungarian in the German text, Mora signals not just that translation is unable to carry across all that a text might say. She alludes as well to the internal differences within languages by emphasizing the theme of unavailability. To this constellation of ideas about translation as difference, the dead lover/other (similarly the cypher for the unavailability of meaning in the novel) foregrounds the idea of a remainder which cannot be recuperated. As such, translation can be linked to mourning as the inability to 'carry across'. As Lisa Foran puts it, 'translation mourns the loss of the inevitable remainder of its work'.[41]

It is not for nothing that Mora weaves the leitmotif of Orpheus and Eurydice into the text. This myth of course tells of Orpheus's journey to the underworld in the attempt to retrieve his wife, Eurydice, from the dead and his loss of her for the second time on the boundary between life and death. It is a story about the liminal experience of the opacity of death and the fragmentation that occurs around this limit. Mora's text spatially alludes to the finite separation between life and death with the page layout with the horizontal line. There are allusions to Greek myth here in the different roles accorded to the characters. Kopp experiences excessive grief in the narrative above the line and he carries his wife's ashes and her words in translation on his laptop around Eastern Europe on a journey whose purpose was originally to find revelations about his dead wife. The textual allusions associate Kopp with Orpheus as a lover who cannot be reconciled with the loss of his wife and whose grief propels him on a journey to the land of the dead in the attempt to retrieve her. Of course in the novel, Eastern Europe is then aligned with the underworld itself which humorously displays the power relation between Germany and her Eastern neighbours while alluding to Flora (topographically on the page) as the site of radical alterity who cannot be brought back to life. Kopp's alignment with Orpheus suggests not only European power relations but also an emphasis on gender difference. In the Greek myth the male hero's excessive grief is eventually transmuted into the most powerful lyrical poetry while 'the inaccessible', as the driving force behind his musical outpourings, is aligned with the absent, dead female. Unlike Orpheus, however, Kopp does not express his despair in song, poetry or even speech;[42] at several points in his narrative there is opportunity for him to talk about his grief — to his friend in Berlin or the friendly native Albanians he meets and stays with. That he is unable to express himself even when others open up to him and share their own stories of their personal tragedies means that his despair is displayed as unspoken and unspeakable. Insofar as Kopp's grief is associated with untranslatability, he becomes partially aligned with Flora herself as the textual figure who embodies the idea of the inaccessible through her depression and suicide. Kopp is affected by Flora's words when he reads of her suffering in her diaries and yet often appears himself inarticulate. This positioning of Kopp in relation to the ineffable is used in the novel to expose male agency and auto-genesis as delusional fantasies. It also downplays the *Bildungsroman* notion of male development. Rather than interpreting Kopp as having learnt to be a more sensitive person by encountering the otherness of his wife's words, specifically through his reading of the translated diaries, we could say that he does not rediscover himself because he cannot recognize himself in the (dead) other (and this opacity is emphasized through his inability to understand the Hungarian language). This is not a self-confirmatory encounter or a mode of 'development' through incorporating aspects of the other because Flora cannot be utilized or translated into the self-same without a remainder. If we turn back to Nancy, we could link Kopp's narrative to the destruction of the myth of a fusional model of identity because his experience of the alterity of the other is a discovery of his own existence beyond himself which does not return him to himself. This is not to be understood as a stage in the overall trajectory of 'self-development' whereby the other or the foreign is subsumed for the purposes of self-improvement. Such a model utilizes otherness as constitutive of self. Rather Flora's palpable absence precipitates the thematization in the novel of a more ethical kind of 'inoperative' difference as a, to speak with Nancy, 'withdrawing from the work'.[43]

Conclusion

Flora/Hungarian is an emblem of the untranslatable, 'maximum difference' that cannot be appropriated and is used to stress a non-utilizable difference along Deleuze & Guattari's lines. The association of Flora with the realm of the dead does not turn her into a radically exterior impossibility, however, since the voice beyond the grave emanates from the translated Hungarian diaries. This suggests that Flora embodies non-integration and the disruption of the idea of unity of language and identity. Through the theme of translation between Hungarian and German (and other episodes in the text where Kopp is required to negotiate East European languages or use English as the *lingua franca*), Mora evokes the non-unity of languages. Target and source languages are shown not to be unities that can be translated as one whole language into the other. Translation cannot be understood through identity thinking as it signals the collapse of the ability to compare like with like. Translation and travelling (Kopp driving through Eastern Europe) and the thematization of border crossings are key in Mora's novel and used to highlight non-identity as originary experiences which are disavowed when fusion and identity are promoted. Therefore Mora's privileging of multilingualism and heterogeneity can be linked to Deleuze & Guattari's 'minor literature'. Further, Flora's voice which speaks from beyond the grave in her translated diary entries can be associated with a radical position as being between and outside the two languages, German and Hungarian, as opposed to fused together with them as a subject. To translate these thematic aspects into current debates about migrant and minority literature: Mora is perhaps complaining about the homogenizing tendencies of the culture industry and the utilizing of 'minority literature' to rejuvenate the majority/mainstream. Mora has also publicly criticized an understanding of German language and culture as homogeneous and resists being labelled a 'foreigner' writing in German.[44] Instead she sees herself 'as German as Kafka'.[45] In other words, she wants to fit into German literary culture, but as different, and is calling for an understanding of culture and language as heterogeneous. To this end in her novel she *utilizes* the Hungarian language to turn it into a metaphor for the unassimilable that is both translatable and untranslatable. The difficulty is, of course, that this comes fairly close to putting the minor to work for the enrichment of the majority culture. In order to reveal permanent differentiation and a difference that is not merely translated into the same, Mora's tightrope walk across the abyss involves figuring Hungarian as a minority language turned into a metaphor for otherness to emphasize heterogeneity. While the idea evokes Deleuze & Guattari's image of Kafka's moving homelessly between languages, in Mora's case the author exhibits more agency to manipulate the contemporary discourses around 'minority writing'.

Notes to Chapter 10

1. <https://www.bosch-stiftung.de/en/project/adelbert-von-chamisso-prize-robert-bosch-stiftung>.
2. Ibid. [accessed 2 November 2020].
3. Further references to the secondary literature on Mora and *Das Ungeheuer* are given below. Anke Biendarra, for instance, sees conservatism in the novel itself as it 'does not transcend but reiterates traditional notions of center and periphery'; 'Travel and Trauma in Post-1989 Europe: Julya Rabinowich's *Die Erdfresserin* and Terézia Mora's *Das Ungeheuer*', in *Anxious Journeys: Twenty-First-Century Travel Writing in German*, ed. by Karin Baumgartner and Monika Shafi (Rochester, NY: Camden House, 2019), pp. 29–40 (p. 37).
4. Deleuze & Guattari, *Kafka: pour une littérature mineure*, 1975. There are two translations into English. I am using Robert Brinkley's translation 'What Is a Minor Literature?', *Mississippi Review*, 11.3 (Winter/Spring 1983), 13–33.
5. Deleuze & Guattari, p. 14.
6. Christina Sharpe, *Monstrous Intimacies: Making Post-Slavery Subjects* (Durham, NC: Duke University Press, 2009).
7. Jean-François Lyotard, *Expédient dans la décadence*, in *Rudiments païens* (Paris: Union générale d'éditions, 1977), pp. 115–56 (p. 116), quoted by Robert Brinkley in his introduction to 'What Is a Minor Literature?', p. 16.
8. Ibid.
9. Deleuze & Guattari, 'What is a Minor Literature?', p. 16.
10. This is from a letter from Kafka to Max Brod (June 1921) which Robert Brinkley quotes in Deleuze & Guattari's 'What Is a Minor Literature?', p. 28, note 2.
11. Deleuze & Guattari, p. 22.
12. Ibid.
13. This is a reference to Jean-François Lyotard, *Expédient dans la décadence*, in *Rudiments païens* (Paris: Union générale d'éditions, 1977), p. 116, mentioned by Robert Brinkley in his introduction to Deleuze & Guattari's 'What Is a Minor Literature?', p. 13.
14. Deleuze & Guattari, p. 23.
15. Deleuze & Guattari are often misunderstood in this way in conventional Kafka scholarship. See Carolin Duttlinger, *The Cambridge Companion to Franz Kafka* (Cambridge: Cambridge University Press, 2013), p. 129.
16. On parallels between the literature of Kafka's time and that of the early twenty-first century see Lene Rock's brilliant book *As German as Kafka* (Leuven: Leuven University Press, 2019).
17. Deleuze & Guattari, 'What is Minor Literature?', p. 22.
18. Deleuze & Guattari, 'What is Minor Literature?', p. 25.

19. Lene Rock, *As German as Kafka*, p. 26.
20. Christopher Fynsk, 'Foreword: Experiences of Finitude', xv in Jean-Luc Nancy, *The Inoperative Community*, ed. and trans. by Peter Connor (Minneapolis: University of Minnesota Press, 1991), p. xv.
21. Jean-Luc Nancy, *The Inoperative Community*, ed. and trans. by Peter Connor (Minneapolis: University of Minnesota Press, 1991), pp. 33–34.
22. Andrew J. Mitchell, *The Fourfold: Reading the Late Heidegger* (Evanston, IL: Northwestern University Press, 2015).
23. Nancy, *The Inoperative Community*, p. 14.
24. Nancy, ibid.
25. Ibid.
26. Nancy, *The Inoperative Community*, p. 23.
27. Nancy, p. 24; italics in the original.
28. Deleuze & Guattari, p. 22.
29. Katharina Gerstenberger, 'Post 1989 Geographies in Terézia Mora's *Der einzige Mann auf dem Kontinent* and *Das Ungeheuer*', *German Life and Letters*, 71.3 (2018), 291–307.
30. Gerstenberger, p. 302.
31. Laura Bohn Case, 'Ich bin genauso deutsch wie Kafka', *German Life and Letters*, 68.2 (2015), 211–27.
32. Mary Cosgrove, 'The Slothful Protest: *Acedia* in Terézia Mora's Darius-Kopp Trilogy and Iris Hanika's *Das Eigentliche*', *German Life and Letters*, 74.1 (2021), 47–67.
33. See Teresa Ludden, 'Allegories of Cultural Relations: Interpreting Anne Duden's Reading of Representations of St George and the Dragon', *German Life and Letters*, 57.1 (2004), 69–89.
34. Mora cites many texts that helped her research the topic of depression while writing this novel. She lists, for instance, Andrew Solomon, *Saturns Schatten* (Frankfurt: Fischer Verlag, 2006) in the 'Hinweis' at the back of the novel.
35. Sarah-Christina Henze, 'Transgression des Strichs: Getrennte Perspektiven in Terézia Mora's Roman *Das Ungeheuer*', in *Das Radikale: Gesellschafts-politische und formal-ästhetische Aspekte in der Gegenwartsliteratur*, ed. by Stephanie Willeke, Ludmilla Peters and Carsten Roth (Münster: LIT Verlag, 2017), pp. 85–105.
36. Deleuze & Guattari, p. 26.
37. Lisa Foran, *Derrida, the Subject and the Other: Surviving Translation and the Impossible* (London: Palgrave Macmillan, 2016), p. 125.
38. <https://tereziamora.de/flora_naploja.pdf> [accessed 1 October 2020].
39. See, for instance, Jacques Derrida, 'Living On. Border Lines', in *Deconstruction and Criticism* (New York: Seabury Press, 1979), pp. 75–176 (p. 102).
40. Lisa Foran's gloss on Derrida's *Survie*, in *Derrida, the Subject and the Other*, p. 126.
41. Lisa Foran.
42. Anke Biendarra reminds us that Kopp has an excellent singing voice and is represented singing a pop song while lost in the forest. Biendarra also relates these references to the Orpheus myth but reads Kopp as experiencing catharsis. See her chapter 'Travel and Trauma in Post-1989 Europe' (as note 3).
43. Ibid.
44. See interview with Anke Biendarra, *Transit Journal* (2007) <https://transit.berkeley.edu/2007/biendarra/> [accessed 23 April 2023].
45. See Lene Rock, *As German as Kafka*, pp. 151–63.

CHAPTER 11

Futurity and the People to Come: *futuristen-epilog* — *poeme* by Berkan Karpat and Zafer Şenocak

Margaret Littler

Introduction

This chapter focuses on a co-authored poetic collaboration between the German writer Zafer Şenocak and installation artist Berkan Karpat that draws on aspects of their shared Turkish heritage, twentieth-century modernisms and contemporary scientific thinking. The project began with a series of collaborative art installations in Munich between 1998 and 2008, the contents of which are distilled in the poems in the resulting volume.[1] This material but transient phase of the poems' inception already points to the project's experimental, non-representational nature; an important aim of the entire project was to overcome the separation between art and science, viewing both in terms of creative experimentation and sensory stimulation, rather than representation of a solid state of reality. In this regard it poses a challenge to the established approach of 'intercultural German Studies' with its focus on intercultural dialogue between self and other, as such stable categories are nowhere to be found. Instead it echoes Bruno Latour's characterization of modernity in terms of the absolute separation of nature and culture on the one hand, and the proliferation of hybrids on the other.[2] It may also be situated within the materialist turn towards the post-human[3] and vibrant matter,[4] as a creative intervention that crosses not only ethnic boundaries but those between science and the arts, the human and the non-human, past and future. This essay draws on Gilles Deleuze's philosophy of time in its focus on futurity, not as a temporal dimension but as an openness to the virtual, which is here manifest in the emergent properties of language itself. Viewed from this perspective the poetry is not concerned with representing a reality or community that already exists, but with the conjuring of new possibilities of life, a people to come.

The cycle contains five poems, the first three inspired by great twentieth-century modernists, the poet Nâzım Hikmet (1902–1963), the Russian Cubo-Futurist Velimir Khlebnikov (1885–1922) and the founder of the Turkish Republic, Mustafa Kemal Atatürk (1881–1938). The last two poems take inspiration from literary figures of modernity, Daniel Defoe's Robinson Crusoe, and Georg Büchner's

Woyzeck and Marie, though these too are transformed by encounters with oriental antecedents and literary forms. Throughout the poems are woven references to Sufi mysticism and the poetry of Mevlâna Jalāl ad-Dīn Muhammad Rūmī (1207–1273) and to his spiritual muse and mentor, Shams-i-Tabrīzī [Sun of Tabriz] (1185–1248). The intermingling of vastly different timeframes is central to my discussion here of the second poem in the cycle, 'tanzende der elektrik' [electric dancers],⁵ inspired by the Russian poet and playwright Velimir Khlebnikov, well known for his eclectic fascination with science, ornithology, cosmology, the oriental roots of Russian culture, and his radical linguistic experimentation.⁶ His early poetry, informed by Russian Symbolism and Futurism, engages in a creative play with language in which small shifts in sound bring about complete transformations of meaning.⁷ Karpat and Şenocak's poem plays with repetition and variation in a similarly experimental way, defying fixed identities as much as it derails obvious meanings, and short-circuits chronological time. The poem is a tribute to Khlebnikov, but not to the actual poet as much as to his simulacrum, the multiple personae and many myths he cultivated and that circulated about him.⁸ My aim is not to pin down these components (Khlebnikov's futurism, science, mysticism) to a definitive interpretation, but to observe how the poem sets them in motion in non-totalizing relation, like the molecular motion of matter itself. Karpat and Şenocak's poem combines experimentation with the materiality of language with references to vibrant matter, and evokes medieval Islamic thought in the midst of modernity, its patterns of repetition and variation activating multiple different contexts, never settling into a univocal meaning. This contributes to the poem's futurity in the sense of a radically open literary form, with meanings irreducible to contexts such as cubo-futurism, mysticism, science or indeed minority literature.

Futurism / Futurian / Futurity and the Virtual

Futurity has recently enjoyed a revival of interest in academic German Studies, indicating a renewed engagement with the acceleration so characteristic of modernity that is transforming human experiences of past, present and future.⁹ Leslie Adelson has been at the forefront of this debate with a series of essays culminating in her 2017 monograph on Alexander Kluge.¹⁰ Adelson defines futurity as a problem in thought related to but not reducible to future time: 'Futurity is [...] an analytical tool rather than a temporal domain; the two should not be conflated, though they are, of course, mutually inflected. Futurity in this sense arguably becomes especially pressing when the future emerges not only as an object of thought but also and acutely as a problem in thought'.¹¹ This idea of futurity as a mode of thought rather than an objective point in linear chronology suggests something akin to the Deleuzean view of the problem, not as something to be solved, identified and represented, but as a challenge that propels thought into motion.¹² Elsewhere Adelson discusses Russian Futurism's 'factography' (citing Devin Alden Fore) as a non-representational approach to literature, rather than an aesthetic celebration of the speed of modern life: 'Beyond *faktura*, factography explicitly sought "the reconvergence of force and signification" [...] the aesthetic of factography aimed "not simply to depict life, but to create it anew in the process" of writing'.¹³ Taking inspiration from Adelson's suggestive discussion, I aim to show how such an understanding of futurity liberates Karpat and Şenocak's poem from restrictive notions of 'ethnos'¹⁴ and suggests a resolutely non-representational approach to writing. As a 'problem in thought' futurity unfixes common-sense assumptions about chronological time, stable identities and the very nature of the people addressed by this poetry. It requires an approach to literature as experimentation with rather than representation of reality.

Deleuze's philosophy itself enacts a kind of futurity, with its injunction to live with a heightened sense of the potential of reality and of individuals to change. His very understanding of the real as a dynamic relation between actual and virtual, and of individuals as locations where thoughts and sensations connect with virtual intensities and ideas, implies a departure from intentionality and the consistency of identities, replacing representations with a re-intensification of life, an openness to its potential to become.¹⁵ Of all literary language it is poetry that abandons claims to referentiality, where the identity of a narrating 'I' is not fixed, *and* where significance is most intensely felt — significance understood as the effect of the virtual in the realm of actual things. This is what is understood here as the reconvergence of force and signification.

Karpat and Şenocak's poetry produces such an opening to intensities, those that animated the poetry of the past as well as those that will give meaning to the future. The poetry renounces both a fixed and active subject position to foreground the dynamic forces that flow through it, much as Khlebnikov saw his own poetry as subject to the ebb and flow of language: 'I am futurity's silent ebb | I am silentium's future flow'.¹⁶ According to Richard McKane, Khlebnikov preferred the term 'futurian' to 'futurist', resisting the solidity of a group identity while insisting on the anticipatory force of his writing.¹⁷ Indeed the poet Osip Mandelstam remarked in 1922 that 'it was not language that was Khlebnikov's main obsession, but time'.¹⁸ He developed elaborate theories on the cyclical nature of history based on complex mathematical formulae, and while there is no critical consensus on their significance for his poetry, Ronald Vroon acknowledges that in the 1919 poem 'The Stone Woman', 'the intersecting axes of the ancient past and present-day reality, the macrocosmos of the heavens and the microcosm of the earth, provide coordinates for the poet's theory of temporal progression'.¹⁹ A similar circularity and interconnectivity of time and space pervades 'tanzende der elektrik', which refers to actual times and places (Mongol migrations to Asia Minor, aspects of Khlebnikov's biography), but expands their scope by setting them in motion with other elements (Sufi poetry and cosmology, space travel, the vibrations of matter). Actual contexts and lived presents are thus made to vibrate with unthought and virtual realities, which is what constitutes the futurity of the text.

'tanzende der elektrik': Genesis, Personae, Beyonsense

First published in 1999, this poem was initially performed in a wooden tower erected in Munich's Odeonsplatz, inside which a sound installation accompanied a Turkish oil wrestling match.[20] At the same time sound recordings of words by Velimir Khlebnikov and those of Mevlâna Jalāl ad-Dīn Muhammad Rūmī were played against each other. While this has been viewed as a battle between medieval and twentieth-century utopias,[21] I see them as overlapping and interacting elements in the assemblage of the installation, transforming each other as they do in the poem. Oil wrestling as 'national' Turkish sport has ancient Greco-Roman origins, but was cultivated in medieval Anatolian dervish lodges ('tekke') as the athletic discipline accompanying spiritual training in mystical Islam. One purpose of the oil is to render the contest more a matter of skill than brute strength, and to this day there is an etiquette of respect for defeated older wrestlers. In Karpat and Şenocak's poem oil is both a lubricant and a source of rich assonance connecting otherwise disparate elements; it is sunscreen in the Iranian desert, it lubricates colours and sounds at the start of the poem, and the stars at its conclusion. Sufism is present throughout the whole poetry cycle in references to 'mevmev'[22] (the Persian poet Rūmī) and 'schems' (Shams-i-Tabrīzī). In this poem Sufi dervishes take on a further resonance specific to Khlebnikov's experiences in Iran, where in 1921 he volunteered for a Bolshevik expeditionary force, and became known as the Russian dervish for his eccentric appearance and nomadic wandering. The 'Rosenmullah' ('Gul-Mullah')[23] is one of Khlebnikov's alter egos in the poem, along with 'russland', 'schems', 'chleb'[24] and 'mevmev'. Humorous variations on the names proliferate throughout, including 'der sprachchlebtomane'[25] [Khlebnikov as thief of language] and the 'feder des graphomanen mevmev' [the graphomaniac mevmev's brush]. Khlebnikov famously adopted multiple personae and resisted ascribed identities: when conscripted into the army in 1916 he is quoted by Ronald Vroon as saying 'I am a dervish, a Yogi, a Martian, anything you want, but I am not a private in a reserve infantry regiment'.[26] So, in the poem, all socially produced identities are undermined or humorously mocked in favour of unthinkable and mutable personae.

I present the first section of the poem here in full, to show how it both refers to the installation — the material conditions of its emergence — and encapsulates many of the interlocking motifs developed and transformed in the poem: Khlebnikov's personae, mystical Islam, dizzying variations of cosmic scale, and the emergence of meaning from material variations of language, also engaging in translingual play between German and Turkish. The poem opens with a hailing of words as 'distant friends', and a disarmingly straightforward promise to tell the story of three central characters, who appear here as oil wrestlers, engaged in a 'cubist' form of the contest:[27]

hey worte	[hey words
hey liebe ferne freunde	hey dear distant friends
ich erzähle euch die geschichte vom	i'll tell you the story of the
kubischen ringen	cubist wrestling
von den sprechkapseln in plasma	of the speechcapsules in plasma
die geschichte von den drei körpern in öl	the story of the three bodies in oil
von schems chleb und dem mevmev	of schems chleb and of mevmev
chleb das bin ich der sprachchlebtomane	chleb that's me the language
bin ich eine haarzelle mohammeds	chlebtomaniac
oder der geist eines großen mannes	am i a haircell of muhammad
mit dem namen russland	or the spirit of a great man
	with the name russia
schems den schönen jungen	schems the beautiful boy
schick ich zu den sternen	i send to the stars
ich handle mit sternen	i deal in stars
die hole ich mir aus dem leierkasten	i fetch them from the organ grinder[28]
dem mahlkasten der töne	the grinding box for sounds
mahle zermahle feilsche mit klängen	grind grind up haggle[29] with sounds
male mit der feder des graphomanen	paint with the graphomaniac mevmev's
mevmev	brush
dem schönen schems augenbrauen	beautiful schems' eyebrows
öle meine töne	oil my sounds
in den körpern der drei troubadoure	in the bodies of the three troubadors
die federzüge mevmevs	the brushstrokes of mevmev
...male...	...paint...
...mahalle...	...mahalle[30] / district...
...hane...	...hane / household...
...ahne...	...guess...
...erahne...	...imagine...]

This opening 'stanza' sets up a speaking subject, 'chleb', who is from the outset multiple, embodying both the origins of Islam ('a haircell of muhammad') and 'the spirit of a great man | with the name russia'. This references two of Khlebnikov's personae: the Sufi mystic and the spirit of Russia, and introduces a molecular scale into the poem. Khlebnikov's patriotic identification with Russia is later referenced in a direct citation of his poem 'Russia and Me' that encompasses both his tendency to self-ironizing, megalomaniac identifications, and his fascination with Russia's oriental roots, expressed here as a cell of Muhammad's hair in Russia's beard:

ich russland	[i russia
ich und russland	i and russia
abertausenden hat russland die freiheit	russia has granted freedom to thousands
geschenkt	and thousands
gute sache	a good thing
lange noch wird man daran denken[31]	people will long remember
an das ringen der bartträger	the bearded wrestlers
an die sonnensegel	the solar sail
an die haarzelle mohammeds	the haircell of muhammad
im bart russlands	in russia's beard
russlands gefallene sterne	russia's fallen stars
der freiheit geschenkt	given to freedom]

As in the opening stanza, however, Khlebnikov's patriotic pride merges with Sufi mysticism and the science of space travel. The 'speechcapsules in plasma' from the opening stanza link language to the molecular movements of matter. As electrically charged matter, plasma conducts electricity and generates magnetic fields. It is energetic matter, associated here with language as productive and transformative force. But it is also connected to cosmic phenomena, and stardust as the origin of matter itself. The stars (to which the beautiful schems is dispatched) are a pervasive cosmic image in the whole poetry cycle, and are here related to Khlebnikov's interest in cosmology, and to his patriotic devotion to the heroes of Russia's past.[32] Yeşilada links the stars to language, specifically the 'Sternensprache' [Language of the Stars] that Khlebnikov imagined for the utopian 'new man'.[33] But the 'solar sail' in the quotation above is a lexical link to space travel, locating the stars in the cosmos. The solar sail on a spaceship propels the vessel by the force of the sun's rays, analogous to wind in a ship's sail. Thus the poem develops its own momentum through multiple associations, and requires of its readers the mental agility to operate at different scales and across multiple times simultaneously. Its sustained ambiguity is in a sense similar to the preservation of wave function in quantum physics, where only its collapse inaugurates a single state of being.

In the opening stanza 'chleb' retrieves sounds from a machine, opening up ambiguities between the acoustic and visual meanings of 'töne' [tones], and between the homophones 'malen' [paint] and 'mahlen' [grind], so that sound, colour and mechanical friction are inextricably linked.[34] Language is something produced by material processes, a manipulation of the matter of sound and pigment to produce an image of the beloved Shams, prolonged by the sibilance and assonance of 'ö' sounds in 'dem schönen schems augenbrauen | öle meine töne'. Here the oil is simultaneously that of the oil wrestlers in Karpat's installation, of the paint on the brush, and it is the long vowel sound itself. There follows a list of words inspired by Khlebnikov's own experimental poetry, shifting single letters or morphemes, within and across languages, to marvel at the creative shifts of meaning produced, moving from painting ('male') through a (Turkish) district ('mahalle'), a (Turkish) household ('hane'), to an act of guessing ('ahne') and imagination ('erahne'). They emerge as if mechanically from the barrel organ, not referring to any actual state of the world, but inaugurating the material shifts of language that will resonate with ever greater intensity throughout the poem.

Translator Paul Schmidt notes that Khlebnikov's writing 'displays a perpetual willingness to allow form to form itself. He allows accidents to happen'.[35] Nancy Perloff also writes of the Russian Futurists' sense of wonder at the creative potential of language beyond semantic reference: 'Their poetry, which they wrote in the language of *zaum'*, or "beyonsense," (*za* [beyond]; *um* [the mind]), can be traced to an eclectic range of sources, including the incantations of Russian Orthodox priests and village shamans, the nonsense syllables of nursery rhymes, and the cacophony of the modern city'.[36]

As Ronald Vroon points out, Khlebnikov's Futurism grew directly from his interest in science; verbal experiments with neologisms, the adding and subtraction of prefixes, word lists giving rise to poems, the revival of etymologies long forgotten, were all features of his poetic method. Vroon cites a scientific analogy made by Khlebnikov to describe his method: 'He likens the corrupted, conventional language of the people to Euclid's geometry, and the product of neological discourse to that of Lobachevsky, with its potential for remodeling the world'.[37] Thus he viewed his paralinguistic pursuits as interventions in the structure of the world itself. This is the basis of Karpat and Şenocak's affinity with his work, rather than his nationalist pride; it is the experimentation with language that restores its power to signify, in the sense of the power to connect with virtual intensities. Meaning is not limited to the relationship of signifiers to each other or of signifiers to an outside world. As for Deleuze and Guattari, here meaning extends to the self-organizing potential of matter itself, signs are 'triggers of material processes', not a second-order reality but catalysts for change.[38] In Karpat and Şenocak's poetry the use of lower case defamiliarizes the German words and the absence of punctuation heightens the ambiguity of the syntax, both features contributing to the intensity of the language and deflecting it from a referential reading. Towards the end of the poem a line develops from the shifts of single letters: 'trance trans transi transit', which Yeşilada sees as encapsulating the movement from the mystic to the migrant,[39] but again it draws attention to the power of paradigmatic as well as syntagmatic relations in language, producing connections that are as morphological as they are semantic.

In the second stanza of 'tanzende der elektrik' words themselves are personified as 'caravans of words in flight', which has been interpreted as a reference to the migration of early Turkic peoples from Mongolia into Asia Minor.[40] This is supported by reference to the 'mongols' and 'the twenty-six horsemen from khanat', but there is another level on which the 'caravan of words' is the list of words themselves, and the letters within them, that bear such transformative power, as characterized in the following lines:

a der listige	[a the cunning one
be der barbar	b the barbarian
ka die böse zunge	k the evil tongue
ka[41] ist für alle ein kerker	k is a dungeon for all
zwang zucht und zaum[42]	duress discipline and zaum
zwingburg für fast tote	stronghold for those near death
...	...
ef der zerbrochene	f the broken one
schwingt	vibrates
schwingt in der schlucht voller goldzähne	vibrates in the gorge full of gold teeth
zett auf dem sonnensegel	z on the solar sail
spannt sich in den magnetischen morgen	fills up into the magnetic morning]

These lines both refer to and enact the 'beyonsense' ('zaum') or sound symbolism of Russian futurism building images of imprisonment and duress from the alliteration of 'k' and 'zw', naming the very vibrations that produce the fricative 'f' and envisaging 'z' as a solar sail taught with the sun's radiation. A later configuration of 'ka' and 'zett' across a line break has more sinister connotations, becoming the

German acronym for concentration camp: 'gefangene des ka | zett auf seinem segel' [prisoners of the k | z on its sail]. Even the identity of individual letters shifts radically depending on their position in the poem, as the letter 'k' transforms from a prison to dead and dying concentration camp inmates. This dark allusion is woven into repetitions of 'gold', from the letter 'f' that 'vibrates in the gorge full of gold teeth' to 'ich hurenhändler | stehle den kadavern die worte aus den mündern | die goldenen worte | goldschmuck für meine sterne' [i hourimonger | steal the words from the mouths of corpses | the golden words | gold jewels for my stars]. Repetitions evoke the theft of gold and of language from corpses, and the promise of a new, utopian language, perhaps Khlebnikov's 'Language of the Stars'. This is certainly suggested by the poem's imperative to others, 'pearl seekers', to join in the renewal of language, first the avant-garde from St Petersburg, then others are hailed to join in:

mein gesicht ein wortkäfig	[my face a wordcage
aufgehängt bei den sternen	hung up with the stars
mein gesicht ein aufschlagpunkt	my face a point of impact
für perlensucher	for pearl seekers
...	...
sterne aus petersburg	stars from petersburg
greifen in meinen wortkäfig	reach into my wordcage
holen	collect
perlen aus dem eismeer	pearls from the icy ocean
...	...
kommt zu meinem wortkäfig	come to my wordcage
ihr perlensucher	you pearl seekers
kommt	come
kommt	come]

As McKane tells us, Khlebnikov wanted poets to be 'fishers of the pearls of the Russian language', and he himself delved into Slavic etymology to create neologisms in Russian.[43] But in Karpat and Şenocak's poem further meanings accrue due to the accumulation of variations on the same words, the face is a cage for words and suspended in the stars, not part of an organism or expressive of identity, but embedded in the materiality of the cosmos and productive of language. The repetition and recombination of elements in the poem produces a cumulative effect that repeatedly deflects the gestures to specific places and times. Thus repetition does not produce sameness, rather referential meaning is unmoored and set afloat on the tide of the poem.

Futurity, Folds in Time and the People to Come

The poem's lack of any conventional structures has been noted (regular verse form, patterns of rhyme/metre, even upper case and punctuation), but it acquires a consistency based on repetition and recombination of elements in ever new constellations, not reducible to an unambiguous meaning. This is here related to Deleuze's view of time, which includes chronological progression (a certain expectancy of the future in the present), as well as the sense of a complete past (archived independently of active memory or material traces), and an 'eternal return' that incorporates the virtual, not determined by past identities and sameness. Deleuze sees repetition as fundamental to all three aspects of time, the repetitions of habit and memory (producing stability and consistency) being superseded by the absolute difference of the eternal return, which overcomes the tendency of the other two towards stasis, and is 'a belief of the future, a belief in the future'.[44] What I suggest here is that there is an analogous structure at work in the repetitions of this poem, which are of course actively produced poetic effects, not the passive syntheses of time elaborated by Deleuze. But as for Deleuze, repetition develops a form of expectancy and consistency in the actual poem, and always also introduces difference because each new repetition resonates with new intensities.

Thus the opening lines address words themselves and promise the telling of a story: 'hey words | hey dear distant friends', but in the second, words are in flight ('caravans of words in flight'). In the third stanza, the opening lines are reprised differently: 'hey words | hey dear distant friends | signals fallen out of your box). Words are now signals, fallen out of context, damaged, yet also released from conventional meanings, and Shams is sent to bathe their wounds with soothing sibilance (sch) and assonance (ö): 'schicke euch schems den schönen jungen |um zu ölen eure wunden' [i send you schems the beautiful boy | to oil your wounds].[45]

In a final reprise, the words are dying camp inmates, and 'ka', at once guard and Sufi mystic, looks on:

hey worte	[hey words
hey liebe ferne freunde	hey dear distant friends
aus dem kasten gefallene signale	signals fallen out of your box
gefangene des ka	prisoners of k
zett auf seinem segel	z on his sail
hat seine locken gelöst und sieht uns an	has loosened his curls and looks at us
auf seinen lippen der koran der zahlen	the qur'an of numbers on his lips]

Here 'ka' is simultaneously a subject (the only possible subject of 'hat' and 'sieht'), the first letter of the German acronym for a concentration camp, and a figure from a surreal 1915 prose text by Khlebnikov. This 'Ka' derives from ancient mythology, a protean familiar accompanying human life, 'the Ka is the soul's shadow, its double, its envoy to the world some snoring gentleman dreams of. There are no barriers for the Ka in time; he moves from dream to dream, breaks through time [...] He occupies the centuries as comfortably as he does a rocking chair'.[46] The combination of the mythological and the mundane in Khlebnikov's text has humorous echoes in

Karpat and Şenocak's poem, where the land surveyor 'K' of Kafka's *Castle* and the hero of Orhan Pamuk's *Snow* also come to mind. Khlebnikov's Ka's time-travelling presence, from ancient Egypt to science fiction (he meets a scientist from the year 2222) may also have served as a model for the poem's folding of time, whereby the damage done to language and humanity by twentieth-century fascism may be soothed by the tones of medieval Sufi poetry. The reference to the 'qur'an of numbers' echoes an earlier reference to the 'qur'an of love', and evokes both Sufi theories about the numerical mysteries in the Qur'an, Khlebnikov's 'Gul-Mullah' persona, and his liking for arcane mathematical formulae linking historical events.

Such apparently direct allusions to Khlebnikov's life and work might seem to anchor its meaning in specific identities and histories, but the effect of the poem is still to destabilize identity as a source of meaning. For example the figure of the 'rosenmullah' introduces a series of allusions to Khlebnikov's poem 'The Gul-Mullah's Trumpet', which evokes his travels in Iran,[47] but in Karpat and Şenocak's poem Khlebnikov's journey is projected into later twentieth-century aviation history. The 'i' flies from Moscow to 'tyran' in a dilapidated Tupolev[48] aeroplane that later crash-lands in the desert, sending 'red parachutes' to mingle with 'marines', the disciples of the migrated Mongols, and 'derwisch-uruss-touristen' [dervish-ur-russian-tourists].[49] Times and peoples mingle as Khlebnikov's voyage of discovery becomes a pilgrimage, a plane crash and a tourist expedition all in one: 'notlandung in der wüste | bei den dornenfressern | schöner ort hier etwas zu heiß' [emergency landing in the desert | with the thorneaters | nice place here a bit too hot]. The camels ('dornenfresser', [thorneaters]) echo the 'plasmafresser' [plasma-eaters] of the Mongol invasions, and prefigure 'der menschenfresser' [the people-eater] that later haunts the poem. The poem combines and recombines the same elements in different, increasingly surreal constellations: parachuting Russians crash-landing in the desert, vodka and sun-cream, the cosmonaut, camels, the stars, corpses, and the virgins of Muslim heaven.

The point is that there is no firm point of reference, no one 'people' directly invoked or addressed in the poem, and yet there *is* a hailing ('hey words | hey dear distant friends') and an invitation to join in the poetic venture ('you pearl-seekers | come | come'). In one stanza a repeated 'hu' seems to hail each persona in turn: 'hu schems | hu mevmev | hu rosenmullah | hu'.[50] The 'i' of the poem shifts constantly, at times it is 'i mevmev', at others 'i russia', or 'i hourimonger', but the subject is also emphatically negated. The 'i' is declared a 'deserter' from the caravan of words, and in a repeated couplet the subject appears merely a means to the end of poetry:

ich bin gar nicht mehr ich   [i am not at all i any more
ich bin gar nicht mehr du   i am not at all you any more
nicht mehr russland   no longer russia
bin desertiert   am a deserter
aus der karawane der worte   from the caravan of words

ich weiß ich bin nur mittelmaß   i know i am but medi-ocre
nur ein mittel für ein versmaß   but a medium for a metre]

This recalls Khlebnikov's view of himself as a medium for language, but it evokes also Deleuze's view of the 'dissolved self', the passive location of thought and sensation rather than a self-conscious 'I'.[51] The poem's 'i' is protean, taking on and discarding identities, and above all denying the stability of a national or ethnic identity. The poet is at times a cosmopolitan catcher of voices, a 'hourisinger' in 'chleb's' club along with Shams as 'lead singer':

Stimmenfänger	[voice catcher
kein geschlecht	no lineage / sex
kein vaterland	no fatherland
hurisänger im club von chleb	hourisinger in chleb's club
der stimmenfänger schems	the voice catcher schems
chefsänger bei chleb	lead singer at chleb's]

The human subject is radically decentred in this poem that links the dervish dance to the revolutions of the planets and the random motion of subatomic particles, just as Khlebnikov saw the cosmos and the microcosmos conjoined by the same rational laws: 'stillgedrehter tänzer | in der umlaufbahn | die zehen zerfressen vom mond' [gyrating dancer at a standstill | in orbit | his toes eaten away by the moon]. A repeated quatrain reiterates the cosmopolitans' lack of anchoring in family/sex/nation/Earth, locating them rather as servants and keepers of the cosmos:

kosmopoliten haben kein geschlecht	[cosmopolitans have no lineage / sex
kein vaterland	no fatherland
sind einsame sternenwärter	are solitary star-keepers[52]
dienen der körpersonne	serve the body-sun]

In the 'star-keepers' Yeşilada sees a reference to Khlebnikov's 'Language of the Stars' and she sees the 'body-sun' as the dervish, revolving around his own axis like a planet around the sun.[53] There is certainly a suggestion of analogy between the new man's movement (the cosmopolitan's travels) and the cosmic orbits of the stars, reinforced by the linkage of 'cosmopolitan' and 'cosmonaut' throughout the poem, the shared roots of the words as significant as their semantic content. But this refrain also points to something beyond the actual markers of human identity (sex, lineage, nationality), embodied in the cosmic, rather than merely earthly scope of the cosmopolitan.[54] Once again one must go beyond a metaphorical reading to consider the movements of matter in the poem. The utopian language and dervish dance are mobile components in the assemblage of the poem, not representations of something with a worldly analogue. Khlebnikov's world, Sufi wisdom and modern science are not in tension, but are heterogeneous components in the mobile multiplicity of the poem.

The language of science and technology becomes more insistent towards the end of the poem, with references to vibrating plasma, cells, and the human body as a machine, a poem ('ghasal'), a resonating chamber and source of material for musical pipes. This 'new man' bears little relation to his precursors in twentieth-century futurism:

auf den münzwerfer wartend	[waiting for the coin-thrower
eine münze für meinen sprechapparat	a coin for my speech-machine
eine münze für das ghasel meines körpers	a coin for the ghasal of my body
wortplasma in schwingung	word plasma vibrating
schwingungen in wortplasma	vibrations in word plasma
drehen meinen körper	turn my body
aus meinen knochen die rohrflöte	the reed pipe from my bones
...	...
hier der neue mensch	here the new man
kein sprechender im schatten seines körpers	not a speaking one in the shadow of his body
der elektrische mensch	the electric man
und sein vibrator	and his vibrator
ein gesicht voller geschmolzener worte	a face full of melted words]

Once 'the new man' is explicitly named, it is as a non-dualistic body, an electrically charged assemblage, with language as a vibrating material component. But it is also a body from whose bones the traditional reed pipe can be made, and from which Sufi poetry issues. The face is no longer a cage for words, but a crucible from which new words may be formed. The poem ends with the electrical image in its title, presenting the 'i' as plugged into a 'you' in a way that defies the subject–object relation, suggesting instead a machinic connection producing an electrical current, just as the dust and plasma of the cosmos gave rise to the matter of earthly life. The 'new man' is born out of the microscopic and cosmic level of matter, bringing us back to the fundamental power of life before any human subject. In this the poem achieves the Sufi goal of liberation from the constraints of personality, as suggested by the constant gyration of the dervish dance. But the spiritual enlightenment implied by Shams' name ('Sun of Tabriz') becomes electric illumination ('i light up my own cell | am my own schems'), folding mysticism into modernity:

ich in meiner sternlosen nacht	[i in my starless night
wie kann ich	how can i
du sagen	say you
ferner freund	distant friend
wir sind angekettet	we are chained to the spot
der strom fließt	the current flows
ich glühe am draht	i glow on the wire
bin das neue licht	am the new light
ich leuchte meine eigene zelle aus	i light up my own cell
bin mein eigener schems	am my own schems
im brutkasten der die welten erschafft	in the incubator of the worlds created
aus staub und plasma	from dust and plasma
kubische welten	cubist worlds
derwische	dervishes
tanzende der elektrik	electric dancers]

The poem returns to the cubist wrestling of its beginning, but the worlds it evokes have been taken apart and reassembled over and over in new and unfamiliar forms. The electric dancers, which are also the dancing particles of electric current, emerge from the metastable matter of the poem itself.

The poem undoubtedly takes inspiration from Khlebnikov's language experimentation, his interest in mystical Islam *and* his fascination with science and cosmology simultaneously, and in its title the dynamic potential of electrically charged matter animates the rotations of the dervish dance. As Deleuze and Guattari themselves observed, Khlebnikov invented two languages, each of which following its own line of escape: 'the astronomical, algorithmic, stellar language of pure logic and high formalism, and the underground "zaoum" that works with a pure asignifying material, intensity, sonority, contiguity'.[55] In Karpat and Şenocak's poem, the material, the mystical and the cosmic are not separate nor are they in tension, but move together in productive constellations. Instead of being separated by the inexorable progress of time, the movements of matter pervade both mystical and molecular reality. The wisdom of medieval Islam lies contracted in the vibrating matter of the present, the desert sand and stardust are neighbours in the consistency of the poem's world. Instead of a constituted and represented people the poem hails a new people, and contributes to the conditions of its emergence.

Notes to Chapter 11

1. Berkan Karpat and Zafer Şenocak, *futuristen-epilog — poeme* (Munich: Babel, 2008). The volume has no pagination.
2. Bruno Latour, *We Have Never Been Modern*, trans. by Catherine Porter (Cambridge, MA: Harvard University Press, 1993).
3. Rosi Braidotti, *The Posthuman* (Cambridge: Polity, 2013).
4. Jane Bennett, *Vibrant Matter: A Political Ecology of Things* (Durham, NC: Duke University Press, 2010).
5. This is only one possible translation of the title, which also implies dancers as a component of electricity.
6. See for example Ronald Vroon's introduction to the *Collected Works of Velimir Khlebnikov*, vol. III: *Selected Poems*, trans. by Paul Schmidt, ed. by Ronald Vroon (Cambridge, MA: Harvard University Press, 1997).
7. Khlebnikov was discredited for 'formalism' in the USSR, yet was also known for his patriotic fervour, honouring the heroes of Russian history.
8. I draw here on Deleuze's use of simulacrum as the impersonal individuation that replaces the illusion of the persistence of the same self through time.
9. See Frauke Fitzner (ed.), *Tempo! Zeit- und Beschleunigungswahrnehmung in der Moderne* (= *ZfL Interjekte* 5, ed. by the Zentrum für Literatur- und Kulturforschung Berlin, 2014) <http://www.zfl-berlin.org/publication/tempo-zeit-und-beschleunigungswahrnehmung-in-der-moderne.html> [accessed 25 April 2019].
10. Leslie A. Adelson, *Cosmic Miniatures and the Future Sense: Alexander Kluge's 21st-Century Literary Experiments in German Culture and Narrative Form* (Berlin and Boston, MA: De Gruyter, 2017).
11. Leslie A. Adelson, 'Futurity Now: An Introduction', *The Germanic Review*, 88 (2013), 213–18 (p. 216).
12. D. N. Rodowick points to the contrast in Deleuze's thought between the theorem (that follows an axiomatic logic) and the problem, which confronts thought with the unthought: 'Rather than resolving itself in a method or model of knowledge, or freezing itself in a proof, thought is pitched into movement, without finality or resolution, by an unanswered question'; *Gilles Deleuze's Time Machine* (Durham, NC: Duke University Press, 1997), p. 199.
13. Leslie A. Adelson, 'Experiment Mars: Contemporary German Literature, Imaginative Ethnoscapes, and the New Futurism', in *Über Gegenwartsliteratur: Interpretationen und Interventionen. Festschrift für Paul Michael Lützeler zum 65. Geburtstag von ehemaligen StudentInnen*, ed. by Mark W. Rectanus (Bielefeld: Aisthesis Verlag, 2008), pp. 23–49 (p. 41).

14. Adelson restricts this to 'the re-working of *ethnos* in a newly expanded European framework, in which Turkish histories also circulate', 'Experiment Mars', pp. 42–43.
15. James Williams, *Gilles Deleuze's Difference and Repetition: A Critical Introduction and Guide* (Edinburgh: Edinburgh University Press, 2013), p. 7.
16. Khlebnikov, *Selected Poems*, p. 9.
17. Richard McKane (ed.), *Ten Russian Poets: Surviving the Twentieth Century* (London: Anvil Press, 2003), p. 49.
18. McKane, *Ten Russian Poets*, p. 50.
19. In Khlebnikov, *Selected Poems*, p. 11.
20. The tower might have been inspired by the Symbolist salon of Vyacheslav Ivanov, known as 'The Tower' in St Petersburg, which Khlebnikov frequented in 1908, see McKane, *Ten Russian Poets*, p. 49. But it also appears in the poem as a 'freudenturm' [tower of pleasure] in which heaven's virgins dance like dervishes.
21. Karin E. Yeşilada, *Poesie der dritten Sprache: Türkisch-deutsche Lyrik der zweiten Generation* (Tübingen: Stauffenburg, 2012), p. 413.
22. The whimsical nickname 'mevmev' refers to Rumi's honorific title Mevlâna, identifying him as a member of the Mevlevi dervish sect.
23. See Khlebnikov's poem 'The Gul-Mullah's Trumpet' (1921).
24. This name clearly derived from that of Khlebnikov is also the Russian word for bread.
25. This humorous play on 'kleptomaniac', 'Khlebnikov' and 'Ottoman' recalls the punning title of Şenocak's fourth prose work of the 1990s *Der Erottomane* (1999).
26. Khlebnikov, *Selected Poems*, p. 1.
27. The poem spreads across seventeen unnumbered pages, in unnumbered sections of varying lengths, which I will call 'stanzas'. This makes precise referencing problematic, but is also in keeping with the poem's structuring principle of repetition and variation from which ever new constellations emerge.
28. 'Leierkasten' is literally 'barrel organ', but the English designation of its operator is much closer to the ambiguous imagery of this poem.
29. 'Feilschen' actually means 'to haggle', but here it also implies 'feilen' [to file] due to the proximity of 'mahlen' [to grind].
30. Both 'mahalle' and 'hane' are words from Arabic that have entered Turkish.
31. See 'Russia and Me': 'Russia has granted freedom to thousands and thousands. | It was a really terrific thing to do, | people will never forget it', Khlebnikov, *Selected Poems*, p. 94.
32. See the poem 'We want to be familiars of the stars', in which the stars are heroes of Russian history and culture, invoked to 'Restore our fathers' spirit / to this dreary, doubtful land' (Khlebnikov, *Selected Poems*, pp. 35–36 (p. 36)).
33. Yeşilada, *Poesie der dritten Sprache*, p. 416.
34. The genre designation of the collection 'poeme' (rather than the more usual 'Gedichte' — poetry) from ancient Greek 'ποιεῖν' implies material production rather than individual genius.
35. Khlebnikov, *Selected Poems*, p. vii.
36. Nancy Perloff, 'Sound Poetry and the Musical Avant-Garde: A Musicologist's Perspective', in *The Sound of Poetry / The Poetry of Sound*, ed. by Marjorie Perloff and Craig Dworkin (Chicago, IL: University of Chicago Press, 2009), pp. 97–117 (p. 99).
37. Khlebnikov, *Selected Poems*, p. 7.
38. Mark Bonta and John Protevi, *Deleuze and Geophilosophy: A Guide and Glossary* (Edinburgh: Edinburgh University Press, 2004), p. 4.
39. Yeşilada, *Poesie der dritten Sprache*, p. 416.
40. Yeşilada, *Poesie der dritten Sprache*, p. 415.
41. Khlebnikov published a surreal prose text entitled *Ka* in 1915. To the contemporary reader this also recalls Kafka's novel *Das Schloß* [*The Castle*] (1926) with its hapless protagonist 'K'.
42. German 'Zaum' means 'bridle', thus echoing in German the constraint of 'Zwang' and 'Zucht', while also evoking the anarchy of the Russian futurists' 'beyonsense'.
43. McKane, *Ten Russian Poets*, p. 49.
44. Gilles Deleuze, *Difference and Repetition*, trans. by Paul Patton (London: Continuum, 2004), p. 113.

45. This resonates with 'öle meine töne' in the first evocation of Shams in the first stanza.
46. Velimir Khlebnikov, 'Ka', in *Collected Works of Velimir Khlebnikov*, vol. II: *Prose, Plays and Supersagas*, trans. by Paul Schmidt, ed. by Ronald Vroon (Cambridge, MA: Harvard University Press, 1989), pp. 56–74 (p. 56).
47. Khlebnikov, *Selected Poems*, p. 221. McKane notes that Khlebnikov's poem was also called 'Tiran without the t', as a punning clue to its origins in the poet's travels in Iran, *Ten Russian Poets*, p. 81.
48. Soviet aviation pioneer Andrei Tupolev (1888–1972) was persecuted in Stalin's purges but became a leading aircraft designer from the 1950s.
49. 'Uruss dervish' is how the traveller is hailed in Khlebnikov's 'The Gul-Mullah's Trumpet' (*Selected Poems*, p. 223). While Khlebnikov's 1915 text 'Ka' refers to a Sikorsky aircraft, the Tupolev was a later Russian design.
50. Yeşilada notes that 'hu' is the cry that often ends the dervish dance (*Poesie der dritten Sprache*, p. 415, note 132). The word 'Hu' also occurs in Khlebnikov's text 'Ka', where the soul is divided into the Ka, the Hu and the Ba, — the Hu referring to man's goodness (Khlebnikov, 'Ka', p. 56).
51. Gilles Deleuze, *Difference and Repetition*, p. 100.
52. Die Sternwarte is an observatory, but astronomer is 'der Astronom'. The poem invents a noun 'Sternenwärter' and the expression 'die Sterne warten', which is humorously mechanical.
53. Yeşilada, *Poesie der dritten Sprache*, p. 416.
54. Elsewhere in the poem the cosmopolitan seems also to be without a determinate language, as s/he cannot translate: 'könnt übersetzen die worte | wär ich kein kosmopolit | nur ein kosmonaut' [if i could translate the words | i wouldn't be a cosmopolitan | only a cosmonaut].
55. Gilles Deleuze and Félix Guattari, *Kafka: Toward a Minor Literature*, trans. by Dana Polan (Minneapolis: University of Minnesota Press, 1986), p. 76 (translation amended).

CHAPTER 12

Minor Literature, Minor Discourse and the Representation of Eastern Europeans Working in Britain

Monica Ali's *In the Kitchen* and Marina Lewycka's *Two Caravans*

Pamela McCallum

Midway through Marina Lewycka's *Two Caravans*, a 2007 novel about migrant workers in Britain's agricultural sector, Andriy, a young man from eastern Ukraine, finds himself on the crowded streets of central London. Fascinated by the abundance of the city — well-dressed pedestrians, towering buildings, shop windows filled with desirable objects — he inadvertently nudges a woman walking quickly, her stylish high heels clicking along the pavement.[1] Her only reaction is a brisk dismissal. Andriy realizes that the cheap fabric and formless cut of his Eastern European shirt and trousers, the worn imitation leather of his shoes and belt, make him invisible to the fashionable woman. Her glance fails to acknowledge his presence on the street, consigning him to an incontestable nothingness in her eyes. This brief episode can productively be read alongside another description of Eastern European workers in the popular news media. In 2016 the London newspaper *The Daily Express* published an article on the Lincolnshire town Boston.[2] With a market dating from the twelfth century and a site directly on the Greenwich meridian, the town might be expected to signify typical rural England, but journalist Chris Roycroft-Davis conveys very different impressions. He describes walking through streets lined with a Baltic nightclub, a hairstyling shop with Eastern European staff, a Polish delicatessen, a Latvian bakery, and pavements peopled with young, boisterous migrants whose voices fill the air with unfamiliar languages. Queueing to purchase a newspaper, he must wait behind a Russian and a Pole, only to meet a Lithuanian at the cash register. Later when he retreats to that most British of community spaces, a pub, the server is a young Polish woman. If Andriy was invisible on the streets of central London, here Eastern Europeans are hyper-visible: lively, jostling bodies and a soundscape of syllables from disparate languages.

These two images — an unnerving obscurity and an intense presence — map out positions occupied by Eastern European workers in Britain. The invisibility that Andriy feels in the face of an affluent Londoner is part of a broad economic approach to sales and marketing that isolates the final product from its conditions of production: in a supermarket, displays of clean radishes, tomatoes, spring onions, other fruits and vegetables, work to dislocate the produce from any consideration of planting, growth and harvest. It all appears unmarked by a prehistory of labour, by bowed bodies, by hands grasping and pulling. Just as the prosperous London woman may never consider the work that makes possible her luncheon salad, so the young migrant on the street is invisible to her. From another point of view, in a town like Boston near sites of labour (in this case, the rich fenlands), the bodies of Eastern European migrants acquire an intense visibility, even claiming space with shops and sites of leisure. Yet there is still a different sense in which the obscurity and the conspicuousness of the migrant body are linked: both representations of migrants reinforce nationalist discourses that have become increasingly vocal in the twenty-first century. Invisibility preserves the fantasy of homogeneous communities, while hyper-visibility fosters unease and apprehension about a seemingly overwhelming otherness. When the European Union (EU) expanded on 1 May 2004, among the new members were seven former Soviet Bloc countries: the Czech Republic, Estonia, Hungary, Latvia, Poland, Slovakia and Slovenia. With economies ravaged by the breakup of the Soviet Union, it is unsurprising that many citizens of these new EU nations utilized freedom of movement to seek work in western Europe. It is also, sadly, unsurprising that the influx of labourers from Eastern Europe gave rise to a range of anti-migrant discourses — Roycroft-Davis's investigation of Boston is a restrained example — all of which have intensified following the June 2016 referendum in which Britain narrowly voted to leave the EU. How might literature be read as an intervention into these populist discourses of anxieties, frustrations and alarm? How might novels offer a counter-discourse to narratives of fear that depict a nation confronted at every turn with an unwelcome otherness? Ashley Dawson points out that 'unlike the often abstract and globalizing theories that undergird policies of "managed migration" today, [texts of literature] illuminate the specific factors that spur and sustain migration and, in doing so, challenge the xenophobic discourses that dominate the public sphere in the global North'.[3] In what follows I explore two novels published after the accession of Eastern European nations to the EU — Monica Ali's *In the Kitchen* (2009) and Marina Lewycka's *Two Caravans* (2007), titled *Strawberry Fields* in North America — to foreground a counter-discourse, or an expanded understanding of minor discourse, that contests anti-migrant depictions of Eastern European labourers in Britain. As a minor element within British immigrant literature, predominantly texts by first- or subsequent-generation writers with affiliations to the British Empire, novels about Eastern Europeans offer distinctive perspectives on processes of othering and strategies of resistance within working lives.

In any discussion of minor literature, the conventional point of departure is Gilles Deleuze and Félix Guattari's book *Kafka: Towards a Minor Literature*.[4] As they argue, in minor literature, language is dislodged from customary usages. For Franz Kafka, who had learned Czech in his childhood, knew Yiddish from his Jewish culture, and experienced the official German of Habsburg bureaucracy, the German in which he wrote his novels and stories is, in their words, 'affected with a high co-efficient of deterritorialization' (*Kafka*, p. 16). In Prague, German is pressed out of its zones of familiarity such as Berlin or Vienna. It inhabits spaces within and around other languages, is adapted to ethnic dialects, and undergoes a process of becoming minor, which can be seen in syntactic inversions, fragmented sentences, abandoned articles. Minor literature takes shape within a major language, exaggerating some aspects, weakening others, to produce new forms of writing, as, for example, in Algerian or Québécois French, in Black American English, or in the various creole forms of European languages in the Caribbean.

It is this twisting and reimagining of language that gestures towards the second characteristic of minor literature, its intimate proximity to politics. Within the close, constricted sites of minor literature what may seem unique is always coupled with politics; a singular character or action, as Deleuze and Guattari put it, 'becomes all the more necessary, indispensable, magnified, because a whole other story is vibrating within it' (*Kafka*, p. 17). In their view, it is not so much that minor literature constructs allegorical figures representing political perspectives, but instead that, in the crowded spaces of a minor text, commercial and economic relations, social authority and subordination, personal hierarchies within the family, all ultimately highlight political stories of domination and resistance. In this way, by becoming political, minor literature acquires a 'collective value' (*Kafka*, p. 17). Here, a writer's enunciations provide a mapping of a community to come, for a creative grasping of future possibility, a collectivity that finds tentative form within minor literature. In the following decades, other scholars extended these discussions. In the late 1980s, within the emergent discipline of postcolonial studies, Abdul JanMohamed and David Lloyd drew on Deleuze and Guattari's reflections on minor literature to examine the 'alternative practices and values which are embedded in the often damaged, fragmentary, hampered, or occluded' texts written by displaced and colonized populations.[5] Taking an altered, but comparable position, Bert Olivier suggests that Canadian thinker Naomi Klein's books *The Shock Doctrine*, on interventions into disaster zones, and *This Changes Everything*, on the climate crisis, produce counter-discourses that parallel minor literature. From her linguistic strategy of substituting new combinations of nouns and adjectives ('disaster capitalism', 'climate crimes') to her stress on communities and alliances, Klein's writing infiltrates and destabilizes dominant discourses.[6] In these cases, minor discourse conjures up conditions of possibility within writing for telling different stories squeezed out from between the lines of major discourses.

One of the stories that Monica Ali's *In the Kitchen* and Marina Lewycka's *Two Caravans* share is the enfolding and compressing of politics into novels that recount the lives of those who are marked by the appearance of a variant racism. Drawing on Ambalavner Sivanandan's term 'xeno-racism', Petra Tournay-Theodotou calls attention to a form of othering that 'is not restricted to persons of a darker complexion, but rather extends to the newer category of impoverished and displaced whites'.[7] Xeno-racism mobilizes the structural dynamics of racism against those perceived as different others, signified not by skin colour, but by poverty. Just as racism utilizes darker skin colour to counter a recognition of common humanity, so gestures, sounds of accents, patterns, intonations, intensities of speech, particularities of clothing, all of which deviate from an imagined norm of 'Englishness', are taken as markers to racialize impoverished migrants. Within such a perspective, xeno-racism situates Eastern European migrants in Britain in a position parallel to Black and minority ethnic immigrants from the former British Empire, at the same time that their lack of connection with Britain and its colonial histories inserts an asymmetry into the relationship. They inhabit a complex intersection where, from the perspective of xeno-racism, practices of othering neutralize the apparent privilege of whiteness when it is accompanied by poverty and unfamiliar languages.

At the centre of *In the Kitchen* is Gabriel Lightfoot, head chef at a luxury hotel in London, who is on the cusp of achieving his longstanding ambition to own a restaurant. Having grown up in an industrial textile town in Yorkshire, now ravaged by the transfer of production to South and East Asia, he appears to have achieved success in the ever-expanding service sector of the capital. Gabriel's hopes begin to slide off course when an Eastern European worker intrudes into his life: Yuri, a Ukrainian night porter, mysteriously dies in a fall while living in the subterranean corridors, the storage areas, of the hotel. The figure of Yuri's dead body haunts Gabriel as he pursues his dream of opening his own restaurant. The novel, often read as a 'condition of England' narrative,[8] follows the chef as he grasps at happiness with his girlfriend Charlie, attempts reconciliation with his family when his father faces a terminal illness, negotiates financing for his long-desired restaurant, investigates unlawful activities in the hotel, succumbs to a psychotic episode — most likely bipolar disorder, from which his mother also suffered — and ends up for a very brief time working as an agricultural labourer. The personal and professional interconnect and traverse each other, opening out onto larger questions of politics, economics and globalization. Just as Deleuze and Guattari claim that politics crowds into the texts of minor literature, so the clash of class, status and mobility coalesce in Gabriel's profession of chef. From one perspective, he is required to organize food, with attention to presentation and style, for the upscale events that take place in the hotel; high-level management figures consult him; his personal attention to customers is valued as part of the 'dining experience'.[9] All of this establishes him as a professional in a service sector that generates enormous profits from the luxury market in central London. Yet from another perspective, the scars on his hands from burns and cuts mark him as a labourer; he navigates a workplace made dangerous by grill flames, boiling water and sharpened knives; his 'office' contains 'a surfeit of air-conditioning duct', a 'plastic seat' (*Kitchen*, p. 11), a worn 'Formica' desktop (*Kitchen*, p. 19), all of which suggest factory production and manual labour, in a space bearing 'the indelible stamp of generations of toil' (*Kitchen*, p. 25). Older industrial production and contemporary service industries intersect on the body of the chef and in the spaces he traverses.

These tensions and contradictions are thrown into relief by the inescapable material presence of a corpse, which eventually derails Gabriel's individual aspirations. When Yuri's body is found on the floor in the lower levels of the hotel, his only possessions are a few personal items (a change of clothes, a razor, cooking utensils). The sole trace of a lifeworld in Ukraine is 'an old photograph of a woman with a cleft chin and two little girls in big coats' (*Kitchen*, p. 31). Somewhat surprisingly, Gabriel's reactions are neither to the blood on the floor, nor to the distortions of the fallen body, but to the human sensibility of an intelligent man. 'He had a wise face, had Yuri,' Gabriel reflects, gazing on the body, 'easy to miss when he was a man in a green boiler suit', and, in death, 'his blue and kindly lips had parted, as if ready to dispense good advice' (*Kitchen*, p. 32). Bit by bit, he learns more details about Yuri's life. The girls in the creased photo are now young women studying at university. Another kitchen worker informs him of an unknown past: 'Yuri was an engineer also. Full qualifications. He understood very well the machines' (*Kitchen*, p. 84). Significantly, Gabriel's slippage from standard English syntax into Yorkshire dialect ('had Yuri'), echoed in his subordinate's unusual phrasing ('very well the machines'), reinforce the intimation that Yuri's death wrenches Gabriel away from his plans for his own restaurant, dragging him back into the working-class environment of his northern boyhood and of the kitchen. For the hotel's senior managers, the death is little more than an irritation (police inquiries, the formalities of an inquest), but for Gabriel it is the beginning of a haunting that continues throughout the narrative.

A corpse underneath spaces of luxury is also a poignant reminder of the co-existence of lawful businesses alongside darker criminal activities. Ali's fictional hotel corporation, the PanContinental Hotel Co., is an amalgam of the British InterContinental Hotels Group (IHG) and the Singaporean Pan Pacific Hotels, a combination that unites the West with the Far East, and is a potent symbol of globalization. Behind the opulent appearance of dining spaces and rooms in PanContinental's London property lurks a sex-trafficking ring run by three employees. In their book *Deviant Globalization*, Nils Gilman, Jesse Goldhammer and Steven Weber stress the overlap among legitimate and illicit businesses. The same infrastructure (airports, international motorways, railways, ports, hotels and so on) that exists to facilitate global travel and trade is also utilized by global crime, which takes shape at, in their words, 'the intersection of ethical indifference and regulatory inefficiency'.[10] The very hotel in which Gabriel hopes to build his reputation as a first-class chef is also the 'headquarters' of a group trafficking young women into the sex trade.

This is perhaps the place to note that a second Eastern European, a trafficked sex worker, Lena, also intrudes into Gabriel's life.[11] His generous, but misplaced, efforts to assist are diminished by the obsessive sex he imposes on her. Deeply damaged by her experiences, isolated in London, terrified that traffickers will find her again, she has ended up living in the hotel basement with or alongside Yuri, in what Margarida Esteves Pereira calls 'a limbo of painful statelessness'.[12] Lena comes from Mazyr, an oil refinery city in southern Belarus, close enough to Ukraine to have suffered significant fallout from the 1986 nuclear catastrophe in Chernobyl. When Gabriel encounters her waiting outside the hotel in the night — 'a streetlamp shrugged a sodium glow over the girl, and he had the sensation she was floating in the circle of orange light. [...] Shadow obliterated her eyes' (*Kitchen*, pp. 103–04) — it seems as if global criminality, brutal sex trafficking, and environmental degradation, have all come together in the slight figure of a very young woman.[13] Indeed, the struggle to survive in London leads her to ethically questionable acts: she enlists Gabriel to retrieve Yuri's hidden money for her; she offers sex for shelter, later angrily demanding payment, and when, in the grip of psychosis, Gabriel empties his bank account for her, she disappears with the money, some eight thousand pounds (*Kitchen*, pp. 112, 106, 440, 497). If Yuri is the reliable worker, willing to offer his engineering expertise on a porter's meagre pay, trying all the while to support his family, Lena is a young woman whose humanity has been eroded by the ruthless exchange economy of trafficking which identifies her only as an object to be sold.

Why would the death of a migrant worker press so intrusively into Gabriel's conscious and unconscious mind? One possible answer is suggested in Judith Butler's *Frames of War* where she argues that precariousness is intrinsic to all human lives. As she puts it,

> Precariousness implies living socially, that is, the fact that one's life is always in some sense in the hands of the other. It implies exposure both to those we know and to those we do not know; a dependency on people we know, or barely know, or know not at all. Reciprocally, it implies being impinged upon by the exposure and dependency of others, most of whom remain anonymous.[14]

For Butler, this state of precarity is inherent to all social formations in which human beings live. While it is tempting to think of precarity primarily in the context of impoverished populations in the developing world who have no access to clean drinking water or medical care, she points out that it is equally evident, though significantly moderated, in wealthy nations. Lives there also lie in 'the hands of the other' (*Frames*, p. 14), dependent on municipal workers to provide safe water and sewage disposal, on transit drivers, on those who grow, harvest and transport food, on air traffic controllers and on a host of others, nearly all of whom remain unknown. To recognize this precarity as fundamental to human life is to also acknowledge that all lives are interconnected with others and their loss inspires grief. That Gabriel initially expresses emotion over the death in only the most cursory and conventional manner — 'he should have sent someone out for flowers' (*Kitchen*, p. 32) — suggests an initial refusal to recognize the life lost. Yuri dies with, in Butler's words, 'no regard, no testimony, and ungrieved' (*Frames*, p. 15), at least in Britain. From the point of view of the hotel, Yuri proves to be a disposable person, a migrant labourer whose loss can be carelessly discounted because he is so easily replaceable. As Nikolai, a Russian doctor, whose flight from political threat has led him to the position of a kitchen worker, comments, 'The significance of Yuri's death is that it is insignificant. That is why it is so troubling' (*Kitchen*, p. 463). For Gabriel, Yuri's loss is initially inconsequential: he remains simply another migrant worker in the hotel, whose labour as a night porter and in repairing the kitchen machinery went unnoticed. Just as politics and collectivity crowd into minor literature, so the affiliations in Gabriel's life as head chef, hierarchies of authority and subordination, embed him inextricably within the workforce of the hotel kitchen, interconnected with all those who work under his supervision. It comes as no surprise, then, that after death this reliable man with a kindly expression returns to haunt the chef who ignored him in life.

In dreams that successively intensify to nightmares (*Kitchen*, pp. 115, 165, 236, 360), Gabriel revisits, as if returning to a primal scene, his first glimpse of Yuri lying dead on the floor. The dreams have an allegorical tone, a search for a corpse, death surrounded by food, which may represent, as Tournay-Theodotou writes, a 'nation which, in its eternal, insatiable greed, literally "feeds off" the body of people like Yuri'.[15] Each begins with a hallucinatory descent through 'phosphorescent light' (*Kitchen*, p. 115), 'viscous violet light' (*Kitchen*, p. 360), or an oxymoronic 'dark-light' (*Kitchen*, p. 165). In the first three dreams he catalogues the details of the body, beginning always with Yuri's feet, taking note of dry skin, yellowing nails, the lines of each instep, seemingly obsessed with the minutiae of a man he scarcely knew in life.[16] In a bizarre parody of the restaurant industry, the chef calls out, 'Who will feed me? [...] Bring me food' (*Kitchen*, p. 165), and miraculously piles of food appear around the body. What might these dreams — becoming nightmares — signify? At a fundamental level, feet suggest both the journey of migration and the exhaustion of work (aching feet, workers on their feet all day). Feet also form the base of the standing body, just as the labour of migrants (agricultural work, repetitive cleaning, even sexual services) often provide foundational tasks. The food that appears in the dream — satay pork, filo stuffed with feta and spinach — are dishes brought to London by many generations of other cultures. An implicit answer to Gabriel's question, and what he experiences when he finds himself picking spring onions on a farm, is that migrants will feed you. All of this is subordinate to Gabriel's increasing intimacy with the corpse. In the first dream, he confronts the corpse where he first saw it; in the second he eats alongside the body; eventually, he reaches out to touch the man's skin and to share food, placing a piece of chicken 'gently between Yuri's black lips' (*Kitchen*, pp. 115, 165, 236). Read in this way, these uncannily repetitive dreams begin to coalesce around a desire that longs for human relations, the very connections erased by the working hierarchy of the hotel. The most terrifying nightmare — a decaying body, rotting food, maggots and flies (*Kitchen*, p. 360) — signals the futility of Gabriel's fantasy that he might recognize Yuri as a fellow human being sharing a workplace, or rather, that his attempts have come too late.

The final section of the novel depicts Gabriel's plunge into a psychotic mania that parallels his hallucinatory dreams. Driven by an agitated impulse 'to descend into the world and see what he could do' (*Kitchen*, p. 494), he terrifies a neighbour, leaves a child crying in the streets, empties his bank account for Lena, and works for two days as a farm labourer. Most significantly, the experience of psychosis brings him into contact with another Ukrainian, Olek, a man whose time in England has included sleeping rough, working in meat-processing, in construction and agricultural sectors. Using a strategy also evident in *Two Caravans*, the language of their exchanges employs linguistic twists, phrasings that might be read as the inarticulate English of a migrant, but that also signify beyond the register of realism. After a short break from picking spring onions, Olek nods to Gabriel, 'Must working' (*Kitchen*, p. 513), which is easily understood as 'we must return to work'. Yet, the deceptively simple phrasing conveys other implications. The weight of 'must', without a subject, suggests the pressures (devastated economies, persistent impoverishment, repressive regimes) that motivate migrants to seek work in western Europe. At the same time, the correct 'ing' ending hints at a gap between the achievements of the speaker and the work undertaken: Olek has a university degree in mathematics. In this way, as Deleuze and Guattari argue, a simple two-word phrase becomes saturated with politics. Linguistic entanglements, equally dense, are evident in a similar later exchange. Olek mentions a woman he met in London; they have lost contact, but he wants to find her again. Gabriel replies that in the vast expanse of London locating her is unlikely, to which Olek responds, 'Not good chances. [...] But must asking question' (*Kitchen*, p. 520). The phrase may refer to the man's determination to try to discover his friend; it may also refer to the question he subsequently asks Gabriel about mathematical chance. Both these possibilities logically fit into the men's conversation, however halting it might be. Still, the imperative of 'must', together with the present participle 'asking', hints at a continual process of questioning, opening onto the larger issues implicit within the novel: how and why is the labour around the growing, harvesting and production of food, fundamental to human survival, so often undervalued? What responsibilities does a society owe to migrants, trafficked persons and refugees within its borders? How might citizens engage with these pressing matters? An attitude of continual questioning is intimated as an orientation towards the world.

Earlier, in a drunken conversation with Nikolai about his dreams, Gabriel responds aggressively to the Russian's suggestion that the recurring nightmares may imply a sense of responsibility for Yuri's death: 'How could that be my fault?' (*Kitchen*, p. 376). It is not so much a personal responsibility for an individual death, but rather an overall ethical consequence that, in Nikolai's words, signifies 'a feeling of responsibility — for the world in which we live, for the kind of world in which there will always be more Yuris, struggling to exist' (*Kitchen*, p. 376), that is, a recognition of Butler's insistence that the precarity of human life implies its interconnections. As Nikolai recasts it, the dream-work within Gabriel's unconscious mind extends a respect for Yuri's humanity to the local social, cultural and political spaces in which people live, and opens up the possibility of wider, global contextualization. The novel, however, circumscribed by its largely realist form, conveys only how these ideas might be concretized in a restricted personal sense — Gabriel's reconnections with his own family; his defence of a young migrant worker on the farm, an act of defiance that produces no positive result; the possibility of a reunion with his former girlfriend Charlie — not how actions might address wider social divisions.[17] At the same time, readers can hardly leave the novel without an awareness of Nikolai's words, without a sense that the transformations of globalization mean countless migrants throughout the world struggle to survive, and that the story of Gabriel's ineffectual gestures may nonetheless shape incentives for human connections and resistances to oppression.

Similar questions about human communities and future possibilities are raised in Marina Lewycka's *Two Caravans*. Doris Lechner describes the novel as 'an Eastern European variation on a British or postcolonial theme', underscoring its affiliations with the large body of writing about newcomers to Britain from former colonies.[18] The narrative takes shape within a world of globalized labour where a business styling itself as 'Human Solutions' (*Caravans*, p. 75) imports workers for farms, care homes, food processing plants and other services, thereby supplying employers' desires for a flexible workforce to whom they owe little or no responsibility. Five characters enter the United Kingdom legally (three EU citizens from Poland, Yola, Marta and Tomasz; and a Malaysian and a Chinese student, Soo Lai Bee and Song Ying, whose questionable language school has facilitated visas). They are joined by three others whose documentation is less firm (Ukrainians, Irina and Andriy, an African, Emanuel). Like *In the Kitchen*, the novel depicts the co-existence of legitimate business pursuits alongside deviant forms of globalization: growers hire both documented and undocumented workers; traffickers haunt the sites of agricultural labour for access to young women far from home. *Two Caravans* focuses on Irina, a nineteen-year-old from Kiev, in Britain for a summer of strawberry picking, who finds herself unexpectedly pursued by a gangster Vulk (the pronunciation suggests *vovk*, 'wolf' in Ukrainian) with intentions to lure her into the sex trade. In distinct contrast is Andriy, a young man from Donetsk, a traditional coal mining area, who flees the bleakness of ravaged industries in Ukraine's eastern districts. While starkly depicting the divisions of the Ukrainian nation, with large urban areas seeking connection with Europe and the eastern borderlands oriented towards Russia, Irina and Andriy also find themselves between two empires. They leave past Ukrainian affiliations to the failed Soviet empire and Eastern Bloc alliances, and enter a British space marked by historical memory of worldwide empire and, in Paul Gilroy's terms, a postcolonial melancholia that cannot relinquish memories of transnational power.[19] Instead of the idealized England of Irina's expectations (summer gardens, dappled sunlight, conversation and tea), the two participate in an exacting economy where their inexpensive labour is necessary to maximize profits. At the same time, even within these dreary and hazardous spaces of work, Lewycka's text installs unsettling, disruptive turns of language to represent both vulnerabilities and risks, together with alliances and collectivities, among migrant communities.

The language of *Two Caravans* has resonant connections with Deleuze and Guattari's return to a discussion of minor literature in their subsequent book, *A Thousand Plateaus*. Its characteristics, they argue, 'make language stammer, or make it "wail," stretch tensors through all of language, even written language, and draw from it cries, shouts, pitches, durations, timbres, accents, intensities', or, in Gregg Lambert's summary, 'make the sequences vibrate' and 'open the word into unexpected internal intensities'.[20] Linguistic style in Lewycka's *Two Caravans* alters and restructures English in the narratives of the migrants. Like the passages in Ali's novel, these writing strategies cannot be described as merely reproducing 'broken English' in an attempt to depict realistically different accents and voices. Rather, the novel dismantles and reassembles language to draw attention to affection and care, fear and terror, wonder and laughter, within both the speech of individuals and the collectivity of the migrant community.[21] Ronald Bogue comments that minor literature generates 'evidence of the atmosphere within which represented affects communicate with one another over, above and through the words'.[22] In *Two Caravans*, circulation of affect in stylistic distortions and linguistic inventions of the text articulates a depth of emotion and collective affiliations among a very disparate group who grope towards communication in their common, second language, English.

Shortly after her arrival at the strawberry farm, Irina reflects on her fondness for studying English, recalling her imaginary constructions of the country: 'I had pictured myself walking through a panorama of cultivated conversations, like a painted landscape dotted with intriguing homonyms and mysterious subjunctives: *would you were wooed in the wood*' (*Caravans*, p. 18, italics in original). In this brief memory of a classroom pronunciation exercise, whose pleasing repetition of vowels and consonants almost seems to create a non-referential fragment of poetry, Irina articulates her desire for romance in England. The phrasing and the subjunctive 'would you were', almost never used in contemporary spoken English, underline that she has acquired the language in school and through reading, just as her mental repertoire of courtship and romance have come from books, film and other media.[23] It is perhaps no surprise that the conventional figure of 'love in a wood' finds an ironic inversion when Vulk, intent on rape, pursues her through a forest in Kent. At the same time that the phrase expresses past and present longings — her love of the English language, her desire to meet the English men and women whose images she has created in her imagination — it also inscribes a future nightmare embedded in networks of exploitation that wind through the Balkans and Eastern Europe to a young Ukrainian woman in England.

Later in the novel the dangers facing Irina are refracted in a condensed, but expressive phrase through which Emanuel conveys the desperation he and Andriy feel when they fear she may have been trafficked.[24] He reports a confrontation with Vulk in Dover: 'Andree asked him the whereabeing of the beauteous strawberry picker Irina' (*Caravans*, p. 153). In contrast to the normal usage (where or whereabouts), the neologism 'wherebeing' conveys dense resonances. With its existential connotations, 'being' underlines both the two men's concern for Irina's welfare and the risks she faces. She has endured a harrowing flight from Vulk, spent a fearful night hiding in the forest, followed sounds of traffic to a road, and joined another group of strawberry pickers (*Caravans*, pp. 56–58, 60–63, 71–73, 81–82, 92–94). Although neither Andriy nor Emanuel is aware of her disturbing experiences, the echo of wellbeing in 'wherebeing' distinctly evokes their anxieties about what might have happened to their friend. Further, Emanuel's account is written in a letter to his sister, words that cannot be delivered because he does not know her address; the letter is consigned to 'a bag full of crumpled papers' under his bed (*Caravans*, p. 11). Language here is multiply displaced. Initially, the conversation between Andriy and Vulk is shifted into reported speech so that readers are given no descriptions of vocal timbre or facial expression; the unfamiliar noun 'wherebeing' must carry the weight of readers' impressions of Andriy's concern for Irina. Then, the communicative function of language is disrupted within a letter that cannot be delivered. Finally, conventional English usage of the present participle as a noun is here linked to 'where', normally an interrogative adverb associated with spaces and sites, journeys and distances. All of these strategies impart affiliations with the migrants themselves, with their dislocations in a strange country, with their desires, hesitations, and commitments to one another.

This is the sense in which minor literature, according to Deleuze and Guattari, emerges as a space saturated with the political. At the same time that *In the Kitchen* and *Two Caravans* tell the stories of the death of a Ukrainian man in a British workplace or Eastern European and other migrants who enter Britain seeking work in the agricultural sector, representations of global migration, privatization of social services, transformation of agriculture into factory farming, disparities of wealth between northern and southern areas of Britain and between eastern and western Europe, bound up with the secretive, illegal underside of globalization, labour exploitation and human trafficking, all crowd into the two novels' narratives. To the extent that readers engage with Gabriel's tentative, humane gestures towards Yuri, a man already dead, with Irina's mental images of England and the English language, with Emanuel and Andriy's heartfelt anxieties for another migrant, they will have encountered, if only in the safety of reading, a lifeworld of impoverished others struggling to exist alongside and among spaces of abundance in the West. In a period when anti-migrant attitudes and policies have become prominent throughout western European nations, *In the Kitchen* and *Two Caravans* construct minor discourses that imagine new collectivities initiated through mutual recognition of common humanities.

Notes to Chapter 12

1. Marina Lewycka, *Two Caravans* (London: Penguin, 2007), pp. 191–92. Further references to this edition are given after quotations in the text. This chapter was written and mostly revised before the Russian invasion of Ukraine in February 2022. It is appropriate here to note that both novels, published more than a decade earlier, incorporate tensions and dislocations — the devastation of post-Soviet economies, repression in Putin's Russia, differing allegiances in western and eastern Ukraine — which form part of the complex intersections between the two nations.
2. Chris Roycroft-Davis, 'Boston: THE Most Segregated Town in the UK', *Daily Express*, 31 January 2016 <https://www.express.co.uk/news/uk/639715/Boston-THE-most-segregated-town-in-the-UK> [accessed April 2019]. I am grateful to Ben Blyth for bringing this article to my attention.
3. Ashley Dawson, 'The People You Don't See: Representing Informal Labour in Fortress Europe', *ARIEL*, 40.1 (Jan. 2009), 125–41 (p. 126).
4. Gilles Deleuze and Félix Guattari, *Kafka: Toward a Minor Literature*, trans. by Dana Polan (Minneapolis: University of Minnesota Press, 1986). Further references to this edition are given after quotations in the text.
5. Abdul JanMohamed and David Lloyd, 'Toward a Theory of Minority Discourse', *Cultural Critique*, 6 (1987), 5–12 (p. 10).
6. Bert Olivier, 'The Possibility of a "Minor Discourse" that Deterritorialises Neoliberalism Politically', *Journal of Literary Studies*, 33 (2017), 1–24 (pp. 16, 21).

7. Petra Tournay-Theodotu, 'Fortress Britain: Hospitality and the Crisis of (National) Identity', in *On the Move: The Journey of Refugees in New Literatures in English*, ed. by Geetha Ganapathy-Doré and Helga Ramsey-Kurz (Newcastle upon Tyne: Cambridge Scholars Press, 2012), pp. 11–25 (p. 12). The term xeno-racism is introduced in Ambalavener Sivanandan, 'Poverty is the New Black', *Race and Class*, 43.2 (2001), 1–5.
8. For a detailed, insightful reading of *In the Kitchen* as a 'condition of England' novel, see Janice Ho, *Nation and Citizenship in the Twentieth-Century British Novel* (New York: Cambridge University Press, 2015), pp. 179–90.
9. Monica Ali, *In the Kitchen* (London: Random House, Black Swan, 2009), p. 89. Further references to this edition are given after quotations in the text.
10. Nils Gilman, Jesse Goldhammer and Steven Weber (eds), *Deviant Globalization: Black Market Economy in the 21st Century* (London: Continuum, 2011), p. 3.
11. Louisa Waugh, *Selling Olga: Stories of Human Trafficking and Resistance* (London: Weidenfeld and Nicolson, 2006) provides an account of trafficking women from the former Soviet Union. Ali also lists books she consulted on trafficking under 'Acknowledgements' (*Kitchen*, p. 555). Pietro Deandrea, *New Slaveries in Contemporary British Literature and Visual Arts: The Ghost and the Camp* (Manchester: Manchester University Press, 2015), pp. 110–14, discusses the invisibility of young women like Lena.
12. Margarida Esteves Pereira, 'Transnational Identities in the Fiction of Monica Ali: *In the Kitchen* and *Alentejo Blue*', *Journal of Postcolonial Writing*, 52.1 (2016), 77–88 (p. 80).
13. Pei-chen Liao, '"Seeking Out the Periphery" in the Shadows: Monica Ali's *In the Kitchen* and Contemporary Writing of Britain', *NTU Studies in Language and Literature*, 28 (2012), 87–115, offers an extensive analysis of darkness and obscurity around Lena.
14. Judith Butler, *Frames of War: When is Life Grievable?* (London: Verso: 2009), p. 14. Further references to this edition are given after quotations in the text.
15. Tournay-Theodotu, 'Fortress Britain', p. 22.
16. In a parallel act, Gabriel's compulsive sex with Lena always begins with her feet, as if he is trying to conjure these spectral migrants into a life they are not permitted to have in Britain: he 'rubbed gently on the heels, marvelling at how truly she was flesh and bone, his Lena, his ghostly girl' (*Kitchen*, p. 307). It is important to note that Dave Gunning, 'Ethnicity, Authenticity, and Empathy in the Realist Novel and its Alternatives', *Contemporary Literature*, 53.4 (2012), 779–813, interprets Gabriel's acts as a will to dominate Lena: 'The quest to know the body of Lena, as much as to know her history, is for Gabe a pursuit of mastery over her, through which he hopes to shore himself up' (p. 791).
17. Scholars disagree in assessing Gabriel's journey and its implications for the novel. Jopi Nyman, 'A Carvery of Hybridity: Monica Ali's *In The Kitchen*', in *Hybridity: Forms and Figures in Literature and the Visual Arts*, ed. by François Specq, Catherine Pesso-Miquel and Vanessa Guignery (Newcastle upon Tyne: Cambridge Scholars Press, 2011), pp. 92–101, suggests that the vibrancy of the multicultural kitchen represents an emergent collectivity beyond the racial divisions of imperialism. Similarly, Christoph Houswitschka, 'Cosmopolitanism and Citizenship: Identities and Affiliations in Monica Ali's *In the Kitchen*', in *Transcultural Identities in Contemporary Literature*, ed. by Julie Hansen and Carmen Llena Zamorano (Amsterdam: Rodopi, 2013), pp. 71–91, stresses how the kitchen blurs boundaries of class, ethnicity and race to challenge traditional social divisions. From a different viewpoint, Sarah Brouillette, 'The Pathology of Flexibility in Monica Ali's *In the Kitchen*', *Modern Fiction Studies*, 58.3 (2012), 529–48, suggests that Gabriel's accommodation with neoliberal capitalism 'can simply allow one to continue to participate in it with impunity, and without suffering undue mental anguish' (p. 532).
18. Doris Lechner, 'Eastern European Memories? Marina Lewycka's Novels', in *Facing the East in the West: Images of Eastern Europe in Contemporary British Literature, Film and Culture*, ed. by Barbara Korte, Eva Ulrike Pirker and Sissy Helff (Amsterdam: Rodopi, 2010), pp. 437–80 (p. 446).
19. Paul Gilroy, *After Empire: Multiculture or Postcolonial Melancholia* (London: Routledge: 2004).
20. Gilles Deleuze and Félix Guattari, *A Thousand Plateaus: Capitalism and Schizophrenia*, trans. by Brian Massumi (Minneapolis: University of Minnesota Press, 1987), p. 104, and Gregg Lambert, 'The Bachelor Machine and the Postcolonial Writer', in *Postcolonial Literatures and Deleuze:*

Colonial Pasts, Differential Futures, ed. by Lorna Burns and Birgit M. Kaiser (London: Palgrave, 2012), pp. 37–54 (p. 40).
21. In a parallel argument, Oliver Lindner, '"East is East and West is Best?": The Eastern European Migrant and the British Contact Zone in Rose Tremain's *The Road Home* (2007) and in Marina Lewycka's *Two Caravans* (2007)', *Anglia*, 127.3 (2009), 459–73, suggests that Lewycka uses distortions in the migrants' English to highlight social othering (p. 468).
22. Ronald Bogue, *Deleuze on Literature* (London: Routledge, 2003), p. 108.
23. Irina's images of England draw on her readings, together with memories from popular media. For instance, she believes English men to be 'incredibly romantic', recalling 'a famous folk legend about a man who braves death and climbs in through his lady's bedroom window just to bring her a box of chocolates' (*Caravans*, p. 20). The 'folk legend' is not rooted in the distant past, but rather derives from a television advertising campaign for Cadbury's Milk Tray chocolates that portrays a 'James Bond' figure braving fanciful obstacles to give sweets to an unseen woman.
24. For analysis of the networks of trafficking in the novel see Pamela McCallum, 'Representing Migrant Labour in Contemporary Britain: Hsaio-Hung Pai's *Chinese Whispers* and Marina Lewycka's *Strawberry Fields/Two Caravans*', *Negative Cosmopolitanisms: Cultures and Politics of World Citizenship After Globalization*, ed. by Eddy Kent and Terri Tomsky (Montréal: McGill-Queen's University Press, 2017), pp. 130–48.

CHAPTER 13

Reinventing Europe from the Margins: Theatre on the Periphery

Madelena Gonzalez

Minority Theatre: Resisting Cultural Homogenization

In the aftermath of Brexit,[1] Europe has never been a more contentious and contested entity, not only within the United Kingdom but also elsewhere on the Continent where the rise of new nationalisms is questioning both the very idea and ideal of a European Union. This chapter is about the mapping of alternative Europes along regional rather than national lines, resistance to the homogenizing forces of globalization, and live theatre in an increasingly digital world. Using Gilles Deleuze's discussion of the concept of the minority as a starting point, it shows how peripheral identities can reimagine and broaden what it means to be European; specific examples of cross-cultural collaboration can bring to light hidden commonalities between seemingly disparate and far-flung communities.

This chapter focuses on two theatre productions: a recent example of collaboration between Welsh and Breton theatre practitioners on the performance of *Merch yr Eog/Merc'h an Eog* [*The Salmon's Daughter*], a multilingual piece performed in Welsh, Breton, French and Creole and which toured Wales, England and Brittany in 2016–17, and *Bewnans Ke* [*The Life of Saint Ke*], the revival of a Cornish drama dating from 1500 and rediscovered in 2000.[2] The first is set in present-day Wales and Brittany and addresses the clash between globalization and traditional ways of life. The second deals mostly with the deeds of the eponymous character who comes into conflict with King Teudar, the Breton king of Cornwall, part of its narrative being loosely based on Henry VII's crushing of the Cornish rebellion in 1497. Both plays suggest an idea of a different kind of European affinity across borders where ancient traditions and myths, as well as a preoccupation with issues relevant to contemporary life, such as environmental concerns, affirm but also question, national, regional and minority identities.

The Salmon's Daughter is the result of several years of collaborative research and discussion between The Welsh Language National Theatre of Wales, based in Carmarthen and *Teatr Piba*, a Breton theatre company in Brest. One of the aims of the project was to see how specific regional languages could be made accessible to a wider audience in the globalized world which the two companies inhabit. Both were particularly keen to stress the European dimension of the play and to bring to the forefront the historical, geographical, linguistic and cultural links between Wales and Brittany, neglected hitherto.

The staging of *The Life of Saint Ke* is part of the *An Gwari Meur* ('the great play' in Cornish) project which aims to deliver the first performance of the play since the Middle Ages in its original Cornish location and community. This planned performance of the play provides an opportunity to examine the local, national and global politics of identity that surround *Bewnans Ke* as a cultural artefact. In traditionally political terms, the play participates in the debate about Celticity as an identity, and the third-wave 'Celtic Revival' taking place in contemporary Britain (with its wider resonances in Scottish and Welsh politics, especially after the UK's decision to leave the EU in June 2016). The case study of Cornwall is interesting both in its own right and in comparison with Scotland, Wales and other 'Celtic' regions (Brittany, the Isle of Man, Galicia etc.) where mysticism and myth are major themes within identity politics.

Both plays are good examples of what can be termed minority theatre, the simplest definition of which is theatre outside the mainstream. However, various scholarly publications on this category of drama suggest a more complex definition. Focusing on the representation of specific communities, languages or identities does not imply lack of relevance to other groups. In fact, as I have argued previously, one of the most interesting aspects of this type of theatre is how it positions its identity in relation to the mainstream and interacts with it.[3] It is important to recognize the 'wider resonance' of minority theatre, its potential for 'representing the universal at the same time as reclaiming the specific'.[4]

In the light of this, it is helpful to refer to Gilles Deleuze's 'One Less Manifesto' in which he proposes a flexible and open framework for his definition of minority, summarized in two main points:

> First of all, minority denotes a state of rule, that is to say, the situation of a group that, whatever its size, is excluded from the majority, or even included, but as a subordinate fraction in relation to the standard of measure that regulates the law and establishes the majority. In this context we can say that women, children, the South, the third world, etc., are still minorities, as numerous as they are. But then, let us take this first meaning literally. There follows a second meaning: minority no longer denotes a state of rule, but a becoming in which one enlists.[5]

The insistence on this notion of 'becoming' as a key alternative characteristic of the minority is particularly relevant to the examples discussed here, for it is precisely theatre's provisional nature, its constant and ongoing poetics of process which enables it to question and to challenge fixed aesthetic, social, linguistic and political paradigms so effectively. This fluidity rests on a principle of what Deleuze calls 'continuous variation' as a way of escaping from the system of power enshrined in the majority and its use of language and art. For theatre to free itself from the dominant, it must 'transmit everything through continuous variation as on a creative vanishing line that constitutes a minor tongue in language, a minor character on the stage, a set of minor transformations in relation to dominant forms and subjects'.[6]

Thanks to its constitutive instability and heterogeneity, minority theatre seems ideally situated to 'deduct the elements of power or majority'[7] and provide a potential variable to mastery or to what Deleuze calls 'the power or despotism of the invariant',[8] as the examples we will analyse here, indeed show.

In fact, both plays have something to tell a wider audience about the challenges facing the very concept of community in a post-Brexit Europe. In contrast to the UK's Referendum vote and the rise of extremist parties across Europe, they do not suggest a return to a form of unexamined nationalism but rather transcend their own constitutive localism in order to uncover the latent connections and proximity between supposedly disparate and distinct communities, the historical, geographical, linguistic and cultural common ground which they share. The very nature of theatre as a collaborative process encourages this.

Indeed, theatre provides a visceral, embodied and lived experience in a provisional and collective space, and as such is very different from the detached consumption of words or images that characterize our interaction with the ubiquitous screens that now surround us, as Susan Yankowitz, the American playwright and novelist, reminds us,

> The screen, be it computer or television, is a tangible intervention that inevitably distances the viewer. There may be times when one wants to play with that artifice [...] technology can be artfully employed for such effects. For me, though, those are best used as adjuncts to what is at the centre of our theatre and our humanity: living bodies and voices making contact in the same time and space.[9]

In other words, the liveness of theatre is a metaphor for living itself. The theatre constitutes a privileged arena for the airing of social problems and concerns within the community, enabling ethnic, cultural and linguistic minorities to construct visible responses to their marginalization by laying claim to, and potentially legitimizing, a specific identity.

The two examples we have chosen seem ideally placed to resist categorization and interpellation by the mainstream and the homogenizing cultural consensus attendant on globalization. They highlight very clearly questions of identity and belonging and it is perhaps no surprise that both have emerged in places with a strong regional character. In Wales and in Cornwall, the Referendum vote was largely in favour of Brexit and thus, against Europe — in its current form, at least — while Brittany has always cultivated a sense of separateness and sought to maintain a very distinct identity in relation to the Europeanized Parisian mainstream to the east. How can these two theatrical productions help to construct a new idea of Europe in which different cultures meet, touch and greet each other, in order to elaborate a common project while still maintaining a strong sense of place and identity? Are such manifestations a form of reaction and withdrawal, or, on the contrary, a unique opportunity for dialogue, exchange and the construction of new communities, not only across borders and cultures but also within them? Such reflections demand that the concepts of centre and periphery, major and minor, be re-examined in the light of recent political events.

Our basic contention here is that minority theatre can challenge cultural consensus and homogenization, while also aspiring to a certain universality. If we now turn to our corpus, we will see that language and space are key elements thanks to which marginal identities are performed, asserted and questioned, and cultural heritage is brought to the fore.

The Salmon's Daughter: Swimming Against, or With, the Tide of Belonging?

The Salmon's Daughter was co-written by Owen Martell, a Welsh playwright and novelist, and Aziliz Bourgès, a Breton actress, documentary maker and writer of fiction for radio and television. The main text is divided equally between Welsh and Breton with shorter passages in Guadeloupean Creole and standard French, and was co-directed by Sara Lloyd of the Theatr Genedlaethol Cymru, The Welsh Language National Theatre of Wales, and Thomas Cloarec of the Teatr Piba in Brest. The multilingual and multicultural nature of the piece is also reflected in the creative and technical team, including the choice of actors, from Welsh, Breton, Cornish, Black British and American backgrounds. The genesis of the project stemmed from several years of collaboration and exchange between artists and performers in Wales and Brittany. Rooted in contemporary reality, one of its main aims was to break the language barrier and produce a truly binational production.

The Story of Mair, the Salmon's Daughter of the title, raises some important questions about cultural identity, language and tradition. She is a young Welsh woman from a farming background who has moved to Brittany to live with another woman and is working as a teacher. As a lesbian and a foreigner living abroad, she constitutes a minority within a minority and her marginal status is also compounded by her choice of Brittany which has peripheral status in France in relation to the Parisian capital and the heavily centralized nature of government, language and culture in French life. In contrast, Mair mostly speaks to her partner and friends in Breton, reserving standard French only for people outside her immediate circle.

The play opens with a tableau of a man, the Salmon Man, removing two salmon from an aquarium which he cleans before replacing the fish. A short monologue in Creole follows, evoking the 'universal cannibalism of the sea'[10] but also the proximity of humans to this vital element to which, it is implied, we shall all eventually return. This somewhat defamiliarizing opening which introduces the question of identity and belonging, gives way to a more conventional scene, Mair's return to the family farm in Wales for her aunt's funeral. We quickly learn that her aunt's death has thrown into question the future of the farm and a whole way of life. The return to one's roots is thus the starting point for the play, based on the obvious symbolism of the salmon swimming against the tide in order to return to its spawning grounds. Act III of the play is punctuated by several dream-like sequences featuring the mysterious Salmon Man, in which it becomes clear that Mair, a very keen swimmer, identifies with the salmon. At one point, her apartment is temporarily transformed into an aquarium in which she swims alongside the fish. In fact, the salmon, which is also one of the forms taken by the mythical poet and magus, Taliesin, common to both Welsh and Breton heritage, is the leitmotif for the whole play, as its title suggests, and creates a bridging effect between Celtic island culture and Celtic continental culture. The salmon was also chosen as a wider symbol of wisdom and power, familiar to the collective imagination of many northern cultures. The most ancient of animals, the salmon symbolizes hope and renewal through struggle.

As she contemplates buying the family farm, only to decide against this, finally, Mair's trajectory back to where she came from, physically, emotionally and psychologically, is not only representative of the dilemma of the younger generation (her brother is striving for a permanent contract for a job in town), torn between two languages, two cultures and two loyalties, home and away; it is also indicative of the universal dilemma of tradition versus modernity and the imperious need to adapt to a rapidly changing world. The message, to which we shall return shortly, seems to be one of fluid identities, expressed through the mixing of different languages, locations and even realities.

The linguistic aspect is at the forefront of the production. The project was multilingual from its conception but also very much aware of the need to make the performance accessible to as wide an audience as possible. Instead of seeing the different languages as an obstacle to comprehension, they were conceived of as a potential source of innovation. Semantic, poetic and musical correspondences between different languages, and above all, the possibility of overlap between Welsh and Breton, provided concrete possibilities for the writing of the piece but also inspiration for the actors on stage. The proximity between Welsh and Breton, for example, allows characters to communicate more easily across cultures as some words are the same in both languages. The main protagonist's partner, Loezia, who is Breton, is able to break the ice with her prospective mother-in-law thanks to the word 'delicious' (p. 13) which is identical in both languages and immediately creates a sense of community and affinity between the two women as they share tea and cake after the funeral in Act 1, Scene 1 of the play:

> MAM: Encore du gâteau, Loezia ?
> LOEZIA: Merci ! C'est délicieux !
> MAM : Délicieux ! (Ndt: C'est le même mot en gallois et en breton). Bien, on arrivera bien à se comprendre avant que vous ne repartiez en Bretagne. (p. 13)
>
> [MAM: Would you like some more cake, Loezia?
> LOEZIA: Thank you! It's delicious!
> MAM: Delicious! (Translator's note: The word is the same in Welsh and Breton). Well, it looks as if we will be able to understand one another before you go back to Brittany.][11]

However, the needs of a non-Breton-, non-French- and non-Welsh-speaking audience needed to be addressed if the performance were to fulfil its ambition of having something to say to the wider community. The question of translation in minority theatre has been discussed at length in relation to contemporary Canadian dramatists such as Marc Prescott or Jean-Marc Dalpé who write in a mixture of English and French and employ frequent code-switching. As Louise Ladouceur explains, marrying accessibility to authenticity is not always unproblematic:

> To render these plays accessible to a Québécois audience ill-equipped to understand them, one must resort to translation. But not the type of translation usually called upon, which basically consists of translating everything into one single language, effectively erasing the linguistic duality characteristic of these plays and which is essential in representing the francophone reality specific to the context where they take place and which they describe. In order to preserve the multilingual nature of the plays, it is necessary to explore other translative strategies based on the use of performative resources or performance-based translation devices.[12]

Chief among the strategies favoured by Ladouceur, herself a translator, is the sensitive use of surtitles: 'This translative strategy, similar to that of movie subtitles, has several advantages: it is quick and relatively inexpensive, and it allows an audience to see the play in its original form and thus to have integral access to foreign works that otherwise would remain unintelligible'.[13] *The Salmon's Daughter*, however, relies on a more high-tech approach providing simultaneous translation without erasing the original. Thanks to a partnership with The Academy for Research and Innovation at the University of Falmouth, the Mercator Institute for Media, Language and Culture in Aberystwyth, and with Derick Murdoch, a software developer, the performance equipped spectators with a special app, 'Sibrwd' ('whisper' in Welsh) which enabled them to be guided by a hushed voice providing simultaneous translation in French, English, Welsh and Breton on their smartphone or iPad. The whispered translation was careful not to drown out the sound of the action taking place on stage so that spectators were immersed in the musicality of several languages at once. This discreet voice-over was a way of representing the inner world of Mair, the main character, the pronunciation of whose name resembles the French word for 'sea' and whose thoughts flow between Welsh, Breton and French like the waves of the ocean. In this way, each spectator experienced his or her own intimate, sensory journey through the play, providing a good example of how digital technology can enhance live performance.

The staging and scenography also factored in this multilingual element by focusing on key words and concepts. Animated images of these were projected onto a screen during the play in order to guide the audience through the piece. These words were intended to be representative of the multilingual reality of the performance, belonging, as they did, either to one of the Celtic languages, or to the Greek or Latin roots of a word, or even to some form of Globish, that is to say, a sort of simplified global English for non-native speakers.

In the Canadian context, Ladouceur explains how the use of more than one language is starting to be seen as a positive attribute rather than an obstacle:

> In Western Canada, the bilingual dialogue in plays originating from small francophone communities allows them to express their own specificity, but at the same time considerably reduces their circulation in the marketplace of

French cultural products in Canada and abroad. Nonetheless, with the increased value that globalisation gives to multilingual resources, the francophone minorities' bilingualism takes on another significance. Previously looked upon as an inability to fully appropriate French and thus combat Anglicization, it is now seen as an asset, inasmuch as it indicates an ability to function in French and in English, thus providing access to a global marketplace that has adopted English as a *lingua franca*.[14]

Although English is not one of the three main languages of the play we are discussing, the use made of technology to enhance the audience's experience and the way the action is set in a contemporary globalized world suggest that its multilingual nature is not to be seen as a barrier but rather as a creative resource. This is borne out by the portfolio that sets out the artistic objectives of the play, one of which is to 'experiment with ways in which minority languages, rooted in specific locations, can be brought into contact with the modern, globalized world'.[15]

Indeed, intimations of an increasingly globalized and technologized environment are scattered throughout the play in Mair's conversations with her brother on Skype and the setting for Act II which takes place mostly in a luxury Spa Hotel in Brittany with piped music and telescreens showing promotional films in English and French. The lack of authenticity of the spa where Mair meets her friends for cocktails and where most of the customers are wealthy Englishwomen of a certain age is thrown into relief by the conversations in Breton which Mair has with her friends. They discuss cultural and linguistic identity and share nostalgia for a rural childhood, the implication being that the experiences of the younger generation in Wales and Brittany are similar, torn between the dream of an Arcadian past and the pull of a modern urban future. The play hints at the passing of a way of life, the rural idyll, and its replacement by the dictates of money and big business as farms are bought up to be used as holiday homes by wealthy visitors, the 'Waitrose English' (Act II, p. 47),[16] or specialize in niche products for the burgeoning tourist industry. This nostalgia is expressed in the traditional Welsh poem that Mair recites to Loeiza in which the poet is drawn back irresistibly to his childhood home, now abandoned and inhabited by 'strange voices and spirits' (Act II, p. 38).[17] However, the play hints that Mair's fantasy of a glorious return is just that — a fantasy. Her friend, Céline, who does not speak Breton as well as the others, confuses the word 'nostalgia' with 'herpes' (Act II, p. 34), an ironic hint that tradition can be a burden and that Mair's longing for the old ways is an inadequate response to the changes taking place. This is also made clear in the surreal dream sequence at the end of Act I, in which Mair's longing for a return to her origins is transformed into a comic nightmare of plastic inflatable cows that finally burst. After his wife's funeral, Uncle Gwilym announces his intention to sell the farm and move into a comfortable modern bungalow. His fall and subsequent hospitalization at the very end of Act III suggest that he will be relieved of the weight of tradition and the responsibility of the family farm.

The answer to the dilemma of belonging posed by the play seems to lie in a hybrid identity reflected in the final dream-like sequence which constitutes Act IV and the epilogue. We see Mair swimming in a digital ocean, then following a salmon into the aquarium where she is partially transformed into a fish and observed from the outside by the Salmon Man we saw in the prologue. The fact that she is confined within the aquarium would seem to indicate that this hybridity is a compromise. However, the Salmon Man's expository monologue is taken up in French by Mair's mother at the end of Act IV, although she is not supposed to be a French speaker in real life. This unexpected and defamiliarizing twist could be read as a manifestation in dramatic form of the changing nature of identity and belonging, which are portrayed as fluid rather than fixed. The monologue emphasizes the affinity of humans with the sea but also the danger of being overwhelmed by its elemental force; the fact that Mair is seen reading Melville's *Moby Dick* at the beginning of Act IV, reinforces this sense of power and foreboding and wo/man's insignificance in relation to the strength of the ocean. The Tahitian idyll of peace and joy, poetically described by her mother, is nevertheless bounded by the terrors of the deep. On a symbolic level, flowing with the current of a new hybrid identity implies the sacrifice of something visceral, an atavistic sense of belonging and an acceptance of a permanent state of non- or partial belonging to several different cultures and places at once, reflected by Mair's transformation into a hybrid of a salmon and a woman. However, it also represents an escape from an all-engulfing, and, possibly, dangerous, return to origin, symbolized perhaps by the presence of the mother on stage whose final words, asking Mair if she is asleep, are simply greeted by her daughter's silence. The Salmon Man's amused expression as he watches Mair in the aquarium intimates that the compromise should not necessarily be viewed as negative, although her fate suggests that any identity, even when it is freely chosen, is always bounded by some form of constraint.

Space and Place on the Periphery: 'The Great Play' of Cornwall

In Cornwall, the question of identity is focused as much around space as on language. Reclaiming certain historically and culturally significant locations, such as the remnants of the traditional earthen-work theatres or playing places, 'plenys an gwari' in Cornish, is a way of laying claim to a distinct cultural heritage. Due to its geographical location, Cornwall, like Wales, Scotland and Brittany is perceived as marginalized in relation to the metropolitan centre of London. If this results in economic disadvantage, it also frees up a creative cultural space for the mysticism, myth and legend common to traditional Celtic identity. Gibson, Trower and Tregidga highlight this element in their introductory essay 'Mysticism, Myth and Celtic Identity' in the volume of the same name. They explain how places like Cornwall and Brittany are often seen as 'special, mystical and separate from the apparently more mundane, rational England or France', how '[t]he Cornish landscape was spiritualised by reconstructions of ancient rights', and how Celtic revivals have been a means of reviving or inventing traditions in the interests of local self-assertion.[18]

The Life of Saint Ke is a medieval community play rediscovered in Wales in 2000 in the papers of the late Welsh scholar, Professor J. E. Caerwyn Williams. A critical edition of the manuscript with translation was published in 2007 by the

University of Exeter Press, edited and translated by Graham Thomas, formerly of the Department of Manuscripts and Records at the National Library of Wales, and Nicholas Williams, a leading expert in the Cornish language. The phrase used locally to describe the play *An Gwari Meur* or 'the great play' indicates the importance the Cornish community attached to an art form that was completely theirs in the Medieval and Early Modern period. At that time, plays were local, community events, organized around parishes and staged in earthen-work theatres unique to Cornwall.

The politics of space are central to the play text of *The Life of Saint Ke*. It is worth noting that the eponymous hero Ke is an outsider who has travelled over the sea from a place called Colon, most probably in Brittany. The first half of the play centres on the struggle for spiritual and territorial ascendancy between the new Christian arrival and the pagan and sanguinary King Teudar, also of Breton origin. Soon after landing, Ke begs from Teudar a few acres of land, which he is able to plough with the miraculous aid of wild stags, but the condition is that he must refrain from speaking against pagan gods. Finding this impossible to do, it is not long before the future saint is thrown into prison and tortured. When his persecutor finally relents, he agrees to give Ke as much land as he can enclose while the king takes his bath. Thanks to the intervention of a wise woman who prepares embrocations and ointments for the sovereign's toilet, the bath takes so long that Ke is able to enclose a vast tract of some of the most fertile land in the kingdom. The triumph of a progressive non-violent Christianity in harmony with its natural environment acts as a sort of founding myth for the identity of the locality, the Kea parish in central Cornwall, where the largest village is still known as Playing Place, in which the partial remains of a medieval theatre where the play was first performed are to be found.

One of the most important aspects of the play is indeed its collective and communal aspect as an outdoor site-specific event, staged over two, or possibly three days of performance. As Coleman explains, a 'plen an gwari' or playing place is not a Greek-style semi-circular amphitheatre with a passive, seated audience but is an outdoor, fully circular enclosure with a wide, flat central area surrounded by earth or stone banks, so, basically, a theatre in the round. It is supposed that the audience would not be confined to seating around the edges but would fill the entire arena. Coleman defines the 'plen an gwari' form as

> a theatrical convention in which the audience throngs through a circular space; high platforms around the outside of the audience (and sometimes one central platform) act as permanent stages often associated with a particular character, performers parade on these platforms but may also descend and pass through the audience, the audience moves on foot to gain a good view, to make way for action happening on the ground and to get the best immersive experience.[19]

The emphasis is thus on movement through space, on action and on the coming together of a community to bear communal witness to its cultural heritage, thus reaffirming its specificity and significance in relation to its identity. However, the Cornish tradition is also interesting for other reasons. Although frequently marginalized in conventional studies of early English drama, it is now believed by scholars that it may contain vital keys to understanding pre-Shakespearean theatre practice.

Today, the plan to revive the play, driven by Will Coleman, author, musician, storyteller and founder of Golden Tree Productions, an organization set up to develop cultural projects that promote Cornwall and its history, is an important affirmation of a specific cultural heritage which has wider resonance for Celticity. Coleman's research suggests the strong likelihood that similar sites and structures existed in Wales, Scotland and Brittany, and further afield in Europe.[20] It is important to remember at this juncture that the debate on Celticity is not just restricted to the British Isles, but stretches to other regions such as Brittany and Galicia, as the work of Gibson, Trower and Tregidga reminds us.[21] The strong links between Cornwall and Brittany are an integral part of *The Life of Saint Ke* and of the legend of the saint, which probably originated in Brittany. A twelfth-century life of St Ke in Latin has been lost but a seventeenth-century French translation by a Breton monk, known as Albert le Grand, shows many correspondences between the French and Cornish texts. *The Life of Saint Ke* and other surviving Cornish plays have a significant amount of Breton content, but also pan-European elements. Indeed, Coleman suggests that they are closer in both form and content to Continental plays than to English ones. He reminds us of the pan-European nature of religion and theatre in the Middle Ages due to the power and influence of the Roman Catholic Church and explains how the Franciscan monks who settled in Cornwall from the 1230s made a point of spreading the tradition of outdoor mystery plays in the local vernacular.[22] When coupled with a strong sense of a distinct Cornish identity, amply illustrated by the historical chronicles of the time, for example, William of Malmesbury's *Chronicle of the Kings of England* (1125), it is easy to see how such plays may have come to represent a symbolic re-enactment of the founding myths of a community and an affirmation of regional or even 'national' Cornish identity, as Coleman claims: 'some plays were a deliberate assertion of Cornish language and identity in the face of the imposition of English language and orthodoxy'.[23] Comparing *The Life of Saint Ke* and *The Life of Saint Meriasek*, another Saints Play, rediscovered in the 1860s, he explains the specific nature of these works in relation to the English mainstream:

> Both plays celebrate a Celtic saint who is 'not on the approved list', both root the action exactly in the parish of the performance, both plays give a deliberately trans-national context to an intensely local sense of identity; both plays have explicit links with Brittany (and thus with Catholic Europe).[24]

The second part of the play, which shifts to King Arthur's struggle against the Roman Empire, would certainly seem to bear out the hypothesis of a wider perspective. After a break in the manuscript at line 1251, St Ke disappears and the scene changes. Significantly, it opens with Duke Cador of Cornwall proclaiming his intent to seek out Arthur at his court in Wales in response to the Roman Emperor's demand for tribute. Although Arthur is in Wales, he is referred to as

'Arthur the Cornishman' throughout the play and, according to Armstrong and Hodges, 'When the author or authors of the *Bewnans Ke* imagined how the rest of the world saw Arthur, his Cornishness was most important'.[25] In the same way, they feel that the play 'affirms the longstanding imbrication of the Arthurian legend with the geographical place of Cornwall, its language and its people'.[26] In the stage directions and, somewhat confusingly, Arthur is referred to as 'Arthur, King of Britain (which is now called England)' (1397).[27] For Armstrong and Hodges, this is part of the dynamic of shifting identities at the time and 'the movement of one cultural group to collectively dominate those which could loosely be identified as "British" while still maintaining some of their original, Celtic, individual, regional identities'.[28]

Arthur is next shown receiving a long list of nobles and allies, some of whom, such as Bedivere, Mordred, Gawain or Augelus of Scotland, are familiar from Geoffrey of Monmouth's *History of the Kings of Britain* (1136). He then proceeds to reject the authority of Rome and send the Emperor Lucius's legates back empty-handed. While demonstrating 'a fierce regional pride',[29] the play bespeaks a much more comprehensive awareness of the geopolitics of the time. Indeed, appearances of Rome's allies in the persons of the rulers of Africa, Babylon, Boetia, Crete, Egypt, Phrygia, Spain and Syria, aligned against Arthur's Welsh court and his allies from Cornwall, Scotland, Norway, Dacia, Iceland, Gothland, Cracow and Castile, suggest an integrated worldview which stretches beyond the boundaries of Europe. Armstrong and Hodges underline the extent to which Cornwall's maritime location and trading profile opened it up to far-flung locations, rather than turning it back on its English hinterland: 'Cornwall [...] was more likely to be in stronger, more consistent contact with ports in Wales, Ireland, Brittany, and elsewhere on the continent than with the English nation — *Anglia* — of which it was supposedly a part'.[30] The language of the play reflects this. It is mostly written in Middle Cornish with stage directions in Latin but it contains a smattering of English, while French words and phrases are scattered throughout. Armstrong and Hodges draw some interesting conclusions from the multilingual nature of the play: 'the polyglot effect of these multiple languages underscores the fact of Cornwall's contradictory cosmopolitan (especially in its port cities) and rural natures'.[31] This echoes some of our remarks about identity in *The Salmon's Daughter* and suggests that the hybrid nature of peripheral cultures and locations and their inhabitants, torn between conflicting impulses, has a basis in historical fact and persists today.

The outcome of Arthur's refusal to pay tribute is war and he sets out for Rome leaving his nephew Modred in charge.[32] The latter conspires with Arthur's wife Guinevere and usurps the throne while Arthur triumphs over Lucius. On his return, Arthur gathers his allies once again and clashes with Modred while Guinevere waits in a castle. At this point, the manuscript breaks off and the rest is lost. The conclusion remains a mystery but the final scenes seem to confirm a victory for Arthur (and thus Celticity?) with the defeat of the traitor:

> FIRST MESSENGER *telling the Queen:*
> Hail in your tower, my lady!
> Indeed Modred's bluff has been called.
> Arthur has beaten him violently.
> As true as I am called Jack,
> he will get the worst fate
> and very soon will be dead. (ll. 3294–99)

The remorse shown by Guinevere would also seem to suggest a possible reconciliation with Arthur:

> QUEEN:
> I do not know at all whither I can go.
> Oh, God wishes that I should be in disgrace
> With my leg crossed over the other.
> Alas that it cannot be otherwise! (ll. 3300–03)

Many critics, including Armstrong and Hodges, feel that the most likely hypothesis for the missing ending is the reappearance of St Ke in order to effect a mediation between Arthur and Guinevere.

Sadly, at the present time, the planned performance is on hold due to lack of funding but it is abundantly clear that this rare cultural artefact from a distant epoch and a seemingly marginal location contains some valid insights about progress and integration. The St Ke of the first section is a model of advanced Christian values while Arthur's palace is a rallying place for minorities from Castile to Iceland and a base from which to combat tyranny. The court is portrayed as cultured, civilized and Christian. Arthur himself is a strong and enlightened figure, 'the noblest person who carried a spear' (l. 1603); he is described as 'courteous' (l. 1605) and his person exudes royalty (ll. 1567–68). This contrasts strongly with the pagan tyrant Teudar who dominated the first section of the play with his coarseness and brutality. It would seem to confirm the idea of an integrated and advanced worldview, based on Christian rather than pagan or tribal values. It also shows the periphery triumphing over centralized imperial power (pagan again), thanks to alliances and affinities with other remote peripheral communities who share a similar heritage and are grounded in common myths and a solid sense of place and physical space while also being capable of adapting to difficult political realities. In this sense, the play shows the tables being turned on the majority in a process which calls to mind Deleuze's concept of becoming to which we referred at the beginning of this chapter: 'Minority denotes the strength of a becoming while the majority designates the power or weakness of a state, of a situation'.[33] It is also evocative of Lionnet and Shih's concept of minor transnationalism which, following Deleuze and Guattari, emphasizes the lateral and non-hierarchical network structures of the rhizome: 'The figure of the rhizome suggests an uncontainable, invisible symbolic geography of relations that become the creative terrain on which minority subjects act and interact in fruitful, lateral ways'.[34] It is precisely such fruitful interaction which *The Life of St Ke* brings to the fore.

Europe *autrement*?

The examples presented here suggest some possible perspectives on minority theatre which can help us to understand its place on the European and, indeed, global stage. Not only do they prove that there is a space for popular, regional, local, committed theatre that has not been filled by institutional mainstream theatre, but the plays studied show the potential of minority theatre for representing the universal at the same time as reclaiming the specific. The identity of minority theatre, as discussed in this chapter, is collaborative and desired rather than imposed and assigned, and its frequent staging of the opposition between the dominant and the subordinate can provide a cathartic emancipation from the oppressive power structures of the majority, reinstating agency at the heart of the creative process and its reception, thanks to the recourse to specific histories, languages and cultural memories.

Following Deleuze, such types of theatre can trigger a process of consciousness-raising[35] by helping to create 'a minority consciousness as a universal-becoming',[36] a dynamic impetus for change as opposed to the authoritarian stasis that characterizes the majority. In a public world increasingly dominated by the virtual, the impersonal and the technological, the struggle for visibility, recognition and remembrance of the marginal presences and peripheral identities of minority theatre liberates a space for the temporary intersection of art and life in the community. Not only does this reinstate an active mode of connection within the alienating, dislocated technologized space of contemporary society, but it also substitutes collective idealist aspirations and energy for the ersatz utopia of individual consumption. If, as Michael Kustow avers, theatre constitutes both 'an art and [...] a model for living together',[37] minority theatre implicates its performers, participants and audiences in a transformative experience of exchange and dialogue across borders, while maintaining specificity and reaffirming identity. The Welsh, Cornish, Breton triangle invoked by these two plays escapes the framework of the EU in its current configuration but reactivates age-old links between similar languages, cultures and histories which are nevertheless relevant to contemporary society. These plays suggest that the idea of the 'Welsh European', first used by Raymond Williams in the 1970s, is also valid for the inhabitants of Cornwall and Brittany and that the impetus for reinventing a different kind of Europe may come from the periphery rather than a centre which has bankrupted the original ideal while leaving next to nothing in its place.[38]

Notes to Chapter 13

1. The United Kingdom voted to leave the EU in June 2016, and finally left on 31 January 2021.
2. Aziliz Bourgès and Owen Martell, *Merc'h an Eog/Merch yr Eog* [*The Salmon's Daughter*] (unpublished text supplied by the authors, 2016). *Bewnans Ke/The Life of St Kea: A Critical Edition with Translation*, ed. by Graham Thomas and Nicholas Williams (Exeter: University of Exeter Press, 2016).
3. In the introduction to *Théâtre des minorités: mises en scène de la marge à l'époque contemporaine*, ed. by Madelena Gonzalez and Patrice Brasseur (Paris: L'Harmattan, 2008), I suggest that minority theatre is not simply a representation and affirmation of a specific identity but becomes a sort of laboratory or testing ground for identity (see Madelena Gonzalez, 'Avant-propos', pp. 9–16 (p. 11)). See also Madelena Gonzalez, 'The Construction of Identity in Minority Theatre', in

Authenticity and Legitimacy in Minority Theatre: Constructing Identity, ed. by Madelena Gonzalez and Patrice Brasseur (Newcastle upon Tyne: Cambridge Scholars Press, 2010), pp. ix–xxix.
4. Madelena Gonzalez, 'Minority Theatre in the Age of Globalization', in *Minority Theatre on the Global Stage: Challenging Paradigms from the Margins*, ed. by Madelena Gonzalez and Hélène Laplace-Claverie (Newcastle upon Tyne: Cambridge Scholars Press, 2012), pp. ix–xxiv (p. xxiii).
5. Gilles Deleuze, 'One Less Manifesto', trans. by Timothy Murray, in *Mimesis, Masochism and Mime: The Politics of Theatricality in Contemporary French Thought*, ed. by Timothy Murray (Ann Arbor: University of Michigan Press, 1997), pp. 239–58 (p. 255).
6. Deleuze, 'One Less Manifesto', pp. 251–52.
7. Deleuze, 'One Less Manifesto', p. 247.
8. Deleuze, 'One Less Manifesto', p. 254.
9. Susan Yankowitz in conversation with Caridad Svich, 'In Search of a Common Language', in *Trans-global Readings: Crossing Theatrical Boundaries*, ed. by Caridad Svich (Manchester: Manchester University Press, 2003), pp. 130–36 (p. 135).
10. Aziliz Bourgès and Owen Martell, *Merc'h an Eog/Merch yr Eog* (*The Salmon's Daughter*) (unpublished text supplied by the authors, 2016), Prologue (p. 2); this is my translation of 'le cannibalisme universel de la mer'. Subsequent references are to this unpublished version and will be given in parentheses in the text.
11. All translations are mine unless indicated otherwise.
12. Louise Ladouceur, 'Bilingualism on Stage: Translating Francophone Drama Repertories in Canada', *Trans*, 13 (2009), 129–36 (pp. 134–35).
13. Ladouceur, 'Bilingualism on Stage', p. 135.
14. Ladouceur, 'Bilingualism on Stage', p. 135.
15. Thomas Cloarec was kind enough to give me a copy of this portfolio, the relevant passages of which I have translated into English for the purposes of this chapter.
16. This is my translation of 'tous ces Anglais Waitrose'.
17. This is my translation of 'des esprits et des voix étranges'.
18. Marion Gibson, Shelley Trower and Garry Tregidga, 'Mysticism, Myth and Celtic Identity', in *Mysticism, Myth and Celtic Identity*, ed. by Marion Gibson, Shelley Trower and Garry Tregidga (London and New York: Routledge, 2012), pp. 1–20 (pp. 3–4).
19. See Will Coleman, *Plen an Gwari: The Playing Places of Cornwall* (Kernow: Golden Tree Productions, 2015), pp. 84–89 (p. 88).
20. Coleman, *Plen an Gwari*, pp. 63–67.
21. Gibson et al., 'Mysticism, Myth and Celtic Identity', pp. 3–4.
22. Coleman, *Plen an Gwari*, p. 72.
23. Coleman, *Plen an Gwari*, p. 47.
24. Coleman, *Plen an Gwari*, p. 79.
25. Dorsey Armstrong and Kenneth Hodges, *Mapping Malory: Regional Identities and National Geographies in 'Le Morte Darthur'* (Basingstoke: Palgrave Macmillan, 2014), p. 37.
26. Armstrong and Hodges, *Mapping Malory*, p. 35.
27. *Bewnans Ke/The Life of St Kea: A Critical Edition with Translation*, ed. by Graham Thomas and Nicholas Williams (Exeter: University of Exeter Press, 2016), line 1397. Subsequent references are to this edition and line numbers will be given in parentheses in the text.
28. Armstrong and Hodges, *Mapping Malory*, p. 37.
29. Armstrong and Hodges, *Mapping Malory*, p. 36.
30. Ibid.
31. Ibid.
32. The spelling in the text is Modred and not Mordred as might be expected.
33. Deleuze, 'One Less Manifesto', p. 255.
34. Françoise Lionnet and Shu-mei Shih, 'Introduction: Thinking through the Minor, Transnationally', in *Minor Transnationalism*, ed. by Françoise Lionnet and Shu-mei Shih (Durham, NC, and London: Duke University Press, 2005), pp. 1–26 (p. 2).
35. I am using the term in the sense of making people more aware of personal, social or political issues.

36. Deleuze, 'One Less Manifesto', p. 256.
37. Michael Kustow, *Theatre@risk* (London: Methuen, 2001), p. xv.
38. I am indebted to Thomas Cloarec, Will Coleman and Marion Gibson for their help in preparing this chapter.

CHAPTER 14

Of Boiled Eggs and Rocket Science: Sharon Dodua Otoo's *Herr Gröttrup setzt sich hin*[1]

Áine McMurtry

> Dominant *white* cultural producers typically consider their own art to be universal (and the art of marginalized groups to be less relevant for the mainstream population) — they are usually completely unaware of their own *whiteness* and of the constraints this will have on their perspectives, their creative work, as well as on their potential audience. By way of contrast, most Black and of color artists living and working in Germany are acutely aware of the importance — or at least the influence — of our heritage and our communities. In predominantly *white* contexts, Black artists need to take the dreams, needs and visions of our communities into account and, by doing so, we often develop strategies to disrupt dominant normalities inspired by racist, sexist, homo- and transphobic worldviews. [...] We believe art really can change the world. And we believe such change has the potential to transform societies in a way that we call revolutionary — especially if advocated by those on its margins.[2]

This critique of mainstream cultural production and its role in consolidating exclusionary structures is found in the introduction to *The Little Book of Big Visions: How to be an Artist and Revolutionize the World*, a 2012 essay collection that sets out to bear witness to Blackness in contemporary Germany.[3] The volume's editors, Sharon Dodua Otoo and Sandrine Micossé-Aikins, underline racist forms of language in predominantly white societies and the imperative to engage with 'concepts for which there are no words... yet'.[4] Comprising texts by Black artists, the volume considers the potential of minoritarian voices for both disrupting and conceiving of alternatives to the dominant social order, whilst continuously reflecting on the difficulty of challenging the hegemonic position without reproducing its terms. As articulated in the above lines, it is a plural understanding of community that is said to be crucial for Black artists in reimagining the white status quo. And, in the context of this volume's examination of works that erode identitarian categories and trouble familiar narratives, I wish to explore a fictional German-language text by Sharon Otoo that came to public attention when it was awarded the prestigious Ingeborg Bachmann Prize in summer 2016.

Born to Ghanaian parents in London, Otoo moved from the UK to Germany in 2006 and settled in Berlin, where she became involved in the Black community as an activist, editor and writer. From the perspective of a soft-boiled egg, *Herr Gröttrup setzt sich hin* [*Herr Gröttrup Takes a Seat*] serves up a portrait of the retired Nazi rocket scientist at his breakfast table.[5] In methodological terms, I draw on a posthuman framework to interpret the politics of Otoo's formal challenge to a society in which whiteness is presented as the norm and its privilege goes unnoticed. Otoo's anthropomorphizing play with perspective will be read as a 'becoming other' that serves to disrupt binary oppositions and categorizations. My reading identifies the text's rejection of a representationalist approach — epitomized in the voice of the fictional egg — as a means of enabling an alternative to dualistic conceptual paradigms caught up in oppositions of difference versus sameness, of the ideal and the real, of the original and the copy. Opening up to difference in and of itself could permit an encounter with otherness that — as Elizabeth Grosz has pointed out — 'may prove highly pertinent to feminist attempts to rethink relations between the mainstream and the margins, between dominant and subordinated groups and between oppressor and oppressed, self and other, between and within subjects'.[6] In particular, I draw on Deleuze and Guattari's concept of the 'body without organs'[7] to consider the political significance of the talking egg at the centre of Otoo's non-realist narrative. The concept will be used to elucidate how Otoo decentres the white masculine subject to foreground instead the disruptive potential of material forces that act on bodies, both human and non-human.

The prize jury at Klagenfurt was effusive in its praise for the story's humorous and innovative retelling of a forgotten chapter of German history.[8] The narrative focuses on Helmut Gröttrup, a real-life electrical engineer who helped design the V2 rocket, the long-range ballistic missile that was deployed by the Germans against the Allies in the latter stages of World War II. Otoo has commented that 'Germany's conception of itself as a White country does have something to do with cultural production, with folklore and with the legacy of the genocides which took place during World War II.'[9] As her first German-language text, Otoo has further suggested that the story formed an 'experiment' that developed when she was asked to contribute to a German publication about whiteness and that she responded creatively instead, since the themes she wanted to explore needed to be told in German.[10] Close to the beginning of the story, the fastidious title-figure is introduced as the archetypal German of his generation, complete with sausage dog and proclivity for punctiliousness:

> Helmut Gröttrup, achtundsiebzig Jahre alt, einundneunzig Kilogramm, ein Meter dreiundachtzig, war deutscher Ingenieur (Raketenspezialist, seit neun Jahren pensioniert), Erfinder und Schach-Genie. Die wochenendlichen Radtouren musste er bedauerlicherweise vor zwei Jahren sein lassen, weil er es mit dem Knie hatte. Inzwischen genoss er seinen neuen Status als regelmäßiger Sonntagsfahrer. Gleich nach der Kirche kutschierte er gerne, samt Frau und Wackeldackel, stundenlang die Hauptstraßen entlang, 'Im Frühtau zu Berge' singend, während ihre Hand auf seinem Oberschenkel lag. (pp. 11–12)

[Helmut Gröttrup, seventy-eight years of age, ninety-one kilograms, one metre eighty-three, was a German engineer (a rocket specialist, retired for the past nine years), inventor, and chess genius. To his regret, he had been forced to abandon his weekly cycling tours two years ago due to a dodgy knee. In the meantime, he had come to enjoy his new status as a regular Sunday driver. Straight after church he liked to chauffeur his wife and nodding dog along the main roads for hours on end, singing hiking songs with his wife's hand resting on his thigh.] (pp. 11–12)

The hyper-detail of this satiric description amasses highly specific cultural clichés in its pastiche of the retired German scientist as pedant, who obsessively manages every aspect of his domestic space. In the course of the short narrative, the impact of the patriarch on those around him is spelled out loud and clear, as Gröttrup is shown to patronize and belittle his wife, and to be entirely unaware of the existence of the foreign cleaner, Ada, in their household. The comic denouement comes when the breakfast ritual that every morning sees his wife boil two eggs for exactly seven and a half minutes results not with the desired hard-boiled outcome but in 'sticky yellow chaos' as egg yolk splatters dramatically across Gröttrup's tie. After this point, the narrative focus shifts to the egg who details its decision that morning to provoke Herr Gröttrup simply because it could. And in these shifts of perspective that move between Gröttrup, his wife, and the egg that resists its own hard-boiling, the subversive narrative voice establishes a mode of free indirect discourse that enables oblique commentary on the power dynamics at play in the German household.

Highlighting the text's postmodern engagement with issues such as relations between the sexes and communicative impasse, the Klagenfurt jury was quick to underscore the links between Otoo's text and German-language domestic satires of the bourgeois patriarch made famous in the comic sketches of popular comedian Loriot, *Das Frühstücksei* ([The Breakfast Egg] from 1977, and polemical Austrian dramatist Thomas Bernhard, *Der deutsche Mittagstisch* [The German Lunch Table] from 1978.[11] In this keen resolve, however, to hold up a mirror to claim Otoo's place within German-language literary tradition, the all-white jury gave little attention to aspects of the story that are not so easily recuperated into the Western male canon. Drawing on Jamika Avalon's understanding of Women of Colour as a 'fugitive archive of resistance' and both symbols and agents of change,[12] Sarah Colvin's political interpretation of Otoo's story convincingly differentiates between Loriot's sexist humour which supports normative beliefs and Otoo's 'literary joking' which is understood 'to counter and challenge empowered norms'.[13] In what follows, I will further unpack the theoretical underpinnings and implications of Otoo's anthropomorphizing play with perspective, which will be understood to go beyond bourgeois satire to be read in terms of a 'becoming other' that — according to Deleuze and Guattari in *A Thousand Plateaus* — challenges static identity constructs and carries a political force with the potential to transform power relations and hierarchies.[14] My interest lies in the connection between the fantastical elements in Otoo's narrative and Deleuze and Guattari's concern with what John Noyes terms the 'geographical materialism of desire' that conceives 'bodies outside the impasses of represented subjects and subjective lack'.[15] Noyes's postcolonial reading of Deleuze and Guattari foregrounds their materialist concern with desire as a means of effecting 'reconciliation and redistribution according to a different understanding of what lack is and where it comes from'.[16] In this context, Noyes further references Stuart Hall's definition of the postcolonial as a 're-narrativisation' that 'displaces the "story" of capitalist modernity from its European centring to its dispersed global peripheries'.[17] Against this theoretical background, I will explore Otoo's narrative project to expose the universalizing self-construction of the German scientist who — by means of juxtaposition with the time-travelling egg — is brought into relation with global spaces and eras all too often consigned to the historical margins.

The vital political role of fantastical literary modes has been stressed by Otoo in comments about frustrating biographical interpretations of her early fiction that underscore the need to use experimentation with literary genre to implicate the reader in the narrative:

> I think this focus on 'real' and 'authentic' stories can become voyeuristic and create a barrier between the reader and the text. I guess that's why for my next publications I looked at 'magic realism' and 'afrofuturism' as literary styles to try out — hopefully they work better at encouraging the reader to focus on their own connection to the story.[18]

Famously coined by the cultural critic Mark Dery in his 1994 interview-essay 'Black to the Future', Afrofuturism has been described as 'both an artistic aesthetic and a framework for critical theory' that — according to Dery writing in the US context — refers to 'Speculative fiction that treats African-American themes and addresses African-American concerns in the context of twentieth-century technoculture — and, more generally, African-American signification that appropriates images of technology and a prosthetically enhanced future'.[19] More recently, understanding of the term has broadened to combine 'elements of science fiction, historical fiction, speculative fiction, fantasy, Afrocentricity, and magic realism with non-Western beliefs. In some cases, it's a total reenvisioning of the past and speculation about the future rife with cultural critiques.'[20] Most evident in Otoo's fantastical adoption of the voice of the egg that — in the course of the narrative — describes morphing across space and time, Afrofuturist perspectives are to be identified throughout the text in its troubling of the universalizing white subject.[21] And it is in this radical challenge to anthropocentrism that Otoo's project can be seen to share central concerns with Deleuze and Guattari's materialist philosophy, which rejects binarized paradigms and their regimes of oppression and social subordination.

In narrative terms, Otoo's textual undermining of formalized notions of identity is to be identified in the shifting narrative voice, which — although loosely tied to different viewpoints in the course of the story — never reliably belongs to a single fictional character, as exemplified in the closing lines of the introductory account of Gröttrup. Here, an explicit challenge to the white male protagonist as an apparently unmarked subject category is foregrounded:

> Er freute sich über die Pünktlichkeit der Regionalbahn, die schattigen Stellen in seinem Schrebergarten während des Hochsommers und die kleine,

verlässliche Flasche Underberg am Ende des Tages. Er fand bei Rot über die Ampel gehende Jugendliche, das Anglisieren des Genitivs und das Einfach-drauflos-duzen weniger gut. Wenn jemensch ihn in seiner Gegenwart als 'Christ' bezeichnet hätte, hätte er 'mit Verlaub' korrigiert: Er war überzeugter Protestant. Wenn jemensch ihn allerdings als 'Cis-Mann' bezeichnet hätte, hätte er vor lauter Irritation bestimmt die Augen zusammengekniffen. Und wenn jemensch ihn als 'weiß' bezeichnet hätte, hätte er dies als Synonym für deutsch aufgefasst oder sich gefragt, ob dies als Beleidigung zu verstehen war. Oder beides. (pp. 12–13)

[He was a fan of punctuality in regional trains, shady spots in his allotment garden during high summer and his reliable miniature bottle of Underberg herbal digestif at the end of each day. He was less fond of jaywalking young people, incorrect genitives and uninvited use of the familiar form of address. If anyone had referred to him as a Christian in his presence he would have corrected them 'with all due respect': he was a convinced Protestant. If anyone had referred to him as a cis-male, however, he would no doubt have screwed up his eyes in annoyed confusion. And if anyone had referred to him as white he would have either regarded this as a synonym for German or wondered whether it was to be considered an insult. Or both.] (pp. 12–13)

The faux-anthropological perspective adopted in these lines reverses the standard ethnographic gaze to question the constructedness of the German subject whose rarefied identity is maintained in attempted distinctions from its manifold others. With the unusual coinage of the gender-neutral pronoun 'jemensch', as well as the use of 'cis' as a term from Gender Studies for those whose gender identity matches the sex assigned at birth, the dialectical contrastive mode favoured by the masculine protagonist gives way to a textual troubling of his assumed universality through a questioning of its chosen signifiers. In so doing, Otoo might be seen to devise a creative response to Deleuze and Guattari's reminder that 'mental correctives are necessary to undo the dualisms we had no wish to construct but through which we pass'.[22] In Otoo's text, the pointed reflection on the use of white as flawed shorthand for national identity issues a further unwelcome challenge to the subject unwilling to contemplate any deviation from his own self-image that underscores the dubious racial categories underpinning this construct. To follow Fatima El Tayeb's concept of 'queering ethnicity', the text's 'transgressive approach to concepts of identity' thus 'challenges the European dogma of colour blindness by deconstructing processes of racialization *and* the ways in which these processes are made invisible'.[23]

Otoo's portrayal of Helmut Gröttrup consistently foregrounds the figure's stringent attempts to regulate and control the world around him. The use of militaristic and bureaucratic lexis to characterize interactions between the married couple compounds the portrait of an authoritarian personality who understands any diversion from the norm as an act of insubordination: 'in letzter Zeit erlaubte sich seine Ehefrau einige kleine Fehltritte, die dazu führten, dass er nun alles haargenau kontrollieren musste. [...] Das hatte sich in letzter Zeit als sehr gewinnbringend herausgestellt' (pp. 14–15) [his wife had recently allowed herself a number of minor misconducts, which meant he now had to keep a sharp examining eye on everything. [...] This had proved very advantageous in recent weeks] (pp. 14–15). Here, the introduction of the language of profit to eliminate any margin of error offers oblique commentary on the calculated bid for control and its relation to systems of binary logic and instrumental reason. In this respect, Gröttrup can be read as a fictional instantiation of Deleuze and Guattari's conception of the organism as a body that normalizes and creates hierarchies.[24] As a real-life rocket engineer who went on to invent the smart card, Gröttrup appears to embody the rational male scientist wedded to abstract epistemic models and anthropocentric meta-narratives. It seems no coincidence that, right from the outset of the text, Otoo dramatizes the rational attempt to control the body in instances of exaggerated performativity. The reader is immediately allocated an active role in the textual troubling of the status quo through italicized sets of instructions that indicate how their body should be positioned during the reading process. The narrative begins, for example, with the following directions:

> *Bitte sorgen Sie dafür, dass Sie bequem auf Ihrem Platz sitzen. Es sollte Ihnen weder zu heiß noch zu kalt sein. Kratzen Sie sich ruhig am linken Ellbogen, wenn Ihnen danach ist. Wenn Sie husten oder niesen müssen, wäre jetzt die angemessene Zeit dafür. Die Geschichte sollten Sie ausgedruckt in Ihrer rechten Hand halten. Heben Sie langsam Ihre linke Hand, und halten Sie schließlich damit ihr linkes Auge zu. Nun können Sie anfangen zu lesen.* (p. 9)

> [*Please ensure you are sitting comfortably. You should be neither too hot nor too cold. Feel free to scratch your left elbow, should you feel the need. If you have to cough or sneeze, now would be the appropriate moment. You should be holding the printed story in your right hand. Slowly raise your left hand and hold it over your left eye. You may now start reading.*] (p. 9)

These imperatives immediately thematize the role of culture in controlling and regulating the body, recalling institutionalized rituals and prescriptions, but in their exaggerated performativity they simultaneously mock the hierarchies and mindlessness of cultural consumption. By focusing on the attempt to regulate disparate body parts, the text could further be read to mimic Deleuzean understanding of the organism's inherent drive to organize, hierarchize and control the body's organs in a particular way.[25] As Otoo remarked in a 2015 interview, 'the moment of confusion and uncertainty is a powerful opportunity to unlearn dominance',[26] and the performative character of the fictional interjections implicates the reader in the task of destabilizing hierarchies and acknowledging the significance of situation and point-of-view for the imaginative task.[27] Following the moment of catastrophe and switch to the perspective of the soft-boiled egg, the logical language of cause and effect deployed by the scientist-patriarch gives way to an insistence on chance and impulse as the drivers for action. Further instructions signal this perspectival shift, as the reader is directed to remove the hand covering their left eye and, instead, demonstratively cover their right before reading on. Immediately thereafter, the narrative voice changes to foreground a condition of playful agency:

> Manchmal wache ich auf und denke: Heute bin ich ein Ei.
> Zugegeben: Das passiert mir nicht oft. Wer will schon ein Ei sein? Nicht wirklich rund, nicht wirklich stabil, nicht wirklich attraktiv. Ich habe viel öfter morgens gedacht: Heute bin ich Crème brûlée oder ein Lottogewinn oder ein Sonnenaufgang. Wenigstens haben die Menschen Freude dran! Aber heute wollte ich einfach als etwas Belangloses durchgehen. Keine große Aufregung. (p. 28)
>
> [Sometimes I wake up and think: I'm an egg today.
> Admittedly, it doesn't happen often. Who'd want to be an egg? Not exactly round, not exactly stable, not exactly attractive. I've thought much more often: I'm crème brûlée or a lottery win or a sunrise today. At least people get some joy out of me! But today I just wanted to get by as something insignificant. No big fuss.] (p. 28)

As these lines establish, the choice of an egg as an unstable entity that proves difficult to define and categorize is crucial to its disruptive power. In the subsequent section, the non-human status of the metamorphic egg is underlined when it asserts past and future incarnations as the lipstick worn by Grötttrup's wife for a meeting with a Soviet spacecraft engineer in the 1940s and as the epicentre of an 1862 earthquake in Accra. Here the Afrofuturist refusal to be constrained by conventional space-time boundaries is presented as part and parcel of a wider rejection of categories — and their constitution through language — articulated from the perspective of the soft-boiled egg:

> Als deutsches Ei nicht hart zu werden ist keine so große Leistung. Deutlich schwieriger ist es für mich, auszuhalten, dass ihr Lebenden ausschließlich mittels dieses Gefängnisses namens Sprache kommuniziert.
> Sprachen und ihre Kategorien, o!
> Menschen und ihre Kategorien!
> Sie sind nicht ganz dicht, o! Sie sind nicht ganz dicht. (pp. 39–40)
>
> [It's no great achievement for a German egg, not getting hard. It's much more difficult for me to stand the fact that you human beings use the prison called language to communicate.
> Languages and their categories, o! People and their categories! They're never watertight, o! They're just never watertight.] (pp. 38–39)

As Sarah Colvin has highlighted, 'the egg-being is mutable and fluid' and the gendered linguistic connotations of its limpness in German — as seen, for example, in the coinages 'Weichei' [weakling] and 'keine Eier haben' [having no balls] — suggest 'an absence of hegemonic masculinity'.[28] Building on Ajalon's 'fugitive archive of resistance', Colvin has developed a compelling reading of the egg as 'hermeneutically resistant' and 'outside the law of dominant culture'.[29] However, rather than following her symbolic understanding of the egg which then fixes it nonetheless 'as a quintessential metaphor of hope, potential, or new birth',[30] I wish instead to explore the materialist implications of Otoo's narrative which permit a move beyond dualistic paradigms. And in the egg's metamorphic refusal to be contained in either physical or linguistic form, I identify a further rebellion against the conception of any unitary or stable Self at the centre of discursive power that has compelling affinities with aspects of the materialist thought of Gilles Deleuze and Félix Guattari. To draw out the wider political implications of Otoo's experimental project, this chapter will conclude with consideration of the line of affiliation between the Deleuzean concept of the 'Body without Organs' and Otoo's literary choice of the egg as the vehicle through which to contest the rhetoric of the German patriarch.

The 'Body without Organs' is a phrase taken from the playwright Antonin Artaud, which Deleuze first employed in *The Logic of Sense* (1969) and further developed with Guattari in both volumes of *Capitalism and Schizophrenia*. Here, the term is conceived as a means of escaping what they consider the shortcomings of traditional psychoanalysis and its privileging of the world of the articulating, self-defining and enclosed subject. Instead, the Body without Organs is proposed as the 'antidote [...] to this articulate and organised organism' that finds its prototype in the egg.[31] In *A Thousand Plateaus*, the correlation is elucidated as follows:

> A BwO is made in such a way that it can be occupied, populated only by intensities. Only intensities pass and circulate. Still, the BwO is not a scene, a place, or even a support upon which something comes to pass. [...] It is nonstratified, unformed intense matter [...]. Matter equals energy. [...] That is why we treat the BwO as the full egg before the extension of the organism and the organization of the organs, before the formation of the strata; as the intense egg defined by [...] dynamic tendencies involving energy transformation and kinematic movements [...]. The tantric egg.[32]

Here, the delineation of the egg as a model without organs that is in a continual process of potential becoming has much in common with the polymorphic egg at the centre of Otoo's story, which similarly functions as 'the unformed, unorganized, nonstratified, or destratified body and all its flows'.[33] The alliance with Deleuze and Guattari's Body without Organs reveals itself as a line of affiliation, rather than any identity or sameness. Implicitly refuting the move from intense egg to extensive organism, Otoos's egg repeatedly voices its commitment to living in the present moment and pokes fun at Gröttrup's compulsion to determine circumstances that he knows virtually nothing about. In contrast to the scientist-patriarch's relentless attempts to control his surroundings, the egg can be seen to occupy an ambivalent border zone between object and subject or — perhaps more precisely — to embody what Jane Bennett identifies as 'vibrant matter' straddling the divide between inert material and vital life.[34] Bennett's study adopts a Deleuzean approach to argue that political theory must better recognize the active participation of nonhuman forces in events by conceptualizing the role of a 'vital materiality' that crosses through bodies, both human and nonhuman. Bennett is concerned with the ethical and political implications of this materialist method for human bodies that do not conform to majoritarian Euro-American models:

> If matter itself is lively, then not only is the difference between subjects and objects minimized but the status of the shared materiality of all things is elevated. All bodies become more than mere objects, as the thing-powers of resistance and protean agency are brought into sharper relief. [...] The ethical aim becomes to distribute value more generously, to bodies as such. Such a

newfound attentiveness to matter and its powers will not solve the problem of human exploitation or oppression, but it can inspire a greater sense of the extent to which all bodies are kin in the sense of inextricably enmeshed in a dense network of relations.[35]

Towards the close of Otoo's narrative, the voice of the egg offers commentary on explicitly politicized contexts in which it acts as a disruptive force when faced with the male embodiments of global power, describing its VIP status as a red carpet that would have liked to trip Helmut Kohl when declaring his fourth term as Chancellor and, twenty years on, claiming to have done so to Robert Mugabe:

> Ähnlich ging es mir vergangene Woche in Berlin, als Helmut Kohl die deutsche Bundestagswahl zum vierten Mal gewann. Zu gerne wäre ich in einem strategischen Moment plötzlich hochgeklappt, so dass er auf dem Weg zum Podest hätte stolpern — eventuell auch hinfallen — müssen. Vor laufenden Fernsehkameras. Dieser Anblick hätte mir gut getan. Es sollte aber diesmal nicht sein (oder ehrlicher: Es ist mir ausdrücklich verboten worden), aber irgendwann einmal werde ich wieder ein wichtiger roter Teppich sein. In ziemlich genau zwanzig Jahren wird ein anderer Politiker Opfer meiner Ungnade sein (er wird Robert Mugabe heißen, wenn nichts dazwischen kommt, und wir werden uns in Harare befinden). Aber ich greife zu weit vor. (pp. 41–42)

> [It was a similar situation last week in Berlin, when Helmut Kohl won the German parliamentary elections for the fourth time over. I would have loved to suddenly flip up at a strategic moment, making him stumble on his way to the stage — and possibly fall. Live on camera. The sight of it would have done me good. It wasn't to be, though, not this time (or to be honest: I was forbidden to do so), but there'll be another occasion when I'm an important red carpet again. In almost exactly twenty years' time, another politician will be the victim of my disfavour (his name will be Robert Mugabe, if nothing comes between us, and we will be in Harare). But I'm getting ahead of myself.] (pp. 40–41)

In these lines, the voice of the egg can be read in Deleuzean terms as an instantiation of those 'intensive flows, which do not correspond with articulated, institutionalised opinions and interests' and 'drive the unconscious machinery of desire as a basis for all political action'.[36] As opposed to a symbolic politics driven by identity, the fictional egg foregrounds a conception of life as material flows able to form productive, continuous connections. The Afrofuturist dimensions of Otoo's fantastical narrative therefore do not posit a representational model that imagines an alternative or counter to the stratified majoritarian order but rather in their associative play that refuses to be bound by either any chronological temporal regime or defined spatial or geo-political realm, a form of Deleuzean micropolitics might be discerned that permits connections, which are local and singular, to gesture towards alternative futures. As a form of repetition, associations elude the model of representation because they take place automatically, linking together singularities, that not only reproduce past events in the present but which — as Ralf Krause and Marc Rölli suggest — extend 'into the virtual depths of a past and a future that cannot be grasped from the field of a living and enduring present'.[37]

According to Deleuze, micropolitical activities are located in submerged processes of becoming that may prepare and provoke significant changes of the majoritarian social order by bringing together 'minorities, becomings, incorporealities, concepts, "peoples"'.[38] Indeed, Otoo has commented quite explicitly on her materialist understanding of her own situation as an author, activist and editor:

> I think of myself as part of a chain, the chain begins centuries ago, and the chain will not end with my death but will continue for centuries after it. I see myself as part of a process, [and] I haven't [...] thought about my end product. [...] The reason why I feel uncomfortable thinking about a legacy is there are lots of 'big man' theories, or 'superhero' theories, you know? It was Christopher Columbus who discovered America, and Martin Luther King is the name, but OK, what was going on with his wife, his best friend and his family? I'm very aware of my networks and I don't like to think of myself as the central person, I like to think of myself as part of a community.[39]

Given the textual — and authorial — preoccupation with drives and connectivities beyond a centralized understanding of power, it seems no coincidence that — in Otoo's story — the voice of the egg forms the only identifiable narrative instance to comment on the apparently marginal figure of Ada, the foreign cleaner said to come to work so early on Mondays and Thursdays that Herr Gröttrup is unaware of her existence. As the figure responsible for bringing the breakfast egg to the Gröttrup household, Ada is attributed a level of insight beyond the other characters.[40] Indeed, the reader is told explicitly that were Frau Gröttrup to talk to Ada more often, she would not only realize that Ada now speaks fluent German, but would be able to access a wealth of information that could allow her the upper hand in the relationship with her husband.[41] The moment of confrontation comes in the final section of the narrative when Herr Gröttrup is surprised to discover Ada in the bathroom sorting through his laundry:

> 'Wer bist du?', stammelte Herr Gröttrup.
> 'Ich bin die Ada.'
> Sie antwortete, als gäbe es nichts Selbstverständlicheres, als dass sie seine Unterhose in der Hand halten würde, während sie sich kennenlernten.
> 'Ada?', erwiderte er. Schweißperlen formten sich auf seiner Stirn.
> 'Ich bin deine Putzfrau.'
> 'Duzen wir uns?'
> 'Sie haben damit angefangen.'
> Wohl wahr. Herr Gröttrup hatte nun mehrere Probleme gleichzeitig. Um sich zu helfen, gab er ihr die Hand. Er wollte sich eigentlich vorstellen. Ada hatte das allerdings als Kontrolle gedeutet — als wolle er seine Unterhose prüfen. Hätte Herr Gröttrup Ada vernünftig angeschaut, wie es sich gehört, wäre er nicht in die Situation gekommen, dass sie sich die Hände schütteln, mit seinem Schlüpfer zwischen den Fingern. (pp. 47–49)

> ['Who are you?' stammered Herr Gröttrup, his astonishment expressing itself in uncharacteristic uninvited use of the familiar form of address.
> 'I'm Ada.'
> She answered as if there were nothing more normal in the world than holding his underpants in her hand as they made their acquaintance.
> 'Ada?' he replied. Sweat beaded on his forehead.
> 'I'm your cleaning lady,' she said, returning the informal tone.

'Did we agree on the familiar form of address?'
'You started it, Herr Gröttrup,' she reverted to the formal.
True enough. Herr Gröttrup now had several problems at once. To rescue himself, he held out his hand to her. He wanted to introduce himself. Ada, however, interpreted his gesture as one of examination — as though he wanted to check his underpants. Had Herr Gröttrup looked at Ada properly, as politeness requires, they would not have ended up shaking hands with his pants between their fingers.] (pp. 47–49)

Ada's performative challenge to the authority of the patriarch is enacted not only in linguistic but also corporeal terms. By following — to the letter — those cultural rituals that seek to stratify, categorize and order, Ada — just like the egg — exposes the mechanisms of control in all their absurdity. This belated foregrounding of the figure of Ada introduces an intersectional critique of the ways in which gender, race and class create overlapping systems of discrimination and disadvantage. Yet Otoo's anti-representationalist method militates against the exclusionary mechanisms inherent in those very linguistic categories, which themselves are caught up in oppositions of difference versus sameness. Instead, I would suggest that Otoo's project might be seen to enable what Michelle Wright has termed a 'diasporic intersubjectivity', which she conceives as a 'dialogic formation in which many subjectivities exist that cannot be organized into thetical and antithetical categories'.[42] To overcome exclusionary discursive tendencies and move beyond the nation where subjectivity is coded male and the migrantized[43] woman remains an 'unsubject' (crucially, we are not given any information about Ada's other languages, country of birth, or ethnicity), the text invokes a model that addresses gender and sexuality as inseparable from issues of race and class. As Otoo has commented, her story gently points out 'that we all have limits to our knowledge and experience. And that no matter how much we think we know, how clever or qualified we are, there are always those who have a different form of insight. And that it would be worth trying to take a step back and finding out more from those around us, especially those who are underestimated far too often.'[44] Through experimental narrative play with radical perspectives, human and non-human, the short story devises a performative means of drawing attention to unseen linkages and forms of community that extend across space and time.

With the award of the Ingeborg Bachmann Prize in July 2016, Otoo was contracted by the major German publishing house Fischer to work her short story into a novel — *Adas Raum* [*Ada's Realm*] — that was published in early 2021.[45] In this novel, Herr Gröttrup does not feature at all, whilst Ada is re-embodied across different historical times and global spaces through four different female characters all bearing that name. The first Ada is a young woman living in West Africa in 1459, the second is based on the historical figure of the mathematician Ada Lovelace and her life in East London in 1848, the third is a Polish woman incarcerated in a Nazi concentration camp in 1945, and the fourth is a woman who has moved from London to Berlin in the twenty-first century facing prejudice due to her skin colour and situation as a pregnant single mother. Through Ada's multiple re-imaginings and re-embodiments, the novel stages a crossing of temporal and spatial boundaries which allows an everywoman to emerge, who figures a materialist conception of life as flows of continuous connection. An unpublished draft when it shot to fame with the Bachmann Prize, the virtual significance of Otoo's short story may further be located in its status as an experimental prototype of the later novel. By opening up zones of indiscernibility and new lines of affiliation through Afrofuturist experimentation on the real, both the short story and the novel emphatically resist the hierarchies and omissions of the present by imagining futures as yet unknown and collectives still to come.

Notes to Chapter 14

1. A longer version of this chapter first appeared in *Forum for Modern Language Studies*; I thank the General Editors and publisher for granting permission (on behalf of the Court of the University of St Andrews) to republish this material.
2. Sandrine Micossé-Aikins and Sharon Dodua Otoo, 'Introduction', in *The Little Book of Big Visions: How to Be an Artist and Revolutionize the World*, ed. by Sandrine Micossé-Aikins and Sharon Dodua Otoo (Münster: edition assemblage, 2012), pp. 10–12.
3. In this article, I follow the editors' choice to capitalize the word 'Black' and write 'white' in small letters: '*"white"* as a political identity does not incorporate the resistance potential that "Black" does'. Cf. Micossé-Aikins and Otoo, *The Little Book of Big Visions*, pp. 12–13.
4. Micossé-Aikins and Otoo, *The Little Book of Big Visions*, p. 11.
5. Sharon Dodua Otoo, *Herr Gröttrup setzt sich hin / Herr Gröttrup Takes a Seat / Herr Gröttrup Sits Down*, trans. into British English by Katy Derbyshire, trans. into American English by Patrick Ploschnitzki and Judith Menzl, ed. by Brittany Hazelwood (Berlin: STILL, 2019). I use the British English translations of the text by Katy Derbyshire in this article.
6. Elizabeth Grosz, 'A Thousand Tiny Sexes: Feminism and Rhizomatics', *Topoi*, 12 (1993), 167–79 (p. 172).
7. Gilles Deleuze and Félix Guattari, *A Thousand Plateaus: Capitalism and Schizophrenia*, trans. by Brian Massumi (London and New York: Bloomsbury, 2013), pp. 117–18.
8. 'Jurydiskussion Sharon Dodua Otoo' <https://bachmannpreis.orf.at/v3/stories/2783488/> [accessed 23 April 2023].
9. <http://www.theafricancourier.de/culture/we-act-as-keepers-of-the-imagination-says-award-winning-sharon-dodua-otoo-on-the-role-of-writers-in-the-struggle-for-a-more-inclusive-society/> [accessed 23 April 2023].
10. <http://www.new-books-in-german.com/take-seat-interview-sharon-dodua-otoo> [accessed 23 April 2023].
11. Cf. 'Jurydiskussion Sharon Dodua Otoo' <https://bachmannpreis.orf.at/v3/stories/2783488/> [accessed 23 April 2023].
12. Jamika Avalon, 'The Fugitive Archive of Resistance: A Metamorphical Narrative', in Micossé-Aikins and Otoo, *The Little Book of Big Visions*, pp. 118–38.
13. Sarah Colvin, 'Talking Back: Sharon Dodua Otoo's *Herr Gröttrup setzt sich hin* and the Epistemology of Resistance', *German Life & Letters*, 73.4 (2020), 659–79 (pp. 674–75).
14. Deleuze and Guattari, *A Thousand Plateaus*, p. 339.
15. John K. Noyes, 'Postcolonial Theory and the Geographical Materialism of Desire', in *Deleuze and the Postcolonial*, ed. by Simone Bignall and Paul Patton (Edinburgh: Edinburgh University Press, 2010), pp. 41–61 (pp. 45–46).
16. Simone Bignall, 'Postcolonial Agency and Poststructuralist Thought: Deleuze and Foucault on Desire and Power', *Angelaki*, 13.1 (2008), 127–49 (p. 138).
17. Cf. Stuart Hall, cited in Noyes, p. 46.
18. <https://www.spreadtheword.org.uk/interview-sharon-dodua-otoo/> [accessed 1 November 2021].

19. Mark Dery, 'Black to the Future: Interviews with Samuel R. Delany, Greg Tate, and Tricia Rose', in *Flame Wars: The Discourse of Cyberculture*, ed. by Mark Dery (Durham, NC, and London: Duke University Press, 1994), pp. 179–222 (p. 180).
20. Ytasha L. Womack, *Afrofuturism: The World of Black Sci-Fi and Fantasy Culture* (Chicago, IL: Lawrence Hill Books, 2013), p. 9.
21. Cf. Priscilla Layne, 'Out of This World: Whence Afro-German Afrofuturism?', *The American Academy in Berlin* (n.d.) <https://www.americanacademy.de/out-of-this-world/> [accessed 23 April 2023].
22. Deleuze and Guattari, *A Thousand Plateaus*, p. 21.
23. Fatima El-Tayeb, *Queering Ethnicity in Post-national Europe* (Minneapolis: University of Minnesota, 2011), p. xix.
24. Cf. 'For Deleuze and Guattari, an organism is a type of body; it is a centralized, hierarchized, self-directed body.' John Protevi, 'Deleuze and Life', in *The Cambridge Companion to Deleuze*, ed. by Daniel W. Smith (Cambridge: Cambridge University Press, 2012), pp. 239–64 (pp. 259–60).
25. Deleuze and Guattari, *A Thousand Plateaus*, p. 201.
26. 'Introduction — On Contested Belonging: A Conversation between Clementine Burnley and Sharon Dodua Otoo', in *Winter Shorts*, ed. by Clementine Burnley and Sharon Dodua Otoo (Münster: edition assemblage, 2015), pp. 7–19 (p. 9).
27. 'I think the content of the instructions also tells a story: the covering of one eye, then the next and finally the instruction to read the text with both eyes open clearly is a reference to the need to access different points of view in order to understand the full picture.' Idra Novey, 'A Conversation between Sharon Dodua Otoo and Idra Novey', in *Herr Gröttrup setzt sich hin*, pp. 67–73 (p. 69).
28. Colvin, 'Talking Back: Sharon Dodua Otoo's *Herr Gröttrup setzt sich hin* and the Epistemology of Resistance', p. 674.
29. Colvin, 'Talking Back', p. 672.
30. Colvin, 'Talking Back', pp. 672–73.
31. Kylie Message, 'Body without Organs', in *The Deleuze Dictionary*, ed. by Adrian Parr (Edinburgh: Edinburgh University Press, 2010), pp. 37–39 (pp. 37–38).
32. Deleuze and Guattari, *A Thousand Plateaus*, pp. 177–78.
33. Deleuze and Guattari, *A Thousand Plateaus*, pp. 50.
34. Jane Bennett, *Vibrant Matter: A Political Ecology of Things* (Durham, NC, and London: Duke University Press, 2010).
35. Bennett, *Vibrant Matter*, p. 13.
36. Ralf Krause and Marc Rölli, 'Micropolitical Associations', in *Deleuze and Politics*, ed. by Ian Buchanan and Nicholas Thoburn (Edinburgh: Edinburgh University Press, 2008), p. 243.
37. Krause and Rölli, p. 247.
38. Kenneth Surin, 'Micropolitics', in *The Deleuze Dictionary*, ed. by Adrian Parr (Edinburgh: Edinburgh University Press, 2010), p. 165.
39. Jendella Benson, 'In conversation with writer and activist Sharon Dodua Otoo', 13 January 2017, <https://mediadiversified.org/2017/01/13/in-conversation-with-writer-and-activist-sharon-dodua-otoo/> [accessed 23 April 2023].
40. 'When I introduced Ada, it quickly became apparent to me that she was the main character of the story. I was intrigued by the idea of writing a main character who barely appears, says very little, and is described even less.' Otoo, 'A Conversation between Sharon Dodua Otoo and Idra Novey', in *Herr Gröttrup setzt sich hin*, p. 72.
41. Cf. Sarah Colvin's detailed analysis of Ada's subordinate status in the bourgeois German household. Colvin, 'Talking Back', pp. 665–66.
42. Michelle Wright, *Becoming Black: Creating Identity in the African Diaspora* (Durham, NC, and London: Duke University Press, 2004), pp. 12–13.
43. Bridget Anderson, 'New Directions in Migration Studies: Towards Methodological De-nationalism', *Comparative Migration Studies*, 7, 36 (2019), 1–13 (p. 2) doi:10.1186/s40878-019-0140-8.

44. Sharon Dodua Otoo and Femi Awoniyi, 'Exclusive Interview with Award-Winning Sharon Dodua Otoo on Writing and the Black Experience in Europe' <https://www.theafricancourier.de/culture/we-act-as-keepers-of-the-imagination-says-award-winning-sharon-dodua-otoo-on-the-role-of-writers-in-the-struggle-for-a-more-inclusive-society/> [accessed 23 April 2023].
45. Sharon Dodua Otoo, *Adas Raum* (Frankfurt a.M.: Fischer, 2021) <https://www.fischerverlage.de/buch/sharon-dodua-otoo-adas-raum-9783103973150> [accessed 23 April 2023].

BIBLIOGRAPHY

ADELSON, LESLIE A., 'Experiment Mars: Contemporary German Literature, Imaginative Ethnoscapes, and the New Futurism', *Über Gegenwartsliteratur: Interpretationen und Interventionen. Festschrift für Paul Michael Lützeler zum 65. Geburtstag von ehemaligen StudentInnen*, ed. by Mark W. Rectanus (Bielefeld: Aisthesis, 2008), pp. 23–49
—— 'Futurity Now: An Introduction', *The Germanic Review*, 88 (2013), 213–18
—— *Cosmic Miniatures and the Future Sense: Alexander Kluge's 21st-Century Literary Experiments in German Culture and Narrative Form* (Berlin and Boston, MA: De Gruyter, 2017)
ADLER, HANS G., *Die Juden in Deutschland: Von der Aufklärung bis zum Nationalsozialismus* (Munich: Kösel, 1961)
AKHTAR, PARVEEN, 'Meeting Ethnic Minorities' Needs', *Assistant Librarian*, 77.9 (1984)
ALCOBA, LAURA, *Manèges: petite histoire argentine* (Paris: Gallimard, 2007)
—— *Le Bleu des abeilles* (Paris: Gallimard, 2013)
—— *La Danse de l'araignée* (Paris: Gallimard, 2017)
ALI, MONICA, *In the Kitchen* (London: Random House, Black Swan, 2009)
ALIGHIERI, DANTE, *The Divine Comedy*, ed. and trans. by Robert M. Durling, 3 vols (Oxford: Oxford University Press, 2007 [1321])
ALMEIDA, DJAIMILIA PEREIRA DE, *Luanda, Lisboa, Paraíso* (São Paulo: Companhia das Letras, 2018)
—— *As Telefones* (Lisbon: Relógio d'Água, 2020)
—— *Esse Cabelo* (Lisbon: Editorial Teorema, 2015)
ANDERSON, BRIDGET, 'New Directions in Migration Studies: Towards Methodological De-Nationalism', *Comparative Migration Studies*, 7.36 (2019), 1–13, <https://doi.org/10.1186/s40878-019-0140-8>
ANDERSON, NEIL D., 'Microgeographies: Galician Narratives of Place (2004–2012)' (unpublished doctoral thesis, University of Chapel Hill, North Carolina, 2014)
—— 'A Critical Geography of Home: Teresa Moure's *A intervención*', *Modern Languages Open* (2016) <http://doi.org/10.3828/mlo.v0i0.111>
ANDERSON, PERRY, *The New Old World* (London: Verso, 2009)
ANOKHINA, OLGA, and EMILIO SCIARRINO, 'Présentation: Plurilinguisme littéraire: de la théorie à la genèse', *Genesis*, 46 (2018), 7–10; 11–33
APPLEYARD, J. A., *Becoming a Reader* (Cambridge: Cambridge University Press, 1994)
ARENDT, BIRTE, *Niederdeutschdiskurse: Spracheinstellungen im Kontext von Laien, Printmedien und Politik* (Berlin: Schmidt, 2010)
ARMSTRONG, DORSEY, and KENNETH HODGES, *Mapping Malory: Regional Identities and National Geographies in 'Le Morte Darthur'* (Basingstoke: Palgrave Macmillan, 2014)
ASHER, KIRAN, and PRITI RAMAMURTHY, 'Rethinking Decolonial and Postcolonial Knowledges beyond Regions to Imagine Transnational Solidarity', *Hypatia*, 35 (2020), 542–47
ASSMAN, JAN, 'Collective Memory and Cultural Identity', trans. by John Czaplicka, *New German Critique*, 65 (1995), 125–33
ATZAGA, BERNARDO, *Obabakoak* (Donostia: Erein, 1988)
—— *Obabakoak*, trans. by Margaret Jull Costa (London: Vintage, 2007)

——— *Soinujolearen semea* (Iruña: Pamiela, 2003)
——— *The Accordionist's Son*, trans. by Margaret Jull Costa (London: Vintage, 2008)
AUDNAL, L., *Der Holzweg* (Berlin: Erich Reiss, 1918)
——— *Die Brandfackel* (Dresden: Piersons, 1929)
AVALON, JAMIKA, 'The Fugitive Archive of Resistance: A Metamorphical Narrative', in *The Little Book of Big Visions: How to Be an Artist and Revolutionize the World*, ed. by Sandrine Micossé-Aikins and Sharon Dodua Otoo (Münster: edition assemblage, 2012), pp. 118–38
BANISTER, PETER, ERICA DURMAN and IAN PARKER, *Qualitative Methods in Psychology: A Research Guide* (Buckingham: Open University Press, 1994)
BARBOUR, CATHERINE, *Contemporary Galician Women Writers* (Cambridge: Legenda, 2020)
BARON SUPERVIELLE, SILVIA, *Les Fenêtres* (Paris: Hors commerce, 1977)
——— *La Ligne et l'ombre* (Paris: Seuil, 1999)
——— *Le Pays de l'écriture* (Paris: Seuil, 2002)
——— *L'Alphabet du feu: petites études sur la langue* (Paris: Gallimard, 2007)
——— *Journal d'une saison sans mémoire* (Paris: Gallimard, 2009)
——— *Al margen/en marge: poesía reunida/poésie réunie* (Buenos Aires: Adriana Hidalgo, 2013)
——— *Le Regard inconnu* (Paris: Gallimard, 2020)
BELPOLITI, MARCO, 'Perché non ricordo gli ebook?', *doppiozero.it*, 9 July 2012, <http://www.doppiozero.com/materiali/fuori-busta/perche-non-ricordo-gli-ebook>
BENJAMIN, WALTER, 'Paris, Capital of the Nineteenth Century' (1939) in *The Arcades Project*, trans. by Howard Eiland and Kevin McLaughlin (Cambridge, MA: Harvard University Press, 1999), pp. 14–26
BENNETT, JANE, *Vibrant Matter: A Political Ecology of Things* (Durham, NC: Duke University Press, 2010)
BENSON, JENDELLA, 'In Conversation with Writer and Activist Sharon Dodua Otoo', 13 January 2017, <https://mediadiversified.org/2017/01/13/in-conversation-with-writer-and-activist-sharon-dodua-otoo/>
BERKERS, PAUWKE, SUSANNE JANSSEN and MARC VERBOORD, 'Assimilation into the Literary Mainstream? The Classification of Ethnic Minority Authors in Newspaper Reviews in the United States, the Netherlands and Germany', *Cultural Sociology*, 8.1 (2013), 25–44 <https://doi.org/10.1177%2F1749975513480960>
BERTHELSEN, CHRISTIAN, 'Greenlandic Literature: Its Traditions, Changes, and Trends', *Arctic Anthropology*, 23 (1986), 339–45
Bewnans Ke/The Life of St Kea: A Critical Edition with Translation, ed. by Graham Thomas and Nicholas Williams (Exeter: University of Exeter Press, 2016)
BIANCIOTTI, HÉCTOR, *Ce que la nuit raconte au jour* (Paris: Grasset, 1992)
——— *Le Pas si lent de l'amour* (Paris: Grasset, 1995)
——— *Comme la trace de l'oiseau dans l'air* (Paris: Grasset, 1999)
——— *What the Night Tells the Day*, trans. by Linda Coverdale (New York: New Press, 1995)
BIENDARRA, ANKE, '"Schriftstellerin zu sein und in seinem Leben anwesend zu sein, ist für mich eins": Ein Gespräch mit Terézia Mora', *Transit Journal*, 20 August 2007, <https://transit.berkeley.edu/2007/biendarra/>
——— 'Travel and Trauma in Post-1989 Europe: Julya Rabinowich's *Die Erdfresserin* and Terézia Mora's *Das Ungeheuer*', in *Anxious Journeys: Twenty-First-Century Travel Writing in German*, ed. by Karin Baumgartner and Monika Shafi (Rochester, NY: Camden House, 2019), pp. 29–40
BIGNALL, SIMONE, 'Postcolonial Agency and Poststructuralist Thought: Deleuze and Foucault on Desire and Power', *Angelaki*, 13.1 (2008), 127–49
BILSKI, EMILY D. (ed.), *Berlin Metropolis: Jews and the New Culture, 1890–1918* (Berkeley: University of California Press, 1999)

BIRDI, BRIONY, KERRY WILSON and SAMI MANSOOR, '"What we should strive for is Britishness": An Attitudinal Investigation of Ethnic Diversity and the Public Library', *Journal of Librarianship and Information Science*, 44.2 (2012), 118–28 <https://doi.org/10.1177%2F0961000611426299>

BIRDI, BRIONY, and MOSTAFA SYED, 'Exploring Reader Response to Minority Ethnic Fiction', *Library Review*, 60.9 (2011), 816–31 <https://doi.org/10.1108/00242531111176826>

BIRDI, BRIONY, and NIGEL FORD, 'Towards a New Sociological Model of Fiction Reading', *Journal of the Association for Information Science and Technology*, 69.11 (2018), 1291–1303

BJERREGAARD, PETER, CHRISTINA V. L. LARSEN, IVALU K. SØRENSEN and JANNE S. TOLSTRUP, 'Alcohol in Greenland 1950–2018: Consumption, Drinking Patterns, and Consequences', *International Journal of Circumpolar Health*, 79 (2020), 1–11

BLAAGAARD, BOLETTE, 'Remembering Nordic Colonialism: Danish Cultural Memory in Journalistic Practice', *KULT-Postkolonial Temaserie*, 7 (2010), 101–21

BLAND, CAROLINE, CATHERINE SMALE and GODELA WEISS-SUSSEX (eds), *Women Writing Heimat in Imperial and Weimar Germany*, special issue of *German Life and Letters*, 72.1 (2019)

BLICKLE, PETER, *Heimat: A Critical Theory of the German Homeland* (Rochester, NY: Camden House, 2002)

BOER, PIM DEN, 'Lieux de mémoire in a Comparative Perspective', in *The Theoretical Foundations of Hungarian 'lieux de mémoire' Studies/Theoretische Grundlagen der Erforschung ungarischer Erinnerungsorte*, ed. by Pál S. Varga et al. (Debrecen: Debrecen University Press, 2013)

BOGUE, RONALD, *Deleuze on Literature* (London: Routledge, 2003)

BOHN CASE, LAURA, 'Ich bin genauso deutsch wie Kafka', in *The Eastern Turn in Contemporary German-Language Literature*, special issue of *German Life and Letters*, ed. by Brigid Haines, 68.2 (2015), 211–27

BONTA, MARK, and JOHN PROTEVI, *Deleuze and Geophilosophy: A Guide and Glossary* (Edinburgh: Edinburgh University Press, 2004)

BOURGÈS, ALIZIZ, and OWEN MARTELL, *Merc'h an Eog/Merch yr Eog* [*The Salmon's Daughter*] (unpublished text supplied by the authors, 2016)

BOYARIN, DANIEL, and JONATHAN BOYARIN, 'Diaspora: Generation and the Ground of Jewish Identity', *Critical Inquiry*, 19.4 (1993), 714–23

BRAIDOTTI, ROSI, *Nomadic Subjects: Embodiment and Sexual Difference in Contemporary Feminist Theory* (New York: Columbia University Press, 1994)

—— *The Posthuman* (Cambridge: Polity, 2013)

BRIONI, SIMONE, 'Orientalism and Former Italian Colonies: An Interview with Shirin Ramzanali Fazel', in *Orientalismi italiani*, vol. 1, ed. by Gabriele Proglio (Turin: Antares, 2012), pp. 215–25

—— '"A Dialogue That Knows No Border Between Nationality, Race or Culture": Themes, Impact and the Critical Reception of Far from Mogadishu', in Shirin Ramzanali Fazel, *Lontano da Mogadiscio / Far from Mogadishu* (Milan: Laurana, 2013), pp. 361–89

—— *The Somali Within: Language, Race and Belonging in 'Minor' Italian Literature* (Cambridge: Legenda, 2015)

——, and SHIRIN RAMZANALI FAZEL, *Scrivere di Islam: raccontare la Diaspora* (Venice: Cà Foscari University Press, 2020)

BROUILLETTE, SARAH, 'The Pathology of Flexibility in Monica Ali's *In the Kitchen*,' *Modern Fiction Studies* 58.3 (2012), 529–48

BUGALLAL, ISABEL, 'La cultura gallega está bien pero limita, prefiero la cultura hecha en Galicia', *Faro de Vigo*, 23 April 2009, <http://www.farodevigo.es/galicia/2009/04/23/cultura-gallega-limita-prefiero-cultura-hecha-galicia/319421.html?pCom=2#EnlaceComentarios>

Burnley, Clementine, and Sharon Dodua Otoo, 'Introduction — On Contested Belonging: A Conversation between Clementine Burnley and Sharon Dodua Otoo', *Winter Shorts*, ed. by Clementine Burnley and Sharon Dodua Otoo (Münster: edition assemblage, 2015), pp. 7–19

Burns, Jennifer, *Fragments of Impegno: Interpretations of Commitment in Contemporary Italian Narrative, 1980–2000* (Leeds: Northern University Press, 2001)

—— *Migrant Imaginaries: Figures in Italian Migration Literature* (Oxford: Peter Lang, 2013)

Butler, Judith, *Frames of War: When is Life Grievable?* (London: Verso, 2009)

Butt, Trevor, and Vivian Burr, *Invitation to Personal Construct Psychology* (London: Whurr Publishers, 1992)

Cabo Aseguinolaza, Fernando, 'The European Horizon of Peninsular Literary Historiographical Discourses', in *A Comparative History of Literatures in the Iberian Península*, vol. I, ed. by Fernando Cabo Aseguinolaza, Anxo Abuín González and César Domínguez (Amsterdam and Philadelphia: John Benjamins Publishing Company, 2010), pp. 1–52

——, Anxo Abuín González and César Domínguez (eds), *A Comparative History of Literatures in the Iberian Peninsula*, vol. 1 (Amsterdam and Philadelphia: John Benjamins Publishing Company, 2010)

Cano, Harkaitz, *Twist* (Zarautz: Susa, 2012)

—— *Twist*, trans. by Amaia Gabantxo (New York: Archipelago Books, 2018)

Caritas and Migrantes, *XXIX Rapporto Immigrazione 2020* (Rome: Caritas, 2021)

Casanova, Pascale, *The World Republic of Letters*, trans. by M. B. DeBevoise (Cambridge, MA: Harvard University Press, 2007)

Castro, Olga, 'Apropriación cultural en las traducciones de una obra (autotraducida): la proyección exterior de Herba Moura, de Teresa Moure', in *Aproximaciones a la autotraducción*, ed. by Xosé Manuel Dasliva and Helena Tanqueiro (Vigo: Editorial Academia del Hispanismo, 2011), pp. 23–44

——, Sergi Mainer and Svetlana Page, 'Introduction: Self-Translating, from Minorisation to Empowerment', in *Self-Translation and Power: Negotiating Identities in European Multilingual Contexts*, ed. by Olga Castro, Sergi Mainer and Svetlana Page (New York: Palgrave Macmillan, 2017), pp. 1–22

Cento Bull, Anna, and Mark Gilbert, *The Lega Nord and the Politics of Secession in Italy* (Basingstoke: Palgrave, 2001)

Chernow, Burt, *Cristo and Jeanne-Claude: A Biography* (New York: St Martin's Press, 2002)

Chitnis, Rajendra, and Jakob Stougaard-Nielsen, 'Introduction', in *Translating the Literatures of Small European Nations*, ed. by Rajendra Chitnis, Jakob Stougaard-Nielsen, Rhian Atkin and Zoran Milutinuvic (Liverpool: Liverpool University Press, 2019), pp. 1–8

CILIP, 'Equalities and Diversity Action Plan', *CILIP — The Library and Information Association*, 2017 <https://www.cilip.org.uk/page/EqualitiesandDiversityAction>

Cinotto, Simone, *The Italian American Table: Food, Family, and Community in New York City* (Urbana, Chicago and Springfield: University of Illinois Press, 2013)

'Cognomi più diffusi? A Brescia Singh batte Ferrari', *Giornale di Brescia*, 17 April 2012, <https://www.giornaledibrescia.it/brescia-e-hinterland/cognomi-pi%C3%B9-diffusi-a-brescia-singh-batte-ferrari-1.1164440>

Coleman, Will, *Plen an Gwari: The Playing Places of Cornwall* (Kernow: Golden Tree Productions, 2015)

Colvin, Sarah, 'Talking Back: Sharon Dodua Otoo's *Herr Gröttrup setzt sich hin* and the Epistemology of Resistance', *German Life and Letters*, 73.4 (2020), 659–79

Cosgrove, Mary, 'The Slothful Protest: *Acedia* in Terézia Mora's Darius-Kopp Trilogy and Iris Hanika's *Das Eigentliche*', in *German Life and Letters*, 74.1 (2021), 47–67

COUNCIL OF EUROPE, 'European Charter for Regional or Minority Languages', 5 November 1992, article 1 <https://www.coe.int/en/web/conventions/full-list/-/conventions/rms/090001680695175>
CRONER, ELSE, *Die moderne Jüdin* (Berlin: Axel Juncker, 1913)
DABYDEEN, DAVID, and NANA WILSON-TAGOE, *A Reader's Guide to Westindian and Black British Literature* (London: Hansib Publications, 1997)
DAMROSCH, DAVID, *What is World Literature?* (Princeton, NJ: Princeton University Press, 2003)
DAWSON, ASHLEY, 'The People You Don't See: Representing Informal Labour in Fortress Europe', *ARIEL* 40.1 (2009), 125–41
DEANDREA, PIETRO, *New Slaveries in Contemporary British Literature and Visual Arts: The Ghost and the Camp* (Manchester: Manchester University Press, 2015)
DELEUZE, GILLES, 'One Less Manifesto', trans. by Timothy Murray, in *Mimesis, Masochism and Mime: The Politics of Theatricality in Contemporary French Thought*, ed. by Timothy Murray (Ann Arbor: University of Michigan Press, 1997), pp. 239–58
—— *Difference and Repetition*, trans. by Paul Patton (London: Continuum, 2004)
—— *Cinema 2: The Time Image*, trans. by Hugh Tomlinson and Robert Galeta (London: Continuum, 2005)
——, and FÉLIX GUATTARI, *Pour une littérature mineure* (Paris: Minuit, 1975)
——, and FÉLIX GUATTARI, *Kafka: Toward a Minor Literature*, trans. by Dana Polan (Minneapolis: University of Minnesota Press, 1986)
——, and FÉLIX GUATTARI, 'What Is a Minor Literature?', trans. by Robert Brinkley, *Mississippi Review*, 11.3 (Winter/Spring 1983), 11–33
——, and FÉLIX GUATTARI, *A Thousand Plateaus: Capitalism and Schizophrenia*, trans. by Brian Massumi (Minneapolis: University of Minnesota Press, 1987)
DELGADO, LUISA ELENA, *La nación singular: fantasías de la normalidad democrática española (1996–2011)* (Madrid: Siglo XXI, 2014)
DENNY, NEIL, 'The Importance of Ethnic Inclusion', in *Books for All: A 16-page Special on Books, Diversity and Your Business* (London: The Bookseller, May 2006)
DEROBERTIS, ROBERTO, 'Da dove facciamo il postcoloniale? Appunti per una genealogia della ricezione degli studi postcoloniali nell'italianistica italiana', *Postcolonialitalia.it*, 17 February 2014, <http://www.postcolonialitalia.it/index.php?option=com_content&view=article&id=56:da-dove-facciamo-il-postcoloniale&catid=27:interventi&Itemid=101&lang=it>
DERRIDA, JACQUES, 'Living On. Border Lines', in *Deconstruction and Criticism* (New York: Seabury Press, 1979), pp. 75–176
DERY, MARK, 'Black to the Future: Interviews with Samuel R. Delany, Greg Tate, and Tricia Rose', in *Flame Wars: The Discourse of Cyberculture*, ed. by Mark Dery (Durham, NC, and London: Duke University Press, 1994), 179–222
DIBABA, YARED, *Platt is mien Welt* (Hamburg: Quickborn, 2009)
—— *Mien Welt blifft Platt* (Hamburg: Quickborn, 2011)
—— *Moin tosomen!* (Hamburg: Quickborn, 2014)
—— *Ünnerwegens* (Hamburg: Quickborn, 2016)
DIRLIK, ARIF, 'Globalization, Indigenism, Social Movements, and the Politics of Place', *Localities*, 1 (2011), 47–90
DODUA OTOO, SHARON, *Herr Gröttrup setzt sich hin / Herr Gröttrup Takes a Seat*, trans. by Katy Derbyshire / *Herr Gröttrup Sits Down*, trans. by Patrick Ploschnitzki and Judith Menzl, ed. by Brittany Hazelwood (Berlin: STILL, 2019)
——, and FEMI AWONIYI, 'Exclusive Interview with Award-Winning Sharon Dodua Otoo on Writing and the Black Experience in Europe', *African Courier*, 26 October 2016, <https://www.theafricancourier.de/culture/we-act-as-keepers-of-the-imagination-

says-award-winning-sharon-dodua-otoo-on-the-role-of-writers-in-the-struggle-for-a-more-inclusive-society/>

—— *Adas Raum* (Frankfurt: Fischer, 2021)

DOMÍNGUEZ, CÉSAR, 'Historiography and the Geo-Literary Imaginery: The Iberian Peninsula: Between *Lebensraum* and *espace vécu*', in *A Comparative History of Literatures in the Iberian Península*, vol. I, ed. by Fernando Cabo Aseguinolaza, Anxo Abuín González and César Domínguez (Amsterdam and Philadelphia: John Benjamins Publishing Company, 2010), pp. 53–132

DOPICO, MONTSE, 'O amor de mãe tópico tem uma leitura antipolítica', *Praza Pública*, 13 October 2014 <http://praza.gal/cultura/7994/lo-amor-de-mae-topico-tem-uma-leitura-antipoliticar/>

DUTTLINGER, CAROLIN, *The Cambridge Companion to Franz Kafka* (Cambridge: Cambridge University Press, 2013)

D'EAUBONNE, FRANÇOISE, *Le Féminisme ou la mort* (Paris: Pierre Horay, 1974)

ECO, UMBERTO, 'The Language of Europe is Translation', ATLAS: *Assises de la traduction littéraire*, Arles, 14 November 1993

EHLERS, CHRISTIANE (ed.), *Chartasprache Niederdeutsch: Rechtliche Verpflichtungen, Umsetzungen und Perspektiven* (Bremen: Bundesraat för Nedderdüütsch, 2014)

ELBESHAUSEN, HANS, and PETER SKOV, 'Public Libraries in a Multicultural Space: A Case Study of Integration Processes in Local Communities', *New Library World*, 105.3/4 (2004), 131–41<https://doi.org/10.1108/03074800410526767>

ELLIS, ROBERT RICHMOND, 'Homoeroticism and the Ever-Recurring Illusion of Selfhood: The Argentine "Life" of Hector Bianciotti', *Revista Canadiense de Estudios Hispánicos*, 22.3 (1998), 431–46

EL-TAYEB, FATIMA, *Queering Ethnicity in Post-national Europe* (Minneapolis: University of Minnesota, 2011)

ENWEZOR, OKWUI, 'A Question of Place: Revisions, Reassessment, Diaspora', in *Transforming the Crown: African, Asian and Caribbean Artists in Britain, 1996–1996*, ed. by Mora Beauchamp-Byrd and M. Franklin Sirmans (New York: Caribbean Cultural Center, 1997)

EPPS, BRADLEY S., and LUIS FERNÁNDEZ CIFUENTES, *Spain Beyond Spain: Modernity, Literary History, And National Identity* (Lewisburg, PA: Bucknell University Press, 2005)

ESTEVES PEREIRA, MARGARIDA, 'Transnational Identities in the Fiction of Monica Ali: *In the Kitchen* and *Alentejo Blue*', *Journal of Postcolonial Writing*, 52.1 (2016), 77–88

FARIAS DE ALBUQUERQUE, FERNANDA, and MAURIZIO IANNELLI, *Princesa* (2013 [1994]), <http://www.princesa20.it/>

FEINBERG, ANAT, 'Abiding in a Haunted Land: The Issue of Heimat in Contemporary German-Jewish Writing', *New German Critique*, 70 (1997), 161–81

FERREIRA, ANA PAULA, 'Lusotropicalist Entanglements: Colonial Racisms in the Postcolonial Metropolis', in *Gender, Empire and Postcolony: Luso-Afro-Brazilian Intersections*, ed. by Anna Klobucka and Hilary Owen (London: Palgrave Macmillan, 2014), pp. 46–69

FERREIRA, PATRÍCIA MARTINHO, *Órfãos do Império: heranças coloniais na literatura portuguesa contemporânea* (Lisbon: ICS, 2021)

FIEKER, CORNELIA, *Das literarisch ambitionierte niederdeutsche Hörspiel* (Leer: Schuster, 1985)

FITZNER, FRAUKE (ed.), *Tempo! Zeit- und Beschleunigungswahrnehmung in der Moderne* (= *ZfL Interjekte* 5, ed. by Zentrum für Literatur- und Kulturforschung Berlin, 2014), <http://www.zfl-berlin.org/publication/tempo-zeit-und-beschleunigungswahrnehmung-in-der-moderne.html>

FLOOD, ALISON, 'Evaristo and Carty-Williams become first black authors to win top British Book awards', *The Guardian*, 29 June 2020 <https://www.theguardian.com/

books/2020/jun/29/candice-carty-williams-bernardine-evaristo-first-black-authors-to-win-top-british-book-awards>
FORAN, LISA, *Derrida, the Subject and the Other: Surviving Translation and the Impossible* (London: Palgrave Macmillan, 2016)
FRANSELLA, FAY (ed.), *The Essential Practitioner's Handbook of Personal Construct Psychology* (Chichester: John Wiley & Sons, 2005)
FYNSK, CHRISTOPHER, 'Foreword: Experiences of Finitude', in Jean-Luc Nancy, *The Inoperative Community*, ed. and trans. by Peter Connor (Minneapolis: University of Minnesota Press, 1991), p. xv
GAL, SUSANNE, 'Language and Political Spaces', in *Language and Space: An International Handbook of Linguistic Variation*, ed. by Peter Auer and Jürgen Erich Schmidt (Berlin and New York: De Gruyter Mouton 2010), pp. 33–49
GASQUET, AXEL, *L'Intelligentsia du bout du monde* (Paris: Kimé, 2002)
GERSTENBERGER, KATHARINA, 'Post 1989 Geographies in Terézia Mora's *Der einzige Mann auf dem Kontinent* and *Das Ungeheuer*', *German Life and Letters*, 71.3 (2018), 291–307
GIBSON, MARION, GARRY TREGIDGA and SHELLEY TROWER, 'Mysticism, Myth and Celtic Identity', in *Mysticism, Myth and Celtic Identity*, ed. by Marion Gibson, Garry Tregidga and Shelley Trower (London and New York: Routledge, 2012), pp. 1–20
GILMAN, NILS, JESSE GOLDHAMMER and STEVEN WEBER (eds), *Deviant Globalization: Black Market Economy in the 21st Century* (London: Continuum, 2011)
GILMAN, SANDER, *The Smart Jew: The Construction of Jewish Superior Intelligence* (Lincoln: University of Nebraska Press, 1996)
GILROY, PAUL, *After Empire: Multiculture or Postcolonial Melancholia* (London: Routledge, 2004)
GIORDANO, ALBERTO, 'Situación de Héctor Bianciotti: el escritor argentino y la tradición francesa', *Hispamérica*, 28.84 (1999), 3–12
GIULIANI, GAIA, 'L'italiano negro: la bianchezza degli italiani dall'Unità al Fascismo', in *Bianco e nero: storia dell'identità razziale degli italiani*, ed. by Gaia Giuliani and Cristina Lombardi-Diop (Florence: Le Monnier, 2013), pp. 21–65
GONZALEZ, MADALENA, 'Avant-propos', in *Théâtre des minorités: mises en scène de la marge à l'époque contemporaine*, ed. by Madelena Gonzalez and Patrice Brasseur (Paris: L'Harmattan, 2008), pp. 9–16
—— 'The Construction of Identity in Minority Theatre', in *Authenticity and Legitimacy in Minority Theatre: Constructing Identity*, ed. by Madelena Gonzalez and Patrice Brasseur (Newcastle upon Tyne: Cambridge Scholars, 2010)
—— 'Minority Theatre in the Age of Globalization', in *Minority Theatre on the Global Stage: Challenging Paradigms from the Margins*, ed. by Madelena Gonzalez and Hélène Laplace-Claverie (Newcastle upon Tyne: Cambridge Scholars, 2012)
GONZÁLEZ, OLGA, 'La présence latino-américaine en France', in *Migrations latino-américaines*, special issue of *Hommes et migrations*, ed. by Olga González, 1270 (2007), 8–18
GONZÁLEZ FERNÁNDEZ, HELENA, *Elas e o paraugas totalizador: escritoras, xénero e nación* (Vigo: Xerais, 2005)
GREENHALGH, LIZ, and KEN WORPOLE, *Libraries in a World of Cultural Change* (London: UCL Press, 1995)
GROSZ, ELIZABETH, 'A Thousand Tiny Sexes: Feminism and Rhizomatics', *Topoi*, 12.2 (1993), 167–79
GRUTMAN, RAINIER, 'Diglosia y autotraducción vertical', in *Aproximaciones a la traducción*, ed. by Xosé Manuel Dasilva and Helena Tanqueiro (Vigo: Editorial Academia del Hispanismo, 2011), pp. 69–92
GRYDEHØJ, ADAM, 'Unravelling Economic Dependence and Independence in Relation to

Island Sovereignty: The Case of Kalaallit Nunaat (Greenland)', *Island Studies Journal*, 15.1 (2020), 89–112

GUERENA, SALVADOR, and EDWARD ERAZO, 'Latinos and Librarianship', *Library Trends*, 49.1 (2000), 138–82

GUNNING, DAVE, 'Ethnicity, Authenticity, and Empathy in the Realist Novel and its Alternatives,' *Contemporary Literature*, 53.4 (2012), 779–813

HALBERSTAM, JACK, *The Queer Art of Failure* (Durham, NC: Duke University Press 2011)

HALL, STUART, 'Conclusion: The Multicultural Question', in *Un/Settled Multiculturalisms: Diasporas, Entanglements, 'Transruptions'*, ed. by Barnor Hesse (London: Zed, 2000), pp. 209–41

HANSEN, DÖRTE, *Transfer bei Diglossie: Synchrone Sprachkontaktphänomene im Niederdeutschen* (Hamburg: Kovač, 1995)

—— *Altes Land. Roman* (Munich: Knaus, 2015)

HARVEY, DAVID, *The New Imperialism* (Oxford: Oxford University Press, 2003)

HAUSCHNER, AUGUSTE, '[review of] *Der Weg ins Freie*', *Die Hilfe*, 15 (1909), 39–40

—— *Rudolf und Camilla* (Berlin: Egon Fleischel & Co, 1910)

—— 'Rahel Levins Sendung', *Das literarische Echo*, 17 (1914/15), cols 267–70

HEGER, ANNIE, 'Editorial', *Plattart: Festival Neue Niederdeutsche Kultur 10. bis 19. März 2017*, p. 1 <https://oldenburgische-landschaft.de/uploads/live/aktuelles/103/programmheft2017.pdf>

HENRIQUES, MARIA ADELINA, 'A emigração PALOP em Portugal: o caso dos doentes evacuados', *Sociológico*, 22 (2012), 53–62 <http://doi.org/10.4000/sociologico.573>

HENZE, SARAH-CHRISTINA, 'Transgression des Strichs: Getrennte Perspektiven in Terézia Mora's Roman *Das Ungeheuer*', in *Das Radikale: Gesellschafts-politische und formal-ästhetische Aspekte in der Gegenwartsliteratur*, ed. by Stephanie Willeke, Ludmilla Peters and Carsten Roth (Münster: LIT, 2017)

HERMANN, GEORG, 'Der deutsche Jude und das Großstadtproblem', undated typescript, Georg Hermann Collection, Leo Baeck Institute New York, section V, 9 pages

—— *Die Nacht des Doktor Herzfeld* [1912] in *Doktor Herzfeld: Die Nacht / Schnee* (Berlin: Das Neue Berlin, 1997), pp. 7–265

HIGONNET, PATRICE, *Paris: Capital of the World*, trans. by Arthur Goldhammer (Cambridge, MA: Harvard University Press, 2002)

HIRSCH, AFUA, 'Why does it take a white face to keep us interested in African stories?', *The Guardian*, 5 October 2013

HO, JANICE, *Nation and Citizenship in the Twentieth-Century British Novel* (New York: Cambridge University Press, 2015)

HØEG, PETER, *Frøken Smilla's Fornemmelse for Sne* (Copenhagen: Rosinante, 2010)

HOLST, EMMA QVIRIN, 'Frederiksen siger undskyld til grønlandske eksperimentbørn', *Altinget* (2020), <https://www.altinget.dk/artikel/frederiksen-siger-undskyld-til-groenlandske-eksperimentboern>

HOOPER, KIRSTY, 'Girl, Interrupted: The Distinctive History of Galician Women's Narrative', *Romance Studies*, 21.2 (2003), 101–14

HOUSWITSCHKA, CHRISTOPH, 'Cosmopolitanism and Citizenship: Identities and Affiliations in Monica Ali's *In the Kitchen*', in *Transcultural Identities in Contemporary Literature*, ed. by Julie Hansen and Carmen Llena Zamorano (Amsterdam: Rodopi, 2013), pp. 71–91

HUMBLE, MALCOLM, 'Monism and Literature in the Later Years of the *Kaiserreich*', in *Science, Technology and the German Cultural Imagination*, ed. by Christian Emden and David Midgley (Oxford: Peter Lang, 2005), pp. 57–79

HUNDAL, SUNNY, 'Why Multiculturalism Matters', *The Guardian*, 19 March 2007 <http://www.theguardian.com/media/2007/mar/19/mondaymediasection8>

Huss, Werner, *Geschichte der Karthager* (Munich: C. H. Beck, 1985)
Ibarluzea, Miren, 'Itzulpengintzaren errepresentazioak euskal literatura garaikidean: eremuaren autonomizazioa, euskal historiografiak eta eta itzultzaileak fikzioan' (unpublished doctoral thesis, University of the Basque Country, 2017)
——, and Mari Jose Olaziregi, 'Autonomización y funciones del subcampo de la traducción literaria vasca contemporánea: una aproximación sociológica', *Pasavento*, 4.2 (2016), 293–313
'"Ich bin mit allen Sinnen in die Sprache und Kultur eingetaucht": Interview mit Yared Dibaba', *Bildungsthemen*, 1 (2016), 12–14
Igartua, Ivan, and Zabalza, Xabier, *Euskararen historia laburra. Breve historia de la lengua vasca. A Brief History of the Basque Language* (Donostia: Instituto Vasco Etxepare, 2012)
Iser, Wolfgang, *The Act of Reading: A Theory of Aesthetic Response* (Baltimore, MD: Johns Hopkins University Press, 1978)
JanMohamed, Abdul, and David Lloyd, 'Toward a Theory of Minority Discourse', *Cultural Critique*, 6 (1987), 5–12
Jay, Paul, *Global Matters: The Transnational Turn in Literary Studies* (Ithaca, NY: Cornell University Press, 2010)
Jensen, Lars, 'Introduction: Denmark and its Colonies', in *A Historical Companion to Postcolonial Literature: Continental Europe and its Empire*, ed. by Prem Poddar, Rajeev S. Patke and Lars Jensen (Edinburgh: Edinburgh University Press, 2008), pp. 59–62
——'Charter Companies', in *A Historical Companion to Postcolonial Literature: Continental Europe and its Empire*, ed. by Prem Poddar, Rajeev S. Patke and Lars Jensen (Edinburgh: Edinburgh University Press, 2008), pp. 67–68
——, and Kristín Loftsdóttir, *Whiteness and Postcolonialism in the Nordic Region: Exceptionalism, Migrant Others and National Identities* (Farnham: Ashgate, 2012)
Jerónimo, Miguel Bandeira, and José Pedro Monteiro, *História(s) do presente: os mundos que o passado nos deixou* (Lisbon: Tinta-da-china, 2020)
Johnson, Catherine, 'Where are Britain's black writers?', *The Guardian*, 5 December 2011 <http://www.theguardian.com/commentisfree/2011/dec/05/where-are-britains-black-writers>
Jürgens, Carolin, *Niederdeutsch im Wandel: Sprachgebrauchswandel und Sprachwahrnehmung in Hamburg* (Hildesheim: Olms, 2015)
Kafka, Franz, *Diaries, 1910–1923*, ed. by Max Brod, trans. by Joseph Kresh, Martin Greenberg and Hannah Arendt (New York: Schocken Books, 1976)
——*Diarios, 1910–1923*, trans. by Feliv Formosa (Barcelona: Lumen-Tusquets, 1995)
Karpat, Berkan, and Zafer Şenocak, *futuristen-epilog — poeme* (Munich: Babel, 2008)
Keith, Michael, and Steve Pile, *Place and the Politics of Identity* (London: Routledge, 2004)
Kellman, Steven G., *The Translingual Imagination* (Lincoln: University of Nebraska Press, 2000)
Kelly, George A., *The Psychology of Personal Constructs* (New York: W. W. Norton, 1955)
Kendall, Margaret, 'Keeping Multiculturalism on the Agenda: Strategies for Actions in Public Libraries', *Library Review*, 41.1 (1992), 25–33
Khan, Sheila, *Portugal a lápis de cor: a sul de uma pós-colonialidade* (Coimbra: Almedina, 2015)
Khlebnikov, Velimir, 'Ka', in *Collected Works of Velimir Khlebnikov*, vol. II: *Prose, Plays and Supersagas*, trans. by Paul Schmidt, ed. by Ronald Vroon (Cambridge, MA: Harvard University Press, 1989), pp. 56–74
——*Collected Works of Velimir Khlebnikov*, vol. III: *Selected Poems*, trans. by Paul Schmidt, ed. by Ronald Vroon (Cambridge, MA: Harvard University Press, 1997)
Kilcher, Andreas, *Metzler Lexikon der deutsch-jüdischen Literatur* (Stuttgart: J. B. Metzler, 2012)

Kilomba, Grada, *Plantation Memories: Episodes of Everyday Racism* (Münster: Unrast Verlag, 2010)
—— *Memórias da Plantação: Episódios de Racismo Quotidiano* (Lisbon: Orfeu Negro, 2019)
Kippur, Sara, 'Pour ou contre une littérature-monde?: Héctor Bianciotti, Silvia Baron Supervielle, and the Case of Argentina', *Contemporary French and Francophone Studies*, 13.2 (2009), 211–22
Kline, Elizabeth, and Barbara Williams, 'Managing Users' Expectations of E-books', in *Adapting to E-books* (London: Routledge, 2009), pp. 249–55
Kloss, Heinz 'Abstandsprachen und Ausbausprachen', in *Zur Theorie des Dialekts*, ed. by Joachim Göschel et al. (Wiesbaden: Steiner, 1976), pp. 301–22
Korneliussen, Niviaq, *HOMO Sapienne* (Nuuk: Milik, 2014)
Krafft-Ebing, Richard von, *Psychopathia Sexualis: Mit besonderer Berücksichtigung der conträren Sexualempfindung. Eine klinisch-forensische Studie* (Stuttgart: Ferdinand Enke, 1894 [1886])
Krause, Ralf, and Marc Rölli, 'Micropolitical Associations', in *Deleuze and Politics*, ed. by Ian Buchanan and Nicholas Thoburn (Edinburgh: Edinburgh University Press, 2008)
Krische, Paul, *Heimat! Grundsätzliches zur Gemeinschaft von Scholle und Mensch* (Berlin: Paetel, 1918)
Kundera, Milan, *Les Testaments trahis* (Paris: Gallimard, 1995)
Kustow, Michael, *Theatre@risk* (London: Methuen, 2001)
Ladouceur, Louise, 'Bilingualism on Stage: Translating Francophone Drama Repertories in Canada', *Trans*, 13 (2009), 129–36
Lambert, Claire M., 'Library Provision for the Indian and Pakistani Communities in Britain', *Journal of Librarianship and Information Science*, 1 (1969), 41–61
Lambert, Gregg, 'The Bachelor Machine and the Postcolonial Writer', in *Postcolonial Literatures and Deleuze: Colonial Pasts, Differential Futures*, ed. by Lorna Burns and Birgit M. Kaiser (London: Palgrave, 2012), pp. 37–54
Langgård, Karen, 'Greenlandic Writers', in *A Historical Companion to Postcolonial Literature: Continental Europe and its Empires*, ed. by Prem Poddar, Rajeev S. Patke and Lars Jensen (Edinburgh: Edinburgh University Press, 2008), pp. 71–72
—— 'Oral/Past Culture and Modern Technical Means in the Literature of the Twentieth Century in Greenland', *Acta Borealia: A Nordic Journal of Circumpolar Societies*, 25.1 (2008), 45–57
Latour, Bruno, *We Have Never Been Modern*, trans. by Catherine Porter (Cambridge, MA: Harvard University Press, 1993)
Layne, Priscilla, 'Out of This World: Whence Afro-German Afrofuturism?', *The American Academy in Berlin* (n.d.), <https://www.americanacademy.de/out-of-this-world/>
Lazarus, Nahida Ruth, *Das jüdische Weib* (Berlin: Siegfried Cronbach, 1896)
Lechner, Doris, 'Eastern European Memories? Marina Lewycka's Novels', in *Facing the East in the West: Images of Eastern Europe in Contemporary British Literature, Film and Culture*, ed. by Barbara Korte, Eva Ulrike Pirker and Sissy Helff (Amsterdam: Rodopi, 2010), pp. 437–80
Lefebvre, Henri, *The Production of Space*, trans. by Donald Nicholson Smith (Oxford: Blackwell, 1991)
Leine, Kim, *Kalak* (Nørhaven: Gyldendal, 2007)
Lewycka, Marina, *Two Caravans* (London: Penguin, 2007)
Liao, Pei-chen, 'Seeking Out the Periphery in the Shadows: Monica Ali's *In the Kitchen* and Contemporary Writing of Britain,' *NTU Studies in Language and Literature*, 28 (2012), 87–115
Library Advisory Council, *Public Library Services for a Multi-Cultural Society*, 2nd edn (London: Commission for Racial Equality, 1997)

LINDNER, OLIVER, ' "East is East and West is Best?": The Eastern European Migrant and the British Contact Zone in Rose Tremain's *The Road Home* (2007) and in Marina Lewycka's *Two Caravans* (2007)', *Anglia*, 127.3 (2009), 459–73

LIÑEIRA, MARÍA, 'Literary Citizenship and the Politics of Language: The Galician Literary Field between 1939 and 1965' (unpublished doctoral thesis, University of Oxford, 2015)

LIONNET, FRANÇOISE, and SHU-MEI SHIH, 'Introduction: Thinking through the Minor, Transnationally', in *Minor Transnationalism*, ed. by Lionnet and Shih (Durham, NC: Duke University Press, 2005), pp. 1–23

LITERATURES ACROSS FRONTIERS, 'Translation Statistics from LAF', 13 April 2015, <http://www.lit-across-frontiers.org/new-translation-statistics-from-laf/>

LOFF, MANUEL, 'Estado, democracia e memória: políticas públicas e batalhas pela memória da ditadura portuguesa (1974–2014)', in *Ditaduras e Revolução: democracia e políticas de memória*, ed. by Manuel Loff, Filipe Piedade and Luciana Castro Soutelo (Coimbra: Almedina, 2015), pp. 23–143

LÓPEZ LÓPEZ, LORENA, *Ainda invisíveis? Narradoras e margens na literatura galega contemporânea* (Santiago de Compostela: Através Editora, 2022)

LUBOWICKA, AGATA, 'Mellem det (post)koloniale, det (post)nationale og det globale: en analyse af Niviaq Korneliussens *HOMO Sapienne*', *Folia Scandinavica*, 24 (2018), pp. 39–55

LUCAS, ISABEL, ' "Uma rapariga africana em Lisboa": interview with Djaimilia Pereira de Almeida', *Público*, 2 October 2015, <http:77www.publico.pt/2015/10/02/culturaipsilon/entrevista/uma-rapariga-africana-em-lisboa-1709352>

—— ' "Djaimilia Pereira de Almeida: não é só raça nem género, é querer participar na grande conversa da literatura": interview with Djaimilia Pereira de Almeida', *Público*, 20 December 2018, <https://www.publico.pt/2018/12/20/culturaipsilon/noticia/djaimilia-1854988>

LYBERTH, JUAAKA, *Godt i vej*, trans. by Lars Wind (Nuuk: Milik, 2014)

LYNGE, HANS A., 'Juaaka Lyberth', *Nordic Co-operation* (2014), <https://www.norden.org/en/nominee/juaaka-lyberth>

LYOTARD, JEAN-FRANÇOIS, *Expédient dans la décadence*, in *Rudiments païens: genre discursif* (Paris: Union générale d'éditions, 1977), pp. 115–56

MANN, BARBARA E., *Space and Place in Jewish Studies* (New Brunswick, NJ: Rutgers University Press, 2012)

MANTEROLA, ELIZABETE, *La literatura vasca traducida* (Bern: Peter Lang, 2014)

MARTÍNEZ-GIL, VÍCTOR, 'Modernidad, política e ibericidad en las relaciones literarias intra-peninsulares', in *Anejo IX: Literaturas ibéricas: teoría, historia y comparativas*, special issue of *Revista de filología románica*, ed. by Juan Miguel Ribera Llopis, Óscar Fernández Poza and Diego Muñoz Carrobles, 9 (2015), 31–44

MASSEY, DOREEN, *Space, Place and Gender* (Cambridge: Polity, 1994)

—— *For Space* (London: Sage, 2005)

MATA, INOCÊNCIA, 'Estranhos em permanência: a negociação da identidade portuguesa na pós-colonialidade', in *Portugal não é um país pequeno: contar o 'império' na pós-colonialidade*, ed. by Manuela Ribeiro Sanches (Lisbon: Cotovia, 2006), pp. 285–315

—— 'Uma implosiva geografia exílica', *Público*, 14 December 2018, <https://www.publico.pt/2018/12/14/culturaipsilon/critica/implosiva-geografia-exilica-1854334>

MATHIS-MOSER, URSULA, and BIRGIT MERTZ-BAUMGARTNER, *Passages et ancrages: dictionnaire des 'écrivains migrants' en France depuis 1981* (Paris: Champion, 2011)

MCCALLUM, PAMELA, 'Representing Migrant Labour in Contemporary Britain: Hsaio-Hung Pai's *Chinese Whispers* and Marina Lewycka's *Strawberry Fields/Two Caravans*', in *Negative Cosmopolitanisms: Cultures and Politics of World Citizenship After Globalization*, ed. by Eddy Kent and Terri Tomsky (Montreal: McGill-Queen's University Press, 2017), pp. 130–48

McKane, Richard (ed.), *Ten Russian Poets: Surviving the Twentieth Century* (London: Anvil Press, 2003)
Medeiros, Paulo de, 'Memórias Pós-Imperiais: *Luuanda*, de José Luandino Vieira, e *Luanda, Lisboa, Paraíso*, de Djaimilia Pereira de Almeida', *Língua-Lugar: Literatura, História, Estudos Culturais*, 1 (2020), 136–49, <http://doi.org/10.34913/journals/lingua-lugar.2020e211>
Meegan, Richard, 'Doreen Massey (1944–2016): A Geographer Who Really Mattered', *Regional Studies*, 51.9 (2017), 1285–96
Meisel-Hess, Grete, *Die sexuelle Krise: Eine sozialpsychologische Untersuchung* (Jena: Eugen Diederichs, 1909)
—— 'Die Judenfrage in romantischer Behandlung', *Der Weg*, 3 (1911), cols 801–05
Message, Kylie, 'Body without Organs', in *The Deleuze Dictionary*, ed. by Adrian Parr (Edinburgh: Edinburgh University Press, 2010), pp. 37–39
Micossé-Aikins, Sandrine, and Sharon Dodua Otoo, 'Introduction', in *The Little Book of Big Visions: How to Be an Artist and Revolutionize the World*, ed. by Sandrine Micossé-Aikins and Sharon Dodua Otoo (Münster: edition assemblage, 2012), pp. 10–12
Miguélez-Carballeira, Helena, 'Inaugurar, reanudar, renovar: a escrita de Teresa Moure no contexto da narrativa feminista contemporánea', *Anuario de estudos galegos* (2006), 72–87
Ming 2, Wu, and Antar Mohamed, *Timira: Romanzo meticcio* (Turin: Einaudi, 2012)
Mitchell, Andrew J., *The Fourfold: Reading the Late Heidegger* (Evanston, IL: Northwestern University Press, 2015)
Moestrup, Mette, 'Forord', in Niviaq Korneliussen, *HOMO Sapienne* (Nuuk: Milik, 2014), pp. 9–12
Moreda Rodríguez, Eva, 'Addressing Gender Gaps in Contemporary Galician-Language Fiction: The Cases of Úrsula Heinze, Silvia Bardelás and Beatriz Dacosta', in *Women's Lived Experiences of the Gender Gap*, ed. by Angela Fitzgerald (Singapore: Springer, 2021), pp. 59–71
Moretti, Franco, *Distant Reading* (London and New York: Verso Books, 2013)
Moure, Teresa, *A intervención* (Vigo: Xerais, 2010)
—— 'Teresa Moure: "Os prexuízos contra o galego aumentan por mor da inepcia dos gobernantes"', *La Opinion Coruña*, 23 May 2010, <http://www.laopinioncoruna.es/cultura/2010/05/23/teresa-moure-prexuizos-o-galego-aumentan-mor-da-inepcia-gobernantes/387141.html>
—— 'Sobre encrucilhadas, normas ortográficas e independência', *Praza Pública*, 27 March 2013 <http://praza.com/opinion/981/sobre-encrucilhadas-normas-ortograficas-e-independencia/>
—— *Herba moura* (Vigo: Xerais, 2005)
—— *Hierba mora* (Barcelona: Lumen, 2006)
—— *La jornada de las mujeres-árbol* (Barcelona: Ronsel, 2006)
—— *La palabra de las hijas de Eva* (Barcelona: Lumen, 2007)
—— *A intervención* (Vigo: Xerais, 2010)
—— *Artes subversivas para cultivar jardines* (Gijón: Hoja de Lata, 2014)
—— *Black Nightshade*, trans. by Philip Krummrich (Sofia: Small Stations Press, 2018)
—— *The Operation*, trans. by Philip Krummrich (Sofia: Small Stations Press, 2021)
—— *La morelle noire*, trans. by Marielle Leroy (Lille: La contre allée, 2024)
Nancy, Jean-Luc, *The Inoperative Community*, ed. and trans. by Peter Connor (Minneapolis: University of Minnesota Press, 1991)
Naum, Magdalena, and Jonas Nordin (eds), *Scandinavian Colonialism and the Rise of Modernity: Small Time Agents in a Global Arena* (New York: Springer, 2013)
Neto, Maria da Conceição, 'A República no seu estado colonial: combater a escravatura, estabelecer o "indigenato"', *Ler História*, 59 (2010), 205–25

Nicholls, Peter, 'Introduction', *Critical Quarterly*, 37.4 (1995), 1–3
Nichols, Catherine, 'Homme de Plume: What I Learned Sending My Novel Out Under a Male Name', *Jezebel*, 4 August 2015, <http://jezebel.com/homme-de-plume-what-i-learned-sending-my-novel-out-und-1720637627?utm>
Nielsen, Kristian H, 'Transforming Greenland: Imperial Formations in the Cold War', *New Global Studies*, 7.2 (2013), 129–54
Nochlin, Linda, 'Why Have There Been No Great Women Artists?', in *The Feminism and Visual Culture Reader*, ed. by Amelia Jones (London: Routledge, 2003), pp. 229–33
Nogueira, María Xesús, Laura Lojo and Manuela Palacios (eds), *Creation, Publishing and Criticism: The Advance of Women's Writing* (New York: Peter Lang, 2010)
Nora, Pierre, 'Between Memory and History: *Les Lieux de Mémoire*', *Representations*, 26 (1989), 7–24
Novey, Idra, 'A Conversation between Sharon Dodua Otoo and Idra Novey', in *Herr Gröttrup setzt sich hin / Herr Gröttrup Takes a Seat*, trans. by Katy Derbyshire / *Herr Gröttrup Sits Down*, trans. by Patrick Ploschnitzki and Judith Menzl, ed. by Brittany Hazelwood (Berlin: STILL, 2019), pp. 67–73
Noyes, John K., 'Postcolonial Theory and the Geographical Materialism of Desire', in *Deleuze and the Postcolonial*, ed. by Simone Bignall and Paul Patton (Edinburgh: Edinburgh University Press, 2010), pp. 41–61
Núñez Seixas, Xosé María, 'La(s) lengua(s) de la nación', in *Ser españoles: imaginarios nacionalistas en el siglo XX*, ed. by Javier Moreno Luzón and Xosé María Núñez Seixas (Barcelona: RBA, 2013), pp. 246–86
Nyman, Jopi, 'A Carvery of Hybridity: Monica Ali's *In The Kitchen*', in *Hybridity: Forms and Figures in Literature and the Visual Arts*, ed. by François Specq, Catherine Pesso-Miquel and Vanessa Guignery (Newcastle upon Tyne: Cambridge Scholars, 2011), pp. 92–101
Olaziregi, Mari Jose (ed.), *Writers in Between Languages: Minority Literatures in the Global Scene* (Reno: Center for Basque Studies-University of Nevada, 2009)
——— 'La literatura vasca y sus ansiedades', in *Interacciones entre las literaturas ibéricas*, ed. by Francisco Lafarga, Luis Pegenaute and Enric Gallén (Bern: Peter Lang, 2010), pp. 345–52
——— 'Going Global: The International Journey of Basque Culture and Literature', in *The Routledge Companion to Iberian Studies*, ed. by Laura Lonsdale and Manuel Delgado Morales (London: Routledge, 2017), pp. 547–57
———, and Lourdes Otaegi, 'Pensamiento y crítica literaria en euskera en el siglo XX', in *Pensamiento y crítica literaria en el siglo XX (Castellano, Catalán, Euskera, Gallego)*, ed. by José María Pozuelo Yvancos et al. (Madrid: Cátedra, 2019), pp. 417–604
Olivier, Bert, 'The Possibility of a "Minor Discourse" that Deterritorialises Neoliberalism Politically', *Journal of Literary Studies*, 33 (2017), 1–24
'Once autores rexeitan a "análise negativa da cultura galega" de Varela', *La Voz de Galicia*, 25 January 2010, <http://www.lavozdegalicia.es/ocioycultura/2010/01/26/0003_8252185.htm> [accessed 10 March 2022]
Opening the Book, 'Reader-Centred Approach', *Opening the Book*, 2013 <http://web.archive.org/web/20150315230244/http://openingthebook.com/reader-centred-library>
Palma, Milagros, *El mito de París: entrevistas con escritores latinoamericanos en París* (Paris: Indigo and Côté-femmes, 2004)
——— *Le Paris latino-américain: anthologie des écrivains latino-américains à Paris* (Paris: Indigo and Côté-femmes, 2006)
Parati, Graziella, *Migration Italy: The Art of Talking Back in a Destination Culture* (Toronto: University of Toronto Press, 2005)
Parekh, Bhikhu, *Rethinking Multiculturalism: Cultural Diversity and Political Theory* (London: Macmillan, 2000)

Parry, Benita, 'Aspects of Peripheral Modernism', *Ariel: A Review of International Literature in English*, 40.1 (2009), 27–55
Paulin, Martine, 'Langue maternelle et langue d'écriture', in *Langues et migrations*, special issue of *Hommes et migrations*, ed. by Claire Extramania, 1288 (2010), 118–28
Pearl, Nancy, *Now Read This*, II: *A Guide to Mainstream Fiction, 1990–2001* (Santa Barbara, CA: 2002)
Pease, Donald, 'Author', in *Critical Term for Literary Studies*, ed. by Frank Lentricchia and Thomas McLaughlin (Chicago, IL: Chicago University Press, 1995 [1990]), pp. 105–17
Perloff, Nancy, 'Sound Poetry and the Musical Avant-Garde: A Musicologist's Perspective', in *The Sound of Poetry / The Poetry of Sound*, ed. by Marjorie Perloff and Craig Dworkin (Chicago, IL: University of Chicago Press, 2009), pp. 97–117
Pisac, Andrea, 'Big Nations' Literature and Small Nations' Sociology', *Etnološka tribina*, 35.42 (2012), 187–206
Poch, Arcadi, and Daniela Poch, *Artivism* (London: Carpet Bombing Culture, 2018)
Poddar, Prem, and Cheralyn Mealor, 'Danish Imperial Fantasies: Peter Høeg's *Miss Smilla's Feeling for Snow*', in *Translating Nations*, ed. by Prem Poddar (Aarhus: Aarhus University Press, 2000), pp. 161–202
——, and Cheralyn Mealor, '"In a little country like ours...": Narrating Minority Identity', *Journal of Postcolonial Writing*, 44 (2008), 193–224
Ponzanesi, Sandra, *Paradoxes of Postcolonial Culture: Contemporary Women Writers of the Indian and Afro-Italian Diaspora* (Albany: State University of New York Press, 2004)
—— *The Postcolonial Cultural Industry: Icons, Markets, Mythologies* (Basingstoke: Palgrave Macmillan, 2014)
Pozuelo Yvancos, José María et al. (eds), *Pensamiento y crítica literaria en el siglo XX (Castellano, Catalán, Euskera, Gallego)* (Madrid: Cátedra, 2019)
'Prémio Literário Fundação Eça de Queiroz atribuído a Djaimilia Pereira de Almeida', *Direção-Geral do Livro, dos Arquivos e das Bibliotecas*, <http://dglab.gov.pt/premio-literario-fund-eca-queiroz-atribuido-djaimilia-pereira-almeida/>
'Prémio Literário Fundação Inês de Castro: Livro de Djaimilia Pereira de Almeida desafia a ativo exercício de interpretação', *Notícias de Coimbra*, 31 March 2019, <https://www.noticiasdecoimbra.pt/premio-literario-fundacao-ines-de-castro-livro-de-djaimilia-pereira-de-almeida-desafia-a-ativo-exercicio-de-interpretacao/>
'Prémios Oceanos 2019', *Oceanos Expressivos da Língua Portuguesa/Associação*, <https://associacaooceanos.pt/premio-2019/>
Protevi, John, 'Deleuze and Life', in *The Cambridge Companion to Deleuze*, ed. by Daniel W. Smith (Cambridge: Cambridge University Press, 2012), pp. 239–64
Proxecto Batefogo (eds), *Árbores que non arden: as mulleres na prevención de incendios* (Vigo: Catro Ventos, 2019)
Prunetti, Alberto, 'Per una critica del cervellone in fuga', *Il lavoro culturale*, 1 April 2016, <http://www.lavoroculturale.org/critica-del-cervellone-fuga-un-punto-vista-working-class/>
Putnam, Robert D., *Bowling Alone* (New York: Simon & Schuster, 2000)
Regueira, Mario, 'Editorial', *Galicia 21*, Issue J (2020), 3–6
Reimóndez, Maria, 'The Rural, Urban and Global Spaces of Galician Culture', in *A Companion to Galician Culture*, ed. by Helena Miguélez-Carballeira (Woodbridge, Suffolk: Tamesis, 2014), pp. 157–74
Remarque Koutonin, Mawuna, 'Why are white people expats when the rest of us are immigrants?', *The Guardian*, 13 March 2015, <https://www.theguardian.com/global-development-professionals-network/2015/mar/13/white-people-expats-immigrants-migration>
Resina, Joan Ramon (ed.), *Iberian Modalities* (Liverpool: Liverpool University Press, 2013)

Riel, Rachel van, *Report to Arts Council Literature Department on Creative Reading Training in Libraries* (London: The Arts Council of England, 1992)
Rock, Lene, *As German As Kafka: Identity and Singularity in German Literature around 1900 and 2000* (Leuven: Leuven University Press, 2019)
Rodowick, D. N., *Gilles Deleuze's Time Machine* (Durham, NC: Duke University Press, 1997)
Rodríguez, Eider, 'Los premios harán un favor a los relatos y al cómic', *El Diario Vasco*, 18 October 2018, <https://www.diariovasco.com/culturas/libros/eider-rodriguez-literatura-20181018001126-ntvo.html>
Romo Feito, Fernando, 'Ideology and Image of Peninsular Languages in Spanish Literature', in *A Comparative History of Literatures in the Iberian Península*, vol. 1, ed. by Fernando Cabo Aseguinolaza, Anxo Abuín González and César Domínguez (Amsterdam and Philadelphia: John Benjamins Publishing Company, 2010), pp. 456–73
Rosenblatt, Louise, *Literature as Exploration*, 4th edn (New York: Modern Language Association, 1983)
Rothberg, Michael, *Multidirectional Memory: Remembering the Holocaust in the Age of Decolonisation* (Stanford, CA: Stanford University Press, 2009)
—— 'Between Memory and Memory: From *Lieux de mémoire* to *Nœuds de mémoire*', in *Nœuds de mémoire: Multidirectional Memory in Postwar French and Francophone Culture*, special issue of *Yale French Studies*, 118/19 (2010), 3–12
Roycroft-Davis, Chris, 'Boston: THE Most Segregated Town in the UK', *The Daily Express*, 31 January 2016 <https://www.express.co.uk/news/uk/639715/Boston-THE-most-segregated-town-in-the-UK>
Rushdie, Salman, *Imaginary Homelands: Essays and Criticism, 1981–91*, 2nd edn (London: Granta, 1992)
Saha, Anamik, and Sandra van Lente, *Rethinking 'Diversity' in Publishing* (London: Goldsmiths Press, 2020) <https://www.spreadtheword.org.uk/wp-content/uploads/2020/06/Rethinking_diversity_in-publishing_WEB.pdf>
Saizarbitoria, Ramon, *Aberriaren alde eta kontra* (Irun: Alberdania, 1999)
—— *Martutene* (Donostia: Erein, 2013)
—— *Martutene*, trans. by Aritz Brandon (Madrid: Hispabooks, 2016)
Santana, Mario, 'Implementing Iberian Studies: Some Paradigmatic and Curricular Challenges', in *Iberian Modalities*, ed. by Joan Ramon Resina (Liverpool: Liverpool University Press, 2013), pp. 54–61
—— 'Translation and Literatures in Spain (2003–2012)', *Revista de Historia de la Traducción*, 9 (2015), <http://www.traduccionliteraria.org/1611/art/santana.htm> [accessed 8 February 2020]
Santoyo, Julio César, 'Autotraducciones: una perspectiva histórica', *Meta: journal des traducteurs/ Meta: Translators' Journal*, 50.3 (2005), 858–67
Sapega, Ellen, 'No Longer Alone and Proud: Notes on the Rediscovery of the Nation in Contemporary Portuguese Fiction', in *After the Revolution: Twenty Years of Portuguese Literature 1974–1994*, ed. by Helena Kaufman and Anna Klobucka (Lewisburg, PA: Bucknell University Press, 1997), pp. 168–86
Sapiro, Gisèle (ed.), *Translatio: le marché de la traduction en France à l'heure de la mondialisation* (Paris: CNRS, 2008)
Sarrionandia, Joseba, *Moroak gara behelaino artean?* (Iruña: Pamiela, 2012)
—— *¿Somos como moros bajo la niebla?* (Iruña: Pamiela, 2012)
Scego, Igiaba, and Shirin Ramzanali Fazel, 'Scrittrice Nomade', *Internazionale*, 22 February 2008
Scheffler, Karl, *Berlin: Ein Stadtschicksal* (Berlin: Fannei und Walz, 1989 [1910])

SCHERLE, NICOLAI, *Kulturelle Geographien der Vielfalt. Von der Macht der Differenzen zu einer Logik der Diversität* (Bielefeld: Transcript, 2016)
SERRES, MICHEL, and BRUNO LATOUR, *Conversations on Science, Culture, and Time*, trans. by Roxanne Lapidus (Ann Arbor: University of Michigan Press, 2011)
SESAY, KADIJA (ed.), *Write Black, Write British: From Post Colonial to Black British Literature* (Hertford: Hansib, 2005)
SHARPE, CHRISTINA, *Monstrous Intimacies: Making Post-Slavery Subjects* (Durham, NC: Duke University Press, 2009)
—— *In the Wake: On Blackness and Being* (Durham, NC: Duke University Press, 2016)
SHIRIN RAMZANALI FAZEL, *Lontano da Mogadiscio* (Rome: Datanews, 1999 [1994])
—— *Nuvole sull'equatore: gli italiani dimenticati: una storia* (Cuneo: Nerosubianco, 2010)
—— *Lontano da Mogadiscio / Far from Mogadishu* (Milan: Laurana, 2013)
—— 'Foggy Dreams Under the Sun Sunshine', in *Moments in Time*, ed. by Writers Without Borders Birmingham (New York: Lulu, 2015)
—— *Far from Mogadishu* (United Kingdom: CreateSpace, 2016)
—— *Clouds over the Equator* (United Kingdom: CreateSpace, 2017)
—— *Wings* (United Kingdom: CreateSpace, 2017)
SHOWALTER, ELAINE, 'Hysteria, Feminism, and Gender', in *Hysteria Beyond Freud*, ed. by Sander Gilman et al. (Berkeley: University of California Press, 1993), pp. 286–344
SIBHATU, RIBKA, *Aulò! Aulò! Aulò! Poesie di nostalgia, d'esilio e d'amore / Aulò! Aulò! Aulò! Poems of Nostalgia, Exile and Love*, ed. by Simone Brioni, trans. by André Naffis-Sahely (Rome: Kimerafilm, 2012)
SISKIND, MARIANO, *Cosmopolitan Desires: Global Modernity and World Literature in Latin America* (Evanston, IL: Northwestern University Press, 2014)
SIVANANDAN, AMBALAVENER, 'Poverty is the New Black', *Race and Class*, 43.2 (2001), 1–5
SOLOMON, ANDREW, *Saturns Schatten* (Frankfurt: Fischer, 2006)
SØRENSEN, AXEL KJÆR, *Denmark-Greenland in the Twentieth Century* (Copenhagen: Museum Tusculanum Press, 2007)
SOULES, ALINE, 'New Types of E-books, E-book Issues and Implications for the Future', in *Adapting to E-books*, ed. by William Miller and Rita M. Pellen (London: Routledge, 2013), pp. 207–28
SPECTOR, SCOTT, *Prague Territories: National Conflict and Cultural Innovation in Franz Kafka's fin de siècle* (Berkeley: University of California Press, 2000)
SPIEKERMANN, HELMUT H., ET AL. (eds), *Niederdeutsch: Grenzen, Strukturen, Variation* (Vienna, Cologne and Weimar: Böhlau, 2016)
SPIVAK, GAYATRI CHAKRAVORTY, *Death of a Discipline* (New York: Columbia University Press, 2003)
—— *An Aesthetic Education in the Era of Globalization* (Cambridge, MA: Harvard University Press, 2012)
STRAUMER, INGRID, 'Plattdeutsches Hörspiel im Aufwind? ', *Quickborn*, 93 (2003), 33–35
STURGES, PAUL, 'Understanding Cultures and IFLA's Freedom of Access to Information and Freedom of Expression (FAIFE) Core Activity', *Journal of Documentation*, 61.2 (2004), 296–305
SURIN, KENNETH, 'Micropolitics', in *The Deleuze Dictionary*, ed. by Adrian Parr (Edinburgh: Edinburgh University Press, 2010)
'Teresa Moure "Os prexuízos contra o galego aumentan por mor da inepcia dos gobernantes"', *La Opinion Coruña*, 23 May 2010, <http://www.laopioncoruna.es/cultura/2010/05/23/teresa-moure-prexuizos-o-galego-aumentan-mor-da-inepcia-gobernantes/387141.html>
THISTED, KIRSTEN, 'Imperiets Genfærd- *Profeterne I Evighedsfjorden* og den Dansk-Grønlandske Historieskrivning,' *Nordlit*, 35 (2015), 105–21

——'Emotions, Finances and Independence: Uranium as a "Happy Object" in the Greenlandic Debate on Secession from Denmark,' *Polar Record*, 56.1 (2020), 1–12

TIRABASSI, MADDALENA, and ALVISE DEL PRÀ, *La meglio Italia: le mobilità italiane nel XXI secolo* (Turin: Accademia University Press, 2014)

TOURNAY-THEODOTU, PETRA, 'Fortress Britain: Hospitality and the Crisis of (National) Identity', in *On the Move: The Journey of Refugees in New Literatures in English*, ed. by Geetha Ganapathy-Doré and Helga Ramsey-Kurz (Newcastle upon Tyne: Cambridge Scholars, 2012), pp. 11–25

TRAIN, BRIONY, 'Reader Development', in *Reading and Reader Development: The Pleasure of Reading*, ed. by Judith Elkin et al. (London: Facet, 2003), pp. 30–58

TUAN, YI-FU, *Space and Place: The Perspective of Experience* (Minneapolis: University of Minnesota Press, 2001)

UPSTONE, SARA, 'Introduction', in *British Asian Fiction* (Manchester: Manchester University Press, 2013), <https://doi-org.sheffield.idm.oclc.org/10.7765/9781847793539.00004>

URIBE, KIRMEN, *Bilbao, New York, Bilbao* (Donostia: Elkar, 2008)

——*Bilbao, New York, Bilbao*, trans. by Elizabeth Maclin (London: Seren, 2014)

——*Mussche* (Zarautz: Susa, 2012)

——*Lo que mueve el mundo*, trans. by Gerardo Markuleta (Barcelona: Seix Barral, 2013)

VENUTI, LAWRENCE, *The Translator's Invisibility: A History of Translation* (London and New York: Routledge, 2004)

VERBEKE, FREDERIK, 'Paris and the Worlding of Minor/Small Literatures: The Case of Basque Literature', *TSLA: Theoretical Studies in Literature and Art*, 39.1 (2019), 1–14

VILAVEDRA, DOLORES, *A narrativa galega na fin de século* (Vigo: Galaxia, 2010)

——'De autores e de editores', *El País*, 28 May 2010 <http://elpais.com/diario/2010/05/28/galicia/1275041904_850215.html>

VILLEGAS, JEAN-CLAUDE, *Paris: capitale littéraire de l'Amérique latine* (Dijon: Éditions universitaires de Dijon, 2007)

VOLKOV, SHULAMIT, 'Antisemitismus als kultureller Code', in *Antisemitismus als kultureller Code: Zehn Essays* (Munich: C. H. Beck, 2000 [1978]), pp. 13–36

WADIA, LAILA, *Kitchen Sutra: The Love of Language, the Language of Love. L'amore del linguaggio il linguaggio dell'amore* (United Kingdom: Amazon, 2016)

WAUGH, LOUISA, *Selling Olga: Stories of Human Trafficking and Resistance* (London: Weidenfeld and Nicolson, 2006)

WEISS, JASON, *The Lights of Home: A Century of Latin American Writers in Paris* (New York: Routledge, 2003)

WILLIAMS, BRONWYN T., 'A State of Perpetual Wandering: Diaspora and Black British writers', *Jouvert: A Journal of Postcolonial Studies*, 3.3 (1999)

WILLIAMS, JAMES, *Gilles Deleuze's Difference and Repetition: A Critical Introduction and Guide* (Edinburgh: Edinburgh University Press, 2013)

WOMACK, YTASHA L., *Afrofuturism: The World of Black Sci-Fi and Fantasy Culture* (Chicago, IL: Lawrence Hill Books, 2013)

WRIGHT, MICHELLE, *Becoming Black: Creating Identity in the African Diaspora* (Durham, NC, and London: Duke University Press, 2004)

YANKOWITZ, SUSAN, 'In Search of a Common Language' (conversation with Caridad Svich), in *Trans-global Readings: Crossing Theatrical Boundaries*, ed. by Caridad Svich (Manchester: Manchester University Press, 2003), pp. 130–36

YEŞILADA, KARIN E., *Poesie der dritten Sprache: Türkisch-deutsche Lyrik der zweiten Generation* (Tübingen: Stauffenburg, 2012)

YILDIZ, EROL, and MARC HILL, 'Einleitung', in *Nach der Migration: Postmigrantische Perspektiven jenseits der Parallelgesellschaft*, ed. by Yildiz and Hill (Bielefeld: Transcript, 2015), pp. 9–16

YILDIZ, YASEMIN, *Beyond the Mother Tongue: The Postmonolingual Condition* (New York: Fordham University Press, 2012)
YUVAL-DAVIS, NINA, *Gender and Nation* (London and Thousand Oaks, CA: Sage, 2011)
ZALDÚA, IBAN, *Ese idioma raro y poderoso* (Madrid: Lengua de Trapo, 2012)
—— *This Strange and Powerful Language: Eleven Crucial Decisions a Basque Writer Is Obliged to Face*, trans. by Mariann Vaczi (Reno: Center for Basque Studies-University of Nevada, 2016)
ZIELINSKA, MARIE F., and FRANCIS T. KIRKWOOD (eds), *Multicultural Librarianship: An International Handbook*, IFLA Publications, 59 (Munich: K. G. Saur, 1992)

INDEX

Page numbers for illustrations are in *italics*, and for notes in the form 41 n. 3.

absence 147, 151–52, 153
Académie française 20, 22
activism:
  anticapitalist 43–44, 46, 70
  anticolonial 68, 73–74
  antiracist 54
  artivism 43–48
  ecofeminist 41–42, 43–46, 47
  environmentalist 41–48
  Extinction Rebellion 45
  against police violence 54
  Reclaim the Streets 45
  resistance, creative 39, 41–48
addiction 70–71
Adelson, Leslie 158–59
Afrofuturism 206, 209
Afro-Portuguese writing 56–62
agency:
  authorial 154
  impossibility of 152–53
  literary 149
  nonhuman 208–09
  non-identitarian 144–45
  of women 27, 30, 33–34
Ajalon, Jamika 205, 209
Akhtar, Parveen 88
Albert le Grand 196
Alcoba, Laura 22, 23 n. 9
Ali, Monica, *In the Kitchen* 174, 176–80, 183
alienation 61, 103–04
allegory 76, 175, 179
allusions 47, 48, 152, 162, 163–64, 166
Almeida, Djaimilia Pereira de:
  Esse Cabelo [*That Hair*] 56–57, 61
  Luanda, Lisboa, Paraíso 51, 56–62
  As telefones [*The Telephones*] 57
alterity 140, 143–44, 152, 153, 204
  foreignness 71–72, 124, 145
  and gender 149
  language and 147
  and national identity 146
Amazon (company), CreateSpace 121, 130–31
amnesia, cultural 68–69
An Gwari Meur ('the great play' in Cornish) 188
Anderson, Neil 46

androcentrism 40–41
Angola 57–58
Anokhina, Olga 98
anthropomorphization 204, 205
anticapitalism 43–44, 46, 70
anticolonialism 68, 69–71, 73–74
antiracism 54
anti-Semitism 25, 29, 31, 33, 34, 35
appendices 104
appropriation 3, 114, 149
Araújo, Marta 62 n. 5
Argentina 15–17, 19–20, 21
Arkotxa, Aurelia 103
Armstrong, Dorsey 197, 198
Arregi, Rikardo 103
art institutions 46
Arthur (mythological king) 196–98
artivism 43–48
assimilation 16, 17, 25, 30–31, 104, 147, 154
associations 211
Atatürk, Mustafa Kemal 157
Atxaga, Bernardo 103, 104
  Obabakoak 102
  Soinujolearen semea [*The Accordionist's Son*] 102, 104
authenticity 47, 70, 114, 122, 192, 206
  lack of 193
authoritarianism 207–08
  challenges to 212–13
autobiography 18–19, 20–21, 56–57, 71
autonomy:
  political 65, 66, 67, 68
  of self 4–5, 45, 46, 140
  self-translation and 101, 102

Baron Supervielle, Silvia 14, 15–16, 18–20
  Al margen/En marge: poesía reunida/poésie réunie [*On the Margin: Collected Poetry*] 20
  Autour du vide [*Around the Void*] ' 19
  Espace de la mer [*The Space of the Sea*] 19
  Les Fenêtres [*The Windows*] 18, 19
  La Frontière [*The Frontier*] 19
  La Ligne et l'ombre [*The Line and the Shadow*] 15, 16, 17, 18–19, 21
  Le Regard inconnu [*The Unfamiliar Gaze*] 18
  Sur le fleuve [*On the River*] 19

Basque Autonomous Community 98–99
Basque language 98
   difference of 99
   teaching of 99
   translation from 101–02, 103–05
   translation into 101
Basque literature 97–107
Becker, Eric M. B. 56
becoming 5, 175, 188–89, 198, 199, 210, 211–12
becoming other 149, 204, 205
Bellow, Saul 93–94
belonging 31–33, 116, 123–26, 190, 194
Belpoliti, Marco 130
Benjamin, Walter 13
Bennett, Jane 210–11
Berkers, Pauwke 85–86
Berlin 25, 27–28, 29
Bernhard, Thomas, *Der deutsche Mittagstisch* [*The German Lunch Table*] 205
Bewnans Ke [*The Life of Saint Ke*] (play) 187, 188, 194–98
Bianciotti, Héctor 14, 15, 16–17, 20–22
   Ce que la nuit raconte au jour [*What the Night Tells the Day*] 15, 16, 17, 20–21
bilingual texts 131
bilingualism 74, 114–15, 117
Birmingham, UK 125, 127
Black writers:
   British 85–96
   German 203–04
   Portuguese 56–62
bodies 167–68
   control and regulation of 208
   of migrants 173–74, 176, 177, 179
   subjectivity and 205–06, 210–11
'body without organs' concept (Deleuze & Guattari) 204, 210–11
Boer, Pim de 53–54
Bogue, Ronald 182
borders/boundaries:
   crossing 43, 112, 153
   fluid 5
   linguistic 1
   national 2, 5, 43, 124
   need for 21
   object-subject 210
   of selfhood 69–70
   transcendence of 21, 151, 209, 213–14
Borges, Jorge Luis 18–19
Boston, UK 173, 174
Bourgès, Aziliz, *Merch yr Eog/Merc'h an Eog* [*The Salmon's Daughter*] 187–88, 190–94
Boyarin, Daniel and Jonathan 26
Braidotti, Rosi 28, 33–34
Brañas, Alfredo 40
Breton language 187, 190, 191–92
Breuer, Josef, *see* Freud, Sigmund

Brexit 124, 125, 187, 188, 189
Brioni, Simone 121–22
   Somalitalia: Quattro vie per Mogadiscio [*Somalitalia: Four Roads to Mogadishu*] 126
British Asian writing 85–96
Brittany 187–88, 189, 196, 199
Büchner, Georg 106 n. 40
Bozcuk 157–58
Buettner, Elizabeth 60
Butler, Judith 178

Cabo Aseguinolaza, Fernando 99
Caerwyn Williams, J. E. 194
Candé, Bruno 54
Cano, Harkaitz, *Twist* 103
canons, literary 2, 3, 100, 123, 205
   Danish/Greenlandic 69, 79
   French 14–15, 22
   Galician 40–41
capitalism, critique of 43–44, 46, 70
Carty-Williams, Candice 86
Casanova, Pascale 2, 14, 100
Case, Bohn 146, 147
Catalan language and literature 101
Celticity 188, 194, 196
censorship 41
Center for Basque Studies, University of Nevada, Reno USA 102–03
centre vs. margin/periphery 1, 68–70
change 8–9, 111
   see also alterity; difference
children's literature 40
Christianity 195, 196
Christo and Jeanne-Claude 45
circulation 2, 4, 23, 192–93
   of Francophone Latin American writing 13
   of Galician writing 48
   of Greenlandic writing 66–67
   of Italian minority writing 122
class, social 16–17, 20, 26, 176, 212–13
classification 86
Cloarec, Thomas 190
code-switching 192
Coleman, Will 195–96
collaboration 103–04, 122, 132–34, 157
   in theatre 187, 189, 190, 199
collectivity 189
colonialism 3–4, 5
   anticolonialism 68, 69–71, 73–74
   'benevolent' 4
   capitalist/globalist 70
   critique of 69–74
   decolonization 4, 52, 55–56, 66, 131–32
   in Greenland 65–69
   hierarchies of 4
   in Italian literature 122–23, 129

Portuguese 52, 57–58
  see also imperialism; postcolonialism
Colvin, Sarah 205, 209
comedy 205
commodification:
  of land 44–45
  of texts 130–31
  of women 43
communicability 142
communities 183
  construction of 35
  cultural 2
  dynamic 9
  founding myths of 196
  interconnectedness 189–90, 199
  isolation 109
  linguistic 4, 127
  migrant 3–4
  minor literature and 175
  national 1
  see also diasporas
communities, minority 3–4, 188
  African, in Portugal 52–53, 54–56, 57–62
  British 85–86
  cultural identities of 56–58, 117–18
  difference of 140–41
  marginalization of 58–60
  place and 58–59
  voices of 55–56
community theatre 194–95, 199
connection:
  to place 47–48
  to readers 206
  see also interconnectedness
Cornish language 187, 197
Cornwall 187, 188, 189, 194, 195–96, 197, 199
Cosgrove, Mary 147
cosmology 162, 167
cosmopolitanism 30–31, 167
Council of Europe, European Charter for Regional or Minority Languages 111–12
counter-discourse 175
CreateSpace 121, 130–31
creativity 31, 121, 162
  multilingualism and 98, 132, 193
  of reading 89
  as resistance 39, 41–48
  of women 46
Creole language 187, 190
crime 177–78, 181, 182, 183
criticism:
  as dialogue 121
  migrant writing and 123
  writers, collaboration with 133–34
culture:
  diversity in 109, 110–13
  exchange 19–20
  hierarchies of 22–23
  identities and 55, 56, 57–58, 104, 123–26
  imperialism of 46
  institutions of 22
  insularity and 45–46
  literary markets and 104
  mainstream 52, 139, 203–04
  majority 141
  nature, separation from 157
  oral 67
  political value of 98–99
  space and 21, 22
  specificity of 42–43, 46
  transculturalism and 5, 19–20, 22–23

Daily Express (newspaper) 173
Dalpé, Jean-Marc 192
Damrosch, David 100
Danification 66–67
Danish language 66, 73, 74, 111, 112
Danish literature:
  colonialism, critique of 69–71
  Greenland as subject in 67, 68–73
Darío, Rubén 14
Darwin, Charles 28
Datanews (publisher) 122, 129
Dawson, Ashley 174
de Castro, Rosalía, *Cantares Gallegos* [Galician Songs] 40
death 139, 150, 152, 176, 177, 178
  of the other 143–44, 146–47, 149
d'Eaubonne, Françoise 43–44
decolonization 4, 52, 55–56, 66, 131–32
Defoe, Daniel, *Robinson Crusoe* 157
degeneration 27–28
Deleuze, Gilles:
  Cinema 2 5, 122
  Difference and Repetition 166–67
  micropolitics 211–12
  'One Less Manifesto' 188–89
  philosophy of time 157, 159, 165
  and Félix Guattari:
    Kafka: Toward a Minor Literature 2–3, 139, 140–45, 149–50, 169, 174–75
    A Thousand Plateaus 181–82, 204, 205–06, 208, 210, 210–11
Denmark:
  Act on Greenland Self-Government, 2009 66, 68
  colonialism 65–69
  Greenland Home Rule Act 66
  Grundlov (constitution) 66
  imperialism, cultural 66–67
  postcolonial 68
  see also Danish language; Danish literature
Derobertis, Roberto 131

Derrida, Jacques 151
Dery, Mark 206
deterritorialization 5, 122, 139, 140–45, 149, 175
dialogue 121, 122–23, 131
    interdisciplinary 126
diaries 77, 129, 146–49, *148*
diasporas 3–4
    Angolan 51, 57
    language choices among 128
    Somali 125–26, 127–28
Dibaba, Yared 115–18
    Ünnerwegens [*On the Way*] 109, 115–16
difference 2–3, 154, 204, 213
    of Basque language 99
    and identity formation 142
    integration of 146
    maximum/self-differing 142, 143, 144–45, 153
    of minority communities 140–41
    of the other 140, 143–44, 149
    universality of 110–11
    see also alterity; diversity
diglossia 39–40, 114–15
Dirlik, Arif 45
disease/illness 59–60, 75
    psychological 27–28, 179
distance 133, 143, 150
diversity:
    cultural 109, 110–13
    in library collections 87–88, 93–94
    linguistic 111–12
Domínguez, César 99
dreams 179, 180, 190–91, 193–94
du Veuzit, Max 22

Eastern European people 173–74
e-books 128, 130–31
Eco, Umberto 100
ecofeminism 41–42, 43–46, 47
education:
    in minority languages 110, 114, 115
    in translation 104
Egede, Hans 65
Eks&Tra (migrant writers competition) 130
Ellis, Robert Richmond 15, 21, 22
England:
    Birmingham 125, 127
    Cornwall 187, 188, 189, 194, 195–96, 197, 199
    idealized 181, 182
English language 197
    diaspora communication and 128
    Globish 192–93
    translation into 43
English literature 173–85
Enlightenment 33
environmentalism 41–48

Epalanga, Kalaf 56
Epps, Bradley S. 99
equality 30, 33, 141
    power and 72–73, 79, 101–02, 146–47
    see also hierarchies
escape 21–22
Etxepare Basque Institute 104
Europe 34, 199
    definitions of 8–9
    globalized 2
    identities of 34
    migration from 15–17
    migration to 57, 115
European Charter for Regional or Minority Languages 111–12
European Union (EU) 52–53
    expansion of 174
    Overseas Countries and Territories (OCT) 65
Evaristo, Bernardine, *Girl, Woman, Other* 86
evolution 30–31
exchange, cultural 19–20
exile 20, 22
exoticism 78, 87, 99
experimentation, literary 142, 148–49, 158, 159, 162–64, 206
expressiveness 110, 111, 112

factography 158–59
failure 48
family:
    motherhood 28, 33, 44–45
    rejection of 28
Farias de Albuquerque, Fernanda, *Princesa* [*Princess*] 127–28
feminism 35
    ecofeminism 41–42, 43–46, 47
    motherhood and 28, 33
Fernández Cifuentes, Luis 99
Ferreira, Ana Paula 55
Ferreira, Patrícia Martinho 55, 61
fiction:
    experimental 142, 148–49, 158, 159, 162–64, 206
    literary/mainstream 91
    multilingualism in 145, 147–51, 153
    novel form 39–41, 73–76, 77–78
    novel form as 121
    readerships for 88–92
    translation in 103
fluidity 8–9, 188–89
    of identities 159, 190–91, 194, 197, 209
food 176, 179, 205, 209–12
footnotes 104
Foran, Lisa 152
foreigners/foreignness 71–72, 124
    visibility of 145

fragmentation 148–49, 150
France 13–14
  Académie française 20, 22
  Basque language in 98
  Brittany 187–88, 189, 196, 199
  civilization, model of 13–15
  Paris 13–14
French language 187, 190, 194
  Latin American literature in 13–24
  learning of 16–17
  postcolonial use of 15
  style and usage of 18–19, 21–22
  translation into 18–19
French literature, translingual writing in 14–15, 18
Freud, Sigmund, and Josef Breuer, *Studien über Hysterie* [*Studies in Hysteria*] 27–28
Freyre, Gilberto 62 n. 8
Frisian language 111, 112
futurism:
  Afrofuturism 206, 209
  Russian 158, 162–63
futurity 157, 158–69

Gal, Susanne 118 n. 5
Galicia 39–40
  cultural practices of 46–47
  Nova Narrativa Galega [*New Galician Narratives*] 40–41
  reintegrationismo movement 42
  Rexurdimento (Renaissance) 40
  Santiago de Compostela 47
Galician language 39–40
  galego internacional (Galician Portuguese) 42
  translation into 101, 102
Galician literature 101
gardens/gardening 43, 44
Gasquet, Axel 19, 22
gender 15, 149, 212–13
  equality 30
  identities 77, 207–08
  neutrality, in language 207
  and otherness 149
  and power 211
  roles 26–27
Genesis (journal) 98
genre 86, 91, 92
Geoffrey of Monmouth 197
German language 111, 145, 150, 151, 207, 212–13
  'Prague German' 142–43, 175
  see also Low German language
German literature 139–40, 145–54, 148, 157–71, 203–15
  Low German 109–19
Germany:
  Berlin 25, 27–28, 29
  Bundesraat för Nedderdüütsch [Federal Council for Low German] 113
  Hamburg 113
  minority language protection 112–13
  Munich 160
  national identity and 31–33
  Universität Konstanz 102–03
Gerstenberger, Katharina 146–47
Gibson, Marion 194, 196
Gilman, Nils 177
globalization 4, 70, 177, 181, 183, 192–93
Gobard, Henri 143
Golden Tree Productions (theatre company) 196
Goldhammer, Jesse 177
Greenhalgh, Liz 87
Greenland 65–82
  colonization 65–69
  Danish attitudes to 68
  in Danish literature 67, 68–73
  as Danish province 66
  decolonization process 66
  government of 66, 75–76
  independence 66, 68, 74
  Nuuk 71–72, 73, 75, 76–77
  stereotypes of 70–71
Greenlandic languages 66–67, 72
Greenlandic literature 65, 66–67, 73–79
grief 152–53
Grosz, Elizabeth 204
Groth, Klaus 112
Gröttrup, Helmut 204
ground, groundless 139, 141, 144–45, 149, 152
Grydehøj, Adam 80 n. 6
Guattari, Félix, *see* Deleuze, Gilles

Halberstam, Jack 48
Hall, Stuart 2, 206
Hamburg 113
Hansen, Dörte 117
  Altes Land [*Old Land*] 109, 113–15
Hauschner, Auguste:
  Die Familie Lowositz [*The Lowositz Family*] 25, 26–29, 34–35
  Rudolf und Camilla [*Rudolf and Camilla*] 25, 26–29, 34–35
Heger, Annie 110–11
Heidegger, Martin 144, 150
Heine, Heinrich 32–33
Henda, Kiluanji Kia, *Plantation: Prosperity and Nightmare* 54–55
Hermann, Georg 29
Herrera, Francisca, *Néveda: Historia dunha dobre seducción* [*Néveda: Story of a Double Seduction*] 40
hierarchies 176, 178, 179
  alternatives to 211
  class 16–17, 20, 26, 176, 212–13
  of colonialism 4

cultural 22–23
destabilization of 208
refusal of 198
self-translation as challenge to 77–78
High German language 112, 113–15
Hikmet, Nâzim 157
Hirsch, Afua 85
Hjort, Mette 3
Hodges, Kenneth 197, 198
Høeg, Peter, *Frøken Smillas Fornemmelse for Sne* [*Miss Smilla's Feeling for Snow*] 67, 68, 69–71, 72–73, 78
home/homeland 30
  belonging and 31–33
  Heimat 26, 31–33, 35
  invention of 46
  making of 26
  in oneself 78
  return to 16, 19
  translingual writing and 21
homogenization 190
homosexuality 21
Hungarian language 146–47, *148*, 150, 151, 154
Hungarian people 140
hybridity 69–70, 115, 194, 197

identities:
  African 56
  challenges to 205
  construction of 56
  cosmic 167
  cultural 55, 56, 57–58, 104, 123–26
  dynamic 9, 167
  European 34
  in exile 62
  fluidity of 159, 190–91, 194, 197, 209
  formation 142
  Galician 40
  gender 77, 207–08
  hybridity 69–70, 197
  Jewishness 29, 30–31
  linguistic 141
  local/regional 189–90
  of migrants 60–61, 123–24, 176
  minoritized 3
  models of 4–5
  non-identity 139–40, 141, 142–45
  plurality of 86–87
  postcolonial 55, 70
  of readers 4
  regional 116–17, 196
  sexual 15
  theatre and 189–90
  of writers 86–87
identities, national 31–33, 40, 53, 207
  Celticity 188, 194, 196
  Cornish 196
  Danish 68
  German 204–05
  Greenlandic 76, 77–78
  Italian 123–26
  language use and 98–99
  of migrants 176
  otherness and 146
  post-national 30, 34
imagery 110
  see also metaphors
immanence 143, 144, 146
imperialism 196–98
  capitalist 70
  commemoration of 52, 53
  cultural 46
  Portuguese 52, 57–58
  see also colonialism
impurity, linguistic 115
inarticulacy 152–53
indigenous people 54
individuality 144
industrialization 75–76
inequalities 30, 33, 141
  power and 72–73, 79, 101–02, 146–47
  see also hierarchies
inexpressibility 152–53
Ingemann, Bernhard, *Kunuk og Naja* [*Kunuk and Naja*] 67
institutions, cultural 22
insularity, cultural 45–46
integration 140, 146, 198
interconnectedness 211
  community 189–90, 199
  human 178–79, 180, 183
  lateral 3, 5
internationalism 30, 34
interpretation, as violence 142
intersectionality 212–13
intersubjectivity 213
invisibility 145, 173–74
Irigaray, Luce 28
Iser, Wolfgang 87
Islam 160, 166, 167–68, 169
Islamophobia 124–26
isolation:
  of language communities 99, 109
  of small literatures 117
Italian literature 121–34
  postcolonial 122–23, 129–30, 131
  publishing and 127–31
Italy 16–17
  Brescia 124–25
  emigration from 126–27
  Lake Garda 125–26
  Lombard League 125
  postcolonialism 131
  racial laws 122

JanMohamed, Abdul 175
Japanese language 102
Jeanne-Claude 45
Jensen, Lars 68
Jerónimo, Miguel Bandeira 60
Jesus, Maria de Lourdes 129
Jewish people:
    German 25–37
    integration 31, 32, 33
    and space 26, 29–31
Jewishness 29, 30–31
Johnson, Catherine 85
journeys 146, 147–48, 152, 166

Kacimi, Mohamed 18
Kafka, Franz 2–3, 140–45, 175
Kalaallisut (West-Greenlandic dialect) 66
Kaneko, Nami 102
Karpat, Berkan:
    futuristen-epilog — poeme 157–71
    'tanzende der elektrik' [electric dancers] 158, 159
Keith, Michael 45
Kellman, Steven G. 23
Kelly, George 90, 93
Khan, Sheila 55–56
Khlebnikov, Velimir 157, 158, 159, 162–63
    'The Gul-Mullah's Trumpet' 166
    'Language of the Stars' 164, 167
    'Russia and Me' 160
    'The Stone Woman' 159
    in 'tanzende der elektrik' 160–62, 165–67, 169
Kiel, Treaty of (1814) 65
Kilomba, Grada 51, 54, 56
Kippur, Sara 14–15
Klein, Naomi 175
Kline, Elizabeth 128
Kloss, Heinz 118 n. 17
Korneliussen, Niviaq:
    HOMO Sapienne 67, 76–79
    Naasuliardarpi [Flower Valley] 67
Krafft-Ebing, Richard von 27–28
Krause, Ralf 211
Krische, Paul 32
Krummrich, Philip 43
Kundera, Milan 104
Kureishi, Hanif 86–87
Kustow, Michael 199

labour 176, 179
Ladouceur, Louise 192–93
Lambert, Claire M. 88
Lambert, Gregg 181–82
land:
    commodification of 44–45
    connection to 47–48
land art 43, 45

Landa, Mariasun 103
Landau, Elisabeth:
    Ahasver 34
    Die Brandfackel [The Incendiary Torch] 34
    Der Holzweg [The Dead End] 25, 31–35
Langgård, Karen 76
languages:
    ambiguous 163
    'artificial' 142–43
    choices of 147, 190
    communities and 127
    detachment from 18
    emergent properties of 157
    individual, creation of 18–19
    island/isolate 99
    majority 140–45, 175
    materiality of 158, 162
    modes of 143
    mother tongue 132–33
    nonrealist 179–80
    between/outside 145
    proficiency in 130
    regional 111–12
    status of 113
    strategic use of 5–6
    translingualism 14–15
languages, minority 3, 4, 5–6
    education in 110, 114, 115
    liveliness of 110–11
    preservation of 109, 111–12, 115
Latin American literature, in French 13–24
Latour, Bruno 157
Laurana (publisher) 121, 127
Leine, Kim 68
    Kalak 67, 71–73, 78
    Profeterne i Evighedsfjorden [The Prophets of Eternal Fjord] 67, 71
lesbianism 190
Lewycka, Marina, *Two Caravans* 173–74, 181–83
LGBTQ+ writing 76–79
librarianship 87
libraries, public 85–96
    collections, diversity of 87–88, 93–94
    users of 88–89
Life of Saint Meriask (play) 196
Lindenberg, Udo 116
Lionnet, Françoise 3, 198
Lisbon 52, 54–55, 58–60
literature:
    children's 40
    migration 122, 127–28
    political value of 98–99
literatures, minor:
    definitions of 2–5, 122–23, 139–45, 174–75, 181–82
    impossible possibility of 141
    political value of 175, 183

literatures, minority 4, 121–34, 153–54
 e-commerce and 128
 historiography and criticism on 100–01
 literary markets and 127–31
 politicization of 104
 publishing of 129–31
 reception of 129–30
 self-publishing of 130–31
 translation's value to 100
literatures, small 2–5, 97
 isolationism of 117
Lloyd, David 175
Lloyd, Sara 190
localism 189
Loff, Manuel 51–52
Loriot (Vicco von Bülow), *Das Frühstücksei* [*The Breakfast Egg*] 205
loss 61
love, motherly 28, 33
Low German language 109, 110–13
 education in 114, 115
 territory of 112
Low German literature 109–19
Lusotropicalism 53, 54
Lussier, Julie 62
Lyberth, Juaaka, *Godt i Vej* [*Well on Our Way*] 67, 73–76, 78
Lynge, Augo, *Ukiut 300-nngornerat* [*Three Hundred Years After*] 76
Lynge, Hans Anton 76
Lyotard, Jean-François 141

magic realism 7, 44
mainstream:
 cultural 52, 139, 203–04
 in library collections 93
 literary 85–86, 91, 188, 196
 population 52
 publishing 42, 86
 theatre and 188, 189, 196, 199
majority:
 culture 141
 languages 140–45, 175
 minority, enriched by 139, 140, 154
 minority, relationship with 139–40, 151, 153–54, 175, 188, 198
Mandelstam, Osip 159
Mann, Barbara E. 26
Manterola, Elizabete 101–02
marginality 3
 vs. centre 1, 68–70
marginalization 35
 liberation from 25–26
 literary 85–86
 of minority communities 58–60

markets, literary 101, 121
 commodification in 130–31
 culture and 104
 migrant writers and 127–31, 133–34
 minority literatures and 127–31
 online platforms and 121, 128, 130–31
 translated literature in 104–05, 127–28
marriage 26–27, 28
Martell, Owen, *Merch yr Eog/Merc'h an Eog* [*The Salmon's Daughter*] 187–88, 190–94
Massey, Doreen 26
Mata, Inocência 62
materiality 162, 163, 167–69, 211–12
Mathis-Moser, Ursula 14
Maurizio Iannelli, *Princesa* 127–28
McKane, Richard 159, 164
Meabe, Miren Agur 103
Mealor, Cheralyn 69–70
meaning 163–64
 resistance to 150
Medeiros, Paulo de 61
Meisel-Hess, Grete, *Die Intellektuellen* [*The Intellectuals*] 25, 29–31, 35
memorials 52, 54
 to slave trade 54–55
memory 130
 collective 4, 55
 of colonial past 51–52, 61–62
 cultural 5, 51, 52–53, 57
 cultural, lack of 68–69
 knots of memory (*nœuds de mémoire*) 55
 postcolonial 56–62
 sites of memory (*lieux de mémoire*) 53, 55
memory projects 53–54
Mercator Institute for Media, Language and Culture, Aberystwyth 192
Mertz-Baumgartner, Birgit 14
metaphor:
 for assimilation 147, 154
 egg as 205, 209–12
 of escape 21
 historical 46, 61
 impossibility and 141
 scientific 167, 168
methodologies 1–2
Micossé-Aikins, Sandrine 203
migrant writers:
 in France 14–15
 Italian 121–23
 literary markets and 127–31, 133–34
 literary prizes for 140
 reception of 129–30
migrants 58–60, 195
 bodies of 173–74, 176, 177, 179
 communities 3–4

disposability of 178
identities of 60–61, 123–24, 176
(in)visibility of 173–74
language use of 132–33
linguistic skills of 212–13
racialized othering of 176
representation of 140, 173–85
second-generation 61
migration 1, 115–16, 122, 163–64
   African, to Europe 57, 115
   European, to South America 15–17
   Jewish 33
   labour 4
   Latin American, to Paris 17
migration literature 122, 127–28
Miguélez-Carballeira, Helena 42
minor literatures:
   definitions of 2–5, 122–23, 139–45, 174–75, 181–82
   impossible possibility of 141, 144–45
   political value of 175, 183
minority:
   definitions of 3, 139–40, 188–89
   identities 3
   majority, relationship with 139–40, 151, 153–54, 175, 188, 198
minority communities 3–4, 188
   African, in Portugal 52–53, 54–56, 57–62
   British 85–86
   cultural identities of 56–58, 117–18
   difference of 140–41
   marginalization of 58–60
   place and 58–59
   voices of 55–56
minority languages 3, 4, 5–6
   education in 110, 114, 115
   liveliness of 110–11
   preservation of 109, 111–12, 115
minority literatures 4, 121–34, 153–54
   e-commerce and 128
   historiography and criticism on 100–01
   literary markets and 127–31
   politicization of 104
   publishing of 129–31
   reception of 129–30
   self-publishing of 130–31
   translation's value to 100
Mitxelena, Koldo 97–98
mixed-race people 122
mobility:
   class 176
   journeys 146, 147–48, 152, 166
   through time 165–66, 209, 213–14
modernism 14, 157–58
   see also futurism

modernity 75, 157–58, 168, 191, 206
modernization 68, 75–76
Moestrup, Mette 76
Monde, Le (newspaper) 14–15, 22
monolingualism 5, 99–100, 101, 145
monsters/monstrousness 147
Monteiro, José Pedro 60
Monteiro, Yara 56
Mora, Terézia 145–46, 153–54
   Der einzige Mann auf dem Kontinent [*The Only Man on the Continent*] 146
   Seltsame Materie [*Strange Matter*] 140, 145
   Das Ungeheuer [*The Monster*] 139–40, 146–54, *148*
Moreira, Joacine Katar 62 n. 11
Moretti, Franco 100
motherhood 28, 33, 44–45
Moure, Teresa 41–42
   artivism 45–46
   Herba moura [*Black Nightshade*] 41–42
   A intervención [*The Operation*] 39, 41–48
   O natural é político [*The Natural is Political*] 43
   self-translation 42–43
movement 146, 147–48, 152, 166
   through time 165–66, 209, 213–14
movements, sociopolitical 42, 45
multiculturalism 52, 87–88, 124–25, 131–33
multilingualism 2, 4
   in fiction 145, 147–51, 153
   global extent of 98
   and language choice 102–03
   in theatre 191–93, 197
   in upbringing 17, 127
Munich 160
Murdoch, Derick 192
Murguía, Manuel 40
Muslim people 122, 124–26
mysticism 191, 194
mythology 152, 165–66, 191, 194

Nabokov, Vladimir 98
Nancy, Jean-Luc 139, 143–45, 149, 153
narrative 159
   decentred 204, 205, 206, 210–11
   of decolonization 4
   fragmentation 140–41
   metanarrative 43, 208
   non-realist 204, 205–11
   optimistic 29, 33, 34
   perspective 73, 77, 113, 208–09
   readers, implicated in 206
   representational 5, 27
   stream of consciousness 76–77
   subjectivity 20–21, 160
   tropes 56–57
   whiteness of 57

nationalism 189
  ecofeminist 42
  Galician 41, 42
  internationalism 30, 34
  Portugal 52–53
  transnationalism 1, 3, 198
nationality 31–32, 60, 111–12
nation-building 40, 76
neologisms 164, 168, 175, 182–83
Nicholls, Peter 91
Nochlin, Linda 46
nomadism 33–34
non-identity 139–40, 141, 142–45
Nora, Pierre 53, 55
Norddeutscher Rundfunk, 'De Welt op Platt' (TV programme) 115
Norway 65
nostalgia 193
Nouvel observateur (journal) 22
novel form 39–41, 73–76, 77–78, 121
Noyes, John 205–06
Núñez Seixas, Xosé María 98

Ocampo, Victoria 19–20
Olivier, Bert 175
Olsen, Moses 76
openness 5, 26, 30, 31, 33–34, 35
  of readers 89
oral culture 67
orphanhood 61
Orpheus-Eurydice myth 152
otherness 140, 143–44, 152, 153, 204
  of ethnic minorities 58–60
  foreignness 71–72, 124, 145
  and gender 149
  language and 147
  literary criticism and 99–100
  and national identity 146
others 195
  becoming 149, 204, 205
  death of 143–44, 146–47, 149
  opacity of 139, 140
  racialization of 175–76
  self, relation with 143–45
Otoo, Sharon Dodua 203, 204, 206
  Adas Raum [*Ada's Realm*] 213
  Herr Gröttrup setzt sich hin [*Herr Gröttrup Takes a Seat*] 203–15

Palma, Milagros 13, 15
Parati, Graziella 131
Paris 13–14
patriarchy 27, 39, 40–41, 54
  rejection of 28, 42, 43, 46, 48
Pearl, Nancy 91

Pease, Donald 121
PEN World Voices (festival) 100
peoples, new 166–69
performance 160
periphery, vs. centre 1, 68–70
Perloff, Nancy 162
personal construct theory 90, 92, 93
perspectives:
  apersonal 9
  narrative 73, 77, 113, 208–09
Phillips, Caryl 86–87
Pile, Steve 45
Pisac, Andrea 100
place 5
  connection to 47–48
  identity of 195
  lieux de mémoire 53, 55
  minority communities and 58–59
  names 42–43
  of production 19
  social movements and 45
place-making 26, 30
Plattart (Low German language festival, 2017) 110
'plen an gwari' (playing place, theatre) 195–96
plot 91–92
plurilingualism, *see* multilingualism
'Plurilinguisme en Europe Occidentale: La France et L'Espagne' (conference, 2017) 102–03
plurinationalism 98
Poddar, Prem 69–70
poetry 18, 132–33
  Francophone Latin American 20
  Galician 40
  German 157–71
  installation performance of 160
  Sufi 168
Pontoppidan, Henrik, *Isbjørnen-et Portræt* [*The Polar Bear: A Portrait*] 67
Ponzanesi, Sandra 131
Portugal 51–64
  1974 revolution 51–52, 53
  African communities in 52–53, 54–56, 57–62
  Belém Cultural Centre 53
  Colonial War 51–52
  colonialism/imperialism 52, 57–58
  Djass 55
  Estado Novo 51–52, 53
  Exhibition of the Portuguese World 52, 53
  Lisbon 52, 54–55, 58–60
  Lusotropicalism 53, 54
  memory culture of 52–53
  nationalism 52–53
  nationality laws 60
  Portugal dos Pequenitos (park, Coimbra) 53
  postcolonialism in 51–52, 54–55

Portuguese language 40, 58, 59
postcolonialism 4, 53–54, 131–32
  anachronisms of 59
  in Italian literature 122–23, 131
  orphanhood and 61
  in Portugal 51–52, 54–55
  as re-narrativization 205–06
'Pour une "littérature-monde" en français' (manifesto, 2007) 14–15
power:
  imbalances 72–73, 79, 101–02, 146–47
  language use and 74
Praza Pública (newspaper) 42
precarity 178, 180
prejudice:
  anti-Semitism 25, 29, 31, 33, 34, 35
  homophobia 77
  Islamophobia 124–26
  see also racism
Prescott, Marc 192
print books 121, 128, 130–31, 146
privilege 15, 20, 42, 74, 140
  theatre and 189
  of whiteness 176, 204
prizes, literary 20, 22, 153–54
  Adelbert von Chamisso Prize 140
  British Book Awards 86
  Eça de Queirós Foundation Literary Prize 56
  Euskadi Prize 100, 103
  Grand Prix Translation, Japan 102
  Inês de Castro Foundation Literary Prize 56
  Ingeborg Bachmann Prize 203, 204
  National Literary Prize for Narrative, Spain 102
  Nordic Council's Literature Prize 67
  Nordic Prize for Literature 73
  Oceanos Prize 56
  Premio de la Crítica Española 42
  Prix de littérature francophone Jean Arp 20
  Prix du meilleur livre étranger 22
  Prix du rayonnement de la langue et de la littérature françaises (Academie française) 20
  Prix Femina 22
  Prix Médicis étranger 22
  Prix spécial Roger Caillois 20
  Xerais prize for Galician fiction 42
production, places of 19
Proust, Marcel, *À la recherche du temps perdu* 22
proximity 133, 150
public libraries 85–96
  collections, diversity of 87–88, 93–94
  users of 88–89
publishing 104, 122
  Italian 122–23
  minority literatures and 129–31
  online 4, 121, 128, 130–31
  see also markets, literary

queer sexualities 76–78, 79
Queizán, María Xosé 41, 42
  A orella no buraco [*The Ear on the Hole*] 41
Quinzaine littéraire, La (journal) 22
Qur'an 166

race 30–31
  Black writers 56–62, 85–96, 203–04
  whiteness 93, 176, 203, 204, 206–07
racism 54, 56, 58–61, 123–26, 203
  anti-Semitism 25, 29, 31, 33, 34, 35
  denial of 54
  racial laws 122
  in United Kingdom 125–26
  xeno-racism 175–76
Radical Middle Way Institute of Narrative Growth 127–28
radio 114, 115
reader response theory 87, 89
readers:
  characteristics 90, 91–92
  connection to 206
  identities of 4
  narrative, implicated in 206
  openness of 89
  writers, imagined by 87
readerships:
  for Black British/British Asian fiction 90–92
  cultural background and 87
  for e-books 128
  for fiction 88–92
  of Francophone Latin American writing 13
  of genres 92
  within/outside text 150–51
reading:
  creativity of 89
  distant 100–01
  habits and attitudes 88–89
  non-representational 3
  public 85–96
  social capital and 87–88
  sociological model of 88–89
realism 6, 112, 114, 179–80, 181
  magic 7, 44
  refusal of 27, 28, 204
reality, subjective 90, 93
referentiality 159, 163, 164, 182
Reimóndez, María 43
relationality 9
  absence and 147
  actual-virtual 159
  between languages 143, 145, 151
  majority-minority 139–40, 151, 153–54, 175, 188, 198
  self-exteriority 141
  self-other 144, 146, 152–53
  of space 26

religion:
    belonging and 32–33
    Christianity 195, 196
    indigenous 74
    Islam 124–26, 160, 166, 167–68, 169
    mysticism 191, 194
repetition 164, 165, 179, 211
representation 6
    critique of 4
    disruption of 149
    of migrants 140, 173–85
    narrative 5, 27
    refusal of 3, 211
    of translators 150–51
reputation, literary 20, 22
Resina, Joan Ramon 99
resistance:
    to authoritarianism 209–11
    creative 39, 41–48
    to meaning 150
reterritorialization 141, 143
Reuter, Fritz 112
rituals 46–47, 205, 208, 213
Rodríguez, Eider 103
Rölli, Marc 211
Roman empire 196–97
Romany language 111, 112
Rothberg, Michael 5, 51
Royal Greenlandic Trading Department 65
Roycroft-Davis, Chris 173, 174
Rūmī, Mevlâna Jalāl ad-Dīn Muhammad 158, 160
Rushdie, Salman 93–94
Russia 161
Russian Futurism 158, 162–63

Saizarbitoria, Ramón 101
    Martutene 103
Salone del Libro di Torino (book fair) 130
sameness 142, 164, 213
Santana, Mario 101–02
Sapega, Ellen 55
Sapiro, Gisèle, *Translatio* 104
Sarrionandia, Joseba 100
Sarro, Alessandra Atti di 129
satire 205
Scego, Igiaba 129
Scheffler, Karl 29
Schmidt, Paul 162
Schnitzler, Arthur, *Der Weg ins Freie [The Road to the Open]* 28–29
Sciarrino, Emilio 98
Seeskow, Wolfgang, *Altes Land [Old Land]*, radio play 114
self-consciousness 56–57
selfhood 69–70, 139, 166–67
    identity and 141–42
    other, relation with 143–45, 152–53

    unitary, rebellion against 209–10
self-publishing 130–31
self-translation 42–43, 77–78, 101–04, 121, 127–28
Semedo, Luísa 56
Şenocak, Zafer:
    futuristen-epilog — poeme 157–71
    'tanzende der elektrik' [electric dancers] 158, 159, 160–69
separateness 189–90, 194
Serres, Michel 8–9
Sesay, Kadija 86
sex work 177–78, 181
sexualities 15, 71, 72
    homosexuality 21
    lesbian 190
    queer 76–78, 79
Shams-i-Tabrizi [Sun of Tabriz] 158, 160, 168
Sharpe, Christina 63 n. 24, 141
Shih, Shuh-mei 3, 198
Shirin Ramzanali Fazel 121–34
    'Afka Hooyo' [mother tongue] 132–33
    'Foggy Dreams Under the Sunshine' 128
    influence of 122–23
    Lontano da Mogadiscio [Far from Mogadishu] 121–22, 126, 127–28, 129–30, 131
    Nuvole sull'equatore: gli italiani dimenticati [Clouds over the Equator: The Forgotten Italians] 121–22, 129–30, 131
    Transnationalizing Modern Languages (research project) 132
    Wings 126
Sibhatu, Ribka, *Aulò! Aulò! Aulò! Poesie di nostalgia d'esilio e d'amore [Aulò! Aulò! Aulò! Poems of Nostalgia, Exile and Love]* 126
significance 5, 68, 159, 163, 178, 195, 208
Silva, Aníbal Cavaco 53
similes 110
simplicity 112
Simsova, Silva 88
singularity 141, 142, 143–44
Sinnos (publisher) 131
Sivanandan, Ambalavner 175–76
Slava (rapper) 124–25
slave trade 54–55
small literatures 2–5, 97
    isolationism of 117
social class 16–17, 20, 26, 176, 212–13
social problems 70–72, 75
solidity 8–9, 159
Somali language 127, 133
Somalia 121–22, 125–26, 129, 131
Sorbian language 111, 112
Soules, Aline 128
South America 15–16
space 5, 213–14
    cities 27–28, 29–31

claiming of 26, 28–29, 34–35
constructedness of 26, 35
cultural 21, 22
for Jews 26, 29–31
between languages 18
minority communities and 58–59
between nations 22–23
relational 26, 35
rural 28–29, 43
territorial 26, 28
theatre and 195–96
typographic 147–49, *148*, 150, 152
urban 75
space travel 162
Spain:
  Basque Autonomous Community 98–99
  Franco dictatorship 40–41
  imperialism, cultural 46
  literary historiography of 99–100
  literary market in 104
  translated literature published in 101
  see also Galicia
Spanish language 14
  Argentine 17
  as bridge language 102
  translation from 18–19, 101
  translation into 42–43
spatiality, linguistic 111–12
specificity, cultural 42–43, 46
Spector, Scott 2–3
Spivak, Gayatri Chakravorty 10 n. 21, 99–100
stars 162, 167
status, linguistic 113
Storch, Mathias, *Singnagtugaq* [*A Greenlander's Dream*] 76
storytelling 127–28
style:
  in French literature 18–19, 21–22
  linguistic 179–80, 181–83
subjection 141
subjectivity:
  bodies and 205–06, 210–11
  challenges to 206–07
  divided 20–21
  intersubjectivity 213
  narrative 20–21, 160
  nomadic 4, 33–34
  nonhuman 210–11
  vs. selfhood 144
subjects 166–68
Sufism 160, 161, 162, 167
surtitles 192
symbolism 56–57, 59, 162, 163–64, 190–91

Teatr Piba (theatre company) 187–88, 190
technology/technologization 192–93
television 115
temporality 5
  anachronism 59
  futurity 157, 158–69
  past 193
  time travel 165–66, 209, 213–14
territorialism 109, 112, 117–18
territorialization 3, 5, 26, 28
Theatr Genedlaethol Cymru (Welsh Language National Theatre of Wales) 187–88, 190
theatre 187–201
  collaborative 189
  community 194–95, 199
  identities and 189–90
  minority 188–89, 199
  outdoor site-specific 195–96
  scenography 192–93
  surtitles 192
  translation in 191–92
Thisted, Kirsten 68
Thomas, Graham 195
time 5
  anachronism 59
  futurity 157, 158–69
  past 193
time travel 165–66, 209, 213–14
tolerance 33
Torres, Xohana 41, 42
tourism 125–26
Tournay-Theodotou, Petra 175–76, 179
trafficking 177–78, 181, 182, 183
transculturalism 5, 19–20, 22–23
translation 100–05
  as duty 103–04
  education and training in 104
  everyday 131–32
  in fiction 103
  lack of 117
  literary markets and 104–05, 127–28
  minority literature, value to 100–01
  in minority theatre 191–92
  Portuguese to English 56
  prizes for 102
  publishing of 101–02, 129–30
  relationality of 151–52
  self-translation 42–43, 77–78, 101–04, 121, 127–28
  simultaneous 192
  strategic importance of 103
  via surtitles 192
  technologies of 192
  untranslatability 5–6, 142, 149–52, 153
  as world's language 100
translators, representation of 150–51
translingual writing 14–15, 18, 20, 22–23
transnationalism 1, 3, 198

Transnationalizing Modern Languages (research project) 131–32
travel 146, 147–48, 152, 166
　through time 165–66, 209, 213–14
Tregidga, Garry 194, 196
Trower, Shelley 194, 196
Tuan, Yi-Fu 26
Turkey 157–58, 160
Turkish people 157–58
Tvon, Telma 56
typography 147–49, *148*, 150, 152, 163

Unamuno, Miguel de 99
United Kingdom:
　Arts Council East Midlands 88
　Birmingham 125, 127
　Boston 173, 174
　Brexit 124, 125, 187, 188, 189
　　Cornwall 187, 188, 189, 194, 195–96, 197, 199
　East Midlands public libraries 88
　Eastern European workers in 173–74
　England, idealized 181, 182
　minority writing, reading of 85–96
　racism in 125–26
　translated literature published in 127
　Wales 187–88, 189, 199
United Nations Alliance of Civilizations (UNAOC) 127–28
United States of America (US) 125–26
universality 190, 199
　of difference 110–11
　white male, challenges to 206–07
Universität Konstanz, Germany 102–03
University of Falmouth, Academy for Research and Innovation 192
untranslatability 5–6, 142, 149–52, 153
Upstone, Sara 86, 87
urbanization 75–76
Uribe, Kirmen:
　Bilbao-New York-Bilbao 102
　Mussche 102
Uruguay 15–16

Valéry, Paul 16–17, 22
Varela, Roberto 45–46

variation, continuous 8–9
Venuti, Lawrence 103
vernacular 112
Vieira, Father António 54
Vieira, José Luandino, *Luuanda* 61
viscosity 8–9
visibility 145, 173–74
Volkov, Shulamit 31
Voß, Johann Heinrich 112
Vroon, Ronald 159, 162–63

Wadia, Laila, *Kitchen Sutra* 130
wake work 57
Wales 187–88, 189, 199
Weber, Steven 177
Welsh language 187, 190, 191–92
Welsh Language National Theatre of Wales (Theatr Genedlaethol Cymru) 187–88, 190
whiteness 93, 176, 203, 204, 206–07
William of Malmesbury 196
Williams, Barbara 128
Williams, Bronwyn T. 86–87
Williams, Nicholas 195
Williams, Raymond 199
women 15
　agency of 27, 30, 33–34
　autonomy of 45
　creativity of 46
　humanity of 28
　liberation of 27–29
world literature 14–15, 100
Worpole, Ken 87
Wright, Michelle 213
'Writers in Between Languages: Minority Languages in the Global Scene' (conference, 2008) 102–03
Writers Without Borders Birmingham, *Moments in Time* 128

xeno-racism 175–76

Yankowitz, Susan 189
Yeşilada, Karin E. 163, 167
Yiddish language 143, 150, 175

Zaldua, Iban 103

www.ingramcontent.com/pod-product-compliance
Lightning Source LLC
Chambersburg PA
CBHW080223170426
43192CB00015B/2730